*Acclaim for Nicholas D. Kristof and Sheryl WuDunn's*

## THUNDER FROM THE EAST

"Terrific reading . . . a brilliant distillation . . . more than one could have hoped for."            —*The Industry Standard*

"A reporter's book in the best sense of the word. . . . [A]n impressive and well-researched study of the world's most important area."            —*The New York Times*

"They present a compelling case. . . . The variety of their experiences is staggering."            —*The Boston Globe*

"A script that often seems like a TV documentary, with sharp, disturbing images that stick to the brain. . . . This book is a vivid and sometimes lurid reminder that Asians are survivors, and that only a fool would bet against them."
—*The Seattle Times*

"Anyone thinking about doing business or pleasure in the Orient will find this illuminating—and a bit scary."
—*Austin American-Statesman*

"A powerful, poignantly written book about Asia and its people that provides essential information on a dynamic part of the world in the midst of transforming itself. . . . Full of surprises and unforgettable images."            —Walter Mondale,
former vice president and ambassador to Japan

"A genuinely important book with an important thesis about the new Asia and the world. With their usual stylish prose and great reporting, Kristof and WuDunn have written a superb book."            —Thomas L. Friedman,
author of *The Lexus and the Olive Tree*

*Nicholas D. Kristof and Sheryl WuDunn*

## THUNDER FROM THE EAST

Nicholas D. Kristof and Sheryl WuDunn, husband and wife, shared a Pulitzer Prize in 1990 for their coverage for *The New York Times* of the Tiananmen democracy movement in China and its suppression. They are the authors of *China Wakes: The Struggle for the Soul of a Rising Power.* Kristof has served as *Times* bureau chief in Hong Kong, Beijing, and Tokyo; WuDunn was a *Times* correspondent in Beijing and Tokyo, and has specialized in business journalism. Both now work for *The Times* in New York City and live nearby with their three children.

# THUNDER FROM THE EAST

# THUNDER
# FROM
# THE
# EAST

## PORTRAIT
## OF A
## RISING
## ASIA

*Nicholas D. Kristof
and Sheryl WuDunn*

Vintage Books
A Division of Random House, Inc.
New York

FIRST VINTAGE BOOKS EDITION, OCTOBER 2001

*Copyright © 2000 by Nicholas D. Kristof and Sheryl WuDunn*

All rights reserved under International and Pan-American Copyright
Conventions. Published in the United States by Vintage Books, a division
of Random House, Inc., New York, and simultaneously in Canada by Random
House of Canada Limited, Toronto. Originally published in hardcover
by Alfred A. Knopf, a division of Random House, Inc., New York, in 2000.

Vintage and colophon are registered trademarks of Random House, Inc.

All photographs, unless otherwise noted, are by Nicholas D. Kristof.

The Library of Congress has cataloged the Knopf edition as follows:
Kristof, Nicholas D., [date]
Thunder from the East : portrait of a rising Asia / Nicholas D. Kristof and Sheryl
WuDunn.
p. cm.
Includes bibliographical references and index.
ISBN 0-375-40325-6 (alk. paper)
1. Asia.    I. WuDunn, Sheryl, [date]    II. Title.
DS5.K66 2000
950—dc21        00-023046

**Vintage ISBN: 0-375-70301-2**

*Book design by Iris Weinstein*

www.vintagebooks.com

Printed in the United States of America
10  9  8  7  6  5  4  3  3  2  1

**TO OUR CHILDREN:**

*Gregory, Geoffrey, and Caroline*

*with joy that we've all been able to share our Asian adventure*

Ship me somewheres east of Suez, where the best is like the worst,

Where there aren't no Ten Commandments an' a man can raise a thirst;

For the temple-bells are callin', an' it's there that I would be—

By the old Moulmein Pagoda, looking lazy at the sea;

On the road to Mandalay . . .

Where the flyin'-fishes play,

An' the dawn comes up like thunder outer China 'crost the Bay!

—RUDYARD KIPLING, "MANDALAY"

# CONTENTS

# CONTENTS

# AUTHORS' NOTE

*People always ask us: "So how did you manage to write a book together?" As they ask, they usually look us over for any scars acquired in our collegial discussions of early drafts.*

*In fact, Nick has written some chapters and Sheryl others. We have different voices in normal daily conversation, and it seemed wisest to preserve those differences rather than to meld the two artificially. The only exception is the final chapter, which we wrote together.*

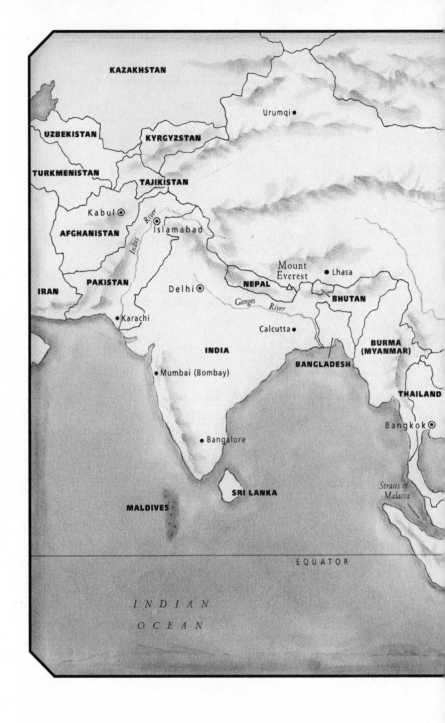

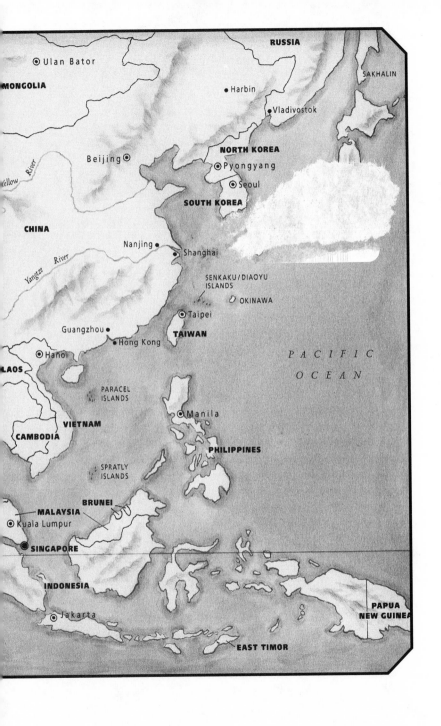

*Part One*

# THE GHOST OF ASIA PAST

*A mob of motorcyclists enters the Indonesian town of Turen, dragging the headless corpse of a "sorcerer" whom they have tortured and killed. Many people were beaten to death or beheaded in a panic over sorcery that arose after the Asian economic crisis devastated Indonesia economically and socially.*

# Search for the Sorcerer

## NICHOLAS D. KRISTOF

*Extremes are followed by changes; changes lead to new opportunities.*

—CHENG YI, AN ELEVENTH-CENTURY CHINESE SCHOLAR
WHO DENOUNCED BELIEF IN MAGIC AND SORCERY

He must have been a raffishly handsome young man, with his bushy eyebrows, large coal-black eyes, high-cheekboned face, and thick mop of black hair dangling over his ears. He looked pale but improbably serene, showing no sign of the torture he had endured, and those eyes were still wide open and frozen in a final instant of surprise. He had a strong, projecting chin, but his head ended a few inches below that chin in a jagged eruption of blood, tissue, and bone. His head had been hacked off with a machete and was impaled on a bamboo stake, and he seemed to be staring at me.

I stared back. That abrupt transition from human flesh to bamboo stake wrenched my gut and paralyzed my legs. I was scared stiff. The mob that had killed him was in front of me now, the killers waving machetes and screaming *Allahu akbar,* God is great. There were about two dozen of them, mostly men in their twenties and thirties, all riding motorcycles slowly down the main street of the little farmtown of Turen, Indonesia.

It was a typical warm afternoon in what seemed a bucolic, prospering community. A tropical drizzle had created a shine on the beautifully paved blacktop road, but there were plenty of trees to shield people from the rain. Comfortable one- and two-story homes lined the road, their walls neatly whitewashed, their roofs made up of pleasant red tile. A few repair shops and small restaurants competed for business, and a billboard advertised "Sun Silk Shampoo" with an image of a young woman with thick, beautiful, black hair. A few bicycle rickshaws were waiting for rides and several pushcart vendors were selling fried rice and noodles. Townspeople were emerging by the side of the road to see what was causing the racket.

It seemed like any of Indonesia's tens of thousands of little villages, except that it had abruptly tumbled into savagery. Some motorcyclists were waving S-shaped machetes, two feet long and bloody, while others wielded sickles that were equally grisly. A few were clenching their fists in power salutes of victory, and they were all grinning happily, cheering and shouting, while the fast-forming crowd on the sidewalk waved back and roared its approval. In the middle of the cluster of motorcycles was a glossy black one, and its driver smiled proudly at the responsibility he had been given. Behind him on the same motorcycle was a long-haired younger man, perhaps twenty years old, his black shirt unbuttoned to the waist, his face gleaming with excitement. Black Shirt was standing up on the footrests, holding on to the driver's shoulder with his left hand, and with his right he was holding up the bamboo stake. Exultantly, he waved it all around, as if he were exhibiting a doll's head on a handle, so that everyone could admire it. Black Shirt was small and skinny, shining with his eagerness to please, and he looked less like a killer than like a proud high-school kid in the center of a homecoming parade.

I was standing under a tree to keep out of the drizzle, and the motorcyclists did not see me at first. But now the cries faded as the mob became aware of the presence of a foreigner. Black Shirt frowned, switched hands and thrust the severed head toward me, he too shouting *Allahu akbar.* The head was raised high, and my eyes locked on the bloody tissue, jagged and ragged, where the neck ended.

Instinctively, I transferred my notebook to my left hand and reached up with my right to feel my own neck. I massaged it absentmindedly with trembling fingers, appreciating its continuity and imagining a motorcyclist's machete arcing down on it and parting the skin.

*Salamet drives his rickshaw near his home in Mojokerto,*
*Indonesia. Here he gives a ride to his eldest son, Dwi.*

. . .

I had come to Java not in search of a beheading but to understand the
upheavals in rural Indonesia caused by the economic crisis in Asia. The
crisis had begun in Thailand in July 1997 and then had devastated once-
booming economies throughout the region, leaving Indonesia worst hit of
all. I was staying in a town in East Java called Mojokerto, where I met
Salamet, a twenty-seven-year-old rickshaw driver. Salamet was a gentle
man with a round face, a drooping moustache, and a pleasing smile. Years
of work as a rickshaw driver, rock-crusher, and gravel-hauler had left him
as strong as an ox, and with roughly the same build. He was of only average height, but he had a barrel chest and a boxer's neck, and he might
have looked intimidating if he hadn't spent so much time gently cradling
his youngest daughter. He would sit back in his rickshaw, his bare feet
dangling out over the footrest, rocking the girl on his knee and griping
about the rising price of food.

The neighborhood seemed as placid as the nearby river running
through the town, but Salamet had been telling me that tensions were
mounting. One day when he was eating a bowl of noodles, he told me

between loud slurps that one bad sign was the rise of sorcery. "Sorcerers are taking advantage of the confusion these days," he warned. Slurp. "There didn't used to be much black magic around, but now it's beginning again." Slurp.

Salamet referred to a series of two hundred gruesome murders in East Java, mostly of Muslim leaders whose bodies were chopped into pieces that were left hanging in the trees. I believed that some army unit was behind the killings, trying to create political instability or even conditions for a coup d'état, but to Salamet and most people in Mojokerto the obvious suspects were sorcerers. Javanese have always believed in black magic and sorcery, and rumors were spreading that the killers wore black and could vanish into thin air. "Those killings—that's the work of sorcerers," Salamet told me confidently. Slurp.

In nearby towns angry mobs began to kill suspected witches and sorcerers. And even in Mojokerto vigilante groups were organized to fight against the sorcerers, whom people called "ninja" after the Japanese warriors. Salamet joined one of these vigilante groups, and the men in it spent their days sharpening their knives and their nights roaming around looking for sorcerers to kill. They were good family men, and I went with some of them to a meeting at the local mosque where a charismatic man named Ahmed Banu was urging the crowd to butcher the sorcerers. Banu and the others greeted me warmly, made sure I was seated comfortably, and then got down to business.

"If we Muslims are being treated like animals, will we stand for it?" Banu asked, his voice rising to a crescendo.

*"No!"* his followers yelled back.

"If we catch the ninja, what should we do? Give them to the police or kill them?"

*"Kill them!"*

"So send this message to your families," Banu added grimly: "When we catch the attackers, we must kill them."

That night, I tossed and turned. Would these villagers, who had been so hospitable to me, actually attack people they suspected to be sorcerers? I wondered whether I had lent credibility to Banu by attending the meeting, increasing the chance that he and his friends would butcher strangers. Finally, I decided that it was all talk and fell into a comfortable slumber. But in the morning, my interpreter brought a local newspaper and I learned that at roughly the same time that Banu was holding his meeting, mobs a bit farther to the south had been tearing apart five men who lacked identification and were consequently suspected of being sorcerers. Two were burned alive and three were beheaded, their heads impaled on pikes and paraded through the nearby towns.

"Where did that happen?" I asked.

"In a little town called Turen," replied my interpreter, a local journalist. As I looked at the articles, I felt revulsion and fear, but in the mix there was also a large dose of curiosity. What kind of people could commit such grotesque acts? How could citizens behead their neighbors? The killings struck me as a modern version of the seventeenth-century Salem witch trials. If there was any sorcery in Indonesia, I mused, it was the economic and social alchemy that left people running around in mobs carrying human heads on pikes. The despair and social disintegration that accompanied the crisis seemed to leave Indonesians particularly inclined to supernatural explanations, particularly vulnerable to manipulation by secret army units, and particularly likely to respond with mob violence to each new threat that appeared to disrupt their lives.

"Let's go," I suggested. "Let's try to find some of the people who did it and talk to them."

It was an odd drive. In journalism you occasionally find yourself careering the wrong way on a one-way street, heading in precisely the direction that you know quite confidently you should be fleeing from. I was tense with apprehension but also soothed by the vivid green countryside we were driving through. It seemed impossible to reconcile the macabre news accounts with a landscape that was tranquil and lovely that morning: paddies sprouting rich green rice plants, dark green forested hills in the distance, occasional coconut plantations with endless rows of palms.

This was the first time in ten years that I had been in this part of East Java, and the economic development over the intervening decade was dazzling. The previous time I had bounced over rutted gravel roads in creaky old buses filled with exhaust smoke. Once a bus had simply let me off on a remote hillside where the road had washed out, and I had been forced to spend the night in a peasant's house, cadging bananas for dinner. Now, just ten years later, I was hurtling along a road that was sleek, paved, and straight, and modern cars and trucks were gliding by clean restaurants and stores. I was traveling on a modern highway to meet mobs that paraded heads on pikes.

When Dante set forth into the Inferno, he was battered by the "sighs, lamentations, and loud wailings resounding through the starless air." I was encountering my own netherworld, with its own wails and laments and cries for help. Since the economic crisis had spread economic and social convulsions through the region, Asia and especially Indonesia had been transformed into something that in its bleakest hours resembled Dante's ninth ring of hell.

As we approached Turen, traffic thinned out and virtually disappeared. We stopped at a regional police station to ask if it was safe, and a senior officer—a tall, stout man with a crisp uniform—assured us pompously that the day had been calm so far. We asked if it might be possible to take a policeman in the car with us for safety's sake, and he frowned.

"No, I'm afraid not," he said. "All the police officers are staying inside the compound here."

"Why?"

He hesitated for a moment, deflated, and then said: "They think it's too dangerous to go out in the streets."

My interpreter went off to chat with some policemen taking their lunch break, and he returned alarmed. The previous night, the policemen had told him, mobs had set up roadblocks in the area, seizing anybody suspicious to execute as a ninja. Even police cars were searched, and two men under arrest had been taken from a police car and lynched. The police officers had run away.

We got back in the car, carefully rolling down the tinted windows so that people could see inside and observe that we were nothing more than friendly visitors. Our blue taxi glided through deserted roads, and thirty minutes later we were in Turen. I told the driver to stay at the wheel and leave the engine running, and I left my camera bag in the car—it was black, and it might be mistaken for a sorcerer's kit.

A gaggle of young men were hanging out on the street by a T-intersection with a little traffic island in the center. I carefully approached the group, introducing myself as an American reporter, and the men seemed friendly and boasted about the events of the previous day.

"One man was killed right here," explained a husky rickshaw driver who said his name was Sukiando. Forty-two years old, dressed in a white T-shirt, blue work pants, and sandals, Sukiando was dramatic and outspoken. He enjoyed being the center of attention as the others pressed around us and offered occasional thoughts of their own.

"Then they cut off his head. Like this"—Sukiando whacked downward several times with an imaginary machete—"and then his head and all the others were displayed right there in the grass." He pointed to the tidy traffic island, its raised sides neatly painted in blue and white stripes. In the center was a well-trimmed bit of grass, but no sign of human heads.

"Somebody moved them last night," he explained, anticipating my question. "Maybe the police. Anyway, there was a big crowd, hundreds of people, and we all had our own weapons. Sickles, knives, machetes, all kinds of things."

"How did you know who to attack?" I asked.

"We attack the ninja," Sukiando explained condescendingly, the way a teacher might explain a point to a particularly thick-headed pupil. The others nodded with faint smiles, trying not to be rude by snickering at my denseness.

"How do you tell who the ninja are?"

"It begins when people see someone suspicious and try to chase him. Sometimes the ninja turns into a cat, and sometimes he stays human. If he stays human, then they cut off his head." Sukiando paused, sighed at the thought of all the beheading that remained to be done, and added: "There are going to be more heads chopped off. Because in every little neighborhood, there are seven or eight ninja who go out every night, and they've got to be stopped."

Suddenly Sukiando cocked his head. "You hear that?" he asked excitedly. "They're coming!" There was a buzz of excitement, and some of the young men rushed onto the road and peered into the distance. There was a far-away clamor of shouting, like the roar of a crowd celebrating victory after a soccer match.

"Who's coming?" I asked.

"They got another ninja this morning. Now they're going to bring him through town."

I rushed to get my camera from the taxi, which was still idling by the side of the road fifty feet away. But the mob was fast approaching, and the last thing I wanted to do was appear to be running away from it. So I trotted backward, a stupid grin on my face. I had just gotten to the car and was reaching for the camera bag when the band of motorcyclists came alongside. I didn't dare turn my back on them, so without the camera I slowly moved to face them. And that's when I saw Black Shirt and the young man's severed head.

Black Shirt and the other motorcyclists stared at me ominously and slowed almost to a halt as they studied me, all the time speaking rapidly in Javanese. The juxtaposition of their savagery and their prudence jolted

*At times of civil unrest, one should worry not just about vigilantes with machetes but also about soldiers with machine guns. Here I ingratiate myself with a few of the troops on the streets in Indonesia at the time of the rioting that overthrew Suharto in 1998.*

me. They drove their motorcycles cautiously, with most of the drivers carefully keeping both hands on the handlebars, and they had put their lights on because of the drizzle. When Black Shirt thrust the young man's head in my direction, I smiled weakly back at the mob. I had tried to work out two escape routes—one by car and the other by climbing a couple of fences and disappearing into the fields—but neither seemed very certain. My heart was pounding in my chest.

As I nervously probed my neck for reassurance, what rocked me was a sense of utter sadness and confusion. This was Java, a gloriously cultured land that had been civilized before Britain and whose people are renowned for their kindness and restraint. This was a nation that the World Bank had hailed as a model for the developing world. But now the Asian economic crisis had contorted it into an example of Asia at its very worst. Suddenly, the *Paradiso* of Asia had become the *Inferno*.

Two conclusions might seem obvious from these economic and social upheavals: First, the Asian economic crisis was a catastrophe of historic proportions. Second, the Pacific Century is over before it began. Asia may hobble back eventually, but when people start running around hacking off each other's heads, they are not on the brink of a middle-class or an industrial revolution.

Yet those are, we think, precisely the wrong conclusions. As Zhao Yi, a Chinese poet, wrote two hundred years ago: *gai guan lun ting.* It means roughly: "You cannot rightly judge a person until his coffin lid is sealed." And although during the crisis Asia was widely measured for its coffin— and sometimes seemed to stretch out inside—it is far too soon to seal the lid. On the contrary, instead of suggesting that the crisis was a catastrophe or that the Pacific Century is over, we will over the course of this book make two very different arguments.

First, *the Asian economic crisis was the best thing that could have happened to Asia.* It entailed a terrible human cost, but it is also helping to destroy much of the cronyism, protectionism, and government regulation that had burdened Asian business. The crisis helped launch a political, social, and economic revolution that is still incomplete but that ultimately will reshape Asia as greatly as the fall of the Berlin Wall reshaped Europe.

This revolution is essential because for all the praise lavished on the Asian business culture, up close it never looked nearly so impressive. Sometimes it looked downright idiotic. I talked to Japanese bankers about their practice of spending thousands of dollars taking their Finance Ministry bank regulators out to $500-a-person expense-account dinners at *no-pan-shabu-shabu* restaurants in Tokyo's Kabukicho red-light district. The attraction of these restaurants is not the *shabu-shabu,* the thinly sliced beef that is dipped into a hot pot in front of the customer. Rather the appeal is the waitresses in short skirts and "*no pan*" (no panties). The restaurants keep water and sake high up, so that the waitresses have to stretch to reach them. One of these *no-pan-shabu-shabu* restaurants, seeking to ensure that customers could appreciate its "special amenities," even put mirrors on the floors. "And if you pay a tip," one official confided, "then the girl will climb on the table and lift her skirt."

Imagine the intellectual level of the discussion at these dinners. Imagine the caliber of Japan's bank regulation.

The Asian economic crisis forced a greater reliance on markets, democracy, and the rule of law. One result is that Tokyo no longer has any *no-pan-shabu-shabu* restaurants. The crisis also meant that Asian countries finally got first-class financial institutions—often American ones—to underwrite the industrial revolution and cultivate deep capital markets.

Just as Britain's economic near-collapse in 1976 and subsequent bailout by the International Monetary Fund laid the groundwork for its renaissance over the next two decades, Asia's upheavals will gradually help clear out the dead wood and reinvigorate the region.

The second argument is broader: Partly because of this forced restructuring, *Asia is likely to wrench economic, diplomatic, and military power from the West over the coming decades.* The "center of the world," to the extent that there is one, has migrated repeatedly over the years. It was China for most of the first millennium B.C., then Rome during the Roman Empire, then China again for well over one thousand years, then Spain in the sixteenth century, then England, and finally America since the late nineteenth century. Now the center of the world may be slowly shifting again, and eventually it will settle in Asia.

The United States is incomparably ahead of Asia in information systems, business management, financial services, and entertainment industries, plus it has the advantage of operating in the international language. But the United States's share of the world's gross domestic product (GDP) peaked in the aftermath of World War II, at about 32 percent. Now America's share of global GDP has fallen to 21 percent, and it is continuing to fall despite the vigor of the American economy in recent years.

This is natural. Poor countries can enjoy "catch-up" growth rates of 5 to 10 percent per year, while mature nations seem unable to average much more than 3 percent. The upshot is that just about every forecast—by the World Bank, by the Asian Development Bank, and by private economists—shows that the East will gain considerably in its share of the global economy in the coming decades. The World Bank's forecasts show Asia's share of global GDP rising from 19 percent in 1950 to 33 percent in 1998, to 55 to 60 percent by 2025. In that year, Asia will still lag behind the West in technology, nuclear weaponry, and per capita incomes, but it will have approximately the same share of global income that the West had at its peak in the 1950s.

This shift of power to Asia is in large part a function of population: Just as the city-state of Venice could not compete with the nation of Spain, and England could not muster the power of a continental nation like America, so it will be difficult for the United States to hold its own indefinitely against the rise of countries in Asia. Sixty percent of the world's people live in Asia, and the proportion will probably reach two-thirds by the middle of this century. In contrast, 5 percent of the world's people live in North America, mostly in the United States.

.   .   .

My smile to Black Shirt seemed to break the ice. He grinned, joked with a couple of his buddies in Javanese, laughed, and nodded to me in a friendly gesture. And then they drove on.

I grabbed the camera from the car and rejoined the group I had been with. The men were abuzz with conversation, and they seemed delighted that another ninja was dead. What jolted me in particular was that these men seemed so ordinary. These were not the dregs of the town but family men who felt threatened and responded in what to them seemed an obvious way. I found them discomfortingly nice. I tried to buy everyone snacks from a pushcart, but they resisted and said that I was the guest and that they should buy a meal for me. One of them bought fried rice for me and paid for it, despite my protests. Having just seen a human head waved around on a pike, the last thing I could do was eat lunch. I mumbled something about my sensitive foreign stomach being unable to deal with street food, and in the end one of the rickshaw drivers ate it.

The incongruities rocked me. I thought again of the Salem witch trials and felt that I had stumbled into a reenactment. There was the same irrationality, the same brutality, the same absurdity, and even greater ferocity—this time the mobs were skipping the trials and brutalizing the corpses. Yet the brutes were uncommonly friendly.

One young man, Sutaryono, who carried a club, sensed my discomfort and tried to take me under his wing. Tall and thin with a pencil mustache and long brown hair, he explained that the ninja seemed to be gaining ground. "If one ninja dies, one thousand more will come up again," he said. "So there are more all the time. Two days ago, there were none around here, and then we killed some and now look how many there are."

"Killing one produces one thousand more?" I asked.

Sutaryono spat in the gravel and nodded gravely. Other heads in the group quickly nodded as well.

"But then isn't it counterproductive to kill them?" I asked. There was a pause.

"We have to kill them," Sutaryono responded heatedly. "They are all over, and they're attacking our Muslim leaders. Last night I saw it with my own eyes. There were three ninja, and when we shone a flashlight at them, they vanished."

"So if they disappear or turn into cats, that means that they are really ninja," I agreed. "But if you kill them and cut off their heads and they don't vanish, doesn't that mean that they were just ordinary people and you made a mistake?"

Another pause. Mohammed Soleh, a thin, earnest man in his late twenties who was better dressed than the others and seemed to be better educated, glared at me. He had said little, but the others clearly respected him and he had seemed from the start to regard me with skepticism. I worried about him.

"If there is a Muslim leader around, then the ninja magic doesn't work," Soleh said in a hard voice. "So if they don't disappear, that doesn't prove anything. In fact, if he can't disappear when a Muslim leader is around, then that just proves he's a sorcerer."

We continued to converse, and I noticed Soleh looking at me with increasing hostility. It was time to go, I said, and I tried again to buy everyone a round of snacks. At that moment another man rushed up and told us excitedly that a convoy of motorcycle vigilantes was driving up. In a minute I could hear them honking and shouting as they approached, and I did not dare flee. I found myself trapped.

Already, if you listen carefully in the West, you can hear the honking and shouting that herald the approach of Asia itself. Even now, our futures are being written, in large part, by the East. That has always been more true than most Westerners realize: New Yorkers speak English rather than Dutch because in the 1667 Treaty of Breda, Holland traded its colony of Manhattan to England, in exchange for the Indonesian island of Run. There was a general cackling among international relations specialists at the time that the Dutch had gotten the better end of that deal. Manhattan was then just a wild island, while Run was the world's leading source of nutmeg. More recently, Asia's influence can be felt each time you listen to a compact disk. Why is the playing time of a CD fixed at seventy-four minutes, forty-two seconds? Because its Japanese developers were determined that it be stretched long enough to contain Beethoven's Ninth Symphony, which is a huge seller in Japan.

The increasing importance of technology in the world today may match the strengths of Asia, which emphasizes math and science in its high schools and turns out far more engineers than any other part of the world. Your laptop computer probably comes from Taiwan and has a memory chip from South Korea. Every day you unwittingly encounter computer software written in Bangalore, India. One Japanese robot can read sheet music and play the piano, and near Kyoto I visited a lab where scientists were building the most sophisticated artificial brain in the world, using techniques that they believe by about 2020 will produce a computer that is smarter than humans.

It would be a mistake to make too much of robots alone, or of Asian economic flexibility alone, or even of Asia's vast population alone. But all this is coming together at the same time, and the business world is being forced to take notice. Even after the Asian economic crisis, top executives at four hundred large American companies reported in a survey that they overwhelmingly see Asia as their major source for future revenue growth. The survey, conducted by Deloitte & Touche, found that 79 percent of the executives believe that Asia will experience the greatest growth in economic influence by 2005, and 47 percent expect Asia to be their greatest area of revenue growth by 2005 (compared to 34 percent who named the United States). Of course, Western executives have always dazzled themselves with their calculations about the potential of the Asian market. George Fisher, as head of Eastman Kodak, did some basic arithmetic: If people in China bought as much film as their relatives in Taiwan, he said, "use of film in the world would rise 50 percent." I am deeply skeptical of the usefulness of these calculations in any time span relevant to a CEO's stock options, but the larger point is valid. As the industrial revolution spreads across Asia, the effects on markets and commerce will be mind-boggling.

Nonetheless, even if we are right and Asia gains weight in the coming decades, growth rates in the high-octane economies of East Asia are likely to be slower in the next twenty years than in the last twenty—say 5 percent or 7 percent growth, not 10 percent growth. One reason is diminishing returns and the smaller potential for catch-up gains. Another reason is demographic: Far more than is generally realized, East Asia prospered in part because of its population structure, and that advantage will now disappear or even become a burden.

What happened was that East Asia improved health care and slashed infant mortality rates, and then afterward cut fertility quickly. The result was a huge baby-boom generation that spilled into the labor force, while there were relatively few elderly people or small children. Between 1965 and 1990, East Asia's working population increased nine times as fast as the number of young and old who together make up dependents. That was a huge onetime advantage and accounted for about one-third of East Asia's economic growth in the boom years. But between 1995 and 2025, the tables will be reversed and the working population will grow only one-fourth as quickly as the ranks of dependents (mostly retirees). Japan, in particular, will face a huge demographic challenge as its labor force shrinks and the number of retirees increases hugely. Indeed, the Japanese government estimates that the country's population will fall almost in half during the twenty-first century. And if Japan's current fertility rates were to continue indefinitely, it would have a population in the year 3000 of only forty-five thousand. So much for buying Japanese property with a long-term view. . . .

Still, the United States and Europe face demographic challenges over the next thirty years that are similar to Japan's. And even if East Asia slows, South Asian countries like India are in an excellent position to speed up. Within Asia, the Indian subcontinent is likely to become relatively more important and Japan relatively less important. Japan and the East Asian "dragon economies" like South Korea, Taiwan, and Hong Kong will slowly lose momentum, while Southeast Asian countries like the Philippines are in a good position to speed up. China's growth rates may moderate, but it will still become steadily more important as the economic anchor of Asia. And my guess is that, relatively speaking, the greatest gains may be made in the traditionally anemic countries of South Asia, such as India and Bangladesh and perhaps Pakistan.

The Indian subcontinent is still an economic and political mess, but it could do far better in the coming decades, and soon people may talk about India's potential with the amazement that they now reserve for China's. Even Bangladesh—the past symbol of hopelessness, dubbed by Henry Kissinger in the 1970s as an "international basket case"—is now turning out very respectable annual growth rates of 5 to 6 percent, better than the United States or Europe. Countries like India and Bangladesh increasingly look like East Asian nations did in the past, as they open their economies and move toward markets and surge because of economic restructuring and catch-up gains. The Indian subcontinent is also perfectly positioned to gain from the demographic bulge moving into the workforce. Indian women now have an average of three babies, down from five in 1980, and the baby boomers are pouring into the labor force. As a result, between 1990 and 2025, India's working-age population will grow more than twice as fast as the number of dependents. While forecasts are extremely uncertain, some extrapolations suggest that by the middle of the twenty-first century, India will be the second-largest economy in the world, after China and ahead of the United States. That would depend on things going more smoothly in India than they ever have, but

*This girl in Dharavi, the Indian slum that is said to be the largest in the world, does not go to school and is unlikely ever to have a decent job. But if India continues to progress, her daughter may have a chance.*

there is at least reason to think that with a heftier contribution from South Asia, the economy of Asia as a whole will continue to gain relative to the West.

So the balance of economic power is slowly shifting. Just as Asia's colonization, squalor, and wars were the outcome in large part of events such as the Industrial Revolution in Europe, in the coming century life in the West will be greatly shaped by outcomes in the East. From the intellectual and economic stirrings along the Mediterranean in the fifteenth century until the Russian Revolution in 1917, the most important historical forces in the world were at work in Europe as it prepared for and eventually launched the Industrial Revolution and a series of political revolutions as well. Then, in this century, America has been the most exciting place in the world: the birthplace of the automotive society, assembly lines, feminism, the sexual revolution, personal computers, and the stock-owning middle class. In the twenty-first century, I think, the most important things in the world will probably be going on in Asia, as the most populous part of the world industrializes, gains economic weight, accumulates military power, and struggles to modernize its ancient soul.

.  .  .

Still, important changes can be pretty awful. In the West, the Great Depression produced not just Franklin D. Roosevelt and the New Deal, but also Adolf Hitler and World War II. That thought was going through my head as I heard motorcyclists shouting *Allahu akbar* as they roared down the main street of Turen. There were fewer motorcyclists this time, about twenty, but as before they were waving machetes and sickles and cheering and honking. One of the motorcycles in the center of the convoy was driven by a pleasant-looking man in his thirties wearing a violet-striped dress shirt, a handsome gold watch, and a black Muslim fez on his head. Behind him was another man of the same age, waving a curved machete in his right hand. From the back of the motorcycle dangled an eight-foot rope that was tied several times around the ankles of a naked, headless corpse that was being dragged along the road. The arms were bound tightly behind the back, and a long smear of blood trailed on the road. It was the body that belonged to the head I had seen.

The motorcyclists were different, though. They seemed less friendly toward me, and several were frowning at the sight of my camera. I put the camera down but they still waved their arms menacingly. They slowed and talked among themselves. I grinned broadly at them with the most supportive, nonjudgmental smile I could muster. They pointed at me. I nodded to them in greeting. They frowned and argued in Javanese. And—may God forgive me—I raised my arm to them in a power salute, giving them an unmistakable sign of approval.

That did it. They relaxed and smiled, and after a bit more conversation in Javanese they continued down the road. I was revolted, at myself as well as at them, but I was even more frightened. I imagined the mob grabbing me and accusing me of being a ninja and hacking off my head. I put my sweaty palm on the back of my neck again. Then, slowly and politely, I excused myself from the young men and fled in the taxi.

It was a long, nerve-wracking ride back through a series of towns whose residents were also on their guard against sorcerers and strangers. Later I found out that three suspected ninja in the area had been beaten to death during the course of the day. As we drove along, my heart was thumping and I looked glassily out the window at the delightfully green landscape. I was struggling to comprehend what I had seen.

The standard comment about Asia is that life is cheap. I heard that from a *Newsweek* correspondent within a few days of my move to Asia in 1986.

He gave me a long account of a trip he had just made through the Philippines and described piles of bodies and a memorable scene of a robber chopping off a businessman's hand with a machete so as to steal his Rolex. "Human life doesn't count for very much here in Asia," the correspondent explained. "People kill each other for nothing." And from afar, hearing about sorcerers or about lower-caste and higher-caste Indians killing each other, perhaps it does sound as if Asians do not much value human life. But on the contrary, the striking thing about Asia most of the time is its tranquillity, even its civility. Crime rates are far lower than in America or Europe, and human relationships are often intricately structured and regulated so as to reduce conflict. I always had to reassure Asian friends going to Washington that they stood a decent chance of returning alive. So it is slanderous to say that life is cheap in Asia, but it certainly is complex.

That is perhaps one good reason *not* to write a book about Asia: It is too overwhelming, vast, and complex. Sheryl and I both speak Chinese and Japanese, and I have traveled through forty countries in the Asia/Pacific region, but what I gain in breadth I sacrifice in depth, and vice versa. No single person can know the entire region intimately; indeed, there are a couple of Asian countries, such as Bhutan and Brunei, that I have never even set foot in. The places we have lived—Hong Kong, Taiwan, China, and Japan—are all in East Asia, and we do not know other parts of Asia nearly so well. Even within East Asia, the only place where we sent our children to local schools (the best way to spy on a society) was Japan. So our experience across Asia has been in the form that the Chinese call *qingting dian shui,* meaning the way a dragonfly skits superficially about the surface of a pond.

Likewise, although we both covered the region for the *New York Times,* we each had our own backgrounds and specialties. Sheryl is a former banker who wrote largely about business and finance; I am a frustrated anthropologist whose main interest is social and political change. Sheryl, as a third-generation Chinese-American growing up in Manhattan, often saw things differently than I did, an Armenian-Polish-Romanian-Scottish-English mongrel who grew up on a sheep and cherry farm near Yamhill, Oregon, population 900. So even the parts of the Asian pond that we skitted about tended to vary, and our notebooks are filled with different kinds of observations.

Moreover, it is easy to argue that "Asia" does not exist and never has; it isn't a single region or culture or people, but rather a geographic fiction to designate the chunk of the world to the east of Europe. There is not even agreement on what Asia includes. When I was a student backpacking in Turkey, I crossed the Bosporus and entered Asia, or so the guidebooks told me. Likewise, geographies suggest that Israel, Jordan, Saudi Arabia, and Iran are all Asian countries.* But Turkey is more in Europe's orbit than Asia's, and just try to find anybody in Hong Kong who thinks of an Israeli or a Saudi as Asian! I have Armenian blood, but I never think of myself as Asian-American. All this confusion about the dimensions of Asia causes occasional problems with the statistics (although the debatable fringes rarely matter much to the overall figures), and there's not much point in being dogmatic about what to include in Asia. For our part, when we write about Asia we generally are referring to the region from Afghanistan in the west to Japan in the east, from the Russian far east in the north to Indonesia in the south. But even this is a vast and diverse terrain. The word "Asia" originated with outsiders—the Greeks, to whom Asia was the place where the sun rose—and so did the concept of such a vast area sharing something in common. And even if one accepts that Asia exists in some sense, it is a bit like the weather: so diverse that it is difficult to generalize about.

There is something to this objection to writing about all of Asia, but I think it is easy to make too much of the point. Geologists usefully generalize about Earth, which is a tad bigger than Asia, and astrophysicists generalize about the cosmos, which is bigger yet. No doubt Asia's variations are greater than those of other continents. But in some ways Asia has been economically and intellectually integrated for thousands of years, making the region greater than the sum of its parts. Traders, missionaries, and scholars have roamed throughout Asia, cross-fertilizing it like honeybees. Indonesians and Polynesians supplied boats and sailors; India gave birth to Buddhism, which spread across East Asia; Vietnam developed key strains of rice; Koreans refined ceramics; Persians improved our understanding of astronomy; and central Asians helped the Chinese develop gunpowder. Asian countries developed together, not in isolation.

It is true, though, that generalizations about any region are risky, and that they are particularly hazardous when we make them about what seems from our standpoint to be an exotic culture. An epiphany at a monastery frames my perspective on this point.

In 1983 I was backpacking around Japan as a penniless law student, hitchhiking rides on any car or truck that would cough to a stop and take

---

* In terms of physical geography, scholars sometimes describe Europe as a peninsula of Asia. But this view is unlikely to be embraced by the average person in London or Paris.

me. I was lugging around the Lonely Planet guide to Japan, and what impressed me most was what it had to say about Japanese women. Judeo-Christian notions of sex as sin had never reached Japan's culture, and so, the book declared, Japanese women have a frank, uninhibited approach to sleeping around. More to the point, the book explained, they are often curious about Western men and sometimes simply walk up to a young American man on the street and lead him off to a hotel for a bit of experimental lovemaking.

All I can say is: Don't count on it.

Immediately after that trip around Japan I went off to Cairo to study Arabic at the American University in Cairo. As it happened, a number of my classmates were Japanese men, and one weekend we all traveled to St. Catherine's Monastery in the Sinai Desert. I bunked with seven Japanese in a little cabin a few hundred yards from some brush that the monks say is the original Burning Bush, and I was wondering how to ask my room-mates if Japanese women really regarded sex as simply one more appetite to be sated. Before I could ask that question, though, the Japanese started grilling me, and all they wanted to know about was American women. Is it true, Takahashi-san asked, his eyes wide as saucers, that American women have a very strong, er, drive? Sato-san inquired: Do American women really go to bed with men as casually as they put on a jacket? Yoshida-san wanted to know: Can anybody just go up to an American woman and say "Sex?" and expect to be led to her bedroom?

No, I protested, startled by the questions. But the more I explained the more skeptical the Japanese became. They thought I was trying to hoard America's women for myself. "I spent a year in the United States when I was in high school," Takahashi-san reminisced, as the other Japanese listened in fascination. "There was a girl in my host family, and one day she and a group of her friends went in the middle of the night to someone's swimming pool—they brought me along. And then, they took all their clothes off. Right there, in front of each other. The girls, too! There was a word for it—I think they called it thin-dipping. I was so embarrassed. But the girls laughed. They just walked around all naked. Girls are like that in America."

Takahashi-san sighed at the memory, turned to me, and added: "I guess that happens a lot?" He and his Japanese friends all looked reproachfully at me, and the room lapsed into a dreamy silence. My credibility was shot.

So we are all projectionists. We each want to uncover something titillating about the other, yet in fact we are all far more alike than we imagine. Living in Asia for the last fourteen years has reinforced that impression: Our perceptions of foreign mores are often rooted minimally in fact and nurtured liberally with our imaginations. Of course, there is something in the notion that Japanese men and women do not have a religious legacy associating sex with sin, and there is a kernel of truth to the vision that some Asians have of American youth culture as a carnal hothouse. But mostly we create mental constructs, much more lurid than reality, and fundamentally we all follow the beat of a similar drummer. This realization came to me that evening as I was interrogated by my Japanese friends at St. Catherine's Monastery, and I have never shaken it. Asia is organized in very different ways than the West, and its cultures and faiths are often a world apart. But fundamentally we are similar enough that we can learn from each other. And as Asia grows more important, we will have to learn more about it.

Asia's lessons are not purely economic ones. In a Gallup poll in 1999, Americans listed their top four national concerns as follows: ethics, morality, and the decline of the family; crime and violence; education; and guns and gun control. Ironically, those are precisely the areas where some Asian countries do offer useful lessons for the West. Asia, by and large, is where the family has remained strongest and crime lowest. Likewise, primary and secondary schools in places like Singapore and South Korea are regularly praised as among the best in the world, and our own experience as parents demonstrates how much better Japanese elementary schools are than most American schools. While Japanese junior high schools and high schools are mind-numbing pressure cookers, the elementary schools are outstanding at teaching not only math and reading but also such values as cooperation and sharing. As for guns, the comparison is perhaps unfair, but Japan went from the nation with the most guns in the world (in the sixteenth century) to the one with just about the least. In all of Japan today, there are about fifty handguns licensed to private individuals, all top-notch target shooters, and although some criminals have guns smuggled in from abroad, an ordinary Japanese is as likely to be struck by lightning in Japan as to be killed with a pistol.

We have spent far too much time in Asia to praise its societies unreservedly. Low divorce rates, for example, simply mean that many men and women are locked for their entire lives into sad and meaningless relationships from which they cannot escape. Asia's children learn their calculus, but they spend so much time with the books that one can question how much they enjoy their childhood. And yet, for all the problems that we saw firsthand around us, we think that Asia has a good deal to instruct us in regard to some of the thorny issues of family and education and civility that in the West have proved most intractable.

As the depravities in Turen suggest, however, Asia's rise is not likely to be smooth. Living in the East taught me to be an optimist, but a grim optimist. My bet is that the Asian economic crisis was not a onetime affair. There will be further turbulence in the years ahead, and it may well get worse. Indonesia may collapse into convulsions, India could fight a nuclear war with Pakistan, and China could be torn apart by secession and civil war. The conflicts and antagonisms that are the legacy of history run deep, impairing economic cooperation. In several Asian countries, nationalism is rising and creating risks of new collisions like those that wracked twentieth-century Europe. The next world war, if there is one, will almost certainly begin in Asia.

There are other reasons for legitimate skepticism about Asia's prospects. The Asean countries in Southeast Asia are talking about an economic union, but European-style integration is many decades away if it ever comes. In addition, in most of Asia the half of the population that is female is hugely underutilized and reflects a tremendous economic potential that is squandered. Asia's industrial revolution is also creating an environmental nightmare that undercuts economic growth and the standard of living. Corruption is entrenched, while markets are often fragile. The Asian economic crisis has brought change, but not enough. Legal systems are still opaque and often useless, banking systems old-fashioned, venture capital scarce, and political leaders reluctant to force through the market-oriented changes that are really needed. More broadly, for five centuries Asia has gone nowhere fast, and so it takes a certain leap of faith to argue that this is finally changing now. Almost anything is possible in Asia, and upheaval is certain.

The same could have been said of America in the late nineteenth century, when the United States was tainted by the Civil War, by the stolen presidential election of 1876, by cronyism that would have made even a Japanese banker blush. The Panic of 1873 sent America into six years of depression, and then the Panic of 1893 led to four more years of economic paralysis. Those were all serious traumas, but in retrospect they were secondary to a great economic boom that changed the world. I think history will show the same to be even more true of Asia.

And to understand where Asia is headed, we need to tackle some mysteries about the past, about an ancient admiral who almost changed the world.

*Priambudi Setiakusuma, head of the temple association at the Zheng He temple in Semarang, Indonesia, praying at the temple. Zheng He's journeys launched the large-scale migration of Chinese to Southeast Asia.*

### CHAPTER TWO

# Why We Speak English

## NICHOLAS D. KRISTOF

*Awake, O ancient East!*
*The moonless night of the Ages*
*Has mantled you in its deep gloom.*
*In your slumber you had vanished in the sea of oblivion.*

*Awake, O ancient East!*
*The many-toned melodies of life have ceased,*
*Like the dying notes of a cricket.*
*When shall the call of light*
*Dance again in your pulse?*
*Awake, O ancient East!*

—RABINDRANATH TAGORE, BENGALI POET (1861–1941)

*A statue of Admiral Zheng He presides in the garden of the Zheng He Museum in Nanjing, China, on the spot where his estate once stood. The museum is now closed indefinitely for lack of interest.*

The old Chinese capital of Nanjing is today an uncommonly ugly city on the Yangtze River. Nanjing is choked with honking cars and broken sidewalks and tired apartment buildings, and the smells of auto exhaust and rotting vegetables and stir-fried noodles mingle with the dust. In one particularly cluttered neighborhood, a two-story white house sits forgotten beside a park where children rollerskate and the elderly do *qi gong* exercises. The house was once an elegant courtyard-style pavilion with soaring eaves and an elaborate garden, and a sign announces in gold-painted calligraphy that it is a museum. But now the museum is deserted, the door is padlocked, the windows are grimy with soot and dust, and another sign says that the museum has been closed indefinitely.

It all seems sad and unfair, because the museum honors Admiral Zheng He, China's Christopher Columbus, and Zheng He could have been one of the world's central figures of the last millennium. If events had gone a bit differently, then he would have led the way for China's settlement of America, Australia, and Africa, and Columbus would be a forgotten figure relegated to some dusty, padlocked museum in Genoa. Zheng He is also fascinating because he is at the heart of one of the central enigmas of history: Why did the West triumph over the East in the last millennium? For most of the last few thousand years, Asia was far more advanced than any other part of the world. In that time, it would have seemed far more natural that Chinese or Indians would dominate the world in the year 2000 than that Europeans would. It would have seemed incomparably more likely that America and Australia would be colonized by Chinese than by the inhabitants of that then-backward island called Britain.

Examining the turning point—and understanding why the West dominated the last five hundred years instead of the East—may lend some insight into the reasons great powers falter, into the potential of Asia, and into the obstacles it will face in recovering its greatness. It seems natural today to think of the West as powerful, to think of the Americas as largely populated by people of European stock, to think of Asia as poor and backward. But it could easily have been different, and one of those crucial moments when history wavered in the balance came in the mid-fifteenth century when China's eunuchs and scholars feuded over Zheng He's voyages. The eunuchs, who included Zheng He, had been castrated as boys and recruited to work in the palace and look after the emperor's harem. Because the emperors wished to be certain that the children of any of their wives were their own, rigorous note-keeping recorded when each

*There is some debate about exactly what Zheng He's grandest vessels, the four-hundred-foot-long treasure ships, looked like. But this model, prepared for a museum in Quanzhou, China, is a reasonable guess.*

woman spent the night with the emperor, and men other than eunuchs had little contact with the women. Partly because proximity breeds power, the eunuchs often rose to important decision-making positions and became advisers to the emperors. The scholars, who had passed a series of local, provincial, and national exams and who reflected the cream of a meritocratic civil service, were supposed to be running the country under the emperor and deeply resented the influence of the eunuchs. Each side had great failings: The eunuchs were often dreadfully corrupt, and the scholars tended to be reactionaries who opposed any reforms, experiments, or explorations.

Zheng He was an unlikely commander of a great Chinese fleet, in that he was a Muslim from a rebel family and was seized by the Chinese army when he was still a boy. Like many other prisoners, he was castrated—his sexual organs completely cut off in a process that killed many boys. But Zheng He was strong as well as brilliant and tenacious, and he grew up to be physically imposing. He was a natural leader who had the good fortune to be assigned as a servant to the household of a great prince, Zhu Di. The prince and the eunuch grew close, and they conspired to overthrow the prince's nephew, the Emperor of China. With Zheng He as one of the prince's military commanders, the revolt succeeded and the prince became China's Yongle Emperor. One of the emperor's first acts (after torturing to death those who had opposed him) was to reward Zheng He with the command of a mighty fleet that was to sail off and assert China's preeminence in the world.

Between 1405 and 1433, Zheng He commanded seven major expeditions, involving the largest naval fleet that the world would see for the next five centuries. Not until World War I did the West mount anything comparable. Chinese records show that Zheng He's fleet included twenty-eight thousand sailors on three hundred ships, the longest of which were four hundred feet long. By comparison, Columbus in 1492 had ninety sailors on three ships, the biggest of which was eighty-five feet long. Zheng He's ships also had design elements such as balanced rudders and watertight bulwark compartments that would not be introduced in Europe for another 350 years.

The ships sailed as far as East Africa and could have gone around the globe. It is difficult to conceive of their magnificence, for each of the grandest ships—the "treasure ships"—had nine masts, huge red silk sails, twenty-four bronze cannon, carved wooden animal heads, and painted sides with large "eyes" in front to see the ocean ahead. The treasure ships had luxury cabins with balconies for the top officers and for foreign princes who would be brought home, and these ships were backed by specialized vessels including horse-carriers, troop transports, cargo ships, two kinds of warships, and water tankers carrying drinking water. The crews included 10 translators, 5 astronomers, 180 doctors and pharmacologists to treat the sick and gather foreign herbs, and even 2 protocol experts to ensure that the Chinese treated foreigners with just the proper degree of politeness.

The sophistication of the fleet underscores how far the East used to be ahead of the West. In a broader sense, it indicates the stakes for the entire world as Asia struggles to get back on its feet. The present situation—with Asia making up a minor part of the world economy—is unusual in historical terms. For the great majority of the last few thousand years, Asia has been far wealthier and more advanced and cosmopolitan than any place in Europe. Several ancient Chinese cities had populations of more than one million at their peak, and by some accounts the Tang Dynasty capital of Changan had almost two million taxable residents in the latter part of the first millennium. In contrast, as late as 1500 the largest city in Europe was probably Naples, with a total population of 150,000. So ancient Asia was the longtime champion of commerce and technology, and one of the central questions for the coming decades is whether it is now ready to recover a part of what it lost.

### ASIA'S LEAD:
### DATES OF INNOVATIONS IN ASIA AND THE WEST

| INNOVATION | ASIA | THE WEST |
| --- | --- | --- |
| Cotton cloth or clothes | 3rd millennium B.C. (India) | 16th century |
| Iron casting | 2nd century B.C. (China) | 13th century |
| Planting with automatic seeder | 1st century B.C. (China) | 1700 |
| Curved iron plows | 1st century (China) | 1700 |
| Paper | 2nd century (China) | 1150 |
| Rotary fan for ventilation | 2nd century (China) | 1556 |
| Wheelbarrow | 3rd century (China) | 1200 |
| Porcelain | 3rd century (China) | 1709 |
| Watertight compartments in ships | 5th century (China) | 1790 |
| Printing with wood blocks | 8th century (China) | 1400 |
| Gunpowder | 10th century (China) | 13th century |
| Bombs | 1000 (China) | 16th century |
| Printing with movable type | 1045 (China) | 1440 |
| Iron-clad warships | 1592 (Korea) | 1862 |

For most of the last four thousand years, Asia accounted for at least two-thirds of the world's gross domestic product, perhaps considerably more. Some scholars even suggest that as recently as the year 1800—when China and India had already been stagnating for centuries—Asia still accounted for 80 percent of the world's GDP. I think that is too high. Angus Maddison, a British economic historian whose calculations I find the most meticulous, argues persuasively that Asia had lost tremendous ground to Europe by the early nineteenth century but that it dominated the world nonetheless. His figures underscore that the real "Asian economic crisis" lasted from about 1820 to about 1950. He concludes that as late as 1820, Asia still accounted for 58 percent of the world's GDP, but that this dropped to a low of 17 percent in 1952. Since then it has risen to more than 30 percent.

### SHARE OF WORLD GDP, IN PERCENTAGES

|  | 1700 | 1820 | 1890 | 1952 | 1998 |
|---|---|---|---|---|---|
| Entire Asia | 62 | 58 | 32 | 17 | 33 |
| China | 23 | 32 | 13 | 5 | 11 |
| India | 23 | 16 | 11 | 4 | 5 |
| Japan | 5 | 3 | 3 | 3 | 6 |
| Europe | 23 | 27 | 40 | 30 | 23 |
| United States | 0 | 2 | 14 | 28 | 21 |

### TOTAL SIZE OF ECONOMY, IN 1990 U.S. DOLLARS

|  | YEAR 50 | YEAR 960 | YEAR 1280 | YEAR 1700 | YEAR 1820 | YEAR 1952 | YEAR 1998 |
|---|---|---|---|---|---|---|---|
| China | 18 billion | 25 billion | 60 billion | 83 billion | 229 billion | 306 billion | 3.8 trillion |
| Europe | 15 billion | 16 billion | 34 billion | 84 billion | 188 billion | 1.8 trillion | 8.6 trillion |

Source: The figures for these two tables are largely from Angus Maddison, *Chinese Performance in the Long Run;* all calculations are based on purchasing power parity. Copyright OECD, 1998

Zheng He's expeditions were not flukes, for Asia had been adventurous about travel since ancient times. American Indians came principally from Asia, of course, and some historians believe that there were repeated infusions of East Asian blood and influence into the Americas by sea over the millennia. For example, historians have found evidence that when China's Shang Dynasty was overthrown in about 1045 B.C., Chinese refugees may have sailed to the Americas and settled among the Olmec people of Mexico and the Chavin tribesmen of Peru. An ancient Chinese chronicle recounts that in the fifth century, a Chinese monk named Hui

Shen traveled with five Afghan monks to a place called the Far East Country, which sounds a great deal like Mayan Mexico.

People in what is now Indonesia also sailed with extraordinary skill, settling distant islands as far as Hawaii and becoming the Polynesians. They also sailed in the other direction, and it is now generally accepted that Indonesians settled Madagascar, the island off East Africa, more than 1,200 years ago. Indeed, the language of Madagascar is still similar to a dialect spoken in Indonesia. That was an extraordinary journey comparable in distance to Columbus's voyage to America. Even more startling, there is some evidence that Indonesians may have landed in Mexico. Scholars have noted similarities between the Sulawesi people of Indonesia and the Otomi tribes of central Mexico, such as in the methods and tools they use to make bark cloth.

Asia was a grand trading network, so vast that in the year 2 A.D. a ship from an unidentified state brought a rhinoceros to China. In 10 A.D., Persian visitors brought the Chinese emperor an ostrich. By the time of the Tang Dynasty in the latter part of the first millennium, China was importing small numbers of African slaves and had a large number of exotic prostitutes. A poet refers to "the Western boy with curly hair and green eyes," and paintings on pottery show a broad range of foreign faces. Records suggest that as early as the seventh century the city of Guangzhou had two hundred thousand foreign residents: Arabs, Persians, Malays, Indians, Africans, and Turks.

Some people believe that Asia's high-water mark came during China's Tang Dynasty, and Tang artistry and poetry is indeed unrivaled. But overall I would argue that Asia's apex was China's Song Dynasty, which ended in 1279. The Song Dynasty was an era of free trade and a huge expansion in shipping and maritime technology. With newfangled developments like the compass and lighthouses, shipping and trade grew enormously. China was the greatest of Asia's civilizations, but it was simply the brightest star in a dazzling constellation of varied peoples and cultures. One simply has to wander the ninth-century stone stupas of Borobudur in Indonesia; dodge the cattle grazing around the stupas in the eleventh-century Burmese capital of Pagan; tour the twelfth-century ruins of Angkor Wat in Cambodia; or pick up a copy of Japan's eleventh-century *Tale of Genji*— sometimes described as the world's first novel—to appreciate the brilliance and diversity of ancient Asia.

*[margin note: brilliance & diversity of Ancient Asia]*

One of the might-have-beens is Karakorum, the capital of the thirteenth-century Mongol empire. Karakorum looks like nothing today—just some old rubble. But it was from these steppes that Genghis Khan's armies set off to kill people on a scale not seen again until civilization arrived in the twentieth century. It is said that Mongol armies killed 90 percent of the population in parts of Persia and effectively destroyed the irrigation system so that agriculture never entirely recovered. Censuses show China's population dropping by thirty million at this time, although it is unclear to what extent one should blame Mongol knives and to what extent disease and dislocation from the Mongol attacks. One of Genghis Khan's grandsons, Batu, conquered Russia, Poland, and Hungary and by some accounts was poised to seize all of Europe, although skeptics say he had run out of grassland for his horses and was ready to turn back. In any case, in December 1241 the khan died, and Batu was summoned home. Western Europe was spared.

Then in the fourteenth and fifteenth centuries Asia began to run out of steam. There was still plenty of greatness to come, but Asia's commitment to free trade was waning, and it was steadily losing its advantage over Europe. Even in the early 1400s Asia could still have triumphed in any collision with Europe. But after Zheng He's expeditions, China—and much of Asia—spun itself a cocoon. That is why I came to be fascinated with Zheng He and wanted to follow his journeys. I wanted to see what legacy, if any, remained of his achievements and to figure out why his travels did not remake the world in the way Columbus's did.

First, I decided to make a pilgrimage to his tomb outside Nanjing. Here was one of the millennium's greatest explorers, a man who almost turned history on its head, and I felt impelled to find some trace of his life. I knew that he had been buried by the Ming emperors in a grand tomb on a hillside, with an inscribed tablet that had vanished a few decades ago and finally been replaced, so I hired a taxi and drove to the hillside. The road petered out from asphalt to gravel to dirt to nothing, so I asked an old peasant for directions. The man, gnarled and weathered, was weeding a vegetable garden beside his house, and he turned out to be a lonely widower eager for a conversation.

"I can't get any work done, I guess," he muttered grumpily. "So where are you from?"

"I'm an American. Where's Zheng He's tomb? Do you know?"

"Right near here. An American?"

"So which direction is the tomb?"

"Right down that path. That'll take you to a bigger path and turn left. An American! Well, well. Let me show you. . . ."

*Tang Yiming, a Chinese peasant, talks about the Zheng He
tomb behind him.*

His name was Tang Yiming. Seventy-one years old, still lithe and
strong, his gray hair was short and ragged; it looked as if he had cut his
own hair with a pair of dull scissors while peering at a cracked mirror. He
tried to be gruff but kept smiling and chatting in spite of himself. He was
impossible to turn off.

Tang accompanied me to a long stone stairway that climbed up the hillside, surrounded by forests and wild grass. We took the stairway to a
rebuilt, modern tomb of white stone. It was solemn and serene, with the
characters for "Zheng He's Grave" on it, plus a bit of Arabic from the
beginning of the Koran: "In the name of God, the gracious, the mer-
ciful. . . ."

As I admired the tomb, I mentioned idly to Tang that it was a pity the
old Ming Dynasty tablet had vanished. "It's one of the mysteries of Zheng
He," I said absentmindedly.

"Oh, yeah, the old tablet," he said nonchalantly. "When I was a boy,
there was a Ming Dynasty tablet here. When it disappeared, the government offered a huge reward to anyone who would return it—a reward big
enough to pay for a new house. Seemed like a lot of money. But the prob-

lem was that we couldn't give it back. We'd smashed it up to use as building materials ourselves. People around here are poor, and they couldn't afford to buy materials to build houses."

"So you . . ." I tried to ask, but there was no stopping Tang.

"Beside the tablet there used to be a turtle-shell tomb protecting the grave of Zheng He," he added. "But in the Great Leap Forward [in 1958], we all set up backyard furnaces to make steel. You know about that? China was going to make more steel than England, and so we all made little furnaces and threw our shovels and cooking pots inside. That was my furnace right over there." He pointed to a hole in the hillside, now grown over with weeds and shrubs. "So then they told us that we had to have a road so that trucks could come and collect the steel. There was this dirt path, but they said it wasn't good enough. We had to put rocks down so the trucks wouldn't get stuck. Well, where could we get rocks? The only thing we could do was smash up the old Zheng He tomb. We broke it up into little pieces and put it on the dirt trail, and it looked okay. But of course we never did make enough steel for a truck to come and get it."

Tang took a puff of his cigarette. I looked at him, taken aback by his admission. On impulse, I mentioned that Zheng He is believed to have died on his last voyage and to have been buried at sea, so there is some doubt about whether there is anything inside the tomb.

"Oh, there's nothing in there," Tang said, a bit sadly. "No bones, nothing. That's for sure."

"How do you know?"

"In 1962, people dug up the grave, looking for anything to sell. We dug up the ground to one-and-a-half times the height of a man. But there was absolutely nothing in there. It's empty."

Chinese records make clear that Zheng He's fleet reached the Kenyan ports of Malindi and Mombasa. Zheng He knew about Europe from Arab traders, and he could have continued around the Cape of Good Hope and established direct trade with Europe. But Europe was a backward region with nothing to offer, as the Chinese saw it. China wanted ivory, medicine, spices, exotic woods, even samples of African wildlife, but it had little interest in European products like wool, beads, or wine. So the Chinese turned up their noses at Europe.

It is normally said that there is no trace in Africa today of Zheng He's trips, but as I conducted my research I came across a few intriguing references to the possibility that one of Zheng He's ships had wrecked off the

*The island of Pate, in the Indian Ocean near Kenya. Chinese sailors from Zheng He's fleet may have shipwrecked here in the fifteenth century, swum ashore, and intermarried with the natives.*

coast of Kenya, in the seas near a tiny island called Pate. It was too enticing to pass up. Any settlement would mark a concrete example of how Zheng He's voyages had left an imprint on distant nations and how it could have left a greater one. So I flew to Lamu, an island off northern Kenya, and hired a boat and a Swahili interpreter-guide to go to Pate and see for myself.

Pate is its own world, without electricity or roads or vehicles. From the sea, the island still looks as it must have in the fifteenth century: a seemingly impenetrable shore of endless mangrove trees. The boatman pulled into a narrow black-sand beach, and I splashed ashore. My interpreter led the way through the jungle, along a winding trail scattered with mangos, coconuts, and even occasional seashells deposited by high tides. Pate was wild and picturesque, but my search was frustrating at first because most of the inhabitants didn't look at all Asian and had never heard of any Chinese. Finally, one sweltering afternoon I strolled through the coconut palms into the village of Siyu, and one of the first people I met was Abdullah Mohammed Badui, forty-four, a light-skinned fisherman. His narrow eyes caught my attention, and so I stopped and chatted with him. He said he was one of fewer than one hundred people left in the Famao clan, and he added: "Legend has it that we are descended from Chinese and others. A Chinese ship was coming along and it hit rocks and wrecked. The sailors swam ashore to the village that we now call Shanga, and they married the local women, and that is why we Famao look so different." Gradually I found other Famao people who looked a bit Chinese and from them a tale gradually emerged.

Countless generations ago, they said, Chinese had been trading with local African kings, and had even been given giraffes by the local kings to take back to China. But one of the Chinese ships had struck rocks on the seaward side of Pate, and the sailors had swum ashore, bringing with them much of the porcelain and other materials from the ship. They had married local women, converted to Islam, and named the village Shanga. Soon afterward, fighting erupted, Shanga was destroyed, and the Famao fled to other villages.

There are hints that there may be something to this tale. The ocean side of Pate island, particularly near Shanga, has many rocks hidden below the surface of the water. And aside from the slight resemblance of some of the Famao to Asians, there is the legend of the giraffes. Chinese records show that Zheng He brought back a number of giraffes to China. They caused an enormous stir because they were believed to be mythical *qilin,* or Chinese unicorns. Likewise, while Chinese ceramics are found in many places along the east African coast, the porcelain on Pate was overwhelmingly concentrated among the Famao, possibly meaning that they had inherited it rather than purchased it from Arab traders. Some ancient Famao graves do not look like Kenyan graves but have dome tops that are sometimes seen in China; the Chinese call them "turtle-shell graves."

Residents of Pate and the other islands of Lamu do a kind of basket-weaving, using thin reeds woven into a triangular pattern, that is common in southern China but unknown in nearby parts of the Kenyan mainland. On Pate, drums are played in the Chinese style more than the African style, and some words that may be of Chinese origin are used in the local dialect. More startling, in 1569 a Portuguese priest named Monclaro wrote that Pate—but no other place in the region—had a flourishing silk-making industry. This seemed incredible to me, but elders in several villages in Pate confirmed to me that their island produced silk until about half a century ago.

The Chinese on Pate, if that is what they were, became stranded when China's leadership decided to end the voyages and keep its fleet at home. The voyages had been backed by the eunuchs and viewed with suspicion by China's traditional elite, the Confucian scholar-officials. The eunuchs have had bad press for the last few centuries, partly because they were extraordinarily corrupt, but one can argue that it was the scholars who got China into a much greater mess. After some brutal power struggles, the scholars reasserted themselves (starting by scratching out the eyes of three eunuchs). The scholars destroyed Zheng He's sailing records, and with the backing of the new emperor they dismantled China's navy. By 1500 the government had made it a capital offense to build boats with more than two masts. In 1525, the government ordered the destruction of all ocean-going ships. The greatest navy in history, which a century earlier had had 3,500 ships (by comparison, the U.S. Navy now has 324), had been extinguished, and China's scholars had decisively steered a course that would lead to poverty, defeat, and backwardness.

China's retreat into isolation amounted to a catastrophic missed opportunity, one that laid the groundwork for the rise of Europeans and eventually Americans. Westerners often attribute their economic edge today to the intelligence, democratic mindset, or hard work of their forebears, but perhaps a more important reason is the foolishness of fifteenth-century Chinese rulers.

*guiding Question*

My search to understand what went wrong with Asia over the last millennium took me to Calicut, India, which was one of Zheng He's main destinations. Located in southwest India, Calicut is the pepper capital of the world. Much of the pepper that Americans sprinkle on their dinners comes from the area around Calicut.

India was one of the great civilizations of ancient times. Its mathematicians probably devised what we call Arabic numbers and knew how to calculate with the zero when the English were still savage tribes. Its astronomers mapped the cosmos and its artisans produced dazzlingly fine cotton cloth when Europeans were still scratching around in uncomfortable woolens. So it is no wonder that in the fourteenth and fifteenth centuries Calicut was one of the great ports of the world—"the great country of the Western ocean," Ma Huan, one of Zheng He's aides, called it in his

*An ice-cream peddler on the beach in Calicut, India, where Zheng He's fleet berthed in the fifteenth century. The pier in the background had to be abandoned in 1989 because it had never been properly maintained.*

memoirs of 1426. In the early fifteenth century, the Chinese fleet in Calicut Harbor symbolized the strength of the world's two greatest powers.

Yet Calicut's significance has been waning steadily ever since, and it has fallen on such hard times that my travel agent booked me mistakenly on a flight to Calcutta. Certainly, it was easy to see why Calicut was no longer a leading international port. Telephone calls to Calicut did not always go through, and my interpreter in Calicut warned me at the last minute that there would be another in a series of general strikes on the day that I was supposed to arrive. "You've got to change your arrival date," he explained. "There'll be no taxis, no buses, no cars on the road."

In the end, my interpreter found a private car, and I got to Calicut smoothly. After arriving, I went to the beach in the center of town to look at the harbor where Zheng He had berthed. The beach was crowded with young lovers and ice-cream salesmen, and it was framed on either side by long piers jutting out to sea. Those piers marked the port of Calicut, but it

*A young woman in Calicut named Rukhiya bathes her children in front of her house, pouring buckets of dirty water over their heads. Far too many Indian children never learn to read and never have access to clean water. In short, not nearly enough has changed since Zheng He visited Calicut in the fifteenth century.*

was immediately obvious that they were unusable. The metal framework remained, twisted and tilted, but the wooden surface had completely crumbled on one pier and partly collapsed on the other.

"The piers got old and no proper maintenance was ever carried out," explained Captain E. G. Mohanan, the head of Calicut Port. "By the time we thought of it, it was not economical to fix it up." So in 1989, trade was halted, and one of the former great ports of the world became no port at all.

Fortunately for Mohanan, caretakers looked after the residence of the port director better than they looked after the piers. So even if the port itself has collapsed, the port director still gets a beautiful house overlooking the crumbled piers, and he even has his own cannon in the front yard.

The saddest evidence of Calicut's stagnation is in the slums. I walked through several poor neighborhoods in Calicut, and it seemed that in some respects life had not improved very much over the last five hundred years. Electricity is rare in the slums, and flush toilets nonexistent. Homes still have thatch roofs, many people are illiterate, almost everybody has parasitic worms, and most houses do not even have outhouses. Instead, slum residents disappear behind a tree or go to the river, and the result is that drinking water is tainted and children die unnecessarily as a result of diarrhea.

Calicut used to be a center for shipbuilding, and for many hundreds of years it has made beautiful wooden ships out of teak. In the shipyards, a few Arab dhows are still being made, like the 136-foot cargo vessel that workmen were hammering on when I visited. Three years in the making, the dhow was just a few weeks from completion.

"People here make the boats without any calculations, without any blueprints," boasted P.O. Basheer, the head of the shipbuilding company, as he stood on the deck. "In other places, shipbuilders use computers, but we depend on craftsmanship. The carpenters lay the keel and then build it from there without ever drafting plans." But perhaps that reluctance to modernize was precisely Calicut's problem: Now countries like South Korea and Japan are the biggest shipbuilders, for Calicut never graduated from handmade wooden boats to machine-made steel ships. "This is a dying business," Basheer admitted. "Ten years ago, there were twenty or thirty of these boats made each season. Now there are only one or two."

As I've said, Asia probably began to stagnate economically in the fourteenth century, but this means only that it did not grow. There was little slippage in per capita incomes until the end of the eighteenth century. Although the evidence is mixed, there is some reason to think that as recently as 1750 Chinese living standards were as high as Europe's, although India's and those of Southeast Asia lagged considerably.

The average Chinese lived longer in the eighteenth century, ate better, and enjoyed more luxury goods than a European of that period. For example, China consumed almost five pounds of sugar per capita in 1750, compared to two pounds in Europe. Another luxury, tobacco, was much more common in China, so much so that even toddlers smoked. The average Chinese used about six pounds of cotton cloth in 1750, compared to less than five pounds in Germany, which was relatively prosperous. Inheritance records suggest that jewelry and furniture were more common among ordinary Chinese than ordinary Europeans as late as the eighteenth century.

Some figures limn the story of Asia's economic history. As late as 1700, well after Asia's peak, India and China each amounted to a larger share of

the world economy than the United States takes up tod
and the United States began to take off, while India and (
Incredibly, per capita incomes in China were actually signi
1952 than they had been in 1280.

### GROWTH RATES IN PER CAPITA GDP
### (ANNUAL AVERAGE COMPOUND GROWTH RATE)

|  | 1700–1820 | 1820–1952 | 1952–1978 | 1978–1995 |
|---|---|---|---|---|
| China | 0.00 | 0.08 | 2.34 | 6.04 |
| India | 0.00 | 0.10 | 1.81 | 2.53 |
| Japan | 0.10 | 0.95 | 6.66 | 2.68 |
| United States | 0.62 | 1.63 | 2.10 | 1.47 |
| Europe | 0.22 | 1.03 | 3.56 | 1.48 |

Source: Angus Maddison, *Chinese Economic Performance in the Long Run.* Copyright OECD, 1998

As Matthew Arnold put it in "Obermann Once More" in 1855:

> *The East bow'd low before the blast,*
> *In Patient, deep disdain.*
> *She let the legions thunder past,*
> *And plunged in thought again.*

*Making $ hot*
*not so hot*
*in china*

So what went wrong? Scholars, politicians, and economic historians
offer a range of reasons, and I find two and a half to be most convincing.

The first is that Asia was insufficiently greedy. The dominant social
ethos in ancient China was Confucianism and in India it was caste, and in
both nations the elites looked down their noses at business. Ancient China
cared about many things—prestige, honor, culture, arts, education, ancestors, religion, filial piety—and making money was well down the list. Confucius had specifically declared that it was wrong for a man to make a
distant voyage while his parents were still alive, and he had condemned
profit as the concern of "a little man." Indeed, Zheng He's ships were built
on such a grand and luxurious scale that the voyages were not the huge
money-maker that they could have been.

Likewise, in India, a high-ranking Brahmin would have lost his caste—
and thus all social status—by making a business trip abroad. For Indian
elites, the focus of life was faith and ritual, not making money. According
to tradition, a Brahmin was supposed to follow a strict code even when
defecating. He was to choose a spot in a field according to complex rules

out distances from the nearest well, temple, and sacred banyan tree. Then he had to hang the Brahmin's sacred thread over his left ear, and while squatting he had to avoid glancing at the sun, moon, stars, or a banyan tree. Afterward, he had to wash his hands and feet with the help of a brass pot, and then scrub his hands again with soil that could not come from a cow pasture, a white ant nest, or any area shaded by a banyan tree. Then he had to wash his hands five more times, beginning with the left; wash his feet five times, starting with the right; and wash out his mouth eight times, spitting out the water to the left each time. That covers only a few of the twenty-three rules for defecation, but it perhaps demonstrates that the elite had other things on their minds than vulgar, temporal concerns like making money. One result was that the rich tended to hoard their wealth in the form of gold or land, rather than recycle it or invest it in commercial ventures.

In contrast to Asia, Europe was obsessed with greed. Portugal led the age of discovery because it wanted spices, and it was mostly commercial shipping and the hope of profits that over the course of the fifteenth century drove Portugal's ships steadily down the African coast and eventually around it to Asia. The profits were vast: Ferdinand Magellan's crew sold a cargo of twenty-six tons of cloves for ten thousand times its cost.

The second reason for Asia's grand failure is related to the lack of greed and had to do with the East's complacency, its tendency to look inward, its devotion to past ideals and methods, its respect for authority, its suspicion of new ideas. Asia lacked the excitement and curiosity of Renaissance Europe, the intellectual ferment that allowed a little country town like Florence to produce or attract in a short space of time Filippo Brunelleschi, Leone Battista Alberti, Leonardo da Vinci, Michelangelo Buonarroti, Niccolò Machiavelli, Francisco Gioccoardomo, Picco della Mirandola, and Girolamo Savonarola. Chinese elites regarded their country as the "Middle Kingdom" and believed they had nothing to learn from barbarians abroad. India had much of the same self-satisfaction, and eventually so did Japan. M.P. Sridharan, a historian, sat on the porch of his home in Calicut and mused: "Indians didn't go to Portugal, not because they couldn't but because they didn't want to."

Fifteenth-century Portugal was the opposite, entirely focused outward. With its coastline and fishing industry, it had always looked to the sea, and rivalries with Spain and other countries meant that it was shut out of the Mediterranean trade. Its only hope to get at the wealth of the East was to go out to the ocean.

The one-half reason is simply that Asian nations were more successful at unifying than European ones. China and Europe are somewhat analogous in terms of their internal diversity, yet China was one nation while Europe was many. The upshot was that China took an all-or-nothing gamble that it lost: When the Confucian scholars reasserted control in Beijing and banned shipping, they in effect condemned all of China. Japan and Korea lost the same gamble when they tried to seal themselves off. In contrast, European countries committed economic suicide more selectively—Portugal slipped into a quasi-Chinese mindset in the sixteenth century, slaughtering Jews, burning heretics, and driving astronomers and scientists abroad, but Holland and England were free to march ahead and take up the slack.

If those were the reasons that held the East back, how does Asia stack up today? Pretty well, I think. The factors that held Asia back for hundreds of years have largely dissipated in recent decades. China in particular has reversed its mindset almost entirely since the fifteenth century: It is now a society that is obsessed with making money and that is curious and outward-looking. Its lack of unity has also been helpful, for Taiwan and Hong Kong were able to test capitalism and prove its merit while Mao Zedong tested socialism. Yet India does not do so well. Although it is changing, India even today is far too inward-looking and much too cool to foreign investment, and it is not a particularly capitalist country. I thought about how India today might be harming itself in some of the same ways as in the fifteenth century, as I dipped my dosa, a south Indian bread, into curry sauce for breakfast at the mayor's house in Calicut.

M.M. Padmavathy, the mayor, is a woman who is young and friendly and unostentatious—and a Communist. Calicut, like several other parts of India, is a Communist stronghold, and Mayor Padmavathy voiced confidence in the eventual triumph of socialism. Wearing a red sari and sitting on a rickety wooden chair in the dilapidated dining room, Padmavathy talked about foreign investment, and the best that she could say is that it is not entirely bad. "We cannot completely rule out foreign investment," she said. "What we are against is the total domination by foreign multinationals."

Because of the trauma of colonization, India is hasty to fault others for its own problems. In discussing the reasons for India's decline with Indian economists, I was struck by the vehemence with which they tended to lay the blame on everybody but their own people. "We were leading once, because we had primary products—pepper, ginger, gifts of nature—that were very valuable," I.G. Menon, an economics professor in Calicut, told me earnestly. "But we were exploited.

"We did not go ahead with an industrial revolution because we had no capital," he added. "Our capital had all gone to England. In Europe, England was the country with the most capital, so it began the Industrial Revolution. But that capital was mostly from India."

As an explanation for what went wrong, this seems to me preposterous. As Nehru himself noted, India had already surrendered its lead long before the Europeans showed up. A country that had pioneered mathematics and medicine and sent shiploads of traders and scholars to places like China and Indonesia should have seemed more likely to colonize England than the other way around. But it lost its edge, and by the time the Portuguese arrived it was a shell. That is why the Europeans, with puny, vastly outnumbered armies, were able to seize India and then plunder it for themselves. "One senses a progressive deterioration during centuries," Nehru wrote. "The urge to life and endeavor becomes less, the creative spirit fades away and gives place to the imitative. Where triumphant and rebellious thought had tried to pierce the mysteries of nature and the universe, the wordy commentator comes with his glosses and long explanations. . . . Indian life becomes a sluggish stream, living in the past, moving slowly through the accumulations of dead centuries. The heavy burden of the past crushes it, and a kind of coma seizes it."

Indian scholars do not always see things this way, and some worry that Western robber barons are about to rape India again with a new kind of colonization. "We have to be internally strong before we can embrace foreign goods," Menon told me sternly. "There can be no partnership between unequals."

I pondered that while rattling back to my hotel in an early model Indian-made Ambassador car, an old clunker like all Indian vehicles. Imported cars have been mostly kept out of India, so the Ambassador had no competition and never progressed. India thus destroyed any hope of building a modern car industry, and my Ambassador was an antique without the charm. In similar fashion, my hotel in Calicut offered high prices and indifferent service, because Indian hotels have been protected from outside competition with foreign chains like Hilton and Holiday Inn.

The Indian subcontinent was one of the great tragedies of the twentieth century. Blessed with tremendous potential—and, as late as 1898, factory wages that were higher than Japan's—it slid into an abyss of mismanagement, bureaucratic paralysis, ethnic antagonisms, and socialist economics. The state has always been powerful in India: At the height of the Mogul Empire from the sixteenth to the nineteenth century, one-quarter of the population worked for the government and at least 15 percent of national income went to the state, compared to 6 percent in England at the time. Alas, the Indian state still does not want to let go. And many Indians convince themselves that foreign countries are plotting to subjugate India; the worst damage that English rule did to India was not to its economy but to its soul.

India reminds me in its insecurities of a Chinese intellectual I know who spent two decades in prison and labor camps and whose entire personality is a nervous tic. He is anxious and unctuous and neurotic and has trouble interacting with others, and I suppose that is what happens to a person who is humiliated for most of his adult life—or to a proud country that is humiliated for several centuries. As V.S. Naipaul wrote, India is "a wounded civilization."

Yet partly because it has been managed so foolishly for so long, India has more potential for growth than any country in the world. In a few decades it will probably surpass China to be the most populous nation in the world, and its baby-boom generation is now pouring into the labor force, just as China's did over the last two decades. Indians do brilliantly everywhere in the world except in India, just as Chinese used to do wonderfully everywhere outside China. If India can shed the two great burdens that have weighed it down for the last five hundred years—social rigidity and a distaste for free economic competition—then it can change Asia and the world. And indeed, change is coming to India, but too slowly. One of the most critical questions for the world in the next decade is how soon India can emerge from its torpor.

One lesson from Zheng He's adventures may apply to the United States. The conventional wisdom in the West about what causes great powers to decline emerges from Yale professor Paul Kennedy's brilliant book *The Rise and Fall of Great Powers.* Kennedy argues that the United States faces the risk of "imperial overstretch" analogous to that faced by Spain in 1600 or Britain in 1900; both countries were humbled because they made strategic commitments that ultimately were too much to handle. Kennedy's book has been enormously influential, and most thoughtful Americans now accept that reaching too far could ultimately bring about the end of the United States's dominance in the world today.

There is something to that parallel with Spain and England. But, coming at it from an Asian perspective, my analogies are different: I see China and to a lesser extent India as models of the decline of great powers. Both fell from global power not because they stretched too far but because they did not stretch enough. Thus it seems to me that America faces not only the Scylla of imperial overstretch but also the Charybdis of imperial understretch. And the United States perhaps fits the Asian pattern more than that of Europe, for there are signs in America today of a disinclination to reach abroad: There are hints of the same kind of haughty arrogance and triumphalism, the same disinterest in foreign cultures and languages, the same self-absorption that ultimately brought down China and India. Large American companies have expanded abroad, but as a whole the United States remains remarkably inward-looking. It is the only industrialized country in the world where foreign books are rarely on the best-seller lists, where foreign movies are almost never box-office hits, where there is an instinctive aversion to the United Nations and to key international treaties, where even many well-educated people do not speak foreign languages. The United States remains remarkably provincial at a time when the world is so globalized, and that is a disequilibrium that will be difficult to sustain.

Zheng He's voyages did have some lingering effects. Some Chinese had already migrated to Southeast Asia in the early part of the millennium, and the Indonesian port of Gresik (now, like Calicut, a sad backwater with a cement plant and not much else) already had one thousand Chinese families when the Chinese fleet showed up in 1406. But it was Zheng He's expeditions that hugely bolstered the Chinese diaspora, leading to the waves of Chinese who moved to Southeast Asia. Those overseas Chinese are now the backbone of economies from Indonesia and the Philippines to Singapore and Thailand.

These overseas Chinese still treat Zheng He as a god—individual Chinese are often promoted after death to become gods, a bit like saints in the West—and the world's largest Zheng He temple is in the Indonesian city of Semarang. It was reassuring to see that even if Zheng He has been largely forgotten within China, he has become a deity in Southeast Asia. "If people want good luck, or if they want a cure for disease, they come and pray to Zheng He," explained Priambudi Setiakusuma, a Chinese businessman who is head of the temple association in Semarang. Priambudi cited the example of a relative of his who had killed a pedestrian with his car and then appealed to Zheng He for mercy. The relative was acquitted of wrongdoing and released from prison. But then he hit and killed another pedestrian, and he had to go once more to appeal to Zheng He. Again, Priambudi explained, Zheng He granted the wish, and the relative got off scot-free for the second time.

"Frankly," Priambudi added after a long pause, "I do not think that the god should have been so lenient."

As I visited places like Semarang and Pate, I mused on the significance of Zheng He's journeys. If ancient Asia had been greedier and more outward-looking, if other traders had followed Zheng He and then continued on, Asia might well have dominated Africa and even Europe. Chinese might have settled not only in Malaysia and Singapore but also east Africa, Australia, and the Americas. What I'd glimpsed on Pate was the high-water mark of an Asian push that simply stopped—not for want of ships or know-how, but strictly for want of national will. How different would history have been if Zheng He had ventured with imperial backing to America? For starters, this book would be written in Chinese.

By calling back Zheng He and renouncing his adventurous spirit, China embarked on a path that ultimately sacrificed five centuries of global leadership for itself and all of Asia. Yet all is not quite lost. Whatever happens in the next few years or even the next decade, our best bet is that Zheng He's spirit will finally triumph in the East. And one of the great ironies is that nothing ultimately will help the East more than the Asian economic crisis and the chaos that it unleashed in places like the private city that Sheryl visited in Thailand.

*Salamet pumps water so that his wife, Yuti, can wash the family clothes at the neighbor-hood pump. Together, they borrowed money to go into business.*

### CHAPTER THREE

# Building Empires

## SHERYL WUDUNN

*Let us all be happy and live within our means, even if we have
to borrer the money to do it with.*

—ARTEMUS WARD, AMERICAN HUMORIST, 1866

He was stocky, short, with a bit of a belly and a roundish face, which some-times bore an expression of hidden power: His thick lips compressed, his olive-colored skin became a mask over his big face, and his dark eyes seemed to pierce right through me. His wide nose and broad cheeks switched from laughter to annoyance in moments. I must have caught him in the latter of those moods in Thailand, when he emerged from a makeshift office like a mayor commanding a city—except that his city wasn't finished yet.

Anant Kanjanapas was cordial, if a bit chilly, the kind of man who got to the point right away. When I met him, he was building an athletic stadium and I had expected some grandiose quarters. Instead, I was surprised to find that his office was made with plywood walls and a tin roof. It was the middle of autumn, and the sun was thumping down on us, but Anant, at fifty-six years of age, looked fresh and crisp in white linen slacks and a Thai-style brown cotton shirt with a geometric print. He barked out a few orders in Thai to his assistants and then he led me to his pride and joy of the moment. I watched as he swiveled back and forth between charm and prickliness. Workers were scrambling to meet a deadline, running to him to consult for a few minutes, then taking away their tape measures or materials. He waved his hand around the arena, with a sense of satisfied accomplishment and a certain delight in the glory of sports. I followed his hand and its grand gesture, but all I saw were immense walls, bare and unpainted, enclosing a large space. I was unimpressed. He took me right to the empty center, and as workers pounded nails and criss-crossed the floor carrying wooden beams, he called for two sofas to be brought to his side. There we sat, specks in a vastness, our voices echoing in the middle of the giant sports stadium.

Anant has always had a knack for the huge and dramatic, and the stadium was a big part of what he envisioned as his own privately run city the size of Boston. Called Muang Thong Thani, the city would revolutionize property development and catapult him from a minor billionaire to a super billionaire—as long as Thailand's economy held up. It was an astonishingly ambitious and dangerous plan, but in some ways it was characteristic of the ambitions and dangers that were gathering in Asia during the long boom.

Making money in Asia in the last few decades has been a bit like making bombs. It's exciting, thrilling, and explosive, and most of the time it works as expected. The rest of the time, as with the Asian economic crisis—well, Anant found out about that firsthand.

Anant, the eldest of eleven children, grew up in a wealthy Chinese family living in Hong Kong. His father, Mongkol Kanjanapas, was born in Bangkok, where he started selling knickknacks on the streets as a teenager before he moved to Hong Kong in the early 1960s. From there, he launched his first watchmaking enterprise, a company that would become his ticket to riches. The family cornered the market as the main agent of Seiko watches in Hong Kong. But the Cultural Revolution in China forced the family back to Bangkok, where they expanded into optical wares and property. Anant moved back to Hong Kong, where he helped the family launch a string of stores, City Chain, that sold watches all over Hong Kong, a city that was fast becoming the watch capital of Asia. When Anant was thirteen, his father sent him to Europe to study English and to get a good education. After a few years, Anant landed at the University of

Switzerland, where he could not only study but also refine his understanding about how timepieces tick. Then his father decided he wanted a toehold in New York, so off went Anant again, ensconcing himself behind the plush curtains of an apartment at the Waldorf-Astoria Hotel. Ambitious and determined, Anant soon helped orchestrate his family's purchase of the Bulova watch company. A dealmaker was born.

Later, his family sold its stake in Bulova to the media mogul Laurence A. Tisch, or Larry, as Anant calls him, and Anant moved back to Hong Kong. He helped his family build a property empire of fifty buildings there, and then they expanded City Chain to Singapore, Thailand, Malaysia, and even Japan. Anant was moving into the ranks of the billionaires—all by a combination of shrewd investment, the odd gamble, and the good luck of being in the world's high-growth region. Economies like those of Hong Kong, South Korea, and Taiwan were growing at rates that were unprecedented in the history of the world. England took fifty-eight years to double its per capita output when it inaugurated the Industrial Revolution at the end of the eighteenth century; America took forty-seven years when it joined a bit later in the nineteenth century. The fastest-growing Asian countries had been doubling their economies every ten years before the crisis.

Steady successes taught Anant that risks paid off, and that big risks paid off big. So Anant began to dream of his biggest project yet. It started one evening in 1973, after he and his parents had just finished dinner at their estate in Kowloon and settled into one of their evening discussions about what they should do next with their business. Instinctively, Anant and his father thought they should do something in Bangkok, for their business in Hong Kong was humming and they wanted a new vista to tackle. Moving into Thailand was a bold move, for Anant knew Thailand as a poor, backward country with open sewers, dirty rivers and canals, and black smoke. Though Anant had grown up mostly in Hong Kong, he had in fact been born in Thailand. Indeed, for years, the name he was most comfortable with was C.P. Wong, which people called him in Hong Kong, and he speaks Thai with a thick Cantonese accent.

Yet Anant was sharp enough to see opportunity for glamour and riches in Thailand, and not just in watches. He talked with his parents about accumulating property in Bangkok, and he proposed that his family build a satellite city outside Bangkok, creating a private community just like those that had been created by Hong Kong's government to relieve congestion. The idea was to build not just a bedroom community for people who worked in central Bangkok, but rather an upscale city with housing and offices alike.

It was an idea that "came in a flash," said Anant in his clipped, Cantonese-accented English. I thought he was sounding a bit glib and raised my eyebrows. "It was not a stroke of genius," he added, with a touch of dry modesty. "It was logic."

Gradually, Anant convinced his family, and he began acquiring real estate in Thailand. They centered their acquisitions on Muang Thong Thani, near the Bangkok Airport, and decided that that would be the site of their new city. As their purchases increased, they eventually acquired the most property in Thailand aside from the royal family, and in 1993, *Fortune* magazine listed the family as the ninety-sixth richest in the world, with $2.1 billion in assets. The following year, profits from the empire hit a record $266 million.

One advantage that entrepreneurs like Anant had was that they did not have to risk so much of their own money. Banks offered the money of their depositors, foreign banks pressed dollar loans into their hands, or Western fund managers lined up to invest in their companies. In Southeast Asia, when Anant was expanding, huge waves of capital were flowing in, driven by capitalists looking for projects in which to invest. This cheap money helped fuel growth throughout Asia. In 1980, for example, bank lending to companies in Thailand was equivalent to 28 percent of the total economy. By 1997, this had reached 105 percent. The money came from German and Japanese banks, American pension funds, and overseas stock investors. But ultimately all this cash rushing into Asia was like air rushing into a balloon, and while it was impressive to look at, there was always the question of whether it would pop.

Anant was so enthusiastic because in Asia it seemed pretty hard to fail. In Thailand, South Korea, Indonesia, and other countries, the governments moved in to rescue tottering companies, and it became evident that the bigger you were, the less likely it was that you would be allowed to collapse. In South Korea, the government had controlled the lending spigots from the very beginning, so that the Korean conglomerates, the *chaebol*, were empires built on bank loans, which were essentially government-supervised funds. Those banks earned a disparaging nickname, "the ATMs of the Finance Ministry," for they handed out loans as directed by government bureaucrats.

After the Asian economic crisis struck, I began hearing more and more people lambaste the Thai, Korean, and Indonesian bankers who had made foolish loans; Western analysts complained to me about the cronyism and bad accounting and corruption that had contributed to the crisis. I admit that all those criticisms are quite deserved. But I was amused at how everyone seemed to have forgotten that it was the Western bankers and fund managers who had been pouring money into these countries—and into projects like Anant's—just as enthusiastically as local bankers had been. If the five-thousand-dollar-a-year bankers in Bangkok were proved to have made senseless investments, so were the million-dollar-a-year emerging-market professionals working on Wall Street.

Barton M. Biggs, sixty-five, the chief global investment strategist for Morgan Stanley Dean Witter & Company, is one of the elders of Wall Street, a gray-haired man whose advice commands the attention of pension fund managers around the world. In an industry that has drifted toward computer models and number crunching, Biggs is a generalist whom I and many others admire for his brilliantly written investment reports that are often funny and always influential. In 1993, in typical by-the-seat-of-his-pants style, he made a weeklong trip to China and came back starry-eyed. I laughed as I heard tales of how his entourage of investors was escorted by police cars through Guangdong Province. After all, I thought, how could he get even a glimpse of the real China that way? Indeed, he may not have known China, but it didn't matter. When Biggs spoke, investors listened. He urged investors to increase their weighting of Hong Kong stocks roughly sixfold, to 7 percent of a global stock portfolio.

"We were all stunned by the enormous size of China," he declared. "Sometimes you have to spend time in a country to get really focused on the investment case. After eight days in China, I'm tuned in, overfed, and maximum bullish." Hong Kong stocks soared at those words, and gained 28 percent over the next seven weeks. Then in August 1994, Biggs declared that the smaller Asian markets—Thailand, Indonesia, and Hong Kong—"will be the best place in the world to be for the next five years."

The confidence in Asia's emerging markets was bolstered after the United States intervened to bail out Mexico in 1994; this bailout, while bitterly criticized at the time, later turned out to be a huge success, and Mexico repaid its loan to the United States ahead of time. Mexico's economy bounced back, and lenders and investors were not terribly injured. But little did we all know that the bailout might have created another problem. The concept of "moral hazard" refers to people taking economic risks because they believe they will be rescued if their bet goes wrong. The Mexican bailout, by its success, created moral hazard and encouraged risky behavior by investors on a much larger scale in Asia. International bank loans to Asia tripled in 1995 and went even higher in 1996.

Biggs was representative of the Wall Street euphoria about Asia. When executives of an obscure Indonesian polyester company called Polysindo visited New York in 1996 to discuss a stock offering, they were granted two meetings with the head of Merrill Lynch, two meetings with the head of Morgan Stanley, and one with the head of Goldman Sachs. No comparable Chicago company could ever have gotten such a welcome.

American investment banks were so eager to arrange stock offerings for the likes of Polysindo that they typically charged Asian companies only about 3 percent of the value of the deal, compared to the 6 percent or more they would charge companies in the United States.

The sense of easy money was infectious, and First World financiers were at least as giddy as financiers in the Third World. American, Japanese, and European bankers were pouring money into those countries in paroxysms of glee. I heard the buzz at cocktail parties in Tokyo and in the white-walled offices of Japanese bankers. With their economy slowing at home and little chance to lend there, Japanese bankers were bumping into each other on the planes to Southeast Asia in an effort to ply their loans on companies in Thailand, Indonesia, and the Philippines.

The growing migration of Western capital to Asia reflected changing attitudes and policies in Western capitals, particularly Washington. The nerve center for international markets was the Treasury building's third floor. That was where Robert E. Rubin, who at the time was Treasury secretary, and Lawrence H. Summers, then his deputy and later the Treasury secretary, shared a spacious suite overlooking the Washington Monument. Summers had been the youngest tenured professor at Harvard, and Rubin had made a fortune on Wall Street, enabling him to take off on vacations with a fly-fishing rod that, as an aide joked, "probably costs more than your house." At one end of their suite, Rubin presided in a spacious office decorated with modern art, family photos—just about all he saw of his family during the week, since his wife stayed in New York and he joined her each weekend—and a few Asian touches such as an antique Japanese flower basket. Behind the desk was a computer, which Rubin used to check the markets every few minutes, and beside it was a scrambler phone to consult with other officials about exchange rate strategy and other national secrets.

At the other end of the suite was Summers's office, covered with photos of his son and twin daughters, and equipped with a small refrigerator stuffed with Diet Cokes (one was usually in Summers's hand). The two men were exceptionally close partners, and when Rubin was puzzled about something, he sometimes wandered over in his stocking feet to consult with Summers. After Rubin became Treasury secretary in 1995, he and Summers spread their passion for free markets; arguably, one result was the long American-led boom in financial markets around the globe. Yet in retrospect Washington's policies also fostered vulnerabilities that were at the heart of the Asian economic crisis. Nick, several colleagues, and I spent many months in 1998 and 1999 searching for explanations to the crisis, and the result was a long series in the *New York Times*. Asian countries themselves clearly made mistakes that were at the heart of the crisis, but it also became clear that the Clinton administration had pushed too hard in the 1990s for financial liberalization and freer capital flows, allowing foreign money to move into these countries and local money to move out. "Financial liberalization was undertaken in countries that didn't have the infrastructure to support it," reflected Ricki R. Helfer, a leading international bank regulator. "That was one of the principal causes of the Asian crisis." Thailand and the rest of Asia may have gotten in trouble largely because of their own mistakes, including poor banking practices and the precariousness of their own economic bubbles. But if those countries had weak foundations, it is partly because Washington helped supply the blueprints.

"I never went on a trip when my brief didn't include either advice or congratulations on liberalization," Jeffrey E. Garten, who was a top Commerce Department official in the Clinton administration, told my colleague David E. Sanger, who reported the Washington end of the *Times* series. "It's easy to see in retrospect that we probably pushed too far, too fast. In retrospect, we overshot, and in retrospect there was a certain degree of arrogance." Garten said that Wall Street was delighted with the push for financial liberalization, and the push by Washington seems to have reflected not only the administration's intellectual sympathy for free financial markets but also the desire to please an important constituency. As Laura D'Andrea Tyson, the former chairwoman of President Clinton's Council of Economic Advisers, put it: "Our financial services industry wanted into these markets." And so while Washington was quick to blame the Asian economic crisis on Third World cronyism, a share of the responsibility has to go to American policies and perhaps to First World crony-ism—an effort by Washington to promote the financial liberalization that would benefit its backers on Wall Street. It was not that the Treasury Department was blindly following the bidding of campaign contributors, because many respected economists around the world agreed that capital flows should be liberalized. But it was an extra incentive that Wall Street contributors were pushing for what many Clinton administration econo-mists believed in anyway.

Anant's private city, Muang Thong Thani, first emerged in architectural blueprints. It would be filled with broad-windowed office towers, tall build-ings, town homes, and traditional suburban-style houses, all set on wide streets following a grid—the antithesis of chaotic Bangkok. And the loca-tion, between Bangkok Airport and the clogged city of Bangkok itself, was perfect. Anant envisioned Muang Thong Thani filling with seven hundred thousand people, maybe even a million.

"We thought that Bangkok was bursting," he told me. "It couldn't expand. Traffic was bad, the air was polluted, so we thought we could give Bangkok a hand." The idea was to build a huge city and run it as a for-profit venture. It was a humongous dream, with the potential to turn Anant into either a multibillionaire or a bankruptcy case. "It was a long-term plan that we were going to send most of the profits from the watch business into the project."

"But why does Muang Thong Thani have to be so large?" I asked, for it was one thing to be big and another to be gargantuan.

"You don't make the maximum profits" from a small development, he explained, because the people next to you also benefit from the crowds you draw and the atmosphere you create. So, he said, "we decided to make one big project," and clean up on all the profits.

Like his wealthy colleagues in many other Asian countries, Anant pushed his projects not just by cultivating the banks but also by winning favors from the authorities—and by browbeating them. Anant's relations with politicians were so close that in 1991 the Thai prime minister appointed him a senator. Since then, Anant has taken his seat in parlia-ment and become one of the very people he was trying to influence. Poli-tics was crucial not only to get approvals for Muang Thong Thani but also for another grand project—a $1.3-billion commuter train that would link his community through a twelve-and-a-half-mile loop around Bangkok. He had conceived of the plan twenty years earlier, and when he finally won government approval, Anant popped open a bottle of champagne and said: "This is not a celebration, but it's a toast to get us ready for further obstacles."

I wondered sometimes if Anant was in part goaded to bigger and bigger projects by competition with his most meaningful rival—his brother, Keeree, who runs another part of the family empire. Keeree had drawn up plans to spend $800 million to build a twelve-mile elevated railway, similar to Anant's, but in a different part of Bangkok. When I raised the issue, Anant denied any rivalry and his son Peter spoke fondly about his uncle. But it did seem strange that they were both vying for financing and permits to build similar but separate train lines.

Muang Thong Thani alone was a multibillion-dollar project, and some of the funds came in when Anant's company, Bangkok Land, listed on the Bangkok stock exchange in 1992.

"What was the reaction from bankers?" I asked. I had heard that there had been a good deal of criticism in banking circles.

"Of course it was positive," Anant said, giving me one of his powerful glares. "Otherwise we couldn't have raised the money." Anant and his family piled on nearly $2 billion worth of bank loans.

As part of the plans for the train, Anant wanted to build a railway depot that would be the tallest building in Asia. Everybody in Asia seemed to want to build the world's tallest skyscraper, and dreams were getting bigger all across the region. But Anant was eclipsed by even more ambitious dreamers. The mark was set instead by the Petronas Towers in Kuala Lumpur, a city in Malaysia that few Americans know much about, let alone travel to. But everyone was racing to the top, and in doing so, Malaysia, a small, newly industrializing country with twenty-one million people, did something that startled many Americans, particularly in Chicago.

Soaring into the Malaysian sky, where not so long ago there were mostly shacks, the Petronas Towers surpassed Chicago's Sears Tower to become the world's tallest building, at 1,483 feet—a $460-million architectural swagger. But like the Asian economic miracle, the Petronas Towers rose from a rickety base. Literally.

When engineers first marked the spot where they wanted to build the towers, they discovered that the limestone bedrock was cratered with caverns, ravines, and steep slopes. After much digging, they hit bedrock just 45 feet below the surface at one end of the site and 590 feet below at the other. In other words, there was a serious risk that the 660,000-ton weight of the twin towers would cause them to "settle" or tip.

The site was moved about two hundred feet away so that both ends of the foundation would rest on soil rather than bedrock and would perhaps settle at the same rate. Even so, specialist surveyors were brought in from Australia to use the latest measuring systems to check twice a day for tilt—the same person using the same instrument at the same time of day—and gaps were engineered into the structure to provide some "give" and allow a tilt of about an inch.

Engineers today say that any amount of leaning is within the tolerance of the design and not enough to make the building come crashing down. In the end, those towers at least put Malaysia on the map for many Americans. At home, people joked that the pride of their country was the "leaning tower of Kuala Lumpur."

Ultimately, some of the boom's most spectacular achievements were the result of an economic bubble fueled by cheap credit. It was a dazzling, shimmering bubble, hauntingly beautiful, but like all bubbles it was prone to pop. Yet throughout Asia and other emerging markets, the problem in the early 1990s was that onlookers focused on the glittering pinnacles rather than the wobbling foundations.

The boom was touching everyone in Asia, even the poor. In the little riverside town of Mojokerto, Indonesia, where Nick had met Salamet, the Indonesian rickshaw driver who told him about the sorcerers, living standards soared. Salamet had grown up barefoot, but now he had begun to wear rubber thongs. And then a friend who worked in an athletic shoe factory got him a pair of rejected shoes, white basketball sneakers. Salamet keeps them under his bed and wears them for special occasions.

His neighbors did even better. A slight forty-year-old named Agus Santoso, too frail a man to make a decent stone-hauler or rickshaw driver, was the talk of the town, for he had managed to learn how to drive a car and had gotten a job driving new automobiles to dealerships all over Indonesia. Every now and then he took a detour and roared into his old neighborhood in Mojokerto in a cloud of dust. The villagers came over and touched the car, and the children peered inside the windows and looked at the dashboard. Santoso earned $400 a month, a colossal sum that had tongues wagging all over the neighborhood. He became the local hero, the fellow the women wished they had married and the men envied behind their grins. Salamet's eyes caressed the lines of the upholstery, and he began to dream that he, too, might learn to drive a car and become a driver just like Santoso.

Even for those remaining in the world of the rickshaw, like Salamet, life was full of promise and progress. Salamet sat on the porch outside his house one day and described the way his life has changed. "The biggest change was electricity, which came about six years ago," he reflected. "It cheers us all up, and at night there's light. And then there's also television now as well. The second biggest change is that the roads here got paved. It used to be that in the rainy season everything got so muddy you couldn't go anywhere. But now we can get around in all seasons, and I can drive the rickshaw and earn a living even after it's rained. The third change is the toilets. They were built four years ago. Until then everybody just used the river, but that was a problem at night. It was far away, and there were snakes that used to bite people."

Although few people noticed it at the time, a growing part of Asia's boom was a bubble. The bubble could be seen in soaring stock prices, and in property prices that rose to the point that a friend of mine living alone in Hong Kong was paying $23,000 a month for his apartment. This bubble could be seen even in Mojokerto. Salamet always used to have to pay cash for purchases. But then in the early 1990s, banks and finance companies began to pioneer a credit system for even the poorest people.

So Salamet and his wife, Yuti, bought a furniture set on installments. They paid for their son Dwi's school uniform on installments as well. Salamet used to rent his rickshaw, a dilapidated contraption that looked like a love seat being pushed by a bicycle. But as the neighborhood prospered, Salamet dreamed of moving up in the world. He borrowed from the bank and picked up a banged-up secondhand rickshaw with a red seat, promising to pay the equivalent of four dollars a month for fourteen months. Salamet thought he would be able to earn the monthly payment in just a few days on his rickshaw, and so it seemed the perfect investment.

Yet ultimately it was all a kind of rickshaw bubble. In 1990, the area had about one hundred rickshaws, and each of the drivers could earn about twice as much as a farmworker. But the advent of rickshaw financing, coupled with the general enthusiasm for moving up in the world, led to an explosion of rickshaws. Soon there were three hundred. "Now there are more rickshaws than the area can support," grumbled Rutiati, a thirty-seven-year-old woman who is a rickshaw agent, arranging financing for Salamet and others in the neighborhood. "There are more rickshaws than passengers."

A wealth of evidence has shown that overhasty liberalization before countries are ready for it can lead to banking chaos and financial crises. But the

United States, carried away in its enthusiasm for markets, led the band-wagon for financial liberalization. "It would be a legitimate criticism to say that we should have been more nuanced, more foresighted that this could happen," Mickey Kantor, the former trade representative and commerce secretary, acknowledged after Asia's crash. Speaking of the risks of financial liberalization without modern banking and legal systems, he said "it's like building a skyscraper with no foundation."

Treasury was the dominant presence in Washington during the Clinton years, and Rubin and Summers won increasing influence because of their skill at marrying international finance and foreign policy. Both were instinctively in favor of free markets and sympathetic to liberalization, and the administration tended to follow that line. It is not that Rubin and Summers were forcing financial liberalization down unwilling throats. Rather, Washington was leading more than pushing, reflecting a broad ideological shift shared by much of the world. "We didn't open up because of the U.S. pressures, but because we wanted the investment," said Bark Tae Ho, an economist at Seoul National University in South Korea. A former Thai official said that the United States had been pressing for capital liberalization, but on an open door. Despite subsequent denials, Washington moved in many ways to promote capital account liberalization, or the free flow of capital.

With countries like Japan and Taiwan, Washington directly argued that capital be allowed to move more freely. As a trade issue, it urged that American investment banks be given access to overseas financial markets, and in April 1997 Rubin pushed to get the seven leading industrialized countries to issue a statement that the International Monetary Fund charter "should be amended to make the promotion of capital account liberalization a specific purpose of the Fund."

Washington was particularly forceful in pushing South Korea to open up, and it dangled attractive bait: If Korea gave in, it would be allowed to join the Organisation for Economic Co-operation and Development, the club of industrialized nations. "To enter the OECD, the Koreans agreed to liberalize faster than they had originally planned," recalled a senior OECD official. "They were concerned that if they went too fast, a number of their financial institutions would be unable to adapt." In retrospect, the Koreans had a point. But at the time, the United States's priority was on twisting Korean arms to open financial markets, rather than on boosting financial oversight.

One reason that liberalization can often be followed by financial crisis is that unless there is strong bank supervision and a culture that backs it, there are plenty of opportunities for corruption and general foolishness. Indeed, sometimes there is a rise in shady dealings, as banks use new powers to make loans to friends or to the family members of senior politicians. That was partly what happened in the U.S. Savings and Loans crisis, and it was partly what happened in Asia. Thailand was famously corrupt, and in 1996 the justice minister accused his own government of taking $90 million in bribes in exchange for handing out banking licenses. When the Bangkok Bank of Commerce collapsed, more than a year before the Thai crisis, it turned out to have 47 percent of its assets in bad loans, many of them to associates of the bank's president. And this was Thailand's ninth-largest bank, operating during a record economic boom.

In the easy money days, there were opportunities aplenty for the small-time businessman who was willing to take on a little risk, people like Sirivat Voravetvuthikun. A Thai-Chinese, Sirivat grew up in a family that valued education and economic security. His father was a hardworking man who had been born in Fujian Province in China, descended from Chaozhou people, a Chinese lineage famed for wandering. In the middle of the twentieth century, this wanderlust took Sirivat's father to Thailand, where he started a small business importing glass and tableware from Japan. The father raised two boys and a girl, and spoke to Sirivat, his eldest, and the rest of his family in the Fujianese dialect of Chinese. From his father, Sirivat learned the ethic of working hard and the trade of commerce. Along the way, he picked up the habit of optimism, which has helped carry him through hard times, and when he gets down, Sirivat lets loose an infectious laugh that tends to cheer him up. It also helped his career that he speaks English, which he began learning in kindergarten. He learned it so well that he was chosen for an American Field Service fellowship when he was eighteen years old, and this allowed him to spend his senior year of high school in Texas.

It was in Texas that Sirivat decided to trace the classic modern pattern for elite Thai: study abroad, return to join a prestigious institution, then work one's way up to a senior post. Sirivat followed the regimen with relish. So after returning home and living in Thailand for two years, Sirivat went back to Texas as a student of finance, first at a small college in McAllen, and then at the University of Texas at Austin. Then he returned to Bangkok and rose rapidly to become a managing director, overseeing brokerage operations at an affiliate of the Bangkok Bank group, one of

Thailand's biggest institutions. In 1988, he went into managing assets on his own, raising $10 million and setting up a fund to invest in Thai stocks. But he unwound that venture in 1994, when the stock market had fallen to half of its peak. That's when he switched to property, with a bit of help from his younger brother.

Sirivat's brother also had a brand-name education—a master's degree in civil engineering from Columbia University and an MBA from the University of Illinois. The brother worked in the real-estate business for Merrill Lynch in Southern California, but after a few years, he came back to Thailand to make his own fortune. He had a grand idea, which was to build a luxury condominium project in the rolling hills of Khao Yai, a three-and-a-half-hour drive northeast from Bangkok.

"To help him, I said I'd do the project," Sirivat said of his brother. "I had good credit, good connections, and I could ask people to buy." They didn't advertise; it was all direct and personal selling. Sirivat approached twenty "big and influential" people and hoped they would tell their friends. He held a big party at the condominium, inviting several dozen people who all drove out in their sparkling cars to view the place and gush over the wonderful landscaping. Early one morning, I drove out to Khao Yai, a sleepy village nestled in the choppy, craggy, tree-topped mountains. Among the coconut and mango trees swaying in the nearby fields I saw two large compounds of condominiums made of adobe. In all, they form a community of twenty-eight luxurious homes, with balconies and swimming pools, beautifully carved stone animals and giant clay pots to hold trees. Sirivat hired an American landscaper, the same company that did the Mirage Hotel in Las Vegas, and sure enough, Sirivat's homes soon appeared like a mirage next to the tin pans and wooden tables of the outdoor restaurant down the road. The entire compound is in a resort with a golf course. In the village nearby, there are modest eateries; the one I went to cleaned its dishes in buckets of water. In contrast, Sirivat's homes look like they belong in Beverly Hills. "Rich people expect that kind of quality," Sirivat explained.

By the spring of 1997, Thailand's economic weaknesses were becoming more apparent, particularly to Thais. Bad debts were sinking many Thai finance companies, persistent trade deficits showed no sign of turning around, and economic growth was slowing. Many of the well paid and supposedly sophisticated Wall Street types didn't see the problems clearly, but ordinary Thais did. Local investors and companies were hedging against the baht and quietly keeping their money in dollars.

A key problem was that Thailand had pegged the value of its currency at twenty-five baht to one dollar. As its economy kept expanding the government kept raising interest rates, which started to soar above interest rates in the United States. So American money flowed into Thailand to take advantage of the high returns.

Meanwhile, Thai companies were running overseas to borrow cheaply in dollars. Both flows worked to break the currency peg, a problem that could be called the Water Bucket Theory of Fixed Exchange Rates. Each day an American earned interest in Thailand was like a drop of water falling into a bucket. The more money Americans poured in to earn interest and the longer they left it there, the more drops of water filled the bucket. But there was risk: Some cowboy could come kick over the bucket, and the peg would collapse. The first try came in May 1997. Tiger Management, the biggest of the investment groups known as hedge funds, began to bet heavily against the baht, and other investors and hedge funds piled on as well. The betting was that Thailand would have to devalue, and soon a financial war was under way between the world's hedge funds and the Bank of Thailand, the Thai central bank.

The Bank of Thailand had a trick up its sleeve, however. On May 15, 1997, it dived into the markets, buying baht, and it simultaneously ordered banks not to lend to foreign speculators. The speculators screamed into their phones, threw chairs across the room, and watched their computer screens in horror as their losses mounted. The only way they could get baht to cover their bets was by borrowing at extortionate rates, which on that day reached 3,000 percent on an annualized basis.

In one day, the hedge funds had lost around $450 million. They called it the day of the "blood baht." But the Bank of Thailand had won the victory at a huge price. Its chief currency trader, Paiboon Kittisrikangwan, had defended the baht by locking up the country's dollars in forward contracts. In other words, Thailand committed itself to using its dollars to buy baht six months or even a year later, at a specified price. The advantage was that Thailand could intervene in the currency markets without—on the surface—using its foreign exchange reserves. But the disadvantage was that in reality its reserves of $30 billion were being whittled away behind the scenes.

Thai officials were furious that American hedge funds and banks were allocating billions of dollars in a bid to force Thailand to devalue the baht—destabilizing the country but winning profits for themselves. The Thais worried about the consequences of such speculative battles on all of

Asia. In May 1997 Rerngchai Marakanond, the central bank chief, sent a secret letter of complaint to Alan Greenspan, the chairman of the Federal Reserve, urging him to rein in American hedge funds and other financial institutions. Rerngchai warned that the attack on Thailand "could have far-reaching implications on the economy both of Thailand and the Asian region" and "threatens to jeopardize the stability of international financial markets."

A similar letter was sent to Hans Tietmeyer, the president of Germany's central bank, noting that one German bank had joined in the attack on the baht. Tietmeyer quickly responded, a Thai official recalled, with a question: Which of our banks? That warmed hearts at the Thai central bank, but the response from Washington annoyed them. The correspondence, made available by a Thai central bank official and confirmed by another government official, shows that the Fed's response came not from Greenspan but from an aide, Edwin M. Truman. The response blandly acknowledged that "large financial firms" can disrupt countries like Thailand but added that these matters were best left to the markets. The Thais felt that the message from Greenspan was: Drop dead.

As Thailand's economy gradually began to fall apart, Thanong Bidaya was on vacation in Hong Kong. Thanong is a well-respected traditional banker, a lean man with at turns an easy smile and a serious determination. He was one of Thailand's most experienced bankers, but he was relishing his time off. He collects antique watches and was planning to go to Macao the next day to look for some to add to his collection when the phone rang in his hotel room. It was the Thai prime minister, asking him to take over as finance minister.

"I told him that if he could not find anyone else, I would do it," Thanong said.

Thanong never got a chance to go to Macao and get his watches. Instead, he flew to Bangkok and spent a few frantic days defending the government's budget until it passed. And then, on the evening of June 27, 1997, he climbed into a blue Mercedes-Benz and zigzagged through throngs of traffic from the parliament building to the Bank of Thailand to meet Rerngchai, the central bank governor.

Thanong's car approached the stately gates to the majestic eight-story Bank of Thailand building, and a guard waved it through. It was about 7:00 p.m. when Rerngchai and Thanong entered a conference room. The two are close friends, and Thanong calls Rerngchai *sempai,* a Japanese term for an older student or colleague, from the time they met while studying in Japan. But this time there was no reminiscing or chitchat. Thanong wanted to know how much the country had left in foreign reserves, the economy's lifeline to the outside world, for foreign bankers scrutinized the size of the reserves when they lent dollars to a country. Rerngchai, who came with a couple of assistants carrying piles of charts and memos, gave his friend the shock of his life.

Thailand was broke. Rerngchai explained that after subtracting the dollars that had been committed in forward transactions (nearly $29 billion), Thailand had $1.14 billion in foreign exchange reserves, a paltry sum equivalent to just two days of imports.

Even though he was finance minister and one of his country's most experienced bankers, Thanong was totally surprised and stunned by the news. The hedge funds had won, and Thailand had lost. On the spot, he told Rerngchai that Thailand would have to drop the peg with the dollar and float the baht. It was a step that central bankers had dreaded for months. They had done everything they could to avoid floating, which they feared would prompt a sharp devaluation of the baht, a collapse in property values, and a loss of confidence in the banking system. But if they didn't float it, Thailand would go broke defending its currency, so it was a choice between two horrors.

"I said I didn't see any choice in dealing with the situation," Thanong told me. "So I told the governor I would take responsibility."

On July 1, Thai Prime Minister Chavalit Yongchaiyudh declared that the baht would never be devalued. That night, if anybody had noticed, the lights burned brightly behind the terraced windows at the Bank of Thailand. Officials stayed up all night, first calling major central banks around the world to warn them of what was coming. Then, at 4:30 a.m., central bankers called the homes of the heads of all Thai banks and major foreign banks in Bangkok, summoning them to an emergency meeting that would begin at 6:00 a.m.

At the meeting, Thailand announced that the baht would no longer be pegged against the dollar. It would float freely.

The Asian economic crisis had begun.

When the bomb exploded, the little guys like Sirivat were the first to feel the blast. Thailand's economy plunged into recession and then depression, and demand evaporated for the kind of luxury weekend retreats that Sirivat was selling. He had been feeling the squeeze as the economy began drying up, and though his condominiums were not even entirely completed, already they were becoming unsalable. Of the twenty-eight condos, he had managed to sell seven—but now the buyers stopped making payments. All the condos remained empty, making it less enticing for anyone else to move in. Sirivat had bought twelve acres of land, and the condominiums were supposed to be only the first phase of his project. Phases two and three had also been planned, but now they were crumpled up, abandoned on the drawing board.

Sirivat hired guards to watch the place and water the gardens, but the grounds began deteriorating anyway. The water in the main swimming pool turned green with algae, and the nine giant clay pots were emptied of their fancy trees. Some of the clay tiles began chipping off the entryways. Fallen leaves covered the ground. Sirivat was sickened by the sight.

He had cobbled together an equity investment of $1.25 million, with the help of his wife, his brother, and a couple of friends. But the banks poured in the most. "If they hadn't lent so much, I don't think I would have done this project. It would have been too much of a burden to put in all of it as equity." The banks are not impressed with their culpability, though. They are suing Sirivat for debts that with interest have reached $15 million.

Sirivat no longer talks to his brother much. When I pressed him, he got touchy and said he doesn't know where his brother is these days. But at least his condominiums are just a small compound of twenty-eight homes.

Anant, on the other hand, is stuck with an empty city. Construction of Muang Thong Thani slowed nearly to a halt with the crisis, and it has become a modern ghost town. The sidewalks are smoothly paved and relatively dirt-free, the storefronts at the outskirts of the city are neat and tidy. Muang Thong Thani initially offered four million square feet of office space—good for at least forty thousand office workers—and thirty thousand finished condominium units. Anant hadn't yet embarked on the other 320,000 condos he had planned to build.

On one side of Muang Thong Thani, there are rows of small townhouses, cookie-cutter, cement-brick, two-story homes. As I edged closer, it became clear that they were not only empty, they were not even completed—bricks were only partially laid out and entire floors were only half-built, as though construction workers had dashed away in the middle of a workday. Windows were mere holes in the wall. The roofless, gray, ghostly structures looked like they had been abandoned in a hurry, and the weeds had grown six feet high.

Along another stretch of the city was a second group of about one hundred unfinished homes, all of them not far from a small model street with different kinds of houses, each marked with a sign on the outside: "The Californian," read one; "Paris," said another. There were faded splashes of light green and pink against gray cement. These were the samples the customers were to pick from. But when I scrutinized these model homes, even they looked weathered, with the paint peeling, the gardens untended. A couple of signs had fallen off their hinges. A small dog roamed the narrow street, alone. Nearly everyone had fled Muang Thong Thani, and places like it were seen as symbols of the excesses of the past. In a larger sense, Muang Thong Thani's problems—and all of Asia's—were a consequence of an ailment that first became evident thousands of miles to the northeast, on the crowded streets and in the extraordinary restaurants of Japan.

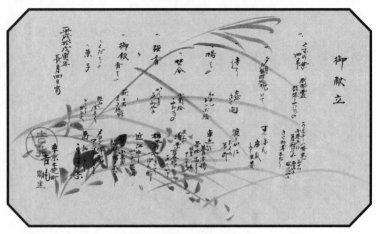

*This is the menu from my dinner at Kiccho restaurant. Written vertically, right to left, it lists the ten-course meal we were all served.*

### CHAPTER FOUR

# Bellyache in Japan

## NICHOLAS D. KRISTOF

*After firing so many workers
I felt like a sculpture
Dashed to pieces.*

—HAIKU POEM BY A JAPANESE BUSINESSMAN
(*ASAHI SHIMBUN*, POETRY COLUMN, 1999)

On a small back street at the east end of the Ginza district in Tokyo is a plain brown door to an old two-story building that looks as if it might be a warehouse. Instead, the door leads to Kiccho, perhaps the most exclusive restaurant in the world.

Not that any customer actually has to open that door. The moment a limousine pulls up (no one arrives at Kiccho by subway), the hostesses outside open the car doors and sweep the guests inside into their private room. Other hostesses in each of the other rooms carefully keep their guests from leaving during that time, so that no one ever knows who else is dining in Kiccho that evening.

The Ginza branch of Kiccho is so exclusive, in fact, that it chooses its patrons, rather than the other way around. R.W. Apple Jr., then the *New York Times* Washington bureau chief and a legend for both his journalism and his expense accounts, visited Tokyo in 1993 and asked the bureau to make a reservation for him at Kiccho. A secretary called up Yugi-san, Kiccho's manager, to make the reservation. "I'm sorry," Yugi-san replied, "but that would be very difficult. We do not take reservations from people other than our regular customers." My predecessor as the *Times* Tokyo bureau chief asked Prime Minister Kiichi Miyazawa for help, and with Miyazawa's introduction Apple was able to go to another Japanese *ryotei* restaurant— just one notch below Kiccho.

By the late 1990s, Japan's economy was in deep trouble and restaurants like Kiccho were less arrogant. Corporate entertainment budgets were being cut, and it was hard to fill tables. So when a friend, the head of a Fortune 500 company in the United States, asked me if I could arrange a family dinner with him at Kiccho, it turned out to be relatively easy. Partly because Kiccho was hurting, Yugi-san agreed instantly. The problem was simply the price: Kiccho's basic charge was one hundred thousand yen per person, not including drinks, geisha, tax, or the customary gratuity. At the exchange rate at the time, that meant almost $1,000 per person. Going full-bore, with geisha and the best sake, would have brought the bill up to $1,500 per person.

I didn't know how much my friend was willing to pay, but this seemed wildly excessive. Sheryl and I counteroffered $500 per person. "No, absolutely not," Yugi-san said firmly. "We can't offer an appropriate level of service for such a sum." So we raised our bid to a base of $600 per person, plus extras such as drinks, and she reluctantly agreed—and even sent us a nice gift package of special Kiccho foods, a kickback to us for booking dinner at her restaurant.

Kiccho was renowned for its splendor, cuisine, and service, but in fact it should have been notorious as an emblem of a rotten system. Meals at Kiccho were always paid for by expense accounts, and so the money was shareholders' money—and that never counted for anything in the old Asia. When Asia tumbled into its economic crisis, the reason was partly that this rotten system had been transplanted from Japan to much of Asia. Japan was often described as the lead goose in a V-formation, determining direction, with all the other Asian countries flying along behind it. In this case, the Japanese goose led the flock straight into a typhoon.

Japan has an overarching importance in the region that is twofold. First, it is by far the largest economy in Asia, four times the size of China's at present exchange rates.* Indeed, Japan accounts for nearly two-thirds of the entire Asian economy. Second, it is the economic pace-setter, a role model for the region. Alas, it was not a very good role model in terms of nurturing a profit-driven market economy.

Thus for all our expectations for Asia as a whole, the country that has been its main economic engine is sputtering and there is little sign of any overhaul that would revive it. Japan's economic structure and, more important, its psychology—its commitment to egalitarianism—are entrenched and raise considerable doubts about whether Japan can recover the vibrancy that it showed in the 1980s. At the heart of Asia, this colossus is deeply ambivalent about economic competition and seems unlikely to produce the kind of strong political leader who could bring crucial if wrenching changes. This weakness is sad for all of us who admire Japan, and it is also damaging for Asia as a whole.

What Japan taught its Asian partners was to muffle competition and ignore the rights of shareholders. Corporate executives in Japan in recent decades hijacked their companies and ran them for their own benefit, rather than that of shareholders. Of course, this happens everywhere to some extent, and it is clearly seen in the pay for corporate tycoons in the United States. But in no major part of the world were shareholders so scorned and ignored as in Asia, and expensive entertainment was an index of that. On any given evening in New York or Paris there may be some tycoons who host meals that cost $500 a person with wines, but the tabs almost never get to $1,000 a person. In contrast, Tokyo has about a dozen top-class *ryotei* restaurants like Kiccho, and on any given evening perhaps two hundred people eat dinner in Japan for $1,000 a person, including accompaniments such as drinks and geisha.

The hijacking of corporations by employees was characteristic of the Japanese model of development. This model arose from Japan's pell-mell rush to modernize beginning in the late nineteenth century. Japan transformed itself in many ways in the Meiji era, but it never really committed itself to free markets. It could well have been described as the world's

---

* An alternative way of measuring an economy's size is to use not exchange rates but purchasing power parity, or PPP. This attempts to adjust for differences in costs among countries, and using these calculations China's GDP is already bigger than Japan's and is the second-largest in the world, after the United States's.

most successful communist country. Capitalists—those who provided the capital, the shareholders—rarely had much influence, and power went to those who regulated capital in the bureaucracy or who spent it in the business world. The inattention to shareholders meant that the ethos of companies was to get bigger rather than to earn profits or pay dividends.

This lust for market share was mimicked around Asia after World War II. There was no single model of development in Asia, for Hong Kong pursued laissez-faire cowboy capitalism while Singapore thrived on state-planned capitalism and Indonesia tried kickback capitalism. But a common theme tended to be a Japanese-style drive for size over profitability and an obliviousness to the interests of shareholders. Companies relied on creative accounting and took shortcuts, and for a long time it worked. In South Korea, Kim Woo Chung started the Daewoo Group in 1967 with $18,000 of borrowed money and turned it into one of the world's biggest conglomerates—and, unfortunately, also one of the most indebted. He grabbed market share and glory, but his shareholders never had a clue as to what was going on, and finally in 1999 Daewoo virtually collapsed in the aftermath of the Asian crisis.

Sheryl and I showed up along with my friend the American chairman and three of his guests at 7:00 p.m. at the door of Kiccho. Four hostesses in silk kimonos greeted us by name and did their best to look thrilled to see us. They helped us take our shoes off and then led us down a corridor to a tatami room with a beautiful scroll on the wall—an early autumn scene, since it was September. We sat on the floor, and then a new round of hostesses came to welcome us and kneel in front of us in the traditional *seiza* position and thank us for coming, and then Yugi-san walked in and bowed to us. Yugi-san was in her sixties, graying pleasantly, elegant in a spectacular silver kimono with a dark blue *obi*, or belt. She served each of us an aperitif of Kiccho's homemade plum liquor. It was deliciously sweet, and its strong fragrance wafted through the room and mixed with the equally delicious tatami aroma.

Then Yugi-san announced that it was time to move. We were ushered into an elevator and taken to the second floor, where Yugi-san led us into a huge room, the size of a typical Tokyo apartment. It was decorated with a lovely seventeenth-century scroll of calligraphy by a famous scholar and by gold and black lacquer boxes that once belonged to a *daimyo,* or feudal lord.

The first treat was the menu. One was given to each of us, not so that we could choose our food—there is no real choice at Kiccho—but to inform us of the ten-course meal we were to be served. The menu was written in black calligraphy, top to bottom and right to left, but the catch was that it was written in the kind of ancient, high-brow Japanese that young people have trouble understanding. It was titled, for example, not "Menu" but "We Respectfully Present." About two feet wide and one foot tall, printed on Japanese-style *washi* paper made from mulberry and other bark, the menu had a beautiful and subtle watercolor painting of grass and flowers, with a red Kiccho seal on the left. The plants were all suggestive of September: pink *hagi* flowers, golden eularia reeds, and violet *kikkyo* flowers. The menu's mix of colored drawing and black calligraphy was straight out of the Japanese artistic tradition. I've kept my copy, and I'm still thinking of framing it. Indeed, the one reason I may not frame it is that it is so seasonal that I could hang it only for a few weeks in September.

Seasons are enormously important in Japan, and the old Japanese calendar had twenty-four key dates that marked the changing weather. These are closely observed by traditional Japanese: Fine restaurants and the most discriminating private homes are careful to rotate their decorations once every couple of weeks or so to match the changing seasons. Our own visit to Kiccho fell in early September, after the traditional date of *Shosho* (manageable heat) and right before *Hakuro* (white dew), and so the food, clothing, ornaments, art, and servingware all reflected themes of that period in early autumn. Even the hostesses took care that their kimonos, *obi,* and hairpins matched the season. Sheryl and I have a lovely antique *byobu,* a Japanese painted screen, and I'm convinced that one reason why I could buy it at a reasonable price is that it shows cherry blossoms: No self-respecting Japanese could display it except in late April or early May, when cherry trees are actually blossoming, and so most of the time it would languish in a closet. But foreigners can get away with anything, and no Americans will think it strange if they see our *byobu* hanging in mid-winter.

The first course at Kiccho was a delicate combination of shrimp, okra, grilled squid, burdock root, matsutake mushrooms, eel rolled around burdock root—and a bit of chrysanthemum flower, because chrysanthemum is an autumn flower. Like all the foods, this course was presented in antique or rare porcelain; this dish was presented in an Oribe saucer the shape of a *biwa* violin. The hostess lifted the lid for me, and I saw food as delicate on the eye as it would be on the palate. Each morsel had been carefully hand-rolled and tied up in edible seaweed and looked dainty and lovely.

Then the hostesses brought out Makiewan gold-lacquered soup bowls. They lifted the lids in unison, and inside the bowls was a clear soup made of soft-shelled turtle and a rare melon, flavored with the tartness of squeezings of ginger. It was a bit like a fish broth, but the taste was mild and redolent of strange flavors and spices that I could not identify. Each course was small, little more than a stimulus to the palate, and so after a few delicious spoonfuls it was gone.

In the postwar period, Japan offered the useful lesson to Asian countries that capitalism could provide a route for poor countries to catch up with the West. But too often Japan's success was explained incorrectly. From the 1970s through the early 1990s, many Americans decided that the lesson of Japan's boom was the smooth functioning of "Japan, Inc.," where bureaucrats and executives together planned their assaults on foreign ramparts. Some American scholars warned that unless the United States followed Tokyo's model of industrial planning, Japan would corner the market for microchips and America would end up making potato chips.

Asian countries bought the argument about the virtues of industrial planning, which spread throughout the region. But in fact the initial premise has been shown wrong. Japan thrived not because of its government planning, but in spite of it. Japan's Ministry of International Trade and Industry—MITI, which used to inspire calls for a similar body in America—turns out to have a pretty poor record. For example, it strongly pressured Honda to stick with motorcycles and not to make cars. MITI also failed dismally to nurture first-class industries in chemicals, aircraft, and computer software, despite enormous effort, expense, and protection from imports.

Indeed, Japanese government efforts seemed to result more often in failures than in success. One careful study of sectors that succeeded and those that failed found that the main difference was competition. In some sectors, such as detergents or securities trading, there were only a few key competitors (often because the government thought that businesses would do better if they did not have to waste energy at home competing in a crowded marketplace). The result was that companies in those sectors got lazy and failed to become competitive internationally. In contrast, Japanese industries that thrived—fax machines, air conditioners, cars—were characterized mostly by brutal domestic competition that forced innovation and cost-cutting.

A similar picture is evident in finance. Japan used regulations to rig the system so that consumer savings were lent to industry at below-market interest rates. In the short term, this financial structure helped Japanese industry, and similar systems were used to funnel credit to companies in South Korea, Indonesia, and other nations. But in the long run, all this government meddling was disastrous. It meant that bond markets and financial securities never developed very well in most of Asia, and that corporations depended on bank lending for their capital. That was dangerously unstable to start with, but it was made worse because in Japan— and much of Asia—bank lending tended to be based more on relationships than on creditworthiness. Borrowers had long-standing ties to their banks (often nurtured in places like Kiccho or in *no-pan-shabu-shabu* restaurants), and bankers made loans to companies because they always had.

The most rigid of these relationships in Japan were among the *keiretsu,* or families of companies. The importance of these relationships was driven home to me while I was still studying Japanese in New York at the Japan Society. The language lab was funded by Toyota, and so one day Toyota sent a couple of people by to see how it was doing, and I met them along with Sheryl and a Japanese friend. We joked about what kind of car we would get in Tokyo—we promised a Toyota—and I had a brainstorm. My Japanese friend drove a Lexus, so I pointedly asked her: "So what kind of car do you drive?" I assumed that she would say a Lexus, that the Toyota people would laugh proudly, and that everybody would be in a good humor.

Instead, it was as if I had told some bawdy joke. The mood became tense, and my teacher awkwardly dodged the question, and there was a long silence. She and the Toyota people were clearly embarrassed, and I felt terrible for putting her on the spot. So a few days later, I apologized to her. "I'm sorry for the other day," I said. "I thought you drove a Lexus."

"Oh, I do," she said.

"Oh? I thought Lexus is made by Toyota."

"Oh, it is."

"Oh? Then why didn't you tell those men from Toyota? They would have been happy."

"It's a bit complicated. My husband works for Sumitomo, which is in the same *keiretsu* as Mazda. So I should drive a Mazda. But instead I drive a Toyota Lexus. Those men from Toyota might know where my husband works, so they would know that I should drive a Mazda. It would be awkward for everybody if I said I drove a Toyota."

.    .    .

The hostesses cleared the turtle soup and then came in with the third course, sashimi, or raw fish. The sashimi was arrayed on an unusual kind of ceramic decorated with chrysanthemums. That evening's sashimi was particularly rare: freshwater *watari* crab, which has wonderful but tiny bits of meat and is available only briefly in the autumn. It was served with okra and myoga ginger to enhance the crab's natural flavor.

My hostess, a woman in her forties in a sky-blue kimono, chatted with me as she waited on me, and that is when the meal began to sour. Sheryl was the only other Japanese speaker there, and so the hostess—who had seemed the sweetest thing ever to wear a kimono—began to light into me.

"You've set too low a limit for such an important guest," she scolded me, tenderly but firmly. "We can't serve him properly when you set this kind of limit. Why don't you raise it to one hundred thousand yen per person? That's the only proper way to treat someone so special."

"No, I can't do that," I said firmly. "And sixty thousand yen per person already seems like quite a bit to me."

She pouted. And when my friend the chairman asked for a white wine, she hurriedly presented him with a bottle of Chablis, on behalf of Kiccho. "That's just for him," she told me in Japanese. "I know you're a bit tight, so we thought we would present it to him. You'll have Japanese sake, right? Because we can't give Chablis to everyone."

"Look," I replied, annoyed, "drinks were not included in my limit, and we will pay for drinks. We can afford them. But yes, I will have Japanese sake rather than Chablis."

When the chairman did not touch his crab, Yugi-san was concerned and quickly offered him smoked salmon as an alternative. She could not have been more gracious, but meanwhile my hostess was turning into a virago. "You see, we have to make a present of this salmon to the chairman," she said disingenuously. "We won't charge you, so don't worry. But you really should raise the limit to one hundred thousand yen per person to treat him properly."

It was an odd feeling. I had never ordered a meal one-quarter so extravagant, and yet no restaurant had ever made me feel like such a cheapskate.

As the lead goose, Japan was the first of the flock to fly into turbulence. Its bubble economy peaked at the end of 1989, and it spent the 1990s falling down to Earth. Instead of warning the other geese, it urged the flock straight on into the Asian economic crisis. And then for a decade, Japanese politicians simply bickered instead of striking a new course. Japan had twice shown itself capable of breathtaking changes—in the Meiji era and again after World War II—but in the 1990s it was paralyzed.

One essential problem was Japan's quasi-communist psychology, which led to outlandish expenses, distrust of competition, and abysmal efficiency. A deep commitment to egalitarianism meant that Japan spent vast sums of money absurdly. On Ikarajima, a sleepy islet that is home to only 350 people, a dazzling new $125-million bridge rises like a mirage to connect it to a neighboring island. There used to be a ferry that took fifteen minutes to make the crossing, but then the government decided to improve the life of people on Ikarajima by building them the bridge—at a cost of $357,000 per resident.

The same mentality of utter indifference to costs can be seen in a newly refurbished elementary school in the little village of Ichinosetakahashi, on the slopes of Mount Fuji. The principal's office has a gleaming new bell and loudspeaker system to broadcast messages and summon the student body from recess. But during my visit in 1998, I quickly realized that it would be simpler to yell through the window for Daiki Saito to come in.

Daiki, a seven-year-old with a mischievous sparkle in his black eyes, is the only student in the entire school. He is the only child living in the village, and although there is another school only twenty minutes away it lies in a different administrative area and so it was deemed inconceivable to send him there. The government therefore spent $100,000 renovating an abandoned schoolhouse and then hired a principal and a first-grade teacher to tutor Daiki. It costs $175,000 a year to run Daiki's school. This is exceptional but not unique, for Japan has several other schools with just a single student, and 14 percent of all the country's elementary schools have fewer than fifty students in all grades.

When the school bell rang in the morning, Daiki and the teacher bowed to each other and began their lessons. She cajoled him through his Japanese class and then through arithmetic, and then they ate lunch together: She sat at the teacher's desk and he at his student desk in front of her. During physical education class, she and Daiki raced around the schoolyard together, and then Daiki practiced vaulting over her back.

As a Japanese taxpayer, I was appalled at this waste of money and at the resulting 65 percent marginal personal tax rates, but it was difficult to find Japanese who were equally outraged. Many Japanese seemed profoundly

*Daiki Saito vaults over his teacher in physical education class at his school near Mount Fuji, Japan. Daiki is the only student in the entire school.*

*The first-grade teacher and Daiki bow to each other at the beginning of class.*

torn, for they worried that efficiency would come at the expense of egalitarianism and social harmony. I found this view enormously admirable and utterly impractical. When I spoke to Daiki's principal, Tomishige Yazaki, he was not in the least apologetic about the expense. "If we just pursued efficiency," he said, "the world would become a very dry place, with no sensitivity."

The fourth course at Kiccho was the fried foods. These included succulent *kuruma* prawns, eggplants carved into the shape of a bamboo tea whisk, and delectable green soybeans, all with tastes and textures that complemented each other. They were served on platters decorated with red dragonflies, which multiply each autumn.

The prawns were followed by a fifth course, simmered vegetables served in a covered bowl with a chrysanthemum design. A rich sauce covered lily bulbs and paper-thin tofu skins that had been carefully dried.

The sixth course was, I thought, the very best. The hostesses brought out tiny hibachi, setting one beside each of us, and putting a small wire grill on top. When the coals glowed red, the hostesses began grilling huge matsutake mushrooms. The mushrooms were perfect to start with, and the hostesses flipped them over and over with chopsticks until they had a hint of crispness on the outside and were hot and juicy on the inside. The dressing was a combination of soy sauce and vinegar made from *ponsu,* a Japanese citrus juice. I could have lapped it up.

The seventh course at Kiccho was Ohmi beef, barbecued for us individually by our hostesses on the tiny charcoal hibachi beside us. Ohmi beef, like Kobe beef, is raised to have perfect marbling of fat and meat, and the pampering of steers is legendary. Cattle-raisers sometimes even massage the steers' backs so that the meat will be more tender (and more pricey).

The grilled beef was served with a mustard dressing and soy sauce. This beef was so tender that it just about melted in the mouth, and it combined with the tangy dressing perfectly.

The beef was followed by a rice dish, traditionally the last of the main courses. Kiccho served the rice in a golden Makiewan lacquered bowl with a cover, decorated with pictures of *hagi,* the autumn flower, and of an insect called *suzumushi,* whose name means "bell-ringing insect." *Suzumushi,* whose chirps sound like a bell only if you have drunk quite a bit of sake, also appear each autumn. When I lifted the lid, I found fragrant steamed rice with ginkgo nuts and tiny shrimp, decorated with pieces of *hagi* flower.

. . .

In a sense, Japan is too civilized for a market system. To revive its economy, Japan desperately needs to create losers. Companies need to lay off excess workers, tiny rice shops need to be replaced by more efficient supermarkets, and failing banks need to go bankrupt. But Japan is deeply uncomfortable with the idea of losers.

When my sons Gregory and Geoffrey went to Sports Day at their Japanese kindergarten, Sheryl and I went to cheer, but it wasn't really necessary. There were three-legged races and basketball shoots and all kinds of games, but somehow at the end of the day no one won and no one lost. There were no prizes for the fastest runner, or for the best basketball shooter; instead, every child got a small prize. The point of Sports Day was not to divide students by recognizing individual excellence but to unite them by giving them a shared experience. When drama teachers select a play to perform, they choose one in which there is no star, just a lot of equal parts—which makes for first-rate student harmony and second-rate drama.

Building teamwork in Japan starts from birth. When our third child, Caroline, was born in Tokyo, the hospital explained that the mothers were to nurse their babies all together in the same room at particular mealtimes. So on her first day of life, Caroline was effectively told to discipline her appetites to adjust to a larger scheme with others.

This civility and egalitarianism shape just about every aspect of life. When the Japanese translation of *China Wakes,* the book that Sheryl and I had written about China, was published, we were pleased that the first reviews were positive. But we were frankly surprised when every single Japanese review was positive, and I remarked on that to a Japanese friend. "Oh, that's the only kind of book review there is in Japan," he explained. "There are no mean book reviews. Just nice ones."

The ninth course was a dessert, fruits, served on Kenzan golden chrysanthemum platters first made by the great eighteenth-century potter Kenzan Ogata. The platters were works of art and so was the food. There were mangos, pears, a kind of jumbo grape, and perfectly ripe muskmelons, all carefully sliced for us so that we could pluck each bite free with a fork. The melons were sweet as candy, soft as yogurt, and ludicrously overpriced. Japan has a special soft spot for melons, and prices soar into the stratosphere. The ones we ate at Kiccho probably cost about $100 each, but the very best cost much more than that. Partly for the same reason that Kiccho's prices are ridiculous—the bills are paid for by corporations, with insufficient control over expenses—melons are purchased as gifts in beautiful boxes and presented to business customers as institutionalized bribes. How much can the very best melons go for? In 1999, *Yubari* melons (a bit like cantaloupes) were somewhat smaller than usual because of a lack of sunshine in the spring. But the best ones were still auctioned for 135,000 yen each—or about $1,100 per melon at the exchange rate at the time.

Finally, the tenth course came to conclude the meal. It was another dessert, and it was served on Lalique glass dishes from France ($200 per saucer in Tokyo's department stores). This dessert was an arrowroot cake mixed with sweet bean paste, wrapped in a dried oversized leaf and eaten with a wooden spear. The cake was served with *usucha,* a light green tea whisked from powder, so fine that it must have been just about worth its weight in gold.

I had never had a meal like this in my life.

My window into the soul of Japan is Omiya Cho, a little town in Mie Prefecture, two hundred miles southeast of Tokyo. I found Omiya because a childhood friend was teaching English in the local junior high school in 1994–95, and I visited it about a dozen times. The town itself has a population of 5,700 and is a cluster of farming villages, surrounded by rice paddies and tea bushes in the valleys. Beyond the fields are steep forested hills that surround the town.

Omiya means "Great Shrine," and it is named for a lovely Shinto shrine set in the heart of a 140-acre forest on one side of the town. The forest is dense with thick cedar trees, a bit like the giant redwoods of California, and when a 380-year-old cedar fell in a typhoon in 1990, it was so huge that the shrine was able to sell it for $600,000. The shrine and trees are dedicated to the Sun Goddess, Amaterasu Omikamisama, the legendary ancestor of the emperors. Nobody much believes in the Sun Goddess anymore, but the men in the fields and forests of Omiya still take care not to urinate when facing in the direction of the shrine. And when a local farmer clubbed a fox on the shrine grounds a few years ago, he died soon after the fox—which, a local man told me, pretty much proved that it was not an ordinary fox, but a fox-devil of the kind in ancient Japanese legends.

When in Omiya I always stayed with Zenzaburo and Michiko Yoshida, of the Yoshida *Honke*—the Yoshida main branch—the family that has dominated the town. Twelve generations ago, Zenzaburo's samurai ancestors lost a battle and gave up the sword to become foresters, acquiring huge tracts of forest and farmland around the Omiya area. With each generation, the business was handed down to the eldest son, who under the family rules inherited everything while the other children got nothing. The Yoshida *Honke* live in the nicest Japanese house I have ever seen, a sprawling mansion of endless corridors and bedrooms, almost all of them unused except for storage. There is even a special four-tatami-mat room (four in Japanese sounds like the word for death) that is used solely for the purpose of holding funeral wakes. Two guest bedrooms have dazzling art and overlook a Japanese rock garden with a stream full of orange, black, and white *koi,* or Japanese carp. The home is far nicer than the prime minister's residence in Tokyo and it does justice to the Yoshidas' warmth and hospitality. Each time I stayed with them, I grew more impressed by their civic-mindedness and straightforward goodness. They became some of my favorite people.

Zenzaburo is in his late fifties, casual and friendly with a bit of a pot from too many beers, while Michiko is a dozen years younger, thin, petite, beautiful, and as sweet as sugarcane. Even though she is queen of Omiya, she outbows everyone else to show her humility. I've seen her kneel down on tatami mats and just about knock her head on the floor in front of some ordinary old villager. The Yoshidas have three children: a son in college, Masaki, who will inherit everything and continue the Yoshida *Honke;* a daughter, Naomi, about to enter college and as lovely as her mother; and a younger son, Motoki, who is a budding musician still in high school. When I first got to know the Yoshidas and was invited to stay in their lovely palace, they were on top of the world. It seemed terribly awkward to me that Masaki would inherit everything—one of Japan's greatest homes, huge tracts of forest lands, the prestige of continuing the Yoshida *Honke*— while Motoki and Naomi would have to leave the main branch and would get next to nothing. Sibling resentments must have been enormous in the Yoshida family over the last twelve generations, I thought, and the idea was impressed on me when I met Yoshidas in Omiya who were descended from younger brothers a few generations ago; they lived ordinary village lives with none of the prestige or munificence of the Yoshida *Honke.*

Then, in recent years, the Yoshida fortunes showed increasing stress, and now the children's prospects have virtually been reversed. Masaki will inherit a dying business, and it will be difficult for him to find a wife willing to move to such a remote place. Naomi and Motoki may well end up richer and more prominent than Masaki, in a way that would have been inconceivable in any previous generation.

What went wrong? Some of the Yoshida family's difficulties, such as the slide in lumber prices, are particular to the logging industry. But in general the problem is the same as that faced by many sectors of Japan's economy: A long-sheltered business was exposed to international competition and battered by it. Businesses that had thrived under protectionism faced American companies that had been forged in the furnace of free markets. Japan's timber industry was one of the first to be sacrificed by Japanese politicians to the maw of American trade negotiators. Throughout the 1990s logs and finished wood began to pour into Japan at prices the Yoshidas could never compete with, and 80 percent of Japan's lumber is now imported. "My break-even cost of selling a log in Tokyo is higher than the price of an American log in Tokyo," Zenzaburo complained.

The underlying difficulty—and it was a structural problem throughout Asia—was that business was not run according to market economy principles. The Yoshidas are not profit-maximizers. They pay their employees above-market wages and hire more workers than they should. They produce high-quality timber that they can feel proud of, they build roads and provide land for schools and buttress the economy, but while all this is admirable, it makes them economically inefficient as timber producers. The Yoshidas are among the finest, most honorable people I have ever known and are deeply respected by all who know them, but their very decency and public-spiritedness have undermined their competitiveness.

I always felt a special poignancy about the Yoshidas because I grew up in timber country in western Oregon, and I have patches of timberland there that my family manages. But of course I don't have any full-time employees, while the Yoshidas have a dozen. When I need seedlings planted, I hire the cheapest crew I can find, paying by the piece. To kill the grass and shrubbery that can choke off the young trees, I hire a helicopter to spray herbicide; the Yoshidas worry about the effect of chemicals on the environment, so they hire employees to cut the grass by hand with sickles. I came to realize, over beers in the Yoshida living room, that I am just the kind of vicious, low-cost producer who is driving the Yoshidas out of business.

"It would be much cheaper to hire workers by the hour," Michiko acknowledged, "but my husband always felt that the Yoshida *Honke* had a responsibility to the community, and that people who work for the Yoshida *Honke* should earn a good standard of living. They should be able to feel proud that they work for the Yoshida *Honke.* They should be looked up to. So we hired people full-time, year-round. Now we aren't hiring any new ones, and people understand that times are difficult and they don't expect us to raise wages. But we can't cut wages, and we can't lay people off. That would be unthinkable.

"We feel a responsibility to the community and to the land," she continued. "That's why we don't use chemicals. That's why we built roads. That's why we tried to hire so many workers. But now our costs are so high, and we can't lower them."

One day when Masaki came home from college, Zenzaburo had a father-son talk with him. "We're really in trouble," he said. "If we keep on going as we are now, with all our employees, then to maintain cash flow we'll have to cut down all our trees in just the next few years. And then we'll have nothing for the next sixty years, until the trees grow back. We'll be out of business. The alternative is that if we lay off all our employees, then maybe we can tough it out and survive—at least survive longer. But that's something that would be very hard on our employees, and all this involves you, too. So I wanted to know what you think we should do."

Masaki scarcely pondered. "We can't lay off our employees. We just can't. Whatever happens, we've got to be loyal to them, because they've been loyal to us. I want to stick it out, come what may."

Most business owners in Omiya felt the same way. The paramount concern was not prices or cost but *giri-ninjo,* an ancient Japanese ethic that translates roughly as "duty and empathy." The result throughout Japan, and to a lesser extent elsewhere in Asia, was an economy whose outward facade was skyscrapers and business suits but whose human interactions were still rooted in traditional concepts of honor. These ways of doing business are frustrating and incomprehensible to American officials but would be immediately understandable to any eighteenth-century samurai. And the collision of the international market economy with Omiya's *giri-ninjo* economy was not a pretty sight. Americans may think of Japanese businessmen as ruthless, calculating tigers, but that is true only in sectors that compete abroad. Domestic companies are the opposite. Each time I visited Omiya, I felt more respect for them, and less hope.

One of the most touching figures in Omiya is Takahiro Tanaka, a slim thirty-seven-year-old who could scarcely be a better man or a more foolish businessman. Tanaka is now a logger working for the Yoshida *Honke,* and he came by the Yoshida house one day and chatted with me about how he had lost his business.

*Takahiro Tanaka straps on his sickle in Omiya, Japan, as he prepares to go into the hills to cut grass as part of his new job as a forester. He used to head a family-owned business making pearl souvenirs, but it collapsed, in part because Tanaka never laid off any employees.*

Tanaka had been in charge of a thirty-year-old, family-owned factory making pearl souvenirs and accessories. At its peak it had several dozen employees, but it was just the kind of inefficient factory that had become uncompetitive in Japan because of the surging yen, rising imports, and increasing labor costs. "It just got too hard to compete with imports," he said. "Chinese-made pearls come into Japan and the finished product is the same price as the cost of our materials." So the business steadily declined and lost money year after year. But because of *giri-ninjo,* Tanaka did not take the cost-cutting steps that might have saved the business. "What I thought about most was the employees," he said. "They depended on us. I just couldn't bring myself to dismiss the inefficient ones. I thought of offering the employees less money. I'm sure that they would have accepted if I had offered. But I just couldn't bring myself to do such a thing." So in 1997, Tanaka's business finally closed down, and all the employees lost their work anyway.

"Wouldn't it have been better if you had fired a few of them, and saved the jobs of the rest?" I asked.

Tanaka sighed and nodded. "Oh, yes. I know that would have been better. But I couldn't. I think a person with greater ability might have saved the company, but I wasn't fit for business."

As the meal at Kiccho ended, my harridan hostess got on her high horse again. It was partly my fault, for I asked her about geisha, since Kiccho is one of the few restaurants in Tokyo that still regularly has geisha entertain each evening.

"Yes, geisha always entertain here," my hostess said brightly. "There are some here tonight. You should order some geisha this evening, for such an important person as the chairman. A couple of geisha would be most appropriate."

Hiring a geisha, she said, would cost $500 for three hours, so two geisha would have set us back about $1,000, on top of the dinner bill. I declined.

Geisha are not prostitutes, and they do not normally sleep with customers. They are entertainers, skilled in dance or song or music, and they are also trained to be charming conversationalists and attentive hostesses. Since customers almost never bring wives to a place like Kiccho and the power elite is almost entirely male, the dinner groups are normally all-male, and the geisha are summoned to add some feminine charm and warmth to the gathering. They flirt with the men and pour them drinks and laugh at their jokes. It is an expensive boost to the ego, but the shareholders are paying.

My dinnermates were also interested in the geisha, so I interpreted what my hostess said about them. None of us wanted to pay $1,000 for their company, but in the end Yugi-san ushered five of them into our dining room just to say hello. Their guests had just left, and they were interested in meeting our group—an oddity with the chairman and three women. All five of the geisha had drunk a bit too much, and none were particularly pretty. They wore beautiful kimonos and *obi,* however, and their hair and makeup were perfect. They were not as reticent as I had expected. One even spoke a little English and was eager to try it, boisterously asking us questions and flirting with me. We exchanged cards, and she reached into her *obi* to pull out one of hers, delicately printed with just her name. No phone number.

No major country has so mishandled its economy in the postwar era as Japan did from 1988 through the late 1990s. First, in the late 1980s it opened the floodgates of the money supply, expanding the bubble economy to ridiculous heights (this was partly at the urging of Washington, which wanted Japan to stimulate the global economy). Then when the bubble popped, Japan first ignored the problems as they developed and then in 1997 actually did everything possible to make them worse. That was the year when Prime Minister Ryutaro Hashimoto raised the national sales tax from 3 percent to 5 percent, even though the economy was still struggling to recover from recession. The result, of course, was a dip in consumer spending—and a further dive in Japan's economy. As Sheryl noted, Japanese banks eager for higher returns began to pour their money into Southeast Asia, feeding the bubble there. But with its own economy faltering, Japan cut its purchases of goods from Thailand, South Korea, and Malaysia, helping to set the stage for the Asian economic crisis. It would be much too harsh to say that Japan was to blame for the Asian crisis, but it does have some share of the responsibility.

Why did Japan fail to act to restructure its economy and revive itself? One reason is the weakness of the political system in Japan. No major country has such a capacity to produce nonentities as prime ministers as Japan, but the problem is not so much the individuals as the political structure. Traditionally in postwar Japan, economic affairs were run by bureaucrats in the government ministries, and foreign and security policies were determined by Washington, so there was not much for politicians to do except to take bribes from construction companies and build bullet train lines in their home districts. Even in the prefectures, there is not much opportunity for local politicians to bring about change, because power is so centralized that they have little authority. Moreover, parliamentary constituencies are allocated disproportionately to rural areas, so that the conservative parts of the country are overrepresented and hold back the prospect of reform.

Yet the political system is only one obstacle to change, and the broader one is society itself. There is an expression in Japanese, *nurumayu,* that describes the coziness of a lukewarm bath even after you know it is time to step naked out of the tub and face the chill. Many Japanese say that their nation's cosseted economy is *nurumayu* and they realize it is time to step out—but that the bath is so lulling that they cannot summon the energy to do so just yet.

One reason why Japan has stayed in the bath is that it has underestimated the seriousness of the situation. Japan is a mighty relaxing bath in which to soak, and throughout the 1990s there was remarkably little sense of crisis even as the nation's economy fell apart. The lack of a crisis mentality meant that Japan could not summon the political will to lay off surplus workers, to extinguish insolvent banks, to snuff out the hopes of the kindly old ladies who run rice shops and futon stores. It meant that there was little public pressure on the prime minister to push for the sweeping deregulation—for the market economy—that Japan desperately needs. Yet gradually, far too lackadaisically, it is happening anyway. "Frankly, I'd just as soon stay in the bath," mused Hironori Takayama, a young banker near Omiya. "But these days, even if you try to stay in the bath, the tub will crack and the water will leak out. So if you stay in you risk getting chilly and catching cold. It's not much of a choice."

One of the funniest people in Omiya is Kihachiro Nishimura, a silver-haired old codger who runs the liquor shop and lost in the last race for mayor. He is often a bit loaded on his own liquor, and his shop is usually empty so that if I drop by he summons me to the tatami living room behind his shop and pours me a drink and begins telling me tartly about what is really going on in Omiya. His liquor shop is just the kind of business that survived on *giri-ninjo* and is now dying because of competition from giant stores, and I broached the subject delicately for fear of offending him. I needn't have worried.

"Oh, this store is dying," he said. "I know it. Already, we aren't really making any money. My wife and I, we just do it to have something to putter around in. Nobody will take over this store when we are too old, and in five or ten years it will be gone. That's okay. We need change.

"I once heard a scholar say that the mass media are very unfair to typhoons. The media always report about the damage caused, but never about the benefits of the rain. I feel sorry for the typhoons. Sure they may knock down a few houses. They even kill a few people. But every year they bring the rain that nurtures our paddies and fields so that we can feed our people. The fact of the matter is that we need typhoons.

"Now an economic typhoon is coming through. It'll destroy this store and plenty of other businesses. It'll kill the old way of doing business in this country. But that's a good thing overall. We need to change. We need the rain that it'll bring to nurture new businesses. So it's wrong just to look at the casualties of the typhoon. It's the best thing happening."

Nishimura didn't know it, but he was restating—much more colorfully—the thesis of Joseph Schumpeter, the Austrian economist who hailed the need for "creative destruction." The weak need to be killed off for the strong to grow, Schumpeter argued. Japan was always too concerned about *giri-ninjo* to let the weak expire, but now it is happening. The *giri-ninjo* economy was already under strain, but now it is collapsing in Japan because of the long recession and elsewhere because of the Asian economic crisis.

In Omiya, I could see this process of extinction of *giri-ninjo* in retail stores—every time I visited there were fewer. One of the stores that pretty much collapsed over the course of my visits to Omiya was the little electronics shop of Yachiyo and Nobuhiro Horie, a middle-aged couple who lived in a house just behind their store. These days, the little roadside shop is just a clutter of unsold odds and ends, and is mostly used as a work area for Nobuhiro to spread things out and tinker with them. He is almost never interrupted by customers.

"I have a friend near here, and I was thinking that since her refrigerator was getting old, maybe she would buy a new one from us," said Yachiyo, a giggly woman who served tea in her home and gaily told all about her incompetence as a shopkeeper. "Then one day I was at her house and I saw a new refrigerator! I thought, Hey! Well, I was very curious, but of course I couldn't say a thing. So finally I casually said, 'I see you have a new refrigerator.' But she didn't want to talk about it." Yachiyo shook her head sadly at the loss of business, and added: "Now even my sister buys electrical things in the big stores, like her new washing machine."

Nobuhiro, who had been brooding quietly in the corner, looked up at that and snapped: "And a new television!"

When it was time to leave Kiccho, the hostesses did not, of course, present a bill. Kiccho is never so crass as to ask a customer to pay right there. Instead, Kiccho sends a monthly bill to the office, and a secretary arranges a bank transfer.

Patrons leaving Kiccho are supposed to present a $100 tip to the hostesses. It is an oddity, for tipping is almost nonexistent in Japan, and I didn't realize this obligation until the next day when my secretaries asked whether I had presented the money. So I ignored my responsibility, and the Kiccho hostesses were far too polite to raise the issue.

A few days later the bill arrived by mail. Yugi-san, presumably concerned by my poverty, had not even charged me for drinks, and she had also left the "service charge" line blank (same for the line stating, "companion charge"). So the overall bill was a relative bargain at 388,800 yen. At the exchange rate at the time, that meant the dinner cost only $3,500.

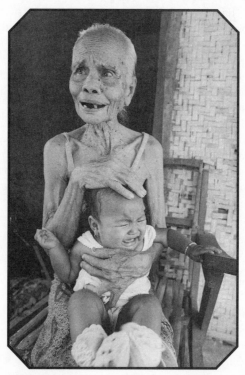

*Sambirah, a great-grandmother, holds baby Maisaroh in her arms. In the worst of the Asian crisis, she said that it did not matter if elderly people like her did not eat, but she could not bear it when the children went to bed hungry.*

### CHAPTER FIVE

# The Blood Baht Spreads

## SHERYL WUDUNN

*If thou be poure, thy brother hateth thee,*
*And alle thy freendes fleen fro thee, alas!*

—GEOFFREY CHAUCER, *THE CANTERBURY TALES,* 1400

On July 2, 1997, as Thailand's newly floated baht plummeted in value, investors were delighted. They phoned in their orders to buy Thai stocks, and this sudden new confidence in Thailand sent the market index soaring that day by 7.9 percent, its biggest gain in more than five years. The devaluation meant that Thai policymakers were admitting past mistakes and facing a new reality, analysts said, and investors were betting that the devaluation would solve Thailand's problems by letting the currency settle at its real value. Some renowned experts were less certain. Barton M. Biggs, the Morgan Stanley Dean Witter strategist who had helped fuel the rush to emerging markets, said on that day that devaluation had created new risks but that Thai stocks were also now cheaper than ever. "So," he said, "you have to weigh the trade-off."

Those initial optimistic instincts—played out the day the baht floated—turned out to be dead wrong. In the ensuing months, the aftershocks from Thailand's devaluation whipsawed around the region and became what is known as the Asian contagion, toppling corporate empires, shutting down plants, folding companies, and breaking up families. Soon leaders of the region were asking why all that was happening. How and why did a devaluation in Thailand hit Indonesia and South Korea? How can it be, as the economist David Hale once said with knowing exaggeration, that "a real-estate crisis in Bangkok set in motion something that has no parallel in human history"?

At the *Times,* we spent a long time looking for answers to that question, and we found that one reason things went so terribly wrong was that Asian executives and political leaders ignored the problems until it was too late. Sometimes they made things worse. But there is plenty of blame to go around, and the Clinton administration and the IMF also badly mishandled the crisis in the early months. Treasury Secretary Rubin and Deputy Treasury Secretary Summers made a catastrophic misdiagnosis of the crisis, one that resulted in Thailand getting insufficient treatment and in other countries being exposed to the infection. Rubin and Summers at first believed that they were facing an isolated economic slowdown in Thailand alone. They felt that the best medicine was an IMF-led bailout based on fresh funds and tough conditions: austerity, high interest rates, and a repair job on the Thai banking system. This kind of program had worked beautifully in Mexico two years earlier, despite the gloomy predictions of critics, and Summers was still basking in the success. Harsh conditions such as sky-high interest rates were an essential element of any recovery, Treasury argued, or else Thailand would simply get into trouble again. Yet in contrast to the Mexico bailout, this time the United States refused to chip in any money. Rubin said he could not contribute because of congressional restrictions, but it would have been possible to get around them. The upshot was that without American participation, the bailout never had credibility. Treasury's failure to chip in is now widely acknowledged to have been an error—a senior State Department official admitted: "In hindsight, it was a mistake."

Tensions also rose because Treasury, even though it was not offering any cash, wanted to run the show. Summers thought that the IMF's proposed program was not tough enough in forcing Thailand to change its ways, and he threatened to scuttle the whole package unless the IMF tightened its conditions. One official who was there recalls Summers warning the IMF: "Where should we cast our 'no' vote?"

The Clinton administration was so adamant about the need for austerity that it blocked Japan from helping out. Officials in Tokyo talked about rescuing Thailand with a big package of loans immediately after the crisis hit, but they did not do so because of Washington's insistence on the need to impose tough conditions on Thailand. Then a couple of months later, Japan again proposed a major bailout of the region, through a $100-billion program called the Asian Monetary Fund. It was hastily prepared, and there are doubts about how well it would have worked, but in the end it was not even tried. The Japanese plan would not have cost the United States a penny, but Rubin fumed about it on the plane taking him to the World Bank meeting in Hong Kong where the plan would be discussed. Rubin and Summers had often shown a deep distrust and distaste for Japanese economic officials, and they met with aides in the forward compartment of the plane—the same plane, an old Air Force One, that had carried Nixon to China in 1972—to nibble on nachos and plot strategy to kill the proposal.

They succeeded, and Japan abandoned the plan. Some American officials regret that. "I think we've all learned a lot of lessons over the last year or so," Stuart E. Eizenstat, then undersecretary of state for economic affairs, told Nick a year after the crisis struck. "Perhaps with 20-20 hindsight, this was an idea that might have gotten more attention." A year after Washington killed its rescue proposal, Japan developed another plan on a smaller scale, this time offering $30 billion under the Miyazawa plan, named after Kiichi Miyazawa, Japan's finance minister at the time. Instead of trying to subvert the proposal, Rubin now called the idea "constructive" and President Clinton hailed it as one of Japan's "important contributions to regional stabilization."

Treasury's error was understandable: It did not realize how many countries the crisis would hit and how deep the economic suffering would be. Nobody else did, either. Indeed, I'm hesitant to criticize Summers because he in particular understood the implications ahead of the rest of us. During the early days of the crisis, after Nick had just come back from a trip to Seoul, Summers asked us whether we thought South Korea would be badly hit. We smiled confidently and said, "Probably not." Summers, more astute than we were, was already trying to figure out how to deal with a possible Korean collapse. In retrospect, he also had much more foresight in his analysis about Kim Dae Jung, then a presidential candidate, than I did. I gloomily wondered whether Kim's traditional support for a stronger labor movement would thwart an IMF program. Summers was more optimistic, arguing—quite correctly, as it turned out—that Kim as president would be able to institute reforms precisely because of his strong labor background. So while I think U.S. officials like Rubin and Summers mishandled the crisis, sometimes catastrophically, my criticism is tempered by humility. Moreover, the mistakes that Rubin and Summers made, while often devastating, were usually reasonable ones to make. Rubin has never openly admitted that his response to the crisis was incorrect, but I think he acknowledges it implicitly. He likes to say, when the topic comes up, that life is a series of bets. If someone offers to flip a coin and gives you two-to-one odds that it will be heads, he says, that is a smart bet to take. And it is still smart to have taken the bet even if you lose. When he says this, Rubin is effectively arguing: *Okay, we screwed up. Our calls were sound ones at the time, but in the end they didn't work out.*

The American-backed IMF policy of harsh measures produced a steady weakening of Thailand's economy. Washington's unwillingness to contribute funds, Japan's failure to contribute for fear of offending Washington, the harsh IMF conditions, the buckling of the banking sector—all these eroded confidence and the economy itself. The baht fell even lower, as investors scurried to convert their baht into the safe haven of dollars, and this forced central bankers to raise interest rates to bolster their weakening currency. These higher interest rates then bankrupted even healthy businesses, eroded confidence in the baht even more, and sent Thailand's economy into a vicious downward spiral.

The weakening of the baht was a particular problem for the thousands of small and large companies that had borrowed in dollars. For example, a Bangkok company might have borrowed $10 million in U.S. currency to develop a luxury Thai property, betting that the exchange rate of twenty-five baht to the dollar would hold as it had for many years. That would mean repaying 250 million baht, and it would seem reasonable if the development could be resold for 350 million baht. But when the baht lost more than half its value, the company would suddenly find that it had to pay back 500 million baht, not 250 million baht. And with the crash in the property market, the finished development might be worth not 350 million baht but only 100 million baht. Suddenly a project that had seemed smart was valued at only 100 million baht with a debt burden of 500 mil-

*As policymakers fumbled, the pain spread to people like Som and Sanguan Chianda, who pray at an altar in their house in Thailand for their son Lamkwan, visible behind them. Lamkwan illustrates the human cost of the Asian economic crisis, for he was sick and needed imported medicine, which soared in price after the collapse of the Thai baht. Without his medicine, he lost his ability to speak and to walk. After Nick wrote about him,* New York Times *readers sent money to help, and two aid organizations, Childreach (the American arm of Plan International) and World Vision, funneled the money to him and bought him medicine and medical attention, saving his life.*

lion baht and soaring carrying costs. That was the formula destroying even many Asian companies that were basically sound.

Treasury and IMF soon realized their mistakes and reversed course, allowing Thailand to ease the austerity, but the damage had already been done. And as Thailand suffered, investors scanned the region and thought they saw the same rags-to-rickety-riches tale in other Asian countries, and they became increasingly leery of the entire region. The jitters spread to Malaysia, Hong Kong, and, most devastatingly, Indonesia. Central bankers in the Philippines saw investors scrambling to sell pesos and buy dollars, putting pressure on the value of the peso. Lending rates soared to 30 percent and officials floated the peso. Taking precautions, policymakers in Indonesia did the same, allowing the rupiah to fluctuate more. The Singapore dollar also dropped in value, and the Malaysian ringgit tumbled. Even the Hong Kong dollar, which is pegged to the U.S. dollar, felt enormous pressure, and on just one day officials spent $1 billion to defend the peg. All of Asia had sunk into a crisis of confidence.

So just as Western capital had poured into Asian markets in the early and mid-1990s, now it began to flood out. For example, after Thailand began to fall apart in the fall of 1997, Barton Biggs made another trip to Bangkok, and this time his advice was grim. "I really went with the idea that Asia was sold out and bombed out and that there must be some attractive values," he said in a teleconference with investors on October 27, 1997, recorded by Bloomberg. "And I've got to say that I was disappointed." Biggs told investors to sell all their holdings in "Developed Asia" markets like Hong Kong, Singapore, and Malaysia, and to cut by one-third their investments in emerging markets like Thailand and Indonesia. In the days after Biggs spoke, the Hong Kong stock market plunged 23 percent over four days.

Biggs put his money where his mouth was. He had bought into emerging markets early in 1997 for his own private portfolio, but now he sold frantically. Records at the Securities and Exchange Commission show that in December 1997 he personally sold $56,000 worth of Malaysian Fund, $650,000 worth of Emerging Markets Fund, $80,000 worth of India Investment Fund, $137,000 in the Pakistan Investment Fund, and almost $1.6 million worth of Asia Pacific Fund. Nervous investors were doing the same thing in fledgling markets around the world, not just Asia. The wave of capital flows to emerging markets, which had reached a peak of $213 billion in 1996, sank to about $60 billion in 1998.

At first, South Korea had seemed immune to the problems. Unlike Thailand and the other countries affected, South Korea was a modern industrialized nation, a member of the OECD. But as other nations were buffeted, gradually Kang Kyong Shik found himself under pressure. A stocky man with a receding hairline that puffs slightly into a neat mat around the back of his head, Kang was at the other end of Treasury's phone calls. The deputy prime minister for economic affairs and a renowned economic planner, Kang was a graduate of South Korea's top university, Seoul National University, and had earned a master's degree from Syracuse University in the 1960s. By the 1990s, he was an elected member in the National Assembly and a prominent proponent of modern economic methods. Appointed finance minister in the spring of 1997, he was at the center of policymaking as the economic crisis began circling the nation. Korea was facing economic troubles and it needed an advocate to carry out financial reforms to restore health to Korea, Inc. Kang cared deeply about transforming South Korea into a true market economy, helping the country shift from an export-oriented power that put growth ahead of all else to an economy that also emphasized stability in that growth. He knew that Korea had to open its markets, deregulate its rigid, archaic financial system, and bring in fair competition. But Kang never had a chance to implement reforms.

By the late summer of 1997, bankers from America and Japan were getting nervous about Asia. They had pulled whatever loans they had in Southeast Asia, and now they were scrutinizing the rest of the region. Some foreign bankers began to refuse to renew their dollar loans to Korean banks, which searched in desperation for other sources of dollars to meet their obligations. In early November, foreign investors suddenly withdrew large batches of capital from South Korea's stock market. Then Japanese banks, under sudden strain from major bankruptcies at home, pulled their short-term loans to Korean banks—about 23 percent of Korea's total short-term loans outstanding. So Kang and his colleagues in the Blue House, the presidential compound, called top policymakers, central bankers, and other staff for an emergency meeting on November 7. The conclusion of that meeting was that Korea would take whatever measures it could on its own, but ultimately it might have to seek help from the IMF. Still, to the public, Kang put on his best face, assuring everyone that Korea was not going to run into problems. When Nick met him for an interview on the day of that meeting, Kang seemed as confident as ever. "Korea is not another Thailand," he said, full of ebullience.

Then the next morning, at 7:30, Kang met with the president's economic secretary over a Japanese breakfast at a local hotel and they discussed the IMF option in more detail. They met again on Sunday to flesh out a final action plan to confront the economic crisis and then presented a proposal to president Kim Young Sam on Monday at 8:00 in the morning. They wanted to disclose a plan to deal with ballooning bad loans. If they could convince investors that their plans were credible, then they might not have to go to the IMF. Kim gave his approval, but meanwhile, the Korean won was slipping, and the Bank of Korea had lent its precious foreign exchange reserves to Korean banks that were in desperate need of funds. The money was unlikely to be repaid, and along with the effort to defend the won, the Bank of Korea's usable foreign exchange reserves had dwindled to about $16 billion, down from a peak just a few months earlier of $34 billion. The smaller sum was barely enough to cover three months of imports, the minimum amount considered financially prudent.

By November 13, things looked grim. Kang tracked down Michel Camdessus, the managing director of the IMF, in Bangkok and invited him to Korea on his way back to Washington. At 3:00 on November 16, a wintry Sunday afternoon, Camdessus landed in Seoul. Kang wanted to avoid the press, so instead of dispatching a black Mercedes-Benz to ferry Camdessus to a luxury hotel in the city center, he sent a staff car to pick up Camdessus and carry him to the downmarket Continental Hotel in the suburbs.

"I couldn't entertain him in the dining room," Kang said, embarrassed even as he recalled the event, and the two men had glasses of scotch in private. "In the hotel room, I asked room service to bring him a sandwich. He had steak instead, of very poor quality." Over this poor meal, Kang secretly asked the IMF for help and won Camdessus's promise of support. The meeting ended at 9:00 p.m. and Kang headed over to the National Assembly, which had objections to his reform bills.

Kang made plans to unveil a new package of measures on November 18 and to tell the world that Korea would seek help from the IMF. Meanwhile, Korea was about to hold a presidential election, so President Kim Young Sam was facing enormous pressure to fix the economic crisis and felt he needed to do something drastic. Moments after Kang presented his final plan to the president, a presidential aide hurried over, mumbling something about a reshuffle. Kang returned to the president's office. Kim was grave. He took Kang's hand and shook it, saying: "You had a hard time. The situation is very difficult, so a reshuffle is inevitable." Kang left the room, realizing that he had been fired.

Barely an hour later, Kang was on a scheduled phone call with Secretary Rubin, explaining Korea's request to the IMF and his own resignation. But Kang's plan to go to the IMF was not announced to the public, and, in fact, that afternoon Kang's successor announced that Korea would not turn to the IMF. As if that were not enough, that evening, the parliament rejected Kang's reform plan.

However, there was no alternative, and three days later, on November 21, Kang's replacement announced that Korea would seek help from the IMF after all. That help turned out to be $58 billion, with lots of strings attached. The Korean public was outraged and on December 18, 1997, it elected a new president, Kim Dae Jung.

Kim's election reflected the political shockwaves rippling through Asia from the crisis. Governments in many Asian countries had derived their legitimacy from their economic performance, under a social contract that was roughly this: So long as the leaders provided strong economic growth, the public would put up with nepotism, corruption, and rigged elections. The Asian crisis shattered that contract, and the result was the thud of falling governments: in Thailand, South Korea, and Indonesia.

Indonesia was hardest hit by the crisis, but what is unclear is whether it had to suffer at all. Some economists make a compelling case that Indonesia was simply the victim of the international equivalent of a drive-by shooting.

Of course, Indonesia had started with some of the same problems as the rest of Asia—the three excesses: excess lending by banks, excess investment by government and corporations, and excess capacity throughout the economy. And corruption and cronyism added to the uncertainty about how bad the problems would get. Yet in contrast to the other countries in the region, when the crisis began in the summer of 1997 Indonesia's trade balance had been in relatively healthy shape and had held steady for years. Indonesia had had a respectable $20 billion in foreign exchange reserves and did not squander them trying to defend its currency. Credit had grown more slowly than in other countries, and there was less indication of a bubble. The government initially reacted with foresight, going to the IMF before any severe problems developed.

Yet in the end, Indonesia's currency lost 85 percent of its value at one point, and the country was savaged by anti-Chinese race riots and the beheading of those supposed "sorcerers." When one adds the deaths from political violence to those from malnutrition, it is clear that the crisis killed thousands of people. "These horrendous things did not have to happen," argues Jeffrey Sachs, the director of Harvard's Institute for International Development. "The crisis was pushed to an extreme that it never had to take."

The brunt of the pain was felt in places like Mojokerta in East Java. Salamet, the rickshaw driver in Indonesia who wanted to kill sorcerers, hadn't even noticed when Thailand devalued the baht and set off the crisis. He never reads the papers, and for several months there was not much impact on his little town of Mojokerto. But by the fall of 1998, a year after

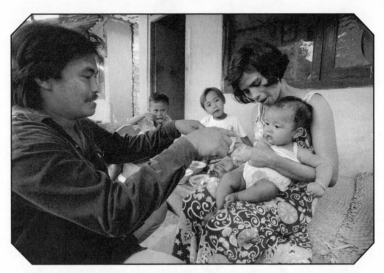

*Salamet plays with his children in front of their home in Mojokerto, Indonesia. During the Asian economic crisis, Salamet fell behind in payments on the rickshaw that he had purchased during boom times. His wife, Yuti (right), argued that the priority should be paying school fees to keep Dwi (center) in school.*

the crisis began, life was miserable there. Salamet spent much of his time sitting on the porch of his little white house, his expression as hard and beaten as the wood on his sagging bench. He stared straight ahead, buffeted by the groans from his fifty-four-year-old mother lying on a mat on the floor inside. "She's dying," he said flatly, as he poured out his story to Nick. "She won't last long. I'm sure of it." From time to time, he went inside to try to comfort her, speaking softly to her in the dim light of the bedroom, but each time he was staggered at the sight. It was a chilling image: she, gasping feebly, too weak to stand or even go to the toilet, and he, too disgusted by the monstrous tumor protruding from her breast. "She's in so much pain," he said weakly, stepping outside again. "It hurts her all the time, every moment. She can't even sleep because of the pain." He slumped.

Salamet is by nature quiet, and when Yuti, his wife, scolds him for not earning enough money he does not shout at her or hit her, as other men in the neighborhood might. "Instead, he just sulks," laughed Yuti, twenty-six, a slight, pretty, brown-skinned woman with jutting cheekbones. So Salamet said little about his mother, and instead he played absentmindedly with the baby, Maisaroh, his eyes twinkling briefly as she grasped his fingers. But most of the time now his face was haggard, as he picked among impossible choices. He sighed as Yuti sat down beside him on the bench, and then they began to quarrel about which expenses to cut.

Should they trim spending on food? They already were down to one or two meals a day. Further cutbacks might leave Maisaroh and her two brothers forever stunted. Should they hold off on making payments on Salamet's rickshaw, which he had purchased just before the crisis hit? They were already four months behind in their payments, and if it were seized for nonpayment then they would lose their livelihood.

Should they stop paying school fees for the eldest child, Dwi, a mischievous second-grader? Already the school was warning them that they must pay for the last two months or Dwi would be expelled.

Or should they stop buying the painkiller for Salamet's mother, which cost about $2 for a month's supply? Yuti argued that the money could be better invested by keeping Dwi in school. Salamet agreed in theory, but his mother groaned so pitifully that he couldn't resist her pleas. "If I had money, of course I would buy her more painkillers," he grumbled, defensive, a bite in his voice. "But now I can't afford to give her much."

One day Salamet and Yuti and little Maisaroh visited Yuti's family in a village twenty miles away. They sat down on the ground beside the hut to chat. No food was served, for there was none; Yuti's family was even worse off than Salamet's. The matriarch, Sambirah, was particularly striking. She didn't know her age but seemed about eighty, and she was so gaunt and frail that she looked as if she might blow away in the breeze. Her rheumy eyes glowed with pride for a moment as she held Maisaroh, her great-granddaughter, in her gnarled arms. Sambirah's pale mouth turned up at the corners, revealing two yellowed teeth, tusks emerging from an expanse of gum. Then the tusks disappeared, and Sambirah's eyes clouded again. She sighed and described how she pawned her sarongs so that the children would not starve.

"I can put up with it if I don't eat," she said in a whisper. "But the children aren't used to it. They cry and cry."

The bewilderment in Salamet's family resonated across the region during the Asian economic crisis. A path that had seemed to mark hope had collapsed into despair, and people who had pushed the Sisyphian rock to the top of the hill now watched it tumble back down.

The sharpest pains resulted from bets going wrong in Washington as well as in Jakarta. As the contagion of the crisis began to spread to Indonesia, officials in Washington had no clue what to do. They knew next to nothing about Indonesia, and the State Department and CIA had lost all credibility during the crisis because they had miscalculated so many times already. The CIA had proven, in the words of one of its top officials, "completely unprepared to deal with questions of an economic nature." So Rubin and Summers were skeptical of the cables coming from Jakarta, but they had no intuitive feel for how to handle them or the Indonesian dictator, Suharto.

"The nature of the crisis was not understood," recalled a senior official who was in the thick of Washington's handling of events. "We didn't really grasp everything that was going on." There was general agreement, though, that Suharto was playing with fire in his flirtation with the idea of trying to bolster the Indonesian rupiah with a currency board, an arrangement where the government would fix the rupiah to the dollar, allow it to be fully convertible, and abandon any independent monetary policy. Though favored by some scholars and used successfully in Hong Kong and Argentina, a currency board is difficult to put into place and probably it would have been used merely as a channel for Suharto's children to move their savings out of the country. So while on a trip to Texas on January 8, 1998, President Clinton telephoned Suharto from Air Force One to urge compliance with the IMF program and to tell him to forget about the currency board. But Suharto stuck to his guns. A White House aide recalled Suharto growling: "Look, I understand that this doesn't cure anything, but the IMF isn't curing anything, either."

Suharto had a point. The IMF and Treasury's approach was making things worse. The IMF had ordered Indonesia to close sixteen banks, thinking that the financial markets would be cheered by a sign that Indonesia was resolutely addressing its bad loan problem. Bad call. "Far from improving public confidence in the banking system," the IMF admitted in an internal document, the closures had triggered runs at two-thirds of Indonesia's banks. That episode was suggestive of what went wrong more broadly in Indonesia: a shattering of confidence.

Washington did not appreciate that Indonesia was particularly vulnerable to a loss of confidence. More than half of Indonesian wealth was in the hands of ethnic Chinese, who amounted to about 3 percent of Indonesia's population. These Chinese were relentlessly discriminated against—were not even allowed to teach their children the Chinese language or to celebrate Chinese New Year—and they were unusually ready to move their wealth overseas at the first signs of distress. All this made it especially important that Indonesia retain confidence and calm; instead, mismanagement in both Jakarta and Washington destroyed the confidence and launched a downward spiral of recession and anti-Chinese riots. Wealthy Chinese were able to leave town, some of them sailing to Singapore and becoming known as the "yacht people," but poorer Chinese were raped, robbed, beaten up, and even killed. Throughout this crucial period, confidence was particularly undermined by comments on and off the record by the IMF and the Treasury Department. Both ridiculed Suharto's budget proposal, which because of exchange rate movements showed a 32 percent spending increase. But three weeks later, having already harmed Indonesia's image irreparably, the IMF quietly approved a budget with a 46 percent spending increase.

People wanted a blood sacrifice; they wanted catharsis. The result was a few political scapegoats whose lives were ruined in an effort to quell the anger of the masses. One of them was Kang Kyong Shik, the ousted South Korean finance minister. In the spring of 1998, a few months after Korea turned to the IMF for help, Kang was arrested and jailed for dereliction of duty and for failure to inform the president early enough of the gravity of the economic crisis. He lingered in a jail cell for 110 days, wrapped in a blue uniform with No. 1199 sewn onto it. His wife, Cho Sam Jin, brought books and magazines to him every day, but gifts of food were not allowed. She also took his laundry to spare him the menial task of having to wash it himself.

Prosecutors charged Kang with several counts, focusing on neglect of duty while he ran Korea's economy but also including abuse of power for pressuring a bank to lend to his friends. His trial was a symptom of the depth of anger in South Korea, as people struggled to comprehend how a miracle economy had faltered. South Koreans seemed to feel overwhelmingly that Kang was partly responsible for the country's pain and that he should bear the penalty. To me, it seemed both ridiculous and remarkable that a nation that had for so many decades accepted authoritarian governments had changed so much that it was putting its leaders on trial for mismanagement. It would be difficult to imagine a U.S. cabinet official going on trial for policy failures.

Newspaper editorials excoriated Kang, unemployed workers blamed him for their predicament, and even scholars argued that the nation's elite officials, long protected and insulated from insult and injury, should be held more accountable for their actions. If convicted, Kang faced the possibility of many years in jail. In spirit, he was already a broken man. When I arranged to see him, he wore a tie and a somber black suit—the first time in months he had worn a suit, he said—and he greeted me in his National Assembly office, in which he had not set foot for months. The wrinkles around his eyes drew a picture of deep strain and suffering on his broad face, and he looked many years older than his age of sixty-three. His ebullience had drained away, he rarely smiled, and there was no humor in his small talk. He had lost so much weight that his suit fell around him in a loose clump, almost hiding the life inside it. As he spoke, however, I could still see an energy, perhaps nervousness, behind his words. He was puzzled by the country's ire, and deeply hurt by it. Kang was a Buddhist, and he had used his time in jail to read many Buddhist teachings, but he also spent many days reading the Bible and asking God why he was being vilified for what he remembered as the most hectic and productive eight and a half months of his public service life. When I asked him how he felt about his plight, he only said: "I lived through those hard times, anyhow. And I succeeded in keeping my health—not only physical, but also mental." Kang did not blame President Kim, saying only: "Kim Dae Jung inherited a very difficult situation. It's quite natural he should find someone to blame for the economic situation."

During those dreary days, he pored over economic literature, partly to see if scholars believed that Korea's economic crisis was the result of his actions. He was deeply relieved that experts did not seem to blame him. I felt sorry for him, but when I asked Koreans what they thought, they were invariably furious with Kang. Many Koreans said that he had lied to the nation, painting a picture of a basically healthy economy just as it was falling apart beneath him. Others said that Kang had delayed confronting the problems and seeking help in part to improve the prospects that his political party would win the presidential elections. Amid the anger, prosecutors demanded a four-year prison term for Kang.

.  .  .

The aftershocks from the Asian economic crisis rippled around the world and sent commodity prices tumbling. Russia and Brazil had their economies battered as well, as major export-earning commodities fetched far less money than before. And like Asia, Russia and Brazil had frailties in their systems, and investors who had been burned in Asia pulled out of Russia and Brazil on a moment's notice. Then in September 1998 the ripples snared Long Term Capital Management, or LTCM, the most glamorous of America's hedge funds. More than a year earlier, the hedge funds had helped to trigger the financial crisis in Thailand, setting in motion a chain reaction that ultimately came back to wobble LTCM. Alan Greenspan, who a year earlier had spurned Thailand's plea to monitor the hedge funds with a cool sermon about the need to follow the message of the markets, held the reins of the Fed when it initiated the rescue of LTCM. After advising other governments to close down troubled financial institutions, the Clinton administration now refused to heed its own advice. That may have been smart, but it smelled of hypocrisy.

Paradoxically, the troubles that felled LTCM were in many respects the same ones that had toppled Thailand and other countries. LTCM and Thailand were both victims of their own success and overconfidence— years of stellar returns had bred a hubris just as their profitability was declining. Of course, Thailand was more troubled by corruption and there are some differences, but each had become overleveraged and overconfident, and both frittered away their capital just as they were facing new kinds of risks. Moreover, they both resisted disclosure, so that investors and creditors never had much idea what their real state of finances was. And, finally, they both had a good deal of bad luck.

Asia got in trouble partly because it was in a transition between the traditional and modern worlds. It had developed modern stock markets, but not modern banking. That dangerous transition phase in which Asia found itself is perfectly captured in the taillights that have been attached to some elephants in Bangkok. Traffic in Bangkok is a nightmare, and there were a growing number of accidents involving elephants and cars. So people began to equip the elephants with trunk lights and taillights so that they could be seen better at night. No doubt it was safer before cars came along, and it will be safer yet after the elephants disappear from the streets, but in the meantime people were getting squashed by the collisions of old and new methods of transport. And that's what happened to Kang. As the judgment day for Kang's trial neared, his friends and colleagues struck back, with forty-one former policymakers signing a petition to protest the precedent of putting on trial an official for the failure of his policies. On August 19, 1999, after a bitter trial process, Kang was acquitted on all major charges. There was one minor conviction, that Kang had pressured state-controlled banks to extend millions of dollars in preferential loans to three financially shaky companies, but Kang was given a suspended sentence. The verdict ended the misery for Kang, and I felt relieved for him. But I also knew that his political career lay in tatters.

For decades, experts will argue about the lessons of the Asian economic crisis. Economists still cannot agree on the causes of the Great Depression, and perhaps they will never entirely concur on the origins of the Asian crisis. Teams of central bankers and IMF officials are still bickering over the usefulness of capital controls and pegged currencies and international rescue packages as ways of preventing similar crises in the future. Still, the crisis leaves Asia with three main lessons.

First, the crisis suggests that as the international economic system grows bigger and more efficient, it also becomes more vulnerable to shocks. The lakes of capital dotting the world have become united into an ocean, and technology can move money in an instant to a distant part of the world where it generates the greatest return. If money can move across the globe in moments, so too can fear and nervousness. And this means that as the lakes yield to the ocean, the storms get bigger and become huge typhoons with tsunami to match. The crisis gave Asian countries a taste of the risks involved in joining the global economic system. Asian countries thought they could take Western capital, expertise, and technology and leapfrog into the advanced world of finance and technology, spewing out improved copycat products at a cost lower than anywhere else. Asian companies financed long-term projects with short-term bank loans, and they had no Plan B if the banks chose not to roll over the loans. They became so used to capital pouring in that they did not contemplate what would happen if it flooded out.

In Asia, one of the best predictors of the crisis turned out to be blindingly simple: the ratio of short-term foreign loans to foreign exchange reserves. In South Korea, the figure was 213 percent at the end of 1996; in Indonesia, it was 181 percent; in Thailand, 169 percent. Other countries were far lower: 77 percent in the Philippines, 47 percent in Malaysia, 36 percent in China. A high ratio like South Korea's meant that while there would be no problem so long as banks rolled over loans, there was not enough cash on hand to pay back foreign banks if the loans were called in—and they were, all of a sudden.

Second, the crisis has taught Asia what some of its responsibilities are, in terms of building genuine markets and systems of laws and regulations. For the most part, Asian countries had planned brilliantly for the physical infrastructure of growth: They built new highways, ports, railroads, airports, universities, and electrical plants. There were bottlenecks, of course, but remarkably few considering the pace of growth. What Asia neglected was the regulatory infrastructure, such as bank supervision and modern accounting systems and rigorous financial reporting requirements. Indeed, Asia tended to boast about its dependence on human relationships rather than legal relationships, and there were regularly snide comments about how America was full of lawyers who produced nothing and Asia was full of engineers who produced new computer chips. Frankly, lawyers never looked so good as after the Asian crisis.

That in turn taught Asia a useful third lesson: humility. The crisis has demonstrated that there is nothing preordained about Asian success, and that it is possible for Asian countries to collapse as well as rise. In particular, as Asian countries modernize, they enter a more competitive world where the going gets tougher. Asian tycoons used to boast that they could make investment decisions in an instant. A Western CEO would bring in teams of investment bankers, lawyers, and accountants before committing to a major deal, but an Asian business leader would commit a few hundred million dollars in an afternoon, without talking to a single lawyer. Now, that doesn't look so smart.

After a long battle with her breast cancer, Salamet's mother finally died in her sleep in November 1998 on the floor of their little house. It was a relief for Salamet that the groans finally ended and that he no longer had to worry about trying to buy her painkillers. But Salamet then found himself faced with another bill he could not pay: the $28 cost of buying a coffin and burying her. In the end neighbors stepped in to lend him the money.

Yet to keep it all in perspective, Salamet is in the worst-off group—the urban poor—in the worst-off country of all, Indonesia, and even he somehow survived. The deprivation and hunger were serious, but the more outrageous depictions of the crisis (coming particularly from aid groups and agencies and journalists) were simply silly. The great majority of people, particularly those in the countryside, were buffered by Asia's natural

*Wilhelmina Boemao, a villager in West Timor, Indonesia, prepares a dinner of a wood called* putak. *Food became so scarce during the Asian economic crisis that villagers ate wild products like* putak *that they never normally touched.*

abundance, free for the asking. In Thailand, for instance, Nick met the family of Maesubin Sisoipha, who were eating bugs for lunch. All the wage earners in the family had lost their jobs, but they were all gathered around a table having a cheerful meal of fried beetles served with mango leaves and rice and fish paste. "Bugs don't taste so bad," Maesubin said cheerfully, bouncing her baby on her knee. "We catch the beetles ourselves. The mango leaves we pick from a tree. The rice we grow ourselves. And we make the fish paste from fish we catch in the river."

One of the hardest-hit areas during the crisis was a village called Toeneke in West Timor, Indonesia. When Nick went there, he met Wilhelmina Boemao, a tall, good-natured woman with short, curly hair, who was preparing her dinner beside her thatch-roofed hut. On the menu that night: boiled wood. Boemao had chopped up chunks of *putak*, a kind of palm tree that grows wild, boiled them into splinters that taste as awful as they sound, or ground the wood into what she calls flour but is actually sawdust. "In the past, I used *putak* to feed pigs, and even they didn't like it," Boemao said with a sad smile. "I never ate *putak*. My grandmother used to talk about eating it in hard times, and my mother may have eaten it once or twice, but in my lifetime, never." Sawdust may be a pretty wretched dinner, but two doctors in the area said that *putak* can be a source of carbohydrates—a bad source, but enough to keep someone alive.

Contrary to some of the initial assertions in the West that the financial crisis had sent Asia twenty or thirty years backward or that it had destroyed the middle class, no one in Salamet's neighborhood thought that their quality of life had retreated even to the level of 1990. Indonesia's GDP dipped 13.4 percent in 1998, putting it back where it was in 1994. South Korea's GDP backed up to where it was in 1996. There are problems with these statistics because of changing exchange rates, but it is impossible to travel in Asia and visit neighborhoods like Salamet's and conclude that the region tumbled back a generation. Salamet has access to a toilet, which he did not have a decade earlier. He has electricity, which he did not have until a few years earlier. His son is still in school, the first in his family to get an education.

On the contrary, the crisis was an imposed breather, a forced opportunity to recuperate and regroup for the rest of the ascent. And the lessons that Asia learned from the crisis—humility, respect for laws and markets and the risks as well as rewards of globalization—may have helped prepare it for an ascent to much greater and more challenging heights.

*Part Two*

# REBUILDING ASIA

*Child prostitutes negotiating with a Cambodian customer in a brothel.*

### CHAPTER SIX

# *Brutal Drive*

## NICHOLAS D. KRISTOF

*First comes the bitterness,*
*Then there is sweetness and wealth and honor for 10,000 years.*

—CHINESE PROVERB

We all have ghosts, and Sriy is one of mine. A Cambodian wisp of a girl, thirteen years old, she had a mischievous grin and luminous black eyes sparkling from an oval face. Her white lace knee-length gown left her golden skin glowing, and her fingernails and toenails were painted ruby red. Then there was the lipstick, a clumsy swath of crimson, so thick and ineptly applied that it was cute, leaving Sriy looking like a little girl playing dress-up.

"This must be a difficult life," I suggested.

"Difficult?" she giggled, the smear around her mouth moving in waves as she spoke. "It's very nice. I get good food and a bed. And look at these nice clothes." Then she smiled, her crimson beak opening wide, as she laughed and grabbed my hand. "Let me show you my bed."

It was late afternoon in the Cambodian capital of Phnom Penh, and the shimmering heat was easing as the sun settled toward the hills. As the temperature dropped from boiling to merely sweltering, the neighborhood along the dirt road was coming to life, with a steady traffic of ox carts, motorcycles, bicycles, and even an occasional car. All along the street were rickety one-story brothels housing teenage girls. Sound carried easily in the evening air, and I could hear girlish laughter and quarrels along the street. Somewhere two dogs were fighting. The open sewer contributed a putrid aroma, but Sriy's brothel itself was painted white and seemed clean and well swept.

I had picked Sriy's brothel at random, walking up the creaking wooden steps with a Cambodian friend who was interpreting for me. The brothel owner, a pudgy woman in her late twenties, had rushed over ingratiatingly. She had a round face, two or three chins, and was dressed in green shorts and a blue T-shirt that clashed, and she beamed at the smell of a foreigner's money. "Okay, okay," she called to me in English. "Come, okay, okay. Welcome! Okay." The working girls stood up from their rickety chairs and walked over, curious at the sight of an American, and Sriy was at the front, joking with a friend, the crimson smear around her mouth so earnest and so overdone that she immediately caught my eye.

I sat down on a folding metal chair at a faded card table by the entrance and told the owner that I wanted to talk to Sriy and her friend. So we sat at the card table, and I ordered Cokes all around—pleasing the brothel owner because she charged a hefty markup on drinks.

"What's your name?" I asked, and because many of the girls are brought in from Vietnam, I added: "Are you Vietnamese?"

"My name is Sriy," she said, and her eyes flashed in annoyance, "and I am Khmer!"

She flirted shamelessly, touching my arm one moment and then pulling back and pretending to be angry. Sriy's aggressiveness made me uncomfortable because she looked so young and physically immature, like a ten-year-old American girl, that her eagerness to sleep with me seemed not titillating but just bizarre. Her manner was also that of a young child: She glowered one moment and then burst into giggles, leaning forward on the card table, which jiggled and threatened to spill our Cokes. We all grabbed the cans to steady them, laughingly sucking up the Coke that had spilled onto our hands.

The brothel owner was watching a Thai pornographic video in the next room, and from our table we could see the corner of the screen and catch the gist of the grunts. "Would you like that?" Sriy asked me mischievously,

*Child prostitutes walk among the brothels of Svay Pak in Cambodia.
Brothel owners do not permit photographs here, so I shot from the waist
without looking through the lens.*

laughing and gesturing to the video, as it spewed out moans and graphic images of oral sex. She and her friend doubled over in laughter, like teeny-boppers at a bowling alley. Sriy reached out to touch my arm and I pulled back, sending her into new paroxysms of laughter. The brothel owner heard the laughter and figured it was time to move us into the cubicles in the back.

"Ten dollars? Okay?" the woman asked. "All night? Okay?"

"No, no," I said. "More Cokes. Four Cokes!"

"You like?" the woman asked me. "You like, okay?" And then she pushed down Sriy's neckline to display her breast—or, rather the nipple of what would eventually become a breast if Sriy were to survive to maturity. Sriy fought half-heartedly, but the woman pinned her hands, and pulled down the dress further. "You like?" the woman asked me, as Sriy looked to the side. "You take girl? Okay? Okay?"

"Just a Coke," I said. "No, four Cokes."

"Just ten dollars," the brothel owner said, switching to Khmer and speaking to the interpreter. "It's a bargain. She's only just lost her virginity. She's practically a virgin."

Then the brothel owner walked around to Sriy's friend and pulled down the top of her dress, too. The friend looked down and to the side as her flat chest was put on display. "Or this one," the owner said. "Look how young and pretty she is."

"Just four Cokes," I repeated stonily.

"Okay, okay," the brothel owner said. "Cokes." She wandered off as Sriy and her friend shrugged and pulled their dresses back up, trying to recover their dignity.

As we waited for the drinks, Sriy began flirting with me aggressively, chasing my knee with her hand and laughing when she saw I was uncomfortable. I pressed again: "But it must be a rough life here, right? Do guys hit you sometimes?"

"No, no, not usually," she said sweetly. "It's pretty comfortable. And we have flush toilets here, which we don't have in the village."

"But you can catch a sickness, right?"

"No, I'm too young," she said brightly.

I paused, frustrated, looking at her skeptically, and keeping my arms back where she couldn't paw them. I wanted to feel sorry for this girl, and she didn't want to let me; all she seemed to want was to sleep with me and take my money. Yet ultimately it was Sriy who gave me a visceral understanding of how Asia would climb its way out of the Asian economic crisis, how it would claw its way back to preeminence. She taught me something of two of the economic pillars of Asia's rise—brutal drive and fantastic flexibility. Her drive consisted of the guts and discipline and stamina that propel many Asians through incredible hardship, their eyes always on some ultimate prize. And Asia's flexibility lies in the mobility of labor and capital to their most profitable uses, as well as the pragmatism to accept outrageous avenues to success. That combination of drive and flexibility helped Asia restructure after the economic crisis and leaves it well positioned for further growth. Sriy helped me understand all that.

Yet at that moment when Sriy was boasting about the flush toilets and other benefits of the brothel, I paused and looked her in the eye, and then asked very quietly: "You mean you want to do this job?"

Sriy's bravado faded. She looked down at her Coke and said nothing. I think she was near tears. There had to be something behind her presence here, for girls didn't just show up for work at brothels like these. For a few minutes, neither of us said anything, and then gently I asked how she came to this place.

"I grew up in a village with my Mom and Dad and brothers and sisters," she began. "But then Dad died in the war, and everything changed. Mom married another man, and he didn't like me," she said. "I wasn't his girl, so he didn't want me in the house. He tried to get rid of me. He used to beat me." The sparkle in her eye gave way to venom. "I hate my step-father," she snarled. "I hate him. I hate him.

"He was the one who wanted to sell me. He forced my Mom to sell me. He made her go along with it. Mom was sick, and she needed money. We didn't have the money for a doctor, and she would have died."

"What was the problem with her?" I asked.

"In here. She was sick in here." Sriy patted her chest. "Her lungs, I think. She couldn't breathe, and she got worse and worse. It was scary, because she had to spend all her time lying down, and she would choke. We wanted to take her to a doctor, but we didn't have money. And so my stepfather said he had to sell me to the city. Mom didn't want to sell me, but my stepfather made her. She was too weak to do anything."

"So did your stepfather take your Mom to the doctor? Did she get better?"

There was a long pause, and I was about to repeat the question when Sriy finally looked up.

"She died." Sriy's eyes glistened, and she held her chin in her hands.

I coaxed and prodded, and it turned out that Sriy had been eleven years old when she had been sold. Her stepfather had used some of the money to help her mother, to no avail. As for Sriy, after working at one brothel for six months, she was sold to another and finally resold to the brothel where I found her.

"You're sure you don't have any diseases?" I asked her.

"I don't think I have any."

"Have you ever been tested for the AIDS virus?"

"No, but I'm clean. I'm very young."

"What do you think of your Mom?"

"Mom's dead now. I can't say anything bad about her."

"But what do you think of your Mom for allowing you to be sold?"

Sriy's eyes grew distant as her thirteen-year-old mind sorted through memories of her mother and some very confusing emotions.

"Mom was sick and needed money. I don't hate her."

"No anger at all?"

Sriy's peaceful expression did not change, and she seemed lost in thought. But she began to play with a piece of brittle plastic on the table, tearing it, breaking it with her slender fingers, violently crushing it into smaller and smaller pieces.

I knew from my interviews with Cambodian aid workers that Sriy and the other girls were real slaves. Mostly teenagers, although a few are just five or six years old, they are the property of the brothel owner who has purchased them, and their only exit comes from sale, escape, or death. Two buildings down the road from Sriy's was the charred wreck of a brothel that had burned a few days earlier. Mixed with the ashes were the bones of two teenage girls who had been locked up in a room after once trying to escape. Nobody knew if they had died of smoke or of the fire itself. Nobody knew their names.

A Cambodian slave's child is also a slave, but one difference from nineteenth-century slavery is that today's Cambodian slaves rarely are allowed to have children. Nearly all are worked to death, catching the AIDS virus within six months of beginning work, and then dying by about the age of twenty. The AIDS virus passes easily to girls like Sriy in part because so many are physically immature, susceptible to vaginal tearing that allows the virus to easily enter the bloodstream.

The thought that transfixed me was this: How could any parents do this? It seemed incomprehensible, a manifestation of pure evil, and so I wanted to confront the parents and understand their mindset. I wanted to shake Sriy's stepfather and ask him how he could do this to a little girl. Could the family really buy a future by killing their daughter?

The cold, cruel discipline that Sriy's parents displayed is one of the lubricants of Asia's great economic machine. Asia arose from pain.

America, aside from the Puritan settlements, was the opposite, nurtured by a profound optimism and a confidence in the manifest destiny not just of the nation but of each family. That is why American university students, cocky and fun-loving, always hoping the exams will be a breeze, have great fraternity parties, and conversely why Asian-Americans often ruin the grading curves. That is why Asian immigrants have come to dominate industries that put a premium not on language ability but on hard work: New Chinese immigrants work in their laundries seventeen hours a day, Koreans dominate the greengrocer business through their willingness to work seven days a week, and more than half of American motels are owned by Indian immigrants (a huge proportion of them Gujaratis surnamed Patel) who succeed because they spend all their waking moments on duty in the motel office. It's not brains but drive that propels Asians into Phi Beta Kappa or the chamber of commerce, and the drive underscores a different outlook about the future. Asians have tended to see not silver linings but storm clouds, and that is one reason why their savings rates are so high; in relation to the fable of the ant and the grasshopper, there is no doubt that Asia abounds with ants.

I am not saying that Asia will rebuild itself by families selling their daughters. Such practices are of course repulsive to most people in the East as well as in the West. But that spirit of ruthless drive and flexibility, manifesting itself in all kinds of ways, is part of Asia's competitive advantage. Asia may have soared in the last half-century, but we sometimes forget that it rose in its own way, Sriy's way. The rise of Asia in the post–World War II era came at the sacrifice of hundreds of millions of young people who worked thirteen-hour days and saved every yen, won, and fen. The characteristic sound of Asia has not been a shout of joy but the hum of machinery. Drive and flexibility forged the Asian miracle, at a tremendous human cost.

There are a couple of caveats here. Much the same could have been said of the Industrial Revolution in the West, when parents sent their children off to be chimney sweeps or to work twelve-hour days at the looms. As Balzac noted of early-nineteenth-century European industry, "no child enters the world without dirty diapers"—industrialization in its early stages is always clothed in wretchedness. Likewise, I have to admit that for all of Asia's pragmatism, it is also the region that has been caught up in some of the great idealistic spasms of the twentieth century, leading to Communist and Nationalist revolutions in China and Indochina and to half a century of foolish socialism in India. To anyone who remembers the Cultural Revolution, when Red Guards ordered people at intersections to go forward on red, the revolutionary color, it may seem odd to describe Asia as pragmatic.

But nothing so cures a country of ideology as having to live with one. That is why there are more genuine Marxists in America than in China. Moreover, if all industrialization is ruthless, the Asian variety seems to me to have been particularly so. Workers in Dickensian London at least had Sundays off; Asian factories in the old days offered no day of rest at all. Even in the 1990s, I talked to Chinese peasant girls in small-town factories in Fujian, Guangdong, and Zhejiang who made toys and shoes and were paid by the piece, who slept in lofts above the factory floor and slipped out of bed to begin stitching by 6:00 a.m. In extreme cases they stopped only at 8:00 or 9:00 p.m. for dinner and then fell exhausted into their beds, and they kept this up seven days a week for three months at a time before enjoying the extravagance of a single day off. Only at Chinese New Year, when they went home to their villages, did they have any real vacation. "Why don't you at least take Sundays off?" I asked one teenage girl in Guangdong. "Oh, I don't want to," she answered quickly. "This way, I can get more money."

The Chinese have a vivid expression for this: *chi ku,* or to eat bitterness. The Japanese have their own term, *gaman,* a word that pops up continually but that is a bit difficult to translate. *Gaman* means persistence and endurance through hardships, and it is as Japanese as sushi. Furthermore, Asia, more than other continents, is a temple to pragmatism. Other cultures put primacy on God, on individual rights, on sacred principles, while Asia by and large has been more accepting of terrible solutions. Western mothers only very rarely would sell their daughters into slavery— and so their whole families sometimes perished. Asian mothers sold their daughters, wept, and prospered. As recently as the first half of the last century, in countries like Japan, China, Korea, and Vietnam, parents frequently sold their children, and it still happens in India, Cambodia, Vietnam, and among the aborigines of Taiwan.

Even today, many Asian societies are the most ruthless in the world. Welfare is almost unknown, and life is a perilous high-wire act. In Japan, which has the best protections, welfare applicants must show that they have no relatives—for the assumption is that family will help out first— and they must accept any job that a social worker arranges for them. Not surprisingly, the number of welfare recipients in Japan has fallen in half since 1960, in the very period in which welfare payments skyrocketed in Western countries.

Elsewhere in Asia, the safety net is even flimsier. South Korea spends 2.1 percent of GDP on social security benefits, the Philippines spends 0.7 percent, and India just 0.5 percent. That compares with 7.5 percent in the United States, 11.7 percent in Germany, and 18.7 percent in France. The lack of an adequate safety net helps explain why the Asian economic crisis was so wretched, and why people like Salamet had to watch his mother die without being able to afford even painkillers.

Yet the utter ruthlessness of letting people tumble from the tightrope and splatter on the floor also helps explain why the region has been so resilient. With no welfare system to rest upon, people have been forced to find something. If they have lost their jobs in a factory, they sell trinkets on the pavement.

The lack of government support, while terribly cruel, had two other positive consequences. First, it meant that Asian governments had sound finances, running budget surpluses as often as deficits. The welfare state never really arose in Asia to swallow up taxes (Japan is a partial exception, because of retirement benefits and the aging of the population), and so governments are small by international standards. Hong Kong allocates 9 percent of GDP to government consumption, Japan and India each allocate 10 percent, South Korea 11 percent, and China 12 percent. In the West, the United States devotes 16 percent of GDP to the government, Germany 20 percent, and the United Kingdom 21 percent. So Asian governments have been among the most fiscally responsible in the world, and have generally maintained low taxes.

Second, the lack of any hope for rescue from governments helped lead to the high savings rates for which Asia is famous. You would save too, if losing your job meant that you would have no income next week. So personal savings rates soared to as high as 40 percent of GDP, while the American savings rate was actually negative in the late 1990s, as Americans dipped into their savings to finance their consumption. This frugality is less visible among younger Asians, but it is still present. Jackie Chan, the kung fu movie star from Hong Kong, is one of Asia's greatest and wealthiest celebrities, but when he travels he washes his own underwear and socks in his hotel room because hotel laundry charges are so high. And when he checks out of a hotel, he takes the remaining soap from the bath, wraps it in the shower cap, and takes it home with him. That's Asian-style thrift.

So how could parents ever sell a daughter, a girl like Sriy, to the horror of the brothels and the almost-certain death that awaits her there? The question nagged at me. Then, a few months after meeting Sriy, I was hiking on a footpath in a remote part of southern Cambodia, and I came to understand.

As I walked gingerly along the winding dirt trail, surrounded by a dense jungle of bushes and leaves and capped by huge, gnarled trees that soared hundreds of feet in the air, as I worried about mines and fretted about the risk of capture by the Khmer Rouge, I heard an unearthly shrieking from somewhere ahead of me: "Aaaaaaaaaaaaeeeeeeeeeeaaaaaah! Aaaaaaaaeeeeaaaaaaah!" Over and over, it resounded in the forest, and

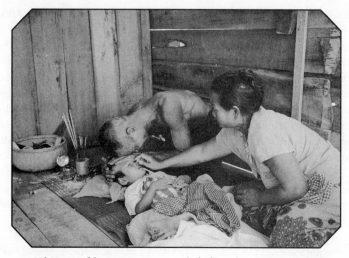

*Yok Yorn and his wife mourn over the body of their son Kaiset, who had just died of malaria.*

even the leaves seemed to wilt at the sound. I shivered, although I wasn't sure if the sounds were human or animal or some trick of the wind. Cautiously I approached and the shrieking became louder and more identifiably human.

Finally the path opened into a clearing with a wooden shack in the center. Several children were clustered outside the shack, shuffling their feet and looking at a gaunt man who was wailing as he knelt beside a figure wrapped in a blanket. I slowly approached and asked one of the older children who the figure was.

"It's my brother," whispered a scrawny teenage girl whose stringy black hair was slightly tinged with brown. "My brother Kaiset. He died this morning of malaria."

The father, a forty-year-old farmer named Yok Yorn, was inconsolable. His eyes were wild, and he seemed manic as he clutched the body of his dead son. Those who say that life is cheap in Asia, that Asians see so much tragedy that they become inured to it, should have seen Yok Yorn that day. One moment he jumped up and shouted to the heavens, then he beat his chest savagely, covered his face with his hands, and sobbed. Finally, he knelt and the savagery melted as he cradled Kaiset in the tattered gray blanket. Yok Yorn held him gently and stared into his eyes. Then tears began trickling down the father's cheeks, and he put his son's body down, ever so carefully, and resumed his frenzy of beating his chest. I gingerly took a few photos from the edge of the clearing, but when Yok Yorn saw me with the camera, he gestured for me to come close. He wanted me to take Kaiset's photograph, so that Kaiset could endure in some form.

"This was the smartest boy in the family," Yok Yorn whispered softly, as he looked down at the body. "And I couldn't save him." The words tumbled out: "We took him to the doctor . . . it was too late. . . . I didn't know it was so serious . . . malaria. . . . He's my second son to die of malaria . . . the other was Thad . . . Thad was sixteen. . . . We moved here to cut down the trees and sell them. . . . We thought we could earn some money, enough to get the kids to school, enough to live . . . but I didn't know the malaria was so bad. . . . Now I have killed my son . . . for a second time." There was a long silence as Yok Yorn looked around at his other seven children, gathered soberly around Kaiset's body. His voice broke as he whispered, "I'm so afraid that my other children will die of malaria as well."

Malaria is curable with medications like larium and mefloquine, but Yok Yorn could not afford them. Nor could he afford $5 for a mosquito net that might save his children from malaria. So two of his nine children were dead so far, and Cambodia's actuarial statistics suggest that more will follow. What overwhelmed me was the waste: Kaiset had died for want of a few dollars, roughly the price of my bottled water that day. And unless Yok Yorn could raise a bit of cash, more of his kids might very well be dead in another year or two.*

So as I stood there awkwardly, embarrassed at invading a family's grief, thinking of my own children, a disturbing thought kept surfacing in the back of my mind, rising again no matter how many times I tried to slap it down: Why not sell the teenage daughter who had spoken to me and save the rest of the children?

The daughter, who was named Phan and was nineteen years old, already had a touch of malaria and might die anyway, but at least such a

---

* Some good came out of Yok Yorn's tragedy. Bernard Krisher, the American publisher of the English-language *Cambodia Daily,* was moved by what I wrote about Yok Yorn and set up a program to provide mosquito nets to poor Cambodians in malarial areas. The program's slogan is "Save three lives for $5," because a chemically treated mosquito net costs $5 and can accommodate three people. Contributions are tax deductible for Americans, and all the money goes to buy nets, as the *Cambodia Daily* covers administrative costs. Information is available at www.fightmalaria.com and www.save3lives.com.

sale would save the others. It would also provide the money to educate the rest of the children and allow them to break out of this endless cycle of poverty. By sacrificing Phan, the family could save the others.

That obnoxious thought gnawed at me. I could never conceive of selling my little daughter, Caroline, into slavery. But neither could I imagine risking the lives of my sons, Gregory and Geoffrey, because I could not raise a few dollars to buy them a mosquito net. And at that moment, as I looked at the sobbing Yok Yorn, as I looked at the corpse of Kaiset, as I looked at the seven remaining children, I felt a flash of sympathy for the mothers who had sold girls like Sriy into brothels. Sriy might die, but perhaps her brothers and sisters were now living and learning because of the money that had been paid for her.

Or perhaps not. I never was able to pin down to what extent Sriy's family benefited from the money gained for selling her, and it is clear that some parents drink the profits from the sale of their daughters. In the Philippines I talked to a woman who sold her son and daughter to a Japanese porn filmmaker so that she could buy a stereo. But some parents who sell their children do use the money intelligently, to clothe and educate their other children. They grieve as much as any parents would, but they see their choice as the best of some terrible alternatives. The greatest advantage of economic development is not that people get refrigerators or cars or electricity. It is that parents never have to face those choices.

Ruthlessness has an impeccable pedigree in Asia. In the Warring States Period of China, 2,400 years ago, there lived a famous soldier-statesman named Wu Qi, who is still read today for his insights into military strategy. Although Wu Qi wanted to be the commander of his country's troops, he knew that the government did not want to put him in charge because his wife was raised in an enemy state. Any normal person would have realized that the situation was impossible and given up. But Wu Qi was as ambitious as he was disciplined, and he pondered the problem over and over: How could he show his absolute devotion to the state? How could he show his hostility to the enemy?

The answer came to him. He murdered his wife. The ruler, impressed by Wu Qi's hatred of the enemy, made him commander. His in-laws may have been displeased, but Wu Qi got what he wanted. His action spawned an expression in Chinese: *sha qi qiu jiang* (kill the wife to get a prize).

That principle, of accepting individual tragedies for the sake of some larger goal, has been studied for centuries as an element of the writings of

Sunzi, better-known as Sun Tzu, the ancient Chinese scholar who was perhaps the greatest military strategist in history. Around 400 B.C., a king heard of Sunzi's military brilliance and asked him to give a demonstration in military training. Sunzi agreed, and according to an ancient chronicle the king then asked, "Can you conduct this test using women?"

"Yes," Sunzi replied. So the king summoned 180 beautiful women from the palace, and Sunzi divided them into two companies and put the king's two favorite concubines in charge of them. Then Sunzi explained patiently to the women the principle of marching, and finally beat the drum to give the signal "Face right." As the chronicle relates, "The women roared with laughter." So Sunzi patiently repeated the instruction and then beat the drum to signal "Face left." This time, the chronicle relates, "The women again burst into laughter." So Sunzi seized the two concubines and accused them of failing to maintain discipline in the ranks and prepared to execute them. The king, who was watching, was appalled and hurriedly asked Sunzi to call it off. Sunzi replied that this was a military matter in which he could not oblige the king, and he cut off the heads of the two concubines.

Sunzi now returned to the drill, and this time the women responded to commands perfectly, not daring to make the slightest noise. Sunzi told the king that the troops were ready for inspection, but the king responded that since his two favorite concubines were dead he did not care. Sunzi declared contemptuously, in words that have resonated over the centuries: "The king likes only empty words. He is not capable of putting them into practice."

Simply the fact that phrases like *sha qi qiu jiang* have been recorded, transmitted, and studied for a couple of thousand years underscores the scholarly discipline and educational tradition of East Asian countries. Education systems teach *chi ku* and *gaman,* for educational investment is a bit like business investment: One must forsake present pleasure for higher future returns. And Asia has the most experience in the world at that. Long before Western countries had bureaucracies to staff, China had national civil service systems in which the brightest young people competed in a series of exams—which they completed only after being double-searched and sealed into bare cubicles for three days, allowed only food, water, paper, ink, and a chamber pot. The very best would pass the highest *jinshi* exam in their thirties, after more than two decades of grueling study, and discipline became a part of the national ethos.

One of those who rose through this kind of Confucian meritocracy (and also through a coup d'état) was Park Chung Hee, the South Korean president in the 1960s and 1970s, a small, wiry man who exemplified the modern idea of *gaman*. Park was an oddity, a strongman who ordered armed forces about at whim but who was shy and awkward and could never look a visitor in the eye. Park was a fervent Communist in the late 1940s and was almost executed for it, but then he changed his mind and after becoming president began arresting, torturing, and sometimes killing those suspected of Communist tendencies. Yet when he was not brutalizing his critics, Park was presiding over an extraordinary economic boom that eventually propelled South Korea into the industrialized world. Above all, Park lived by discipline, and it was this same characteristic that enabled Korea to pick itself up.

The eeriest vignette of Park's rule was in 1974 when he was giving the National Day speech before a huge audience, and a young man raced forward, firing a handgun. The assassin missed Park but hit the president's wife in the head, fatally injuring her and covering her orange gown with blood. In the crossfire a policeman shot and killed a teenage girl who was in the chorus. Park loved his wife and was never the same after that moment; in his diary he described that day as "the longest of my life, the most painful and sad . . . I have cried alone in secret too many times to count."

Yet as soon as the gunman had been seized and carried off, along with the bodies of the First Lady and the high-school girl, Park returned to the podium and completed his speech. The writer Don Oberdorfer, who was there, recalls that Park acted as if nothing had happened. When Park was finished, the chorus, minus the dead girl, sang a few numbers. Finally, President Park stepped wearily from the podium, gathered his wife's shoes and purse from the floor where they had fallen, and left the auditorium. It was a moment of heartbreaking *gaman*.

Nothing captures the difference in attitudes of West and East more than the concept of sweatshops. Nike and other American companies have been hammered in the Western press for producing shoes in grim little factories with dismal conditions. Well-meaning American protesters helped derail the World Trade Organization (WTO) meeting in Seattle in 1999, and one of the key issues was how to put Third World sweatshops out of business. But when I tried to talk to poor Asians about the issue, the reaction I got was usually puzzlement.

*Sariman is a victim of the brutal realities of Third World sweatshops. He used to work in a factory in East Java, Indonesia, but was crippled while working and lost his job. He was saddled with expensive medical bills and had no income, and the factory refused to accept any responsibility. Sariman now makes a living by selling fruit from this pushcart.*

One day I drove out to the great garbage dump on the edge of Jakarta, Indonesia, to talk to people there. The dump covers several hundred acres with hills and valleys and marshes, all composed entirely of garbage. New trucks drive onto the dump constantly, leaving their latest loads of rubbish in random piles. When I tried to enter the dump, the guards stopped me and said I needed to get government permission to go in, but I retreated a few hundred yards and slipped in behind a hill of rubbish. The dump stank and flies swarmed around my head. The ground was a mix of dirt, ash, excrement, and papers, and smoke from scores of fires left a thick haze in the air. Thousands of poor Indonesians, dressed in rags, were picking through the garbage.

I approached one woman who looked to be in her early twenties and was accompanied by a three-year-old boy who trotted and wobbled at her heels. The woman's name was Tratiwoon, and she paused to explain her work. She was short and thin, brown-skinned, with long, black hair tied into a thick ponytail, and she carried a reed basket in which she put dirty

*Tratiwoon and her son pick through garbage in the dump in Jakarta.*
*Her fondest hope is that her son will someday get a job in a sweatshop.*

rags, old magazines, and anything else that could be sold to recyclers. She and her son, who wore only a pair of shorts, were both barefoot, and I wondered how they avoided cuts and infections as they marched around that muck with its broken glass and old wires. Then I quickly realized that they did not avoid them, for I saw sores and scars on both their feet. The boy was helping Tratiwoon pick up rags and papers, and his hands were filthy; I cringed when he thoughtfully put his finger in his mouth.

"I've never gone to school, so this is all I can do," Tratiwoon said, as we watched a bonfire of rubbish nearby. I had gotten used to the stink by now, but the flies infuriated me. I batted them away constantly as we spoke; Tratiwoon and the boy let them settle anywhere, even on their eyes, giving a mild shake of the head to drive them away when they became too numerous. I asked her how old she was, and she laughed gaily and shrugged. "I guess I'm about twenty," she said. "Or thirty. I don't really know. But the boy, he's three. I know that. Yeah, I think he's three.

"I live right over there, on the edge of the dump. Most of us live just outside, although a few people live right in the middle of the dump. They don't pay anything; they just put up some boards, and they have a home. But because I've got the boy, I wanted to live outside the dump. So we walk over every day. The boy helps me pick stuff up. Of course, it's tough for him. He's just a little guy."

Tratiwoon estimated that she earns a bit more than $1 a day for what she rescues from the dump. When I asked her about the sweatshops that I had noticed earlier in the neighborhood around the dump, she beamed and spoke dreamily about how much she would like her son to get a job in one when he is older. But she worried that such a job might be too exalted for him. "He's not going to get an education, so I just don't know whether he can get a job like that."

It was plain that Tratiwoon regarded the worst of sweatshop jobs as far loftier than her own work, and she was right. Even if her son gets only a twenty-five-cents-an-hour job in a hellish little factory with dangerous fumes, he will sweat less and be healthier than if he stays on at the dump. To people like Tratiwoon, a sweatshop represents a leap in living standards. Of course, sweatshops come in all varieties, and some managers are brutal in the way they expose children to dangerous chemicals, deny bathroom breaks, force people to work double shifts, dismiss anyone who tries to organize a union, or demand sexual favors from employees. Sweatshops are also famous for sealing emergency exits or locking workers in at night, with the result that if a fire breaks out the workers burn to death. Third World workers are, of course, furious at such abuses, but they also recognize that they are not typical. In general, there is much less anger in Jakarta or Saigon than in New York or San Francisco at Western companies that operate bleak factories in Asia and pay their workers next to nothing.

I have come to feel that the campaigns against sweatshops are often counterproductive, harming the very Third World citizens that they are intended to help. The effect of these campaigns tends to be twofold. First, in the short term they clearly raise the conditions at existing factories producing branded merchandise for companies like Nike. Second, they raise labor costs and thus encourage mechanization, reducing the numbers of employees needed in the factories. This has been a special problem in India, where huge numbers of people are desperate for work, and yet the regulatory environment has led businesses to mechanize and close off opportunities for the poor. The upshot of these campaigns is to help people who currently have jobs in Nike plants, but to cost jobs overall and to send jobs from the poorest countries to mid-ranking ones. The only thing a country like Bangladesh or Cambodia has to offer is cheap wages, but companies are already wary of manufacturing there because of low productivity, poor infrastructure, and other problems. If in addition companies find themselves embarrassed and scolded for paying terribly cheap wages in those countries, then they will manufacture instead in somewhat richer areas like Taiwan, Malaysia, some parts of Indonesia, or on the Mexican-American border.

What Tratiwoon realized but well-meaning Americans often do not is that the sweatshop jobs are never the bottom tier in a country. Even worse are the standard jobs that the poor drift into: farm labor, day jobs on construction sites, sorting garbage, the sex industry, and begging. And so the risk is that American campaigners against sweatshops end up deterring the American fat cats who hope to exploit cheap Indonesian labor with sweatshop factories. The result would be that Tratiwoon's son would never leave the garbage dump. If Americans want to help Third World citizens in terrible jobs, they would be far better off working with a first-rate development organization like Childreach, the American arm of Plan International, instead of threatening the very jobs that in the poorest countries are an escalator out of despair.

The gap between East and West in thinking about sweatshops came into even sharper focus after the Asian economic crisis. With millions of people losing their jobs, even the most dangerous and blighted work became appealing. In the north of Thailand, I happened to be having breakfast in a village where Mongkol Latlakorn, a quiet, courteous man, was sitting on a nearby bench. He did odd jobs and was hoping to get work as a day laborer. He spoke reverently about his beloved daughter, Darin, a fifteen-year-old of whom he is enormously proud. Darin had gone to school a bit and now had a job in a tiny sweatshop in Bangkok, making clothing for export. She was working nine hours a day, six days a week, for $2 a day.

"It's dangerous work," Mongkol said. "There's lots of machinery, and sometimes it catches her hands. Twice the needles went right through her hands. But the managers bandaged up her hands, and both times she got better again and went back to work."

I muttered something sympathetic about how it sounded awful, and Mongkol looked at me puzzled. "It's good pay," he said wistfully. "I wish I could get a job like that. And I hope she can keep that job. There's all this talk about factories closing now, and she said there are rumors that her factory might close. I hope that doesn't happen. I don't know what she would do then."

This is not to say that Asian values are permanently and profoundly dif-

*A weaver named Misri works in a sweatshop in Gresik, Indonesia, making fabric that is turned into clothing for export. She earns about fifty cents for a long day's work and sleeps on the floor by the looms at night. Such locally owned sweatshops are more common and typically involve worse conditions and lower pay than the Western-owned factories.*

ferent from those elsewhere in the world. There are differences (just as there are variances between the values of my hometown in rural Oregon and those of the block on Manhattan's Upper West Side where Sheryl was raised), but the differences in values among nations are mostly the product of the times and of particular government policies.

Scholars often used to offer cultural explanations for economic growth, and even today it is common to hear that China and Japan are booming because of the intuitive capitalist spirit or ingrained industriousness of the Chinese and Japanese peoples. But explanations based on immutable culture have been discredited, because the enthusiasts could not get their story straight. Confucianism used to be seen as an obstacle to economic growth, because it looked down on commerce; now it is praised as a great boon to growth. Chinese are now seen as industrious; just a decade ago, at least within Chinese factories, they were ridiculed for spending all their time on tea breaks and taking naps. Tamils are an exceptionally enterprising and hard-working people in Sri Lanka, but if this is ingrained in Tamil culture, then what happened to the Tamils in southern India?

Japan is a good example of the problems with explanations based on immutable culture. The Japanese are renowned today for their high savings rates, for their discipline and commitment to hard work and high quality. But a century ago, Japan's savings rates were far lower than in the West. Likewise, foreigners used to be firmly agreed on the laziness and incompetence of Japanese workers. In 1881, a foreigner wrote in a Yokohama newspaper: "The Japanese are a happy race, and being content with little, are not likely to achieve much." As late as 1915, an Australian expert told the Japanese government: "My impression as to your cheap labor was soon disillusioned when I saw your people at work. No doubt they are lowly paid, but the return is equally so; to see your men at work made me feel that you are a very satisfied, easygoing race who reckon time is no object. When I spoke to some managers they informed me that it was impossible to change the habits of national heritage."

Many Japanese themselves shared the bleak assessment of their own abilities. In 1884, a Japanese writer named Yoshio Takahashi even published a book, *The Improvement of the Japanese Race,* in which he argued that Japanese were so inferior to Westerners, mentally and physically, that the only hope was for Japanese men to divorce their wives, marry Western women, have babies, and thus improve the gene pool.

Why Japan and the rest of Asia managed to grow, despite the initially low savings rates and poor habits of workers, remains a complex subject of some debate. Economic growth is not a science but an alchemy, and nobody has managed to come up with a persuasive formula. When Walter Rostow wrote his famous analysis of the origins of growth, he emphasized propensities to save and invest. Alexander Gerschenkron, the great economic historian, responded that Rostow had explained growth by referring to the propensity to grow.

Still, we know a few things about growth. It is basically the result of more inputs or more productivity in using them. The first input is labor, and recent scholarly research has emphasized the demographic aspect of this component of economic growth. After decades of debate, complex statistical work has shown that rapid population increases themselves neither lead to economic growth nor dampen it. What counts is not the overall population but the bulge within it. If a large proportion of people are workers, and only a small proportion are children or aged, then there is a very strong correlation with growth. Economists such as David E. Bloom and Jeffrey G. Williamson have calculated that this surge in workers produced much of Asia's economic miracle and that it will continue to boost Asia's growth rates—especially in the Indian subcontinent and Southeast Asia—in the coming decades. This chart shows what economists call the demographic "gift," measured as the ratio of the growth rate of the working population to the growth rate of the dependent population (such as children or old people):

### DEMOGRAPHIC CONTRIBUTION TO GROWTH, 1965–1990

| | AVERAGE GROWTH RATE OF WORKING POPULATION, 1965-1990 | AVERAGE GROWTH RATE OF DEPENDENT POPULATION, 1965-1990 | STIMULUS TO ECONOMY (RATIO OF FIRST COLUMN TO SECOND COLUMN) |
|---|---|---|---|
| Asia | 2.76 percent | 1.56 percent | 1.77 |
| East Asia | 2.39 | 0.25 | 9.56 |
| Southeast Asia | 2.90 | 1.66 | 1.75 |
| South Asia | 2.51 | 1.95 | 1.29 |
| Africa | 2.62 | 2.92 | 0.90 |
| Europe | 0.73 | 0.15 | 4.87 |
| North America | 2.13 | 1.11 | 1.92 |
| Oceania | 1.89 | 1.00 | 1.89 |
| South America | 2.50 | 1.71 | 1.46 |

### DEMOGRAPHIC CONTRIBUTION TO GROWTH, 1990–2025

| | AVERAGE GROWTH RATE OF WORKING POPULATION, 1990-2025 | AVERAGE GROWTH RATE OF DEPENDENT POPULATION, 1990-2025 | STIMULUS TO ECONOMY (RATIO OF FIRST COLUMN TO SECOND COLUMN) |
|---|---|---|---|
| Asia | 1.61 | 0.99 | 1.62 |
| East Asia | 0.20 | 0.87 | 0.23 |
| Southeast Asia | 1.66 | 0.63 | 2.63 |
| South Asia | 2.11 | 0.90 | 2.34 |
| Africa | 2.78 | 1.88 | 1.48 |
| Europe | 0.00 | 0.48 | −.01 |
| North America | 1.33 | 1.21 | 1.10 |
| Oceania | 0.93 | 1.37 | 0.68 |
| South America | 1.87 | 0.94 | 1.98 |

Source: Compiled from David E. Bloom and Jeffrey G. Williamson, "Demographic Transitions and Economic Miracles in Emerging Asia," National Bureau of Economic Research (NBER) Working Paper 6268.

The philosopher Auguste Comte was, of course, exaggerating when he said that "Demography is destiny." But between 1990 and 2025, Asia will be better positioned demographically to enjoy strong growth than any region except South America, which is too thinly populated to have the same global impact. Southeast Asia and the Indian subcontinent are particularly well positioned demographically, and may be able to use this to gain ground relative to East Asia. Japan's working-age population has already been shrinking since 1995, and South Korea and Taiwan are not far behind in the demographic journey. Even China, in terms of its age structure, is no spring chicken, and the growth rates in its working population have been declining since the 1980s. So the upshot is that the "demographic gift" is coming to an end in East Asia, but that it will become larger in the rest of the continent.

After labor, the second main input to economic growth is capital, to invest in new machines and technologies. Asia's high savings rates provided the capital, at low interest rates. And governments helped create a stable, low-tax environment, with predictable inflation and exchange rates, that also encouraged very high investment.

The least understood part of the growth equation is productivity, which mixes together the inputs and uses them to boost output. Asia's productivity seems to have risen in part because of the investment in human capital, or education. All those dreary childhoods spent hunched over homework paid off economically. Still, it is fair to ask why the education paid off only in recent decades, since Asian countries had enjoyed boundless education, and *gaman,* for many centuries. Evidently human capital is not sufficient for growth, and it is also necessary to be open to new ideas and to the outside world. When Asia got its policies right and did open up, then it was finally able to exploit its human capital. Openness to the outside world, at least in an intellectual sense of sending students to Berkeley or Cal Tech, also helped lead to new ideas for running businesses. In short, with the right policies, Asia's growing pool of human capital helped improve the use of the increasing pool of financial capital. And in all this, there was an essential role for the ruthless drive to prosper—the *gaman,* the ability to eat bitterness, even the willingness to *sha qi qiu jiang*—that characterized much of Asia.

So while I'm generally skeptical of the notion of immutable cultural differences playing an economic role, I accept that there have been some relevant cultural differences. The long tradition of educational self-discipline and more than a thousand years of Confucian stories emphasizing sacrifice and self-abnegation probably made it easier to promote the *gaman* spirit. The result is that, in cross-country surveys, work turns out to be far more important to Asians than to Westerners. When people in various countries are asked how they want to spend their time, Asians and Westerners both give a similar high priority to their families. But Americans and Europeans also say that they want to spend a lot of time relaxing and enjoying hobbies, while Asians are far more likely to say that they want to devote time to their jobs and to studying and taking special classes. Likewise, Asians are much more inclined to say that work is important to them. One needs to take these surveys with a large sprinkle of salt, given the difficulties of fine-tuning them across several languages and cultures, but for what it is worth here is what one poll found about attitudes toward the work ethic around the world:

**MEASURING *GAMAN***

PERCENTAGE OF PEOPLE SURVEYED WHO SAY
"TO DEVOTE ONESELF TO WORK" IS IMPORTANT

| United States | 34 |
| France | 42 |
| United Kingdom | 44 |
| Germany | 68 |
| Singapore | 85 |
| China | 90 |
| Japan | 91 |
| South Korea | 96 |
| India | 98 |
| Indonesia | 99 |

Source: Dentsu Institute for Human Studies

Perhaps the lack of Judeo-Christian religious absolutes encouraged Asian pragmatism. While Westerners grew up with "Thou shalt nots," many Asians grew up with more subtle messages arising from the traditional tales that imbued values into societies. One of these tales, a true one, concerned the Korean King Yongjo, who ruled for fifty-two years in the eighteenth century. There was widespread rejoicing when in 1735 he finally had a son and heir, Sado. But by his teenage years, Sado was killing animals and servants, once beheading a eunuch and carrying the head into his wife's bedroom. By his twenties, Sado was killing attendants in court and even going into town in disguise and killing citizens. Finally, his own mother, the queen, suggested that he must die, and King Yongjo reluctantly agreed.

First, King Yongjo pleaded with his son to do the honorable thing and commit suicide. Sado tried several times to strangle himself, but never quite succeeded. So finally in 1762, King Yongjo summoned court officials and his son to a nearby shrine in honor of the moon—since the moon was a symbol of the prince—and had attendants bring out a large chest. The prince, then twenty-seven, lay at his father's feet, tugging at his robes and crying and pleading for his life. But King Yongjo, despite his own terrible grief, forced his son into the chest and sealed it shut. It took thirteen days for Sado to die, his shrieks echoing around the shrine.

The legend of that grim choice—praised in history as the best thing for Korea—helped inculcate the spirit of sacrifice that eventually caused South Korea to rocket ahead. One can't put too much emphasis on these legends or this culture, for North Korea has been one of the world's worst-performing economies in the same period. But it would be wrong to ignore them altogether.

There are a few arguments that are sometimes made to suggest that Asia's glory days are over:

*Asia's boom was a mirage. Asia simply grew by applying more inputs like labor and capital, rather than by raising productivity. So there is no miracle to reclaim.* This was the argument of the economist Paul Krugman, who suggested that East Asia had grown in the same way that the Soviet Union did in the 1950s, by investing heavily and expanding the labor force. If this were true, then Asia might end up looking like Russia. But Krugman's writings, while a reasonable and provocative critique at the time, provoked further research into Asian productivity, and that research tended to undermine his thesis. Total Factor Productivity, or TFP, the critical aspect of productivity, is very difficult to measure, but in fact subsequent research suggests that it has grown much more in Asia than in America or in any other region of the world. Krugman is right that much of Asia's growth came from piling on inputs, but productivity growth also seems to have been a significant element of Asia's boom. In any case, even if Krugman were right and productivity growth were slowing ineluctably, his argument would suggest a gradual lowering of growth rates over a decade or two—or another half-century in the case of countries that lag the most, such as China and especially India.

*Asian companies prospered simply because they had cheap credit. Now that they pay market rates for their capital, they will no longer shine.* Again, there is something to this theory. Capital tended to be locked at home and funneled to state-favored companies at very cheap rates, and that era is over. But this system also meant that there was no venture cap-

ital and very poor allocation of investments. The new Western-style banking system that is emerging could actually promote an entrepreneurial
boom and stimulate economic growth in the medium and long terms.

*Asia thrived in the industrial age, when the key to success was a
smooth assembly line. But it will stumble in the postindustrial age,
because Asian schools stifle creativity and teach the skills to assemble cars
rather than to design them.* The first problem with this argument is that
Hong Kong and Singapore are among the most successful postindustrial
economies in the world. The second problem is that Asia has thrived in
creative areas like toy design, and no American schoolchild who collects
Pokémon cards or plays Nintendo would dismiss Asia as uncreative.
Indeed, with its strong foundation of training in mathematics and science,
Asia is in an excellent position to prosper in an increasingly technical
information age.

*Asia is in trouble because the language of the future is English, and
Asians aren't very good at it.* Aside from the fact that there are more
English speakers in Asia than in America, there is a point here. The
United States benefits from its native fluency in the international language. On the other hand, Asian countries benefit from proximity to the
largest and fastest-growing markets in the world. In any case, as France
has found, international languages are not immutable; we might remember that a lot more people in the world are native Chinese-speakers than
native English-speakers.

*The secret of Asia's rise was its flood of exports directed at the West. But
now Asia is too big to grow that way.* This is partly true, but it exaggerates
the importance of trade to Asia's economic growth rates. Japan's exports
amount to just 9 percent of GDP, less than the share in the United States
or in most of Europe. Even South Korea's share is just 32 percent, which
is less than the share in Canada or Ireland. Moreover, countries like Thailand and South Korea typically imported more than they exported, so they
suffered trade deficits that in a narrow sense eroded economic growth
instead of contributing to it. It is true that Asian countries cannot rely in
the future on pouring more goods into the American market, but they can
still increase their exports to each other. They can also grow by boosting
their service sectors (small by international standards) and by liberalizing
their economies. So there are still plenty of avenues for economic growth.

The bottom line is that while some of these critiques of Asia have a
measure of truth, none is a reason to regard Asia's boom as over. East
Asian growth rates will slow from diminishing returns, but the Indian sub-

continent's will probably increase. Already India and the Philippines are thriving in one key postindustrial area: the globalization of services. G.E. Capital, for example, has set up a telephone service center in Gurgaon, near Delhi, and bounces calls back and forth to America via satellite. The eight hundred employees at the telephone service center are Indians who speak fluent English and use American names while on the phone. The *Far Eastern Economic Review* described a twenty-three-year-old woman named Pooja Atri who goes to work in Gurgaon each evening—8:00 a.m. New York time—and uses the name Janet Williams to call credit card holders on the East Coast of the United States to remind them to pay their bills. Using her best American accent, based on watching the TV show *Baywatch,* she begins calls: "Hi. My name is Janet and I'm calling from G.E. Capital." Even if the accent is a bit odd, who would think that the call is coming from India?

As telecommunications costs plummet, it becomes easier for countries like India to export these services, for there are huge numbers of college-educated Indians who speak fluent English and can be hired for about $4,000 a year. British Airways, American Express, and other companies have also set up phone centers in India, and there is a thriving business in transcription services. For example, doctors in America use the Internet to send tape-recorded oral histories to companies that hire Indians to transcribe them and return them in a few hours by email. The Philippines, the other Asian country with a bounty of college-educated English-speakers, is also becoming a telephone center for employees whose workdays correspond with American time zones, as they call customers in the United States. If you call or email America Online with a billing problem or technical question, for example, you'll probably be answered by one of AOL's six hundred employees in the Philippines. AOL hires college graduates with degrees in computer science or accounting and pays them a tiny fraction of the wages they would command in the West. This kind of outsourcing of services could become a major boon to countries like India or the Philippines and demonstrates that drive and flexibility will continue to push the region forward, often in unexpected ways.

The economic fundamentals that propelled Asia during its boom years—very high savings rates, very high "human capital," market-friendly policies and extraordinary discipline and pragmatism—all remain in place, while the banking and finance systems are getting better. The Asian economic crisis in many cases has started to bring better political leadership, greater rule of law, increased attention to shareholder interests, and, fundamentally, an increased appreciation for markets. For better or for worse, Asia is a convert to laissez-faire, and the free market economist Milton Friedman has become a hero in much of the East. He is worshipped in Hong Kong, which he has praised as the best-run economy in the world, although there are uncertainties about whether it will stay that way under Chinese rule. Friedman's laissez-faire ideas have much more intrinsic appeal even in China than in the United States, and Chinese Communist Party officials sometimes describe Friedman as their favorite economist. Little Mongolia—barely out of the grasp of communism—is talking about erecting a statue of Friedman on a hill overlooking the capital.

All this means is that Asia is in a strong position to continue to grow, but not necessarily in the same places and patterns as before. Growth will be fueled less by massive investment spending, and more by consumer spending and interregional trade. Moreover, the sources of growth will be less East Asia and more Southeast Asia and the Indian subcontinent. But those are details: The bottom line is that the resurgence of Asia that began in about 1950 is probably going to continue.

The ruthlessness of Asian capitalism sometimes offends me, and it is precisely that ruthlessness that is killing little Sriy in Cambodia. But in a strange way, I find something impressive in the way people can face the most wretched choices and, rather than remaining paralyzed, can choose what they see as the least worst and move on.

In the West, we read of human sacrifices and simply think that they are stupid (except in the context of war, where they have been glorified). Asia's tradition is more ambivalent. Korea's most famous filial child, for example, was a fifteen-year-old girl named Sim Chong, who supposedly sold herself to sailors who wanted to sacrifice a beautiful virgin to the sea. In exchange, she got rice for her blind father to donate to a temple, so that he could pray for recovery of his sight. The tale of Sim Chong's sacrifice was often recounted in songs in nineteenth-century Korea.

Sim Chong songs have disappeared, but the idea has not. I thought of her when I met Lamphan Ngaophumin, a radiant, chipmunk-cheeked girl from a farming village in northeast Thailand near the Lao border. Lamphan, a pretty girl with sparkling eyes and long black hair, was fifteen, just like Sim Chong, and since her mother and father were working in Bangkok she was raised by her grandmother in the village.

The grandmother, Samrong Harwiset, is a solid, no-nonsense peasant

*Lamphan Ngaophumin with her grandmother, who sold her to a brothel in Bangkok.*

in her late fifties. "I'm looking after the five grandchildren on my own," she said as we sat in her house one sweltering afternoon. "Then with the crisis, my daughter stopped sending money from Bangkok." So Samrong and her grandchildren spent the days in the mountains, collecting food for themselves and herbs to sell. But that was not enough, and so Samrong was thrilled when a trader from Bangkok showed up in the village and offered to buy pretty Lamphan for $40 and pay her a wage thereafter.

"If we'd had money, she wouldn't have needed to go," Samrong said unapologetically. "I just wanted her to get money. That way she could help her brothers and sisters." Samrong says the trader told her that Lamphan would work as a maid, but other village girls had been sold to brothels in Bangkok, and all the neighbors say that Samrong knew what she was doing to her eldest granddaughter. Asked about that, Samrong did not deny it. She shrugged her shoulders, paused for a long while, and said, "When you're poor, you'll believe anything."

Lamphan said she was taken by bus to Bangkok and resold to a brothel, where her terrors began. "The brothel owner said, 'I bought you, and I can do whatever I like with you,'" Lamphan said. "They locked me up and I thought I would die. Every day I cried. I tried to slash my wrists, but the cuts weren't deep and they bandaged me up so that my arms eventually healed. Here, you can still see them."

She held out her arms to me, and I could see the scars on both wrists.

"They tried to break my spirit. They said they wanted to teach me that I had to do whatever they wanted, at once, without thinking. So they starved me. They would lock me up for a couple of days and give me no food, only water, and they said they would give me food only when I agreed to give up. Then they brought out a plate of shit. Dog shit. They told me that I had to eat it. I wouldn't, and so they said that they would force me to eat it. They wanted to show that it was useless to fight back."

In the end, Lamphan managed to escape and contact a fellow villager who was also in Bangkok. The police detained Lamphan and returned her to the brothel owner, but then a group of villagers in the Bangkok area came to the brothel and rescued her. They brought her back to the village, and since she never saw a doctor it is unclear whether she has HIV. She doesn't even seem to have thought of that. When I met her, she was simply living with her grandmother again, with no hard feelings.

"Whenever I think about it, I start crying again," Lamphan said. "But I don't blame Grandma. She didn't know. And we needed money." Samrong herself also seemed to think that everything had turned out fine in the end. "It'll be okay," Samrong said soothingly. "She won't have any trouble getting a husband. She's still a very pretty girl."

I had been standing beside Lamphan in the late afternoon sun, hearing her tale. "Well," I said when she finished, "that was an awful experience. But I'm sure you'll never leave this village again."

"Oh, I've got to go," she said, looking down at her feet. "We're running out of money."

"You're going to go? Where?"

"Some friends and I will go to Bangkok again to try to get work. There's somebody in the village who can introduce me to a factory where I would make wicker furniture. I'll be really careful this time."

"Aren't you scared?"

"Of course I'm scared. I'm terrified."

"Then why?"

"I have to do it, because we need to earn a living."

*Sirivat and his wife start their lives anew in Bangkok.*
(Courtesy of Sirivat Voravetvuthikun)

### CHAPTER SEVEN

# *Reinventing Lives*

## SHERYL WUDUNN

*There is nothing more difficult to carry out, nor more doubtful of success, nor more dangerous to handle, than to initiate a new order of things.*

—NICCOLÒ MACHIAVELLI, *THE PRINCE*, 1532

Sirivat Voravetvuthikun looked sadly and slowly around the conference room at the somber faces of his employees. They had crowded into the big room and huddled around the vast teak table in his luxurious Bangkok office.

"I hate to tell you this," he told them, "but we're out of money."

The mood felt like one of those tropical thunderstorms that rip through Bangkok without notice, and the room sparkled with tension and electricity. Sirivat, the Thai-Chinese condominium developer in Bangkok, the Texas-educated investment banker who had invested in his brother's property dream, the high-flyer with millionaire friends, was on the ropes. Now all he had was an empty subdivision and piles of debt, and he and his brother were quarreling bitterly. The twenty-eight condos in Khao Yai were empty; there was no prospect of selling or renting them, and the banks were demanding repayment of loans.

"We cannot sell the condominiums," he said. Two young women employees began crying. "There's nothing I can say that's going to make this right. We're out of cash, and we can't get any more loans. There's no way we can get more money from the bank. And so I can't keep paying all of you unless together we can figure out some way of making money. The property business is broke." He looked around. "Those of you who want to go, just go." He paused and then asked abruptly: "How many are leaving?"

Twenty raised their hands. Sweat trickled down foreheads, and flies buzzed annoyingly at the windows. There were another twenty employees left, and they said they would stay with him.

"Those who didn't raise your hands, what can I do to feed you guys?" Sirivat asked.

There was a sickly silence, as each person thought about upcoming bills. "How about if we opened a restaurant?" one young woman suggested tentatively. "We could cook and wait on tables ourselves."

"But do we really know how to cook that well?" protested another. "And how could we afford to lease a restaurant?" Sirivat also argued against opening a restaurant because he had no capital. Nor did he have the skills to make good food.

"Street food?" another woman suggested.

"There's no money in that," a man argued. "There's no way we could make any money that way."

Then Sirivat's wife, Vilailuck Voravetvuthikun, a petite Chinese-Thai, spoke up for the first time. "Sandwiches," she said earnestly. "Sandwiches!" Everybody looked at her in puzzlement, but she brimmed with confidence. Over the years, she had learned how to make sandwiches for her children and the sandwiches had become a classy snack in their eyes. "Let's make sandwiches and sell them on the street. Nobody in Thailand sells sandwiches, so we'll have our own product. The costs are low, and people like to eat new things. And they taste wonderful. We can make lots of different sandwiches, and we can charge a good price because there's no competition."

So just days later his wife bought a few loaves of bread and made a batch of sandwiches, and Sirivat and his employees set out to sell them on the street. From property salesmen they became street peddlers, and in the beginning they found it humiliating. The first day, they made twenty sandwiches. It took them six and a half hours to sell them all. Then, the police stopped one of Sirivat's sandwich sellers on the street, and Sirivat discovered it was illegal to sell on the street without a license. Sirivat himself was stopped while selling sandwiches, and the police tried to confiscate his box. "I said I would go with my box," he recalled, and so he was briefly detained. But Sirivat, with his education and connections, was undaunted, and he went to see the governor of Bangkok to protest the treatment of street vendors. "I asked for sympathy from the governor. They are not making things dirty, not messing things up. . . . I see honest people selling things, while politicians, they run away like dogs and pigs. . . . If you don't allow them to do this, they'll be thieves, they'll rob. The governor listened to my plea. So he changed." Bit by bit, the rest of Sirivat's luck also changed. Although Thais found the notion of sandwiches curious— most customers had never eaten one—they began to snap them up, even though they sold for the hefty price of 75 cents each. Business began to boom through 1997 and 1998, and Sirivat painted his sandwich boxes with a new logo reading "Sirivat Sandwiches." By 1999, he was again able to pay employees their entire salaries.

Sirivat's new venture was an accident, but it reflected the small restructurings under way in the commercial and personal lives of millions of people across Asia. Thailand is divided by one of Asia's worst income gaps, with the top 10 percent of the country making thirty-seven times what the bottom tenth make, though that is still better than the gap in the United States. But suddenly, everyone felt poor. So rich and poor alike were reconfiguring their lives, picking up what was left after the crisis stole so much. Desperation can fell people and it can also inspire them. Sirivat was stuck with vast losses, piles of debt, and troubles with the banks. Like millions of others, he was forced to find a new livelihood. He hasn't completely found his way, but he has grand dreams once again. And he is dreaming for the future of his kids, two teenage girls and a boy.

"This could be their business in the future," he said. He began to imagine opening sandwich outlets all over Thailand, and he decided that his new career might be better than the old one. "This," he said, with untamed conviction, "is going to be big."

The Asian economic crisis swept millions of people out of their jobs, and plunged many marginal businesses—and a lot of good ones—into insolvency. Yet in a simple, almost perverse way, the restructuring was the best thing that had happened in Asia in a long time, and the biggest problem has been that the restructuring did not go deep enough; the economic crisis was too short to force even more fundamental change. The crisis was beneficial because it forced people like Sirivat to reconsider their businesses and try new ventures. But perhaps more crucial, it was useful because it began to push through important changes in both social attitudes and the structure of Asia's economic system.

In its boom years, Asia was on a narrow railroad track, racing ahead with the speed of a bullet train. But it couldn't go farther or faster on that narrow-gauge track; if it wanted to go places, it needed to shift to the wider and more modern track used in the industrialized world. So the train needed to stop and widen its wheels and Asia needed to liberalize and transform itself so that it could run on the global track. Getting on the right track didn't just mean lifting up the rail cars and widening the wheels. It meant rebuilding the whole railroad system. "It is not just a restructuring of business or industry that we need," said Oh Ho Gen, the hard-nosed, hard-driven executive chairman of the banking industry's Corporate Restructuring Committee in South Korea. "Restructuring is a misleading term. It's redefining our economic system."

The most gaping deficiency was in the financial system, the lifeline of the economy. The Asian boom masked the sloppiness, the slipperiness, the cronyism and the rule by man* that governed the banking systems in Asia. Banks tended to lend to their favored clients, regardless of whether they were good credit risks. Typically, the banks were poorly capitalized and had little understanding of the chances they were taking. It wasn't always their fault, for they often were ordered by government officials to lend to particular companies.

The crisis slowly forced a lot of that to change. It pushed some banks into bankruptcy, and led to some companies being acquired by foreign institutions, which attacked the local laziness in corporate governance. Citibank and G.E. Capital have both taken advantage of the crisis to increase their presence across the region, and many foreign companies are bringing world-class technology, management, and financial scrutiny to countries that never had it. Employees at Japanese carmaker Nissan, which sold a big stake to Renault of France, watched in horror as Renault sent in Carlos Ghosn to run Nissan and eliminate twenty-one thousand jobs. Workers at Japan's bankrupt Yamaichi Securities, whose branch network was acquired by Merrill Lynch Securities Japan, trembled as they

---

* I mean "rule by man" as opposed to "rule by law." But another problem with Asian corporations has been far too much rule by men and not enough by women.

became Merrill staff members and were told that they would be paid according to their performance. Even in Korea there was progress, although sales of banks to foreign institutions took much longer than they should have. After much foot-dragging South Korea finally sold a major stake in Korea First Bank to an American investor group.

So Asia has made tremendous strides since the crisis began, and this restructuring, however incomplete, is threefold: In politics, it has nurtured more democratic governments and a more vigorous news media; in the economy, it has encouraged the use of the market mechanism and greater openness to foreigners; and in society, it has loosened the linkages among elites who used to run countries through what was called "crony capitalism."

And, well, maybe there's a fourth dimension. Ingenuity. Creativity. Sandwiches.

Along a lonely alley in Bangkok, corrugated roofs jut into the air, clamoring for more space. Cement buildings are blackened by city soot. It is the perfect hideaway for someone who has just lost millions of dollars on an exclusive cluster of villas. At the mouth of the alley is a car dealer. The lane curls several times before it reaches a dead end and a row of five-story whitewashed townhouses, a couple of them enclosed by gold-painted gates. Next door is a townhouse with an unassuming gray gate, a balcony with white floors, and down below, a carpet of shoes that people have taken off just before entering the building through a sliding door. This is where Sirivat is being reborn, transformed from illustrious fund manager and property builder into a sandwich tycoon, and one who has learned his lessons.

When I saw Sirivat in his humble new offices, he was a man on the mend, and though flashes of anguish still surfaced, he was brimming with hope and determination. "I don't want to have to borrow a single dollar," said Sirivat, still flinching at the mention of banks. The debt burden from Khao Yai was his nemesis: "Even if I sell sandwiches for 100 years, I still cannot repay." No wonder he now teaches his employees that "Cash is king" and to "Be only as extravagant as you can afford to be." "I had good credit," he said, as we sat in his clean, bare, white-walled office in the front of the building. "The banks kept wanting to give me money, but money is not free. I had to pay interest and now when the business is bad, I can't pay the interest and the bank sues me." But now Sirivat is focused on sandwiches, and he has done so well that he needed more space and rented out the townhouse next door for the same price as the first one,

$430 a month. His transition from white collar to blue collar has had its snags. Five employees left when they found out they would have to get up early to make sandwiches. Now, he provides beds for many of them, and even some married couples send their kids to the grandparents and stay in a room he provides for them.

Sirivat was selling sandwiches at three small kiosks: two in private hospitals and a third in a shopping mall. The rest of his sandwiches were sold on the street from a giant box on a strap, the way an ice-cream man sells at ball games, only this was a downscale version with no ice. "We carry the box," he said. "We sell for breakfast. Bangkok has a traffic problem so people go out early and don't have breakfast. We also sell during lunchtime but sales are not doing well because the sandwich is not a staple." Most of the sandwiches are sold for breakfast or snacks, with lunches making up only 15 percent of daily sales.

When I peeked into the kitchens, I saw cheese, ham, tuna, and racks of bread—expensive bread that comes in packs of eight slices and is made by a Thai-Japanese company. Sirivat gets some discount, but he hopes to negotiate better deals, and in the meantime, he rationalizes. "I use good bread, good ingredients. . . . When you think of sandwiches, think of Sirivat Sandwiches," he said, slipping into his souped-up salesman spiel. I looked at the sandwiches and the refrigerator full of cheeses and meats and it all seemed so blandly American.

"Why didn't you consider noodles? That's a meal all Thais love, no?" I asked. I got an earful. Sirivat wanted to be a contrarian.

"Noodles? Too troublesome. Too much preparation. You have to buy good noodles and pork. You have to boil water, this and that. My wife's idea, it's easy to make. It's not dirty. It's not messy. We sell food that Thais are not used to eating."

The room for making sandwiches takes up a whole floor, separated from the next-door townhouse by a wall. In that room, he bragged about starting an "experimental" lab for new kinds of sandwiches. I held back a chuckle. On a daily basis, the sandwiches are made on a big table—the old teak conference table from his real-estate days. Sirivat makes all sorts of sandwiches: cheese, crabmeat, tuna, and a bit of chicken. He stresses cleanliness, and the room looked clean indeed. But the day was hot and muggy and I couldn't help but notice piles of lettuce and tomatoes wilting in the heat at the center of a nearby table, and they were destined to spend the day outside until they were sold. I hinted at the possibility of spoilage, but none of this bothered Sirivat.

Sirivat explained his strategy in stark terms. "We're really looking at the upper class," he said. "I go to private schools where there are children who can afford it." While the 75-cent price of regular sandwiches is about a half-day's salary for many Thais, Sirivat also offers an after-school kids' special for 50 cents, which helps to get rid of the day's inventory. Sirivat boasts that he doesn't pay for his kiosks, but got all of them through connections. He knew the president of a private hospital and talked his way into setting up a stand there. So even in the midst of this Asian restructuring, cronyism survives.

The chaos of the Asian economic crisis threw everything up in the air. People like Sirivat were trying to shed the burdens of past deals, while thrashing about for a place in the new economy. In these times of confusion and breakdown, Asia's economy is undergoing an especially rapid evolutionary spurt, and a new combination of the old and the new is emerging. Modern phenomena like the Internet are also being hurled at Asia, and it needs to be prepared to embrace the dizzying and tantalizing forces of modernity if it is to thrive. That's the way it works in nature, too. In the evolutionary process, a crisis that produces chaos offers greater options for selection of the fittest. The result is a greater structure and more refined complexity in the evolving system. The emerging system will still rest on the foundations of the old. Many critics rightly decried the slow pace of reform and the resistance to it in Asia, but new systems are not manufactured; they evolve, as the seedlings of the new grow strong enough to replace the old, and for a long time, the old and the new live side by side, like the elephants with the traffic lights on their trunks in Thailand.

It isn't surprising that the rapid economic comebacks in South Korea, Thailand, Malaysia, the Philippines, and even Indonesia slowed the reform process and took away some of the pressures for society to better itself. It takes a remarkable political will to unseat tradition, unless there is a grave jolt from the outside. That's why progress will be fitful, with leaps forward as well as stumbles backward. Clearly, the biggest challenge ahead for Asian leaders will be to toughen the political will and intensify the reforms and restructuring to prevent another hard landing as severe as the Asian financial crisis.

In Asia, the shocks to the old system were forcing changes in the social structure. These took place far more quickly and arguably ran deeper than the lifestyle changes brought about by the phenomenal economic growth of the previous years. Almost everywhere in Asia, countries needed far-reaching economic changes: stronger rule of law, swifter bankruptcy proceedings and accounting standards, better capital and bond markets, and a focus on efficiency and profits. And after the Asian economic crisis, these changes began to take shape. But the most fundamental kind of restructuring is the political one, which lays the groundwork for all the others and allows a country to more swiftly and ably confront similar crises in the future. So although it may have been an Asian economic crisis, the most essential changes in Asia have, in a sense, been the least flashy, the least remarked on: the political restructuring that is changing the way these countries work. The reworking is just a start, and it will take a few decades to stabilize, but the stirrings are visible and the hope is that even now, Asian governments would be more sophisticated and successful in their responses if another economic crisis were to break out tomorrow. It is not that democracies can avoid upheavals, for banking crises have erupted in the United States and other European countries. But the Asian crises erupted because there was little understanding of the risks at the top of the political pyramid. So loose laws and regulations allowed banks to lend through relationships rather than creditworthiness. Capital markets were thin because the government played too much of a role choosing winners and losers, and the press and opposition groups had no independent voice and did not provide enough scrutiny. Has that changed? In varying degrees. In Indonesia, substantially; in Korea, a good deal; in Thailand, a fair amount. But the change is a continuum. Asia wasn't black before, it's not white now.

Of course, the winds of change did not stir everywhere. China remains a big question mark, inching toward greater social and economic pluralism but still energetically rounding up anyone who might challenge the government politically. And Malaysia reacted to the crisis by taking a step back from the global society, with Prime Minister Mahathir Mohamad embroiling the nation in a sordid trial and subsequent imprisonment of his former deputy prime minister, the highly respected Anwar Ibrahim. Yet even there, the episode disillusioned many Malaysians—especially after it was proven that police had beaten Anwar in prison—and politicized young people while giving new life to the opposition. The upshot is probably that post-Mahathir Malaysia will be a more politically open and lively place than if the clash and repression had never taken place.

Political change was greatest in Indonesia, where President Suharto had been one of the longest-serving rulers in the world and often appeared untouchable. The nation had little hope for a vigorous market economy so long as Suharto was still in power and allowing his children and buddies to extract billions of dollars through monopolies and special concessions. One public stock offering before the crisis, for instance, involved a demand that $50 million worth of shares go to a family member of Suharto, according to an executive familiar with the deal. Yet the crisis overturned a political era by forcing Suharto to resign in disgrace, costing his children and buddies their old monopolies. The new president, Abdurrahman Wahid, said that he would abolish the Information Ministry, an anachronistic bureaucracy of fifty-five thousand employees dedicated to censorship and propaganda. Indonesian newspapers have become increasingly aggressive about looking for corruption and cronyism, and a modern civil society is emerging. The opposition party joined the ruling establishment and a more pluralistic political and social system has begun to emerge. After a bitter battle, Indonesia let go of East Timor in 1999, a move that seemed unthinkable a year earlier. Not all of the loosening was good; the beheadings in East Java prove that much. But in most of the economies struck by the crisis, societies are moving toward becoming more open and democratic.

In Thailand, the second-largest economy in Southeast Asia, the crisis resulted in the most effective and least corrupt government that Thailand ever had. Leaders immediately began an economic housecleaning, bankruptcy procedures were made easier, and the economy became more driven by markets and less by cronyism. That didn't mean the new leaders entirely rewrote the country's political makeup, and despite much fanfare, the banking system will still take years to dispose of its mountains of bad debt because leaders are afraid of pushing too far. But there is greater recognition of the fallout from poor banking practices and a realization that even the best of connections can't lift a bad bank out of the mire.

South Koreans responded politically to the crisis with enormous vigor, choosing as their new president Kim Dae Jung, the longtime dissident who had nearly been executed by past dictators. When we first moved to Asia, the American ambassador in Seoul refused to meet Kim, and we would go see Kim for long lunches as he suffered under house arrest with plenty of time on his hands. Now he is the dominant political leader in Asia. At first, many thought that an ex-dissident like Kim was a neophyte at economics and would pander to labor and refuse to push tough economic policies. But Kim was magnificent: He exhorted and educated his countrymen and began removing the shackles of regulations—in banking, in accounting, in corporate indebtedness. He began cutting the cozy three-way ties between the banks and the bureaucrats and the *chaebol*.

By the end of his first year in office, he and his aides had liquidated 144 smaller financial institutions and nationalized two big banks in preparation for selling them to foreigners. His government oversaw the merger of forty-eight institutions and suspended the licenses on fifty-nine others across the country. He set aside $53 billion to help ailing institutions. About half of that was used to add to the thin cushion of capital at the banks. He toughened the oversight of banks. And he put the *chaebol* on notice that they would no longer receive special favors in exchange for campaign contributions. Instead he ordered them to restructure along market lines. Kim told them to lower debt ratios to 200 percent of equity, and he forbade them to cross-guarantee their debts. Korea's mighty *chaebol*s, their feet mostly dragging in the dirt, were humbled, pulled into the world of modern markets by a man more determined than they were.

Jang Chang Ik found out about Asia's restructuring the hard way. It happened when he was in his office at the LG Group, a leading Korean conglomerate, smoking a Korean cigarette. The phone rang, and it was the vice president of personnel, summoning him to his office. Jang walked down the hall to the vice president's office and took a seat, fearing what was coming.

A tall man with droopy eyes, his brows furrowed as if he were constantly fretting about life's problems, Jang filled his working life with task after unending task. He rarely smiled, and at a joke his lips would just curl up at the edges before he went back to his serious work. He was already an upper-middle manager, and he had been rigorously trained for a top spot. His career had also benefited from his high-tech background, for in the army he had worked with computers and developed skills that launched his career as a computer programmer. Later, LG switched him to accounting, planning, and administration, and he trudged up the corporate hill for nearly two decades, clocking long hours and following orders from his bosses until he became one of them. The LG Group was his entire life. The company paid for hospital costs for newborns, it helped finance a car and a home, and it planned retirement. In return, Jang gave it his every waking moment. In his home, he had an LG air conditioner, tall and metallic; an LG clock, prominently posted on the wall; an LG computer near his giant LG television; and his apartment was in a large residential compound for LG employees.

But when Jang took a seat in the vice president's office, there were just a few pleasantries before the news came. "The company is in a bad situation, and it is downsizing," the vice president explained. "The number of directors will be cut, so there isn't much chance that you'll be promoted. Why don't you look for other ways to cope?"

In short, Jang was fired.

He had heard rumors from colleagues that he might be on a list, so he had begun to think about the possibility that he would lose his job. Even with the warning, he was in anguish. He waited nearly four weeks before he told his wife, a sweet, short-haired woman, Kim Gwi Seon. He wanted time to think, by himself, on his own. But in fact his dismissal, in August 1998, liberated him and allowed him to become an entrepreneur. In early January, on the day after he left LG, he put up a shingle on a new steel door. He is now chairman, president, chief executive, and chief operating officer of JCI Information Technology, his new software consulting company, named for his initials. Nearly every day he deals with big challenges like bidding for a contract, hiring a new programmer, and renting more space. He is lucky. His misfortune became one of those moments in life where destruction brings about something creative.

"I considered two options," Jang recalled, as we sat in his crisp new office in a building that housed other electronic start-ups. "I could find a job at another company. Or I could start a company of my own. Thinking about my age, I gave up the first idea and decided to start a company of my own. I had a few ideas. So I met some people in each of those fields and decided that this one would be the best. One area I had thought about was transportation, or distribution, but you need many licenses to open up that kind of business and I thought it would be too much for one individual. And I was much more familiar with the computer world."

Jang's departure from LG turned out to be a blessing not only for him but also, in a tiny way, for Asia. His small company may not become Asia's Microsoft. But there are thousands of tiny start-up ventures like his, all formed in the debris of the Asian crisis. More than a year after the crisis, newly formed companies were outnumbering bankruptcies by about eight to one in South Korea's biggest cities. Some of those new start-ups may be the next-generation Samsung or Hyundai. These new ventures are more nimble than the old behemoths and often more ferocious competitors, and they are bringing a burst of new entrepreneurialism to Asia.

One of the reasons for optimism about Asia's long-term prospects is precisely the upheaval that hurled Jang out of his old job and into a new

*It took a while for Jang Chang Ik to launch his company, but since the day he started in January 1999, he hasn't had a moment to relax. Here, Jang works in his office at his new company, which has been expanding rapidly.* (Sheryl WuDunn)

one. The crisis shook Asia to the core, and slowly a new economy and society are emerging. This newer Asia is more democratic and more entrepreneurial than the old one, and it offers far more hope for the future.

The political restructuring was accompanied by a social one, for in Asia the elites scratched each other's backs and by doing so reinforced their power. Many countries had a kind of aristocracy, not as closed as in Europe in the nineteenth century but still one that largely ruled the political and business worlds and the news media as well. Admission to the aristocracy was largely by educational achievement, wealth, and friendship with the leadership, and the system was rigged so that the children of elites were far more likely than peasant children to end up graduating from the best universities and winning their American doctorates to confirm their own membership in the club.

In Korea, the social establishment was dealt a blow by Kim Dae Jung. Kim was not just from the opposition party but from an opposition region:

Cholla, an economically backward area in the southwest of the country. Many proper South Koreans looked down on people from Cholla and would never want their son or daughter to marry one; people from Cholla had difficulty getting good jobs or being accepted in society, and yet all of a sudden a man from Cholla was president. The elites who had gone to the same schools and intermarried and built up crony capitalism—the bank presidents who had loaned to their friends in industry and accepted oversight from their school chums in the bureaucracy while making campaign contributions to their old pals in politics—suddenly found themselves out in the cold. The shock to the Korean system was huge, but it helped lead to the democratization of Korea's society and economy as well as its political system. There was some affirmative action of sorts: People from Cholla began to rise in the bureaucracy, reporters from Cholla were promoted to editors, and business tycoons found themselves facing bankers from Cholla. The change certainly opened up Korean political society, but it could also lead, as some critics say is happening, to a new cronyism.

The social change in Asia that resulted from the crisis is hard to describe or pin down, and in many ways it was one of culture and values. It was a bit like the fall of the Berlin Wall in twentieth-century Europe, or the collapse of the ancien régime in eighteenth-century France. The old ways of doing things were discredited and pushed aside, even though the replacement system was not always easy to discern. Suharto could have said with Louis XIV *"l'état, c'est moi,"* but his successors probably will never be able to get away with that conceit.

A lot has been said about "Asian values" and about how Asians had a special respect for authority and would tolerate oppression as long as they could prosper. But there are similar strains in Western history as well, in the values of the ancien régime in Europe, where the elites bowed to oppressive authority as long as they could keep their elite status. Moreover, "Asian values" were not purely Asian, for the views of authoritarians like Lee Kuan Yew of Singapore were not so different from those of, say, Plato, with his faith in highly educated philosopher-kings ruling society. The sense of entitlement felt by Asian autocrats—almost a divine right in the case of Suharto, who ruled like a Javanese king—also mirrored certain attitudes in feudal Europe. The modern Asian rulers were often an educational elite, while those in Europe were an aristocratic elite, but the belief in orderliness, the skepticism about democracy, the distrust of hoi polloi were all fairly similar. Even Nick's great-great-grandfather, an aristocratic nobleman in what is now the Ukraine, remarked in 1848 when the serfs were freed by law: "This is terrible; now the peasant is going to take every-thing." He would have agreed entirely with the philosophy of Asia's old leaders, with their belief in order and authority vested in an elite. But that culture has largely died out in the West. In Asia, it is in the process of dying.

The demise of philosopher-kings and authoritarian oppressors in Asia will be even more swift because of the Internet and the fast-changing world of telecommunications and information technology. Political rulers in Asia sustained their grip on power by controlling information. They muzzled the press, stamped out criticism, and squelched dissenters, and so they have every reason to fear the Internet. Not only will the Internet subvert that monopoly on information, but it will also change Asian society far more than it has changed America. Where it hasn't been brought in from the top, democratization is creeping into Asia from the bottom, and it will unseat the entrenched political core if that core doesn't adjust. In China, a country still starved for information, the Internet offers people access to news and information, from simple headlines to chat rooms and stock prices. In the past, access was reserved only for the elite, and com-puters are still a luxury. But as set-top boxes and mobile phones become the key technological devices of the future, people in poorer regions can increasingly participate in the mad walk to modernity. New markets are being built with the Internet in China, and new-age entrepreneurs are amassing money, power, and influence; they are like the Carnegies and the Fords, but they are the Zhangs and the Yips. It is much easier for alliances and groups to form where they were once illegal. Government authorities may try to block sensitive web sites, but the Internet is far too overpower-ing a force for the Chinese government to take on. Officials are already swaying on a tightrope, trying to balance politics and progress, wanting to harness a phenomenal technology but fearing the loss of state control. With each bow they give to the Internet, the pace of change accelerates to bring about more progress, greater openness, and variety in society.

Strangely, Asia's restructuring is going slowest where it is needed most: in the continent's largest economy, Japan. If Japan had taken the initiative early on and embarked on a far-reaching economic restructuring, this would have helped establish a role model for all of Asia and contributed to a new dynamism in the region. But Japanese companies waited a decade before they began seriously to trim staff, close redundant offices, and slash costs. Even then, they were slow to take painful steps to make themselves more efficient and only a very few dared to fire anyone. Some companies resorted instead to corporate bullying to nudge workers out the door. When a major Japanese tire-and-rubber company asked a fifty-three-year-old senior researcher to retire, he refused. So the company moved him to a bare desk in a corner of the factory and told him that every two weeks he would have to turn in a report on the same topic: "My Second Life." For six months, he stubbornly stuck it out, writing about himself until he had nothing left to say. In desperation, he turned to a friend, Kiyotsugu Shitara, who gave him two books on insects and animals, which turned out to be his salvation. "He said, 'I can read about the lives of butterflies and animals and then I can write thousands of reports,' " Shitara, who now runs a union for managers, told me. A year later, he was still writing, and Japan's economy was still struggling. Japan would have been better off if people like him had been fired. Japan's banks, at one point staggering under a burden of hundreds of billions of dollars in bad loans, were the most lethargic in Asia and among the greatest obstacles to achieving a more efficient economy. And no one in the cowardly crowd of government officials was bold enough to take on the banks, except Hakuo Yanagisawa.

If he had been a samurai, Yanagisawa would never have bothered to sheathe his sword. He feints, he darts, he backs his adversary—in this case, the Japanese banking system—against the wall. In the end, the establishment yielded. Not long after Yanagisawa took over as chief regulator of Japan's banking system in the fall of 1998, word raced through town that two bank presidents had committed suicide. It wasn't true, but the rumor captured the fear felt by bank executives that the new demands on them could crush them and cost them their jobs. Yanagisawa bullied five banks into pulling out of international business. Other banks caved in to demands to abolish archaic practices, like *sodanyaku,* in which former top executives continue to draw large salaries and keep company-paid cars and drivers until they die.

"I am convinced this is a time of change," Yanagisawa, sixty-three years old, told me in his grand office, as a bevy of minions scribbled down his every word. He is a Japanese politician whose mix of daring and diplomacy led then Prime Minister Obuchi to tap him to take on the banks. Under Yanagisawa's brief year-long tenure, Japanese banks wiped out their official bad debt from their books and set aside $77 billion as a cushion against good debt that might go bad. It helped that the government gave the banks a first-aid infusion of $64 billion, in return for preferred shares. And the banks buckled to some demands. They agreed to reduce one in three board members, cut bonuses for executives, and shave salaries. More and more employees are afraid of being dismissed. Banks are reevaluating their customers, writing off loans, calling in others, or demanding partial repayments. They are unloading unwanted real estate and selling some bad loans.

As with all of corporate Japan, there are still huge challenges ahead for the banks. Japanese financial institutions have been slow to invest in new businesses and technology in the past couple of decades and were late to move toward Internet banking. They still operate with a herd mentality, and there were several copycat mergers of banks. But the government's Big Bang program, a blueprint for financial deregulation and reform, is bringing about changes in the financial landscape. Thus even in the last of the major Asian countries to embrace reforms, even in one of that country's most lackadaisical sectors, restructuring has arrived, and the impact is rippling throughout the country. Even in the hills of Omiya, there is grim recognition. Michiko Yoshida introduced Nick to a local factory owner, Mitsuo Okura, a wry sixty-two-year-old, lithe, strong, and self-confident. He runs a four-employee factory beside his house, spitting out gobs of black plastic that end up in Toyota and Honda cars. Pictures of his grandchildren decorate the walls in his little office, and he smilingly rebukes his own foolishness for expanding his factory eightfold during the bubble era. His eyes crinkle pleasantly as he acknowledges that his own son and daughter have declined to inherit his little factory. He knows that in the economic competition for survival of the fittest, he will end up in a more ruthless animal's digestive tract, and yet he accepts this with equanimity.

"People complain about the bad economy," Okura said, "but when I look around the house, I've got everything I want. I've got three cars, and most families around here have two or three as well. I've got a couple of televisions, and so do most people. I've got a washing machine, a refrigerator, and so do all my neighbors. Even if no one sees a bright future, there's no feeling of crisis." Okura, it seems, believes he can live off of his accumulated assets, the fat of his land.

Okura is a perfect example of how creative destruction works. Okura's parents were farmers, just as most Japanese were when he was born in the 1930s. Then farming became uncompetitive, and so he started his factory in the 1960s, just as the entire nation was riding a manufacturing boom to prosperity. Okura's factory is likely to collapse before long, but his children have already taken the generational baton in new directions. His daughter is an interior designer and his son is a software engineer who is developing

*Mitsuo Okura works in his factory in Omiya, Japan, making plastic parts for cars. Okura readily admits that his factory will die out, but his family is already making the economic transition to a postindustrial economy.*

"electronic money" for a credit card company. His children's success has comforted him and reassured him that economic change, however brutal, is worthwhile. "Deregulation is inevitable," he said.

The words of a friend, a finance ministry bureaucrat, still echo in my mind. When I asked him whether he thought the program of deregulation would really change Japan, he said: "It may not appear now as a Big Bang, but in ten years' time, when we look back, we will be able to say, 'That was a big bang.'"

Even if the direction has been set, Asia's restructuring is a slow and unsteady process of evolution. Some of the old tycoons are still in the driver's seat, and there has not been any neat resolution of past foolishness. The old messes are not easily cleaned up, and the temptation has been to rely on cronyism and favors to resolve them.

In Bangkok, Anant Kanjanapas struggled to save his empty city, Muang Thong Thani, the satellite town that he had envisioned as a kind of private Boston-sized community. Defeated by the market, he was nonetheless

able to coax the government into helping with the financing of a convenient expressway exit that made Muang Thong Thani highly accessible
and a quick ride from the airport. He also convinced Thailand's Defense
Department to move its entire government staff offices—military barracks
and all—into the satellite town at a cost of $100 million. The Defense
Department now occupies its own tower, and it moved in five thousand
families. The department's move was highly controversial, and critics in
Bangkok cried foul, arguing that the government was helping a private
entrepreneur to survive. Anant is defensive about the unfavorable press he
has received. ("They said the Defense Department wasn't moving in. So
what is all this?" he said, pointing to the new tower that the Defense
Department was in fact moving into.)

"I don't think it's successful," he admitted of Muang Thong Thani, "but
at least we are not sinking. We have problems, of course, like everyone
else." But Anant is dreaming again: He is talking about a big plan to build
a giant entertainment and shopping complex to draw crowds to Muang
Thong Thani.

In his city, though, ordinary people can't rely on government help, so
they are doing their own restructuring. At No. 11 Bond Street in Muang
Thong Thani, Pornsawan Rakthanyakarn bought the building to open a
jewelry store, but then the Asian crisis came. With no one buying jewelry,
she switched plans and opened a drugstore selling everything from Vase-
line Intensive Care Lotion to Pond's Cold Cream to European brandy. She
is willing to sell absolutely anything. Pornsawan, who perches by the cash
register, is a large Thai woman with a big bouffant hairstyle. She offered a
faint smile as I entered, and as she stood up, I caught a glimpse of her
brown flowered print dress. We chatted, and she noticed that I was eyeing
the huge diamond ring on her second finger. "Would you like to buy my
diamond ring?" she asked eagerly.

I asked how much, and she thought for a moment. "It costs five million
baht," she told me. That amounted to $125,000. I passed.

Now, Sirivat sells five hundred to one thousand sandwiches a day and is
broadening into selling snacks, such as dried fish, along with the sandwiches. His latest expansion has been into sushi, and Sirivat Sushi in
boxes can be seen on the streets. Some of his staff wake at 3:00 a.m. to
prepare the morning run of sandwiches. They work for three hours and
then go back to sleep, and then wake up again to prepare for the afternoon
sales shift. When business got so good, Sirivat not only rented the second

townhouse, but also built a passageway connecting the two. He says he is making a 30 to 35 percent gross margin on the sandwiches. As if embarrassed at such low margins, he explains that he uses expensive ingredients, "like mayonnaise," which in Thailand is considered a luxury condiment. He still hasn't mended relations with his brother, though. "What does my brother think? I don't know. I don't want to talk to him. I don't know what he's doing. I don't think he's a very responsible person."

Sirivat has had people already express interest in investing in his business. Investors from Switzerland and Malaysia have inquired about buying a stake, he says. Some businessmen want to franchise his sandwiches, but he hasn't done it yet because "I cannot control quality." Already, he says he's seen some copycats selling sandwiches at lower prices on the streets. "I welcome that. Does it hurt me? I don't believe so." Meanwhile, Sirivat continues to go full-bore toward expansion and promotion. For his high-school reunion, he convinced the organizers to allow him to cater the event and promote his sandwiches. So he brought eight hundred sandwiches with him. Sirivat also offers a deal where if the buyer pays for 250 sandwiches, Sirivat will come and give a speech on the economy. His ultimate goal is to list on the stock exchange. "I don't know when, but I'm preparing in the future. I'll have the business operation listed on the stock market! It's going to be a very good company, a cash company, that's my plan." Before, he says, "many people scolded me, blamed me. 'You're selling sandwiches on the street! Use your brain to do something bigger.'" Now, he says, "every one of those who looked down on me gives me the thumbs up."

*Children sweeping up the grounds of Takihara Elementary School in Omiya, Japan. Japanese schools do not have custodians, and the children do the cleaning each day.*

### CHAPTER EIGHT

# For Shame

## NICHOLAS D. KRISTOF

*Interviewer: "And what do you think of Western civilization?"*
*Mohandas K. Gandhi (thoughtfully): "I think it would be a good idea."*

Just days after we moved to Tokyo in 1995, our son Geoffrey, then a baby, roused Sheryl for a 5:30 a.m. feeding. A few minutes later our bed began to shake. "Wake up, Nick!" Sheryl urged me with a poke. "It's an earthquake!" I grunted and, in an effort to reassure the household, kept sleeping. But it turned out to be the great earthquake that devastated the port city of Kobe and killed 5,200 people. A modern city was reduced to rubble, and for the next few days ordinary middle-class families were thrown back virtually to the stone age, struggling to find water, food, toilets, and shelter. Homes and shops were abandoned, of course, and in America or Europe the result would have been widespread looting, as well as desperate fighting for water, food, and blankets.

Instead, the people of Kobe were majestic in their suffering. They lined up for water and other supplies, never jostling, and nobody climbed through the shattered store windows to help themselves. Even the *yakuza,* the Japanese gangsters, suspended their criminal behavior and tried to improve their image by trucking food to the hardest-hit areas to give it away to the newly homeless.

I was fascinated by these displays of public honesty, and so I kept searching for a case of theft or looting. Finally, I was thrilled to find one. Two young men had entered a shattered convenience store, picked up some food from the floor, and run out. Rumors of this crime spread around town, and finally I was able to find the store and its owner. "Of course, we expect this kind of looting if there's an earthquake in Los Angeles," I noted triumphantly, fishing for a good quote, "but were you shocked that your fellow Japanese would take advantage of the chaos and do such a thing?"

The shop owner looked puzzled. "Who said anything about Japanese?" he asked me politely. "The thieves weren't Japanese. They were foreigners. Iranians, it looked like."

He was right, it turned out. And I always think of that scene when I hear people talk of instability in Asia, because to me it speaks to something very different and something I saw much more often: a moral cohesion and sense of shared values that together create a considerable degree of social stability in Asia. The social fabric of the East is rent or threadbare in places, but on the whole it seems to me stronger and more resilient than that of the West. And in assessing Asia's prospects in the coming decades, one of the important assets that it has working for it is this social fabric—by which I mean strong families, low crime rates, considerable civility, and a broad sense of shared values and destiny. If I had to offer a shorthand for Asia's path to growth, it would be economic flexibility, brutal drive, and social stability.

It may seem strange to refer to social stability with regard to Asia. Revolutions have upended countries from China to Vietnam, riots have beset Korea and Indonesia, and India's Muslims and Hindus periodically kill each other. No place had less stability than China during the Cultural Revolution from 1966 to 1976, Cambodia during the Khmer Rouge nightmare of 1975 to 1979, the Indian subcontinent during partition in 1947, or Indonesia during its spasms of anti-Communist violence in 1965 and 1966. All that has to be acknowledged. And yet somehow Asia emerged, by and large, with its societies surprisingly intact. Indeed, what is most striking about Asia is that for all its upheavals it has largely escaped the different but almost equally enormous turmoil that has strained the family and community in much of the West over the last few decades.

Beginning in the 1960s, a wave of sociological phenomena swept over not just the United States but almost the entire world. Crime soared, especially violent crime. Divorce rates leaped. The proportion of children born to unwed mothers surged, and single-parent households became much more common. An underclass grew in the cities, kept down by drugs and hopelessness, and unable to use education or jobs to climb the escalator to the middle class. These patterns were most associated with the United States, but they were also visible even in deeply traditional societies like Switzerland and developing countries like Brazil. One careful study around the world found that a dramatic weakening had taken place in the family structure in nearly every country of the world—but that some Asian nations were an important exception. Change did come to Asia, of course: Divorce rates across Asia, for example, averaged about 1.5 per 1,000 people per year in the 1990s, triple their level of the 1950s. But even today's rate is less than one-third the rate in the United States.

The writer Francis Fukuyama called these social phenomena that began in the 1960s "the great disruption," and they aroused deep anxiety in the West. These are areas where the East has something to teach the West. The lessons are layered and subtle, and Asia is certainly not a model—think of the families in India who torture their daughters-in-law to extract extra dowry payments, or the Chinese peasants who buy kidnapped women as wives and imprison them in their homes and villages. Asian families remain authoritarian and, for many young people, stifling, and some see the freedom of the American family as the ideal model. Yet for my part, I found it liberating to live in places where Sheryl and the kids could walk around at night, and I think that there is much we can learn from civility and socialization in Asia.

Asia's tightly woven social fabric underpinned economic growth in the good times, but it was particularly visible in times of despair. Many experts had predicted that the Asian economic crisis would lead divorce rates and school drop-out rates to surge, crime to climb through the roof, and hunger and hopelessness to breed violence across the region. There were examples of all these phenomena, but far fewer than had been predicted. During this terrible time, something happened that was entirely unexpected: societies created their own safety net to shield the weakest; families came together to look after in-laws or distant cousins; neighbors helped each other out; temples, mosques, and churches handed out rice; villagers gave each other loans; schoolteachers continued to teach even students who did not pay fees. The human toll of the Asian economic crisis turned out to be not nearly as bad as most experts had predicted, and the main reason was the tight-knit communities and strong families, especially in rural areas.

I saw these mechanisms at work in Salamet's family in Indonesia. I was so moved by his struggle to keep his son in school and hold on to his rickshaw that I made him a present of the money that I calculated he needed. He kept about half but immediately gave the rest to various needy family members and neighbors. In other places, these support mechanisms were more formalized. On a roadless area of the little Indonesian island of Sumba, a dazzlingly beautiful collection of traditional villages,* I came across Bulu Kadi, a fifty-five-year-old peasant with a head of unkempt hair and a machete tucked into his belt. Kadi, though hungry, didn't worry about anybody starving. "The tradition here is that if people don't have food, they can borrow from their neighbors," he said. "If you borrow one sack of rice, you have to pay back two sacks. People always help each other." This is a crude banking system, with 100 percent interest rates, but it has one advantage over Western banking systems: In Sumba, people can borrow when they need the grain, and social pressure means they are certain to pay it back; in the West, people lose access to credit just when they need it most, and the risk of default is very real.

These support mechanisms are fraying in the cities but remain strong in rural areas across Asia. One of the saddest people I met was a thirty-two-year-old Thai woman named Bangon Phailak. A peasant with soft brown eyes and thick black hair cut just above her shoulders, Bangon lived in the village of Ban Wan Yai in a remote corner of northeastern Thailand near the Laos border. Soft-spoken and calm, she seemed unsurprised when I came across her chopping up wild plants to eat. Her shack was made of rough wooden planks loosely nailed together, and Bangon herself seemed rough-hewn in the same way, with weathered brown skin and patched clothes and a surpassing gentleness about the way she moved and spoke. I liked her immediately.

Bangon's problem was her greatest love: her four-year-old daughter, Saiyamon, sitting beside her. The little girl was malnourished and anemic, and although Bangon foraged for food in the woods and fields this was not

---

* Memo to tourists: If you ever plan a visit to Bali, be sure to tack on a side trip to Sumba. There are quick, direct flights from Bali. But Sumba is a different world and one of my favorite places in Indonesia. It is rarely visited by foreigners (in contrast to the clogged beaches of Bali) yet its ancient stone villages are breathtaking.

*Bulu Kadi cuts up a wild root called* wee-ah *in front of his hut. His granddaughter Olpiana is behind him.*

enough. Saiyamon needed rice and milk, which had to be purchased from a store with money. Yet Bangon was herself seriously sick and needed the money for treatment. A doctor had told her that she needed a stomach operation to save her life.

So as Bangon saw it, she faced a choice, one she pondered as she cut her vegetables: What did her daughter need more, food or a mother?

It seemed to me that it would have made sense for Bangon to keep her child hungry and anemic, but at least with a mother to look after her.

*Bangon Phailak with her daughter Saiyamon in front of their house in northeastern Thailand.*

However, Bangon could not face her daughter's tears. She decided to forgo medical care and sacrifice herself.

I was appalled by Bangon's choice but also skeptical. So I went around quietly asking the neighbors if she was really so sick and poor. "She's very sick, no doubt about that," one neighbor said soberly. "She's been to the doctor many times, and she's gotten steadily weaker. Now she can't even do any work in the fields, the way she could just a few months ago." Down the road a bit, a middle-aged woman chimed in: "Everybody feels bad for them, and especially for that little girl. Some folks help them now and then, giving them food or lifts on a motorcycle to the doctor. But now we're all in such a tough bind that people are just thinking about their own families, and no one has cash to help out the neighbors."

Yet when I asked how Bangon paid the doctor, the villagers hung their heads and acknowledged that they had given her cash after all. I am used to people claiming to be far more generous than they really are; in this obscure village I was encountering tremendous generosity that people did not want to admit to. When I walked around Bangon's hut, I was startled to see a little red motorcycle in back. It was old and battered, but it was just about the only possession that I could see.

"Is that yours?" I asked.

"No, no," she explained. "It's my neighbor's. But he lent it to me for as long as I need it, so that I can go to the doctor or take Saiyamon to the doctor."

"Does he charge you for the use of the motorcycle?"

"Oh, no. And he gives me gas."

The civility during the crisis extended to the criminal world. Some people were driven to crime by the Asian economic crisis, of course. But to me, the criminal who was emblematic of that period was not some murderer or bankrobber but rather a fifty-one-year-old South Korean grocer named Chung Kyu Chil. A customer came into his shop one day in December 1998 to find Chung unconscious in a pool of blood, and the ambulance crew found that both his legs ended at the ankles—his feet had been chopped off and were missing. The police were summoned, but Chung could not explain what had happened. He said he had gone to bed drunk, and he could think of no reason why anybody would want to chop off his feet. When the police investigated they discovered that Chung had debts of $230,000, largely acquired by bad bets on the South Korean stock market. They also found that he had recently taken out twenty-four insurance policies that would pay him millions of dollars if he became disabled. At this point, Chung confessed. Desperate, he had asked his best buddy to chop off his feet with an axe and throw them in the Han River.

That was, of course, an attempt at insurance fraud and it certainly was violent, but it is not exactly the kind of violent crime one might expect to see in such desperate times. In spirit, it was closer to the *gaman* and self-sacrifice that propelled Asia during its boom years. And, indeed, for all the alarming predictions about rising crime, in the end crime rates in places like South Korea actually fell as the crisis took hold. The social fabric held.

Just a few years ago, it was fashionable for authoritarian Asian leaders to trumpet "Asian values" and use them to justify their repression. Now that Asians themselves have ousted such emblems of Asian values as President Suharto of Indonesia and elected such symbols of universalism as Kim Dae Jung in South Korea, it is harder to argue that Asians themselves believe in "Asian values," in the sense of a preference for order over freedom.

Yet there is no doubt that there are "Asian values" in another sense, in the plain sense of the values that Asian people hold. Of course these values are different from country to country, city to village, social class to social class, religion to religion, family to family, and so the concept of

Asian values isn't particularly more meaningful than American values or European values. It may seem silly to generalize about societies across Asia, for there are huge variations and some societies are more admirable than others. Yet I believe that two generalizations are valid, and that these help explain not only how Asia rapidly began to bounce back from its economic crisis but, more important, how the region will gain strength and importance in the coming decades. The first generalization is that families are strong and the second is that shame is an important social sanction.

The two factors are interwoven and help provide that sturdy social fabric that underpins much of Asia, for many families stay strong because they would be shamed if they broke apart. And while shame and strong family ties are not universal in Asia, they are widespread. For all the differences between, say, India and Japan, one of the common features is the centrality of shame in the culture. We may find the ethical systems of rural India or Pakistan horrifying; after all, this is where fathers occasionally kill their own daughters for choosing a boyfriend and going out with him instead of waiting for an arranged marriage. But there is no doubt that these systems operate on shame. The fathers are driven to such a horror because of the enormous social humiliation that accompanies a breach of local mores, for in rural areas a girl who goes out with a boy shames her whole extended family. These murders are relatively rare, of course, but they reflect an intricate ethical code that is widespread in Asia and that is typically far more sophisticated and demanding than that of the West. Afghanistan villagers or Javanese fishermen may not have much in the way of a material civilization these days, but their understanding of mutual responsibilities is far more complex than that of Europe or America.

Part of the reason has to do with long histories of people living in close proximity. In contrast to Europeans or, more recently, Americans, the people of India, Java, China, Korea, and Japan have been living cheek-to-jowl for thousands of years. Even today, the numbers are startling: The United States has an average of 29 people per square kilometer; the world as a whole has 44; China has 130; India has 318; South Korea has 461; and Hong Kong has 6,375. The most crowded place on Earth is the urban area of Hong Kong, with 155,000 people per square kilometer, seven times the density of Manhattan. The Indonesian island of Java has one hundred million people in an area about the size of New York State; if the Javanese were Americans, they would have torn each other to pieces long ago. The reason that Javanese do not (except for occasional spasms) is an exceptionally complex linguistic and social code for showing mutual respect. I think it is no accident that, while European or Semitic languages have just a few simple ways of showing formality or respectful distance (for example, *vous* instead of *tu* in French), languages like Korean, Japanese, and Javanese are infused with countless ways of calibrating speech to show a dozen different levels of politeness.*

Japan is the apex of this ethical code for human interactions. Just about every aspect of life is governed by strict social regulations, and social pressures are internalized so that people largely behave well on their own. Taxi drivers wear gloves and keep their vehicles pristine, and one top Japanese government official explained what happened when he was deemed senior enough to be a potential assassination target. "The police installed a closed-circuit camera on the front door of our house," he said, "and they monitored it from a police box down the street. But my wife thought it was a terrible nuisance. From then on, she had to put on her makeup even before taking out the garbage." Though a foreigner, I gradually absorbed the mores, and after a while I became self-conscious about wearing old blue jeans when I took the kids to school. I'm not quite sure why, but it had something to do with being concerned about what other parents thought and feeling sure that if I wore torn blue jeans they would see me as an uncivilized tramp.

This strongly internalized peer pressure to behave appropriately is the essence of Japan's success in suppressing crime. Japan's attitude toward crime reminded me of the "just say no" campaign in America against narcotics, except that in Japan, it never inspired jokes. One of the most touching people I ever met in Japan was a murderer, Fujita, a squat, strong man with short, graying hair framing a gentle face. He spoke quietly, mouse-like, as he sat on the tatami floor of the tiny home in which he lived. He awkwardly held his rough, clumsy hands in his lap, where they matched his rough, fraying, navy-blue work clothes. His demeanor was as sad and frayed as his clothing, and he never looked me in the eye as we spoke, gazing instead at my knees.

A compulsive gambler, he had tricked a neighbor into lending him some money, saying that it was for an investment. Then Fujita gambled it away on *pachinko,* a Japanese variation of pinball, and the neighbor grew suspi-

---

* All these factors make Asian languages on balance much more brutal to study than European languages. There are exceptions, such as Indonesian, which is very easy. But Korean may be the most difficult major language to master, and Japanese, Chinese, Hindi, Khmer, Tamil, Javanese, and other Asian tongues are not far behind.

cious and kept demanding the money back. Finally, in a fit of anger, Fujita smashed his neighbor's head with a hammer and killed him. Fujita, then forty-two years old, quickly confessed and was sentenced to life in prison as his wife and four children sobbed quietly in the back of the courtroom. "The last time I saw them was in the courtroom," he told me morosely. No family members ever visited him during the fifteen years and three months that he was in prison, yet somehow the experience seemed to have left him loving them more than ever. His voice trembled as he spoke of his children.

"There were seven people in my cell, and we used to talk about the day when we would get out, and about how we would be good," Fujita said. "Everyone in the cell was a lifer, and when we were inside the cell and talking, we used to worry about our families. I wouldn't be able to sleep at night. I couldn't get rid of my guilt, my sorrow for my daughters, especially because I couldn't see them at their weddings. Everybody in the prison felt terrible. Some felt so bad about how they had disgraced their parents that they would never go back and see them again." When Fujita was released in 1991, he decided not to go back to his family, for fear of adding to their burden. It was his greatest gift to those he loved, staying away to avoid punishing them. "I've been away for many years, and if I returned it would bring great suffering to my family," he explained. "It's not that people would ostracize me, but they would talk of nothing else."

If Fujita were in America, he might be inclined toward excuses: It happened all of a sudden; I didn't really mean to kill the guy; I was addicted to gambling and wasn't myself; I never had much education; lots of people who do even worse things get shorter sentences; whatever I did doesn't justify the way the prison guards treated me. But Japan does not tolerate excuses, and the whole system places a huge emphasis on cultivating remorse. Police and prosecutors try to get criminals not only to confess their actions, but also to feel bad about them. Even in prison, counselors do their utmost to make felons feel guilty. By forcing criminals to confront the fact that they have done wrong and by harassing them for their moral failings, the system establishes a framework of justice that does not tolerate excuses. In America, there are eddies of society where it is perfectly honorable to mug a stranger or where a young woman will happily accept a gift of a gold necklace that she knows is stolen. Those eddies also exist in Japan, of course, but to a much smaller degree. And the enormous effort by the authorities to make criminals feel guilty makes it difficult for these eddies to offer an alternative moral universe. "None of the prisoners thought that they had been treated unfairly," Fujita said. "Everybody knew that it was his own responsibility that he had ended up in prison."

Although he was already an elderly man, Fujita was working every day and living in a tiny room so that he could save some money. He was trying to give his savings, amounting to several thousand dollars, to the family of the man he had killed. There was no legal obligation to do so, and since he was already out of prison it would not help him with the authorities. But Fujita insisted on offering the money to help atone for his wrongdoing—although the victim's family members refused to let him off that easily: They would not accept the money.

Fujita's attitude as he sat on the floor beside me, hanging his head, speaking slowly and barely audibly, could be captured in a word: shame. As the criminologist James Q. Wilson has argued, shame is one reason why crime rates are so low in Japan, and shamelessness is one reason why they are so high in America. Shame is not entirely a blessing, for it means that Asian societies are unusually judgmental and censorious, a bit like Puritan America, with very little tolerance for free spirits. Misfits in schools are often bullied, and family members of misfits are made to suffer as well. All this earnestness also leaves countries like Japan with a pretty dreadful sense of humor and very little appreciation of irony. Former Prime Minister Keizo Obuchi was one of the few genuinely funny people in Japanese national politics, and I once had a terrific lunch with him in which he spent the whole time cracking jokes—and teasing me for having written that he had the pizzazz of a cold pizza. Then afterward Obuchi held a press conference, and as soon as the television cameras turned on, his humor vanished and he became another colorless, dull, Japanese politician. Aides explained that the public wants a serious leader, not a funny one. Perhaps. My only attempts at irony in speeches in Japan were humiliating—each pause for laughter was followed by a perplexed silence—and I remember my embarrassment when I was reading to Geoffrey in a doctor's office in Tokyo. It was a Power Ranger comic book, and for amusement I told the story in Japanese from the perspective of the monster: He's walking innocently down the street, and all of a sudden these terrorist super heroes attack him, and he has to defend himself. Geoffrey and I were really getting into it, when I felt eyes upon me. I looked around the waiting room, and all the parents were looking at me in horror.

The internalized shame also results in Asians putting enormous pressure on themselves. Lots of people make themselves miserable for no good reason. That is one reason why, in much of Asia, murder rates are low but suicide rates are high. In America, when people explode from unbearable pressure, they kill their neighbors; in Asia, they kill themselves. Indeed, while the Asian crisis did not lead to a leap in violent crime, it did trigger a spate of suicides.

One time I visited my favorite little Japanese town of Omiya shortly after reading about Brandon C. Blenden, a seventeen-year-old in Mississippi who, while drunk, had caused a car crash that killed a four-year-old girl, Whitney Lee. The judge sentenced Blenden to twenty years in prison and also ordered him to write a $1 check each week for the next ten years and send it to Whitney's parents. The judge instructed Blenden to write on the memo line of each check the words "for the death of your daughter, Whitney." The idea was to ensure that Blenden faced a weekly reminder of the devastation he had caused. I mentioned that judge's sentence to some friends, and they told me of a man in Omiya who many years earlier had been driving a car when a boy darted out onto the road. The driver, through no fault of his own, killed the boy. Each year on the anniversary of the boy's death, the man goes to the home of the boy's parents to offer his apologies one more time, to demonstrate his grief and remorse. It is terribly painful to him, and yet he feels it is his moral obligation. Blenden had to be forced by the criminal justice system to accept his responsibility; in Omiya, the pressure was internal, and the man in Omiya embraced the responsibility himself.

How does a society cultivate these kinds of values? The process begins in early childhood, as we found when we sent Gregory and Geoffrey to Japanese nursery schools and kindergartens. At Gregory's kindergarten graduation ceremony, he and the other graduates lined up in front of all of us proud parents and sang together to the teachers: "Because you taught us so much, we became good children. Thank you, teachers. Goodbye, gentle teachers, friends, and goodbye wood blocks that we used to make little houses with. Goodbye, everybody!" The Japanese versions of some Western fairy tales were similarly syrupy. My favorite was a Japanese story about how Goldilocks, after being caught in the home of the three bears, does not run off as in the Western version. Instead, she apologizes for her mistakes, and then she and the bears have a happy meal together and become best friends.

Many Japanese parents teach their children values by having their sons or daughters turn in coins that they find to the police. I decided to do the same. So one day when Gregory found a one hundred-yen coin on the sidewalk, I explained that just because you find something doesn't mean it's necessarily yours. We walked over to the Arisugawa Park Police Box and Gregory handed over the coin to the policeman at the desk. The officer fetched a "found property" form and gravely asked Gregory where he had found it and where he lived and what his occupation was. Then the policeman praised Gregory for his honesty and told him that if no one claimed the coin, in six months Gregory could get it back. The policeman had taken about twenty minutes to fill out the form, and obviously the police were spending far more in administrative costs than the coin was worth. But I can't imagine a better way of teaching property rights.*

It is the same kind of community values that makes the family such a strong institution in Asia. Couples stay together in places like Japan not because they are especially in love, or because they are especially faithful or devoted to each other. In India in 1950, some 90 percent of girls were married by the age of fifteen, often to men they scarcely knew, and divorce was almost unknown. The glue of Asian marriages was not love or compatibility but peer pressure. Husbands and wives cheat on each other and abuse each other, but they stay together—and women do not have babies outside of marriage—because of the fear of humiliation if they do otherwise.

I had read many paeans to Asian family values, but I heard something more realistic and nuanced from Yuri Uemura, a septuagenarian midwife who lived in Omiya. Uemura, a delightful, colorful woman whose face was as weathered as an old baseball and etched with a thousand seams, described her own marriage as strong but unhappy. "There was never any love between me and my husband," she told me, and she added that her husband had never told her that he liked her, had never complimented her on a meal, had never given her a present, had never shown her affection of any kind, and had never even called her by her name. Instead, he summons her with a grunt. "Even with animals, the males cooperate to

---

* Alas, teaching values turned out to be more complicated than I had expected. Gregory was so thrilled by his experience turning the coin in to the police that he began to walk with his head down, scrutinizing the pavement. A week later, he found a one-yen coin, worth less than a penny. Then he came across a ten-yen coin. Gregory wanted to turn the coins in to the police, but I was afraid that if he began appearing constantly, turning in small coins and demanding that the police fill out all the paperwork, they would be peeved. So I put him off, and then fortunately Gregory's Japanese kindergarten had a fundraising campaign to help the poor, and children were encouraged to contribute anything that was theirs—without getting money or help from parents. I told Gregory that it would be okay to give the coins to the poor, and he did so. But he figured out pretty quickly that taking the coins to the police had been only a symbolic gesture.

*Yuri Uemura talks about family life in her home in Omiya, Japan. She has been married to her husband for more than four decades, and their marriage is strong—but unhappy.*

bring the females some food," she said sadly, noting the contrast to her own marriage and a husband who simply beat her. "When I see that, it brings tears to my eyes."

I was startled, because I had gone to Omiya to learn the secret of the strength of Japanese families, and I quickly realized that Japanese couples are not as happy as the statistics indicate. The family structure is rock-solid, but family members are not particularly close. Children and parents, husbands and wives often scarcely communicate except by grunts. Masayuki Ogita, a poultry farmer, explained that he never says anything to his wife because "I kind of feel that there's nothing new to say to her." One survey that asked married men and women in thirty-seven countries about their views on politics, sex, religion, and other issues found that Japanese couples ranked dead last in compatibility, by a huge margin. Another survey revealed that if they were doing it over again, only one-third of Japanese would marry the same person.

Yet Japanese do stay together, and the family remains about as strong as ever. The upshot of all the social pressure is that in Japan only 1.1 percent of births are to unwed mothers—virtually unchanged from 1960. In the United States, the figure is 30 percent. Divorce rates in Japan are rising (although they are still less than half of the U.S. level) but they usually do not involve young children. So single-parent households are stable, accounting for exactly the same proportion as in 1965. As Uemura told me: "I haven't lived for myself, but for my kids, and for my family and for society."

One of the paradoxes is that almost all Japanese families are, in a sense, single-parent households. The father is usually more of a theoretical presence than a homework-helping reality, and expectations of his sexual fidelity are sometimes low. (Japanese wives, when packing their husbands' suitcases before solo business trips to Thailand, have been known to pack a few condoms as well.) Because fathers often stay late in the office or go drinking with work buddies, a national survey found that 30 percent of Japanese fathers spend less than fifteen minutes a day on weekdays talking with or playing with their children. A separate survey of eighth-graders found that 51 percent never spoke with their fathers on weekdays. Yet, surprisingly, it does not seem to matter all that much whether the father is an actual presence or a theoretical one. Those few children in Japan who grow up in single-mother households are at much greater risk than their peers of turning to crime, but children turn out fine if they have a father who is nominally at home even if they never see him.

Of course, shame and strong families are not universal in Asia and they certainly vary from country to country. It seems to me, for example, that shame is much less of a sanction in China—which has a strain of American-style individualism—than in either Japan or India. Likewise, all these social patterns are constantly changing, in the East as well as in the West, and it is common to say that young people in Asia are different from their elders. That is certainly true. Chinese and Japanese no longer promote blind obedience to the elderly by repeating stories of filial piety, like the one about the man who slept naked on his bed so that mosquitoes would bite him instead of his aged parents next door. The foolishness of the old ethos is reflected in the true story of a Japanese girl, Omasu, who in the nineteenth century was summoned to testify at the trial of her father, who was accused of stealing a coin. The girl started to answer the questions, but soon realized that the judge would get her to incriminate her father. There was a pause, and suddenly blood began to gush from her mouth. To keep from saying anything that might harm her father, she had bitten off her tongue. It worked: Her father was acquitted, and a wealthy merchant so admired her filial piety that he married her.

Those old values are fading, and the nuclear family is replacing the extended family. Young Asians are different. But the effect on family and shame is still uncertain, and it is too soon to know whether Asia will follow the trajectory of the West. Japan and China both managed to have a sexual revolution without having an explosion in the number of single mothers. And Japan demonstrates that a country can industrialize, at least for a time, without going through the pattern of rising crime and disintegrating families that characterized industrialization in much of the West.

Economists have found a link between social stability and economic growth, but its causation is a bit uncertain. Of course, there are a few obvious connections. Strong families tend to take responsibility for their own and thus forestall the emergence of a welfare state. The combination of shame and strong families also keeps at bay the pathologies of drugs, gangs, crime, and an underclass. Shame tends to create trust that borrowers will repay money, so people lend to each other and foster mobility of capital. On the other hand, strong families and strong communities in places like China sometimes create corruption, because public officials feel an obligation to give a break to relatives or to people from their hometowns.

I think that social stability also helps because it allows countries to manage crises and bounce back afterward, and it helps encourage political moderation and a somewhat more stable investment environment. The social stability leads people to take the risk of investing in new factories or businesses, in expectation that they will have a chance to reap the returns.

Shame and strong families are also inextricably interwoven in Asia within the education system.

Education is, I believe, an important reason for optimism about Asia's prospects. Schools vary widely, of course, and there are plenty of weaknesses: Chinese cities have a decent primary system but third-rate colleges with places for only 1.8 percent of college-age young people; India is the opposite, allowing far too many children to get virtually no education at all but offering a college education to a relatively impressive 6.4 percent of young people; Afghanistan is an educational catastrophe with barely any schools at all; and Pakistan is not much better. Yet despite some truly awful school systems, by and large Asia is strong in education, especially in elementary schools and high schools. And, as William Butler Yeats noted,

*Fifth-graders at Aso Elementary School in Omiya, Japan, solving a math problem together. The class was broken up in small groups, called* han, *and each was supposed to solve this problem: "Each one-meter segment of a tree weighs 1.2 kilograms. So how heavy is 3.3 meters of the tree? Round the second decimal place and give your answer to one decimal place, and show how you reached the result." Each* han *quickly reached the intermediate answer of 3.96 kilograms, but some had trouble rounding to the desired answer of 4.0 kilograms. Here the four pupils in one* han *show their equations, and they are challenged by the boy standing up at his desk and facing the blackboard. He asks how they got from one equation to the next. The teacher is standing in the back, deferring to the students, as often happens in Japan. The idea is that the students will learn better if they play a central role in the problem solving and in correcting and teaching one another.*

*A girl cleans the hallway of an
elementary school in Omiya, Japan,
during the daily cleanup period.*

"education is not filling a bucket but lighting a fire." The upshot is a population with a strong pilot light, one that not only will be well-trained academically for jobs in an information age, but also one that has imbibed the
side benefits of education, particularly self-discipline.

Education is closely linked to the shame culture in part because the
schools propagate it. Much more openly than in the West, schools teach
values and aim to turn out not just smart young people but also good
ones. In contrast to America, class sizes are large—an average Korean
elementary-school class has thirty-one students—and naturally I asked
about discipline. The teachers acknowledged that it can be difficult to
maintain with thirty or forty pupils in a class. But, particularly in Japan, I
came to understand that what teachers were trying to instill was not discipline but self-discipline.

Since Japanese often complain that their schools are too regimented, I
was startled the first time I walked into a classroom in Omiya. Two boys
were wrestling on the floor, a girl in a bright red dress was throwing a paper
cup in the air and catching it, and two boys were grappling with the

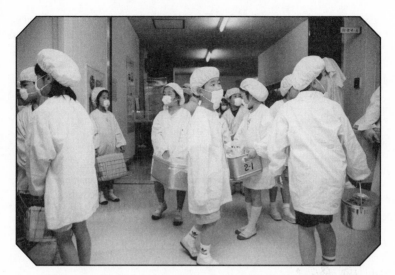

*These are not youthful surgeons, but students at Azuma Elementary School in Yokohama, Japan. These are the children responsible for bringing food from the kitchens to their classrooms, a task that is intended to teach responsibility.*

teacher as he fended them off and spoke with a girl. All the other kids were rushing around and yelling. This was a break, not instruction time, but even when class resumed the chaos subsided only a bit. Then when I was interviewing the principal in the schoolyard, a bouncy fourth-grade girl kept yanking at my arm insistently. She wanted me to join a softball game, but it was the kind of inappropriate behavior that an American principal would have stopped immediately. This principal did nothing, however, and soon the girl pounced on him, tugging at his sleeve and pulling him backward. He asked her to stop, but she would not. And so he put up with it.

Particularly in Japan, teachers do not usually punish students who misbehave; rather they manipulate other students to scold the culprit into feeling guilty. The manipulation is masterful and helps create the internalized codes of harmony that are the backdrop of a civil society. Catherine C. Lewis, an American scholar who sent her children to Japanese schools and has written a terrific book about Japanese education, *Educating Hearts and Minds,* describes a scene she witnessed in a Japanese kindergarten. Several five-year-old boys begin to roll clay balls and drop them on the goldfish in the aquarium, while gleefully shouting, "Bombs away!" The teacher, Mrs. Nomura, noted, "That could hurt the fish." The boys continued, and Nomura repeated that the clay balls could hurt the fish. The boys paid her no heed, and Nomura commented once more, "How sad the class will be if the fish get hurt." Several boys continued to drop the "bombs," but Nomura did not stop them and said nothing further.

An hour later, in the class meeting at the end of the day, Nomura brought up the issue of dropping the bombs and suggested that this might kill the fish. She did not say it is bad to drop the bombs, but she asked the children, "What does everybody think about this?" Some children said that it sounded like fun to bomb the fish. Nomura did not scold them, but she focused on others who said that they did not want the fish to be hurt. "What shall we do about this problem, then?" she asked the students. After some discussion, she had manipulated the students into reaching two conclusions: First, that no one should drop bombs on the fish, and, second, that "if you see someone hurting the goldfish, you should tell them to stop."

That is discipline, Japanese-style. The teacher never told anyone to stop doing something bad, and indeed she tolerated misbehavior. She treated it as a problem for the entire class to solve and led the children through her questions into reaching the desired result. Then she created peer pressure against misbehavior and fostered an arrangement whereby the children would police themselves. Perhaps this did not work perfectly, for it *is* a lot of fun to drop clay balls on goldfish. But it helped provide a foundation of a sense of discipline and morality.

So as to nurture young people who can eventually become an educated and cooperative workforce, schools give children responsibilities from the first grade. In Tokyo, Gregory normally went to Nishimachi, an international school, but in the summer months we sent him to Kougai, the local public elementary school, and he was thrilled by some of the class jobs he was given. His favorite was bringing the lunch from the kitchen and serving it to his classmates, but there were other responsibilities as well. The students rotate among themselves the job of class monitor, teaching leadership and perhaps creating some empathy for a teacher who is struggling to calm an excited class. Within each class, students are also divided into other decision-making groups. The "play group" decides what games to play and who will be on each team, and the "study group" leads the class when the teacher is absent. Yes, that's right: The students themselves are the substitute teachers. When a teacher is sick in Japan, the school does not provide a substitute. "If a teacher is away, then the children work on handouts and homework," Tamotsu Wakimoto, a principal of a school in Omiya, explained to me. "With the first- and second-graders, we would be a bit concerned, so we'd have a teacher look in on them from time to time. But with the older kids, they study quietly." Of course, he added, "if a teacher is gone for a month or more, we would want to get a substitute."

The students also clean the schools. Japanese schools do not have janitors. Instead, they have a daily "cleaning session," in which the pupils are responsible for cleaning the floors, corridors, windows, toilets, and everything else. Gregory and the other students were not much impressed by this system, but I thought it was terrific and served a real purpose. "If we had custodians, I suppose this school would gleam," mused Mizue Hanzawa, a school nurse in Yokohama, looking around a room whose patina could not be described as a gleam. "But it's very important to build responsibility and teach children to clean up the space they use. That's a purpose of education. And I think that this way the kids learn to take care of things." It does not work very well, I should add. Japanese children have rooms at home that are as slovenly as American children's rooms. And the kids on toilet duty during the cleaning session rarely scrub very diligently. Yet graffiti is rare, because the kids don't like scrubbing it off. "Kids write graffiti in pencil," Miyuki Shibahara, an English teacher, told me. "They don't have the guts to write in pen."

After they clean the school, the students get together in small groups to assess their work. In Omiya, I watched as a string bean of a sixth-grade boy, in command of one group of cleaners, gathered his troops and led a brief "confession session." "Did we work together well?" he asked, looking up from his checklist.

"Yes," the others called out.

"Did we use all our time well?"

"Yes!"

"Did we put all the tools away?"

"Yes!" But then the conscience of a shy eleven-year-old girl, Seira, intruded on the self-congratulatory mood. "We didn't really put the brooms away neatly," she piped up. "We just stuffed them in the closet and closed the door." The other children nodded guiltily.

A survey of parents in the United States found that their top three complaints about local schools were drugs and violence, low academic standards, and insufficient emphasis on the basics. In that sense, Asian schools are just what Americans seem to be dreaming of. Drugs and guns

*Children at this school in China's Dabie Mountains learn to work outside of the classroom as well as in it. The community has virtually no budget for a school, so the students and teachers augment the funds by raising vegetables to eat and sell.*

are unheard of in the schools, academic standards tend to be high, and the focus is on the basics. No distinction is made between misbehavior in school and outside. "A neighbor of mine phoned to say that a kid had been smoking in town," Shibahara, the English teacher, told me. "So we passed out paper and asked all the kids to write down anything they knew about this. One boy admitted it. He wrote down that he had done it. So I scolded him, and he began crying. I called his mother down to the school, and she began crying, too."

Yet this Sunday-school earnestness carries only so far. For many years, there have been exceptional cases of students attacking teachers or even killing other students, and in 1997 a fourteen-year-old boy in Kobe beheaded a friend and left the head on a school gate. More commonly, students are rebellious, even if their rebelliousness is more limited than in the West. Instead of taking drugs, the daring students smoke cigarettes.

*Chinese classrooms are bare and shoddy in rural areas, but students all know that the best way to succeed in life is to work hard in school. This is an English class at a school in a remote part of Hubei Province, and one drawback is that the teacher does not speak English. But she tries hard, and so does everybody else. The principal said that if he has a student with disciplinary problems, the most extreme measure he ever has to take is to write a reproachful note and tack it up in the schoolyard. That shames the miscreant into better behavior.*

Instead of burning down their schools, they bleach their hair until it has a hint of brown. The coolest kid I ever found in Omiya was Kazuhiro Fujikura, a fourteen-year-old slugger on the junior-high baseball team. He was pointed out to me as he sat in the hallway, leaning against the wall with his legs sticking out so that people had to walk around him.

"He's so cute," gushed Asaha Shimomura, a ninth-grade girl talking with her girlfriends twenty feet away. I asked if Fujikura was smart, and the girls put their hands to their faces and giggled. "Of course not," Asaha said. "He never does any work." Kazuhiro was a hero partly because of his hair. It broke school rules by extending below his collar, and it was streaked with tan in defiance of the rules against dying or bleaching hair. "The teachers keep giving me guidance," Kazuhiro explained. "They say I should cut my hair and dye it black again." He paused thoughtfully. "I kind of figure that if dying hair is banned, then I probably shouldn't dye it black again."

Education is also connected to the culture of shame in another way: Social pressure keeps children in school and working hard. This is also a link to economic growth, for the result is widespread literacy and a more able workforce.

Academically, Singapore probably has the best public schools in the world, but international studies suggest that South Korea and Japan are not far behind. The most comprehensive study is the Third International Math and Science Study, which in 1997 reported the results of tests conducted on fourth- and eighth-grade students in forty-one countries around the world. The following charts show the top five countries (and the United States, usually trailing) and the mean scores of their students.

**FOURTH-GRADE MATH**

| | |
|---|---|
| 1. Singapore | 625 |
| 2. South Korea | 611 |
| 3. Japan | 597 |
| 4. Hong Kong | 587 |
| 5. Netherlands | 577 |
| 12. United States | 545 |

**FOURTH-GRADE SCIENCE**

| | |
|---|---|
| 1. South Korea | 597 |
| 2. Japan | 574 |
| 3. United States | 565 |
| 4. Austria | 565 |
| 5. Australia | 562 |

**EIGHTH-GRADE MATH**

| | |
|---|---|
| 1. Singapore | 643 |
| 2. South Korea | 607 |
| 3. Japan | 605 |
| 4. Hong Kong | 588 |
| 5. Belgium | 565 |
| 28. United States | 500 |

**EIGHTH-GRADE SCIENCE**

| | |
|---|---|
| 1. Singapore | 607 |
| 2. Czech Republic | 574 |
| 3. Japan | 571 |
| 4. South Korea | 565 |
| 5. Bulgaria | 565 |
| 17. United States | 534 |

Other international studies have reached similar conclusions about the excellence of East Asian schools. Take the following math problem given on a standardized test to junior-high students in several countries:

*A runner ran 3,000 meters in exactly 8 minutes. What was his average speed in meters per second?*
*A. 3.75      B. 6.25      C. 16.0      D. 37.5      E. 362.5*

The correct answer is B, and 38 percent of Japanese students got it right, precisely twice the 19 percent that answered correctly in America. Or take this problem for senior-high students:

$\int (x-1)^2 \, dx$ *is equal to:*

A. $2(x-1) + c$        B. $\frac{1}{2}(x-1)^2 + c$        C. $\frac{1}{3}(x-1)^3 + c$

D. $\frac{1}{3}(x-1)3 + c$        E. $\frac{(x-1)3}{x} + c$

As 83 percent of Japanese students knew, the correct answer is C. Only 30 percent of Americans realized that.

Why do Asian students do better? One reason is that they work harder. The school day is slightly longer and in some countries there is a half-day session on Saturdays, plus summer vacation is much shorter. In Japan, students have six weeks off for summer vacation, and Gregory was given loads of work to do in that time: ideographs, or *kanji,* to memorize and learn to use in writing; a journal to write every day using those *kanji;* arithmetic; science measurements; even music. It would take about two hours a day during his vacation to do properly. The result of all this is that by the time a child in most Asian countries has reached high school, he has two more years of class time than his American counterpart. A thirteen-year-old Filipino, for example, spends 1,467 hours in class a year, and a Malaysian spends 1,230 hours; in contrast, an American student spends about 980 hours and a Swede 741 hours.

A second reason why Asian students do well is simply that education is treated more seriously and reverently than in the West. Teachers are well paid and well respected in the East, and they tend to be first-rate. A study by the Organisation for Economic Co-operation and Development (OECD) found that Korean teachers are the best paid in the world relative to the wealth of the country. The average South Korean elementary-school teacher with fifteen years' experience earns a sum equivalent to $42,000 a year, after adjusting for relative purchasing power, and tops out at the end of a career at $67,000. In contrast, the average American elementary teacher earns $32,000 after fifteen years and tops out at $40,000. The Korean salary is equal to 3.2 times per capita GDP, while an American teacher gets only 1.2 times per capita GDP. Japanese teachers are also paid very well, earning salaries that are generally higher than those of pharmacists or engineers, and so in a typical year there are five applicants for every teaching job. More broadly, there is a strong sense from India to Japan that education is a critical way to get ahead, and a correspondingly strong respect for eggheads. The admiration for teachers in Japan emerges in opinion polls, where teachers are awarded higher prestige than engineers or department heads in city hall. And Taiwan is the closest thing on Earth to the elitist state envisioned in Plato's *Republic,* for it is virtually a doctorocracy—a country run by Ph.D.s. Taiwan's cabinet always has more Ph.D.s from American universities than the U.S. cabinet does. Taiwan's president, Chen Shui-bian, and vice president, Annette Lu, both graduated at the top of their classes at Taiwan's best university and they may be equipped with more intellectual candlepower, at least in an academic sense, than any other president–vice president team in the world.

Often the attitudes toward education are simply snobbish, and Asian intellectuals do not seem to realize that they may not be completely educated no matter how many degrees they have if they do not know how to hammer a nail or wash dishes, if their hands have never been calloused, and if they do not understand the rhythms of an assembly line. Many Asian intellectuals would arrogantly agree with the dictum of Aristotle that the educated are superior to the uneducated "as much as the living are to the dead." Yet even if much of this is prejudice, confusing academic degrees with wisdom, the consequence of all this snobbery is a fierce drive for education—and that is at least a worthy result.

Perhaps the most important factor in the excellence of education in the East is the public understanding of why some people succeed. Cross-country surveys have shown that Americans and Europeans tend to regard the best students as the bright ones and attribute success to intelligence. As kids themselves say of anyone who aces a test: "He's a brain!" Chinese and Japanese alike see things differently. They assume that the best students are simply the hardest-working, and that the C students are not dim but lazy. The result is that there is no excuse for mediocrity, and parents push their children—and kids push themselves—because of the belief that success is just a matter of working harder. A growing body of research suggests that Asian children do well in school because their parents set high benchmarks, which the children then absorb, while American parents are reluctant to push their children too much. So Asian parents set high standards and American parents set lower standards; in each case, the children oblige by doing what is demanded of them.

Singapore, South Korea, and Japan are in the vanguard, but their rever-

*South Korean high-school students sketch classical busts in a "cram" school. Success as an artist in South Korea depends largely on having good academic credentials—i.e., graduating from a good art school—and admission to art school is based mostly on an examination of a student's ability to sketch the same few classical busts. The system underscores East Asia's overemphasis on rote training rather than creativity.*

ence for education is spreading elsewhere on the continent. While the quality of education in Pakistan and Burma is still dreadful, China has dramatically improved its schools, and some first-rate private schools are emerging to compete with the public ones. Most important, India—which mortgaged its future by neglecting education—is finally doing more to bolster its schools. Far too many Indian children are left out of the system and the average elementary-school class still has fifty students, but at least a growing number of kids are finally getting through school. If India can just keep up the progress and accelerate it, the gains will be enormous. And while the Indian educational authorities do not inspire much confidence, the children and parents often do. An Indian journalist, P.P. Abu Backer, whom I met in the southern Indian state of Kerala, took me to his home and introduced me to his family. His fourteen-year-old daughter, Neethu, a pretty chocolate-skinned girl with gold earrings and a blue school uniform, was struggling with her homework, and I asked her how much homework she typically did in a day.

"Usually I get up early and do homework from 5:30 a.m. to 7:00 a.m. before school, and then again from 6:00 p.m. to 9:00 p.m.," she explained, adding that most of her classmates in the English-language school did the same.

"That is normal," Abu Backer assured me. "When children are in English-medium schools and the parents are educated, they are like this. Of course, when examinations come, she must study harder."

Obviously, all this work comes at a price. The emphasis is often on rote learning, so you get some frightfully well-educated young men and women who have no common sense and no social skills. "Trained seals," a Japanese critic called his country's students. Creativity is neglected, and musicians and artists often seem technically brilliant but short on passion. Many more young Japanese than young Americans, for example, learn to play the violin, but while they become technically excellent, few reach the top rank. An American friend who played in a Japanese orchestra told me that the performance had been "surreal"—perfectly rehearsed, but so mechanical, he said, that he "felt sorry for Beethoven." In Korea, I watched art students copying sketches of a few classical busts. They spend years endlessly perfecting these few sketches, because the entrance exam to art school is based on the ability to do them. The result is not great artists but human photocopiers. Moreover, far too much of the education focuses on what was important a couple of decades ago, and there is not nearly enough training in computers and software design. The result is hordes of graduates who are well trained for the 1960s, rather than for the 2000s.

Moreover, young people might well work too hard. "I bring in a video like *Indiana Jones and the Temple of Doom* on a Friday night and offer to lend it to the kids," laughed Matthew Low, an American who taught English in Omiya and the surrounding towns. "But the kids suck in their breath and say, 'I'm afraid I've got work to do.' They have very little enjoyment of youth here. Making out in the back seat of a car, getting a part-time job in the twelfth grade, getting a car—the kids here miss the whole track we get in the United States of money and responsibility."

Matthew had a point, and I confess to many ambivalencies about Asian education—even about its brightest spots, like Japan or Singapore. In particular, the high schools and "cram" schools work students too hard and try to set up assembly lines of knowledge in a way that dulls thoughtfulness. Colleges are not nearly as good in Asia as in America, Europe, or Australia; Japan, in particular, disgraces itself with its third-rate universities. And yet, for all the weaknesses and for all the Saturday-night slogging when kids should be out partying, I think that education as a whole is a reason to be optimistic about Asia's future. The global economy increasingly will depend on educated citizens, and in their focus on education I think some Asian countries are making a strong investment that will pay off in economic growth as well as social stability. In an increasingly globalized world, dependent on new technologies, American and European youngsters will find themselves competing not just with the hard-working Japanese-American boy around the corner but also with the Korean, Chinese, and Japanese who grew up in their home countries and are better educated because of it.

I never did get entirely comfortable with the Asian obsession with education, though. When my son Gregory was a three-year-old in Aiiku nursery school in Tokyo, we got a form from the school at the beginning of our first summer. The nursery school runs year-round, and it asked if we wanted to take any days off in the summer. The form had just a few lines to fill in: "name," "dates of proposed vacation," and "reason for proposed vacation." Reason? I didn't know what to write, but I had a sense that "we need a vacation" would be inappropriate. I asked a Japanese secretary in my office what to write. "Just say 'home visit to America,' " she advised. "That sounds kind of educational."

*Honda's robots, P2 and P3, play soccer in Tokyo. P2 and P3 are the most advanced humanoid robots in the world today and reflect Japan's excellence in robotics.* (Copyright © Honda Motor Company, Ltd. All rights reserved.)

### CHAPTER NINE

# A Land Where Robots Roam

## SHERYL WUDUNN

*"Well, I hope those twenty-first-century machines don't exhibit our
mob psychology . . . I mean, I wouldn't want to end up in a dark alley
with a band of unruly machines."*

—RAY KURZWEIL, *THE AGE OF SPIRITUAL MACHINES*

Ningyocho, or Puppet Village, is a traditional part of town in the northeast
of Tokyo. Along the main strip, shopkeepers sell old oven-fired mugs and
glazed plates and *o-sembei,* or deep-fried rice snacks that come flat,
puffed, rolled, or layered with seaweed. A corner Japanese bakery, with its
piping hot ovens in the back, draws people to its Ningyo cakes and cookies
with red bean paste. A toy shop sells big and menacing Ninja Turtle dolls
and keychains with wooden faces. Another store owner sells dresses with
frills and lace for about $50. There's a shrine that gets extremely crowded
on holidays. It's a bustling few blocks, with the kind of bustle that goes on
at its own pace, oblivious to the modernity of the surrounding Tokyo,
much less the rest of the world.

But slightly off to the side is a grayish, boxy, almost humble little build-ing: the home of the Softbank Corporation. When I passed through the secure doors on the top floor of Softbank, I found myself in a dimly lit foyer with clusters of deep black sofas and two columns of floor lamps. It felt like evening on a quiet and cozy street of outdoor cafes. "Come on in," called out a short, boyish-looking man, who had bounded out from an office toward the back. This was Masayoshi Son, a forty-one-year-old with strong, bright teeth gleaming beneath a big grin. I had expected a more stately fel-low. Instead, Son's eyes danced around as he spoke, and he seemed rest-less in his spacious office. His energetic gait was infectious, and as he led me into his office, I found myself quickening my pace just to keep up.

Masa Son, as some Americans call him, is a personification of the new, high-tech Asia. Sometimes described—not very accurately—as an Asian version of Bill Gates, Son heads Softbank and is Asia's leading Internet player. As a college kid in the 1980s, he had invented the first electronic dictionary in Japan, as he was struggling through American education with his newly acquired English. More than a decade later, he had par-layed an intuitive understanding of Internet commerce into a huge finan-cial empire that made him one of Asia's most admired businessmen. Earlier tycoons made their fortunes building roads or cars or banks or televisions, but Son built his from scratch by betting on the directions of technology. In the way he bridges cultures and takes risks and competes with Americans and Europeans, Son is an example of what is to come. He demonstrates Asia's push into information technology, a push that may have far-reaching consequences for Asia's competitiveness and the world as a whole. One of the fundamental questions that will determine Asia's success in economic development in the coming decades is whether it can master these technologies and profit from them.

One reason Asia is well positioned in technology is that math and sci-ence are built into people's lives much earlier than in the United States. When Gregory was at Kougai Elementary School, a Japanese school in Tokyo, I quickly realized how much better the math teaching was there than in the international schools—and for that matter, in American schools. When I visited Kougai's first-grade classes one Saturday morning (children attend two Saturday mornings a month) near the beginning of the school year, the teacher held up giant flash cards with a number, like THREE. I silently groaned, for I had often heard about the rote learning methods that Japanese schools used. The pupils bellowed back "SEVEN."

I perked up. The teacher's card said FOUR. Students yelled out "SIX." The teacher's card said EIGHT. The kids screamed "TWO." I saw they were responding with the number that added up to ten. The kids yelled the answers as fast as I could have. Then, later on in the school year, I discovered that while children at Gregory's international school were learning to add simple numbers, like 13 and 11, Japanese first-graders were already being drilled on problems like 158 plus 26. And even before they get into school, kindergartners become experts at Pac-Man, Game Boy, and other video games—they have computerized toys on their keychains—so that when they finally get to sit in front of a computer, they are comfortable with new technologies. When Japanese teenagers discovered pagers in the mid- to late-1990s, they developed a pager code to send messages to each other. It was kind of like a numerical Morse code, in which the numbers sounded like phrases. Three-nine, or *san-kyu,* in Japanese, sounds like "Thank you." Other examples are:

| | |
|---:|---|
| 0840 | Good Morning. |
| 530 0906 | I'm so sorry. I'll be late. |
| 49 | An emergency? |
| 14106 | I love you. |

The emphasis on math and science was the result of industrial planning over recent decades, as Asian schools strove to train engineers and scientists who would help build the country's manufacturing base to catch up with the West. In their eagerness to modernize, Asians showed their willingness to adapt to new methods and standards. Asia adopted the metric system to replace old measures such as the *catty,* for weight, and the *li,* for distance. It also (helpfully) abandoned the counting of time by old-fashioned divisions, like the "hour of the dog," which was how time was told in China and Japan as recently as the nineteenth century. Japan still clings to the *tsubo,* and Taiwan to its *p'ing,* for measuring areas. Meanwhile, America still uses the less convenient measures of pounds and feet. Now, its foundation in engineering puts Asia in a strong position to master some of the technologies that will dominate the global economy, but of course it is not clear whether Asian countries will actually capitalize on this educational edge. It is a leap to go from expertise in differential calculus to success in commercializing the technologies of daily life or from mastering the Second Law of Thermodynamics to writing a revolutionary software program. After all, technology, a word that comes from the Greek *tekhne,* means "art" and "craft" as well as "study," and so there is an element of artistry and creativity in shaping a craft for practical use.

Asia's success on that score is mixed. In the first round of the competition to scale the heights of technology, Asia triumphed. It took manufacturing to new efficiencies and levels of quality control, and so Japanese cars, steel, and audio and camera equipment were arguably the finest in the world. Some of these skills were derivative, but Japan's success in taking foreign technologies and improving them and then producing them cheaply was a technological marvel. And Japan is surprisingly clever at design and branding a winning product. Likewise, other countries such as South Korea, Taiwan, and even Malaysia managed to follow along and produce cheaper products with admirable efficiency and quality. The upshot was that much of the household hardware in American homes was designed or built in Asia, ranging from the car in the garage to the television in the den to the boom box in the bedroom.

Then, after winning the first round of the technology battle, Asia faltered. The United States came to dominate the postindustrial technologies of computer software and the Internet. This happened partly because of the proliferation in America of personal computers, the importance of universities and their links to the Internet, and America's advantage in mastery of English, the international language and, at least for now, the language of the Internet. Today, America is well ahead of Asia in postindustrial technologies. So the score is 1-1, with several rounds left to go. I don't know who will "win," and the metaphor of a sports match, of course, is not exactly correct, for each side learns from the other. The rush to top the rival's latest wonder squeezes out more energy and creativity from the one who is second-best. Japan and America also build on and benefit from each other's technologies, so that products get better and all sides, especially the consumer, end up winning.

Masayoshi Son already has become one of the most powerful financial forces in cyberspace, controlling key stakes in more than one hundred different Internet companies in the United States and Japan. He tied up with Microsoft and Global Crossing to set up a fiber-optic cable under the Pacific Ocean to bolster Japan's links to the rest of the world and to interconnect all of Asia. Softbank owns 28 percent of Yahoo and important stakes in Geocities, E-Loans, E*Trade, USWeb, Message Media, and

*Masayoshi Son, a not-entirely-Japanese who became Japan's greatest entre-
preneur, in his office in Tokyo.* (Courtesy of Stuart Isett)

TheStreet.com. Softbank and affiliated companies were soon worth more
than $25 billion, with Son's own stake a nice portion of it, and Softbank
was transformed from a tiny maverick to Japan's fifth-largest company,
surpassing Sony Corporation, Japan's symbol of postwar success, in size of
market capitalization in late 1999. In contrast to other Japanese businessmen who had struck it rich making hardware, Son was fascinated early on
by the World Wide Web and the ethereal linkages that made commerce
possible. "For the next ten years, we do nothing but Internet," Son told me
one afternoon. "Internet is the only focus I am interested in. Because
that's where the whole society is going to have a big revolution. That's
what I'm most interested in."

After the Asian financial crisis stormed through the region, Son and his
high-tech company became a controversial symbol of the regeneration of
Japan and the rest of Asia. He embodied a sense of real hope for the
region, and yet he also reflected an enormous uncertainty. Son has been a
dazzling star, but many stars fall, and skeptics have raised questions about
his tumultuous rise and about his empire, from his accounting practices

to cash flow shortages and even the steep tax bills he faces if he brings back gains from the wealth he accumulates abroad. Market plunges in America could bring him to his knees, and like many new billionaires, he has an empire that could become an empty shell almost overnight. In that sense, Son has personified many of the doubts about Asia's technological future. But whether Son himself emerges triumphant in the end, there seems to be something broader at work. Across the region, there is a growing number of high-tech entrepreneurs, of whom he is simply the most famous. Whatever happens to him, his early successes will have paved the way for others and underscored the growing recognition that technology must be a crucial element in Japan's revival. The late Prime Minister Keizo Obuchi invited him into a close circle of advisors for guidance on reviving the economy. I saw Son after he met Obuchi the first time, and he was beaming and basking in the new status he had just acquired. Son is so down-to-earth that it is hard to imagine him feeling comfortable around Japan's stiff leaders. "It was great," Son said about the meeting with Obuchi. "Right after the meeting, when I was leaving the room, the Prime Minister himself tapped my shoulder saying, 'Go, go, go!' " Son had discussed his ambitious plans for revitalizing small ventures in Japan and Obuchi had told him: "Do it freely."

"This is the beginning of a different Japan," Son continued, breaking out in his great big grin. "Japan is seeming much more open than in the past. For this kind of high-rank, government-established meeting—none of us guys had been invited. None of the venture companies were being invited. Probably I was the first guy, of my age, and our level of company, that they invited to give a speech."

Indeed, Japan's leaders sometimes seem like keepers of tradition, battling to defend the status quo rather than inspiring their people to go charging ahead into the twenty-first century. But even without government inspiration, Japanese companies flourished in high technology by showing flexibility and cleverness in absorbing and adapting new technologies to match national idiosyncrasies. Japanese consumers are not only fickle and finicky, they are sticklers for quality and aesthetics. More important, they have small homes and high energy bills. But luckily enough, so does the rest of the world, outside North America. So if products can pass the Japanese test, they stand a good chance of survival around the world. Thus, Japanese manufacturers took cars and miniaturized them and increased their fuel efficiencies to suit the narrow streets and the expensive oil and gas in Japan; those cars are the best in the business. They took computers and compressed them into flat-screen panels to fit into tiny homes; those screens are in houses around the world. They took cellular phones, cut the up-front costs, shaved their size, and added colors and functions; those phones propelled Japan into the forefront of mobile phone manufacturing and operating technology. Japan even took the mundane American toilet and added bells and whistles—that is to say, water sprays and hot-air jets. Who knows? Japanese toilets may make their way abroad, too.

The same process of remolding, rethinking, and rebuilding technologies also takes place, though to a lesser degree, in South Korea, Taiwan, Singapore, Hong Kong, and parts of nearly all the rest of Asia, including China, Malaysia, India, and Indonesia. In the past decade, these Asian centers have developed a knack for harnessing technology not only as consumers, but also as producers, manufacturing much of the world's computer chips, mother boards, and other hardware.

Most of the rest of Asia wants to follow Japan's path toward technological prowess, though in many cases it is a stretch. Burma, for instance, sometimes appears like an open-air museum of 1940s technology, with vintage cars chugging past colonial storefronts and slowly overtaking ancient bicycles; Burma has been left so far behind that soon all its possessions will be considered antiques, and it may finally be able to trade them for new ones. Likewise, the city of Bangalore, India, is a software center for the world, but the Indian government says that at present rates it will be another century before every Indian family has a toilet.

Yet it remains a distinct advantage that the workforce throughout Asia is increasingly skilled and educated. Marry that with the pragmatism and work ethic that is pervasive in much of Asia and the upshot is that technology is increasingly a pillar of Asia's future economy and that Asians themselves—especially Chinese and Indians—have become major figures in many high-tech start-ups in California and elsewhere. There is no country better than Japan at fusing and cross-fertilizing technologies to create something new, partly because Japan has nearly twice as many scientists and engineers engaged in core research and development as does America. One sees the harvest in patent figures. More than three times as many first filings of patents are in Japan as in either the United States or Europe. Even within the United States, something is striking about the patent filings. Consider this list:

**TOP TEN ORGANIZATIONS RECEIVING PATENTS FROM THE
U.S. PATENT AND TRADEMARK OFFICE IN 1999**

| RANK | COMPANY | HOME COUNTRY |
| --- | --- | --- |
| 1 | IBM | USA |
| 2 | NEC | Japan |
| 3 | Canon | Japan |
| 4 | Samsung Electronics | South Korea |
| 5 | Sony | Japan |
| 6 | Toshiba | Japan |
| 7 | Fujitsu | Japan |
| 8 | Motorola | USA |
| 9 | Lucent Technologies | USA |
| 10 | Mitsubishi Electronics | Japan |

Source: U.S. Patent and Trademark Office

That's right: Of the ten companies with the most patents filed in the United States in 1998, three were American and seven were Asian. It is true that the United States almost always invents the new paradigms and that Japan's contribution is mostly derivative. But it is the Japanese derivations that often transform those paradigms into popular new products. And there is every reason to believe that the two sides can work together (they already are), that alliances between technology companies in Asia and America will increase, and that Asian technologies will have more and more of an impact on Americans and Europeans.

In the past, the global competition focused on filling the consumer's garage and living room or den, and Asia boomed as it made the cars and televisions and stereos to fill those demands. But in the next twenty years, the competition will be to fill every single room of the house. The big companies, particularly in Japan, envision a time when houses are thoroughly wired and computerized, and they aim to dominate that wave of sales as well. Even if American companies maintain their edge in computer software and Internet commerce, Asian companies may dominate the business of providing smart toilets and smart refrigerators that blur the distinction between object and computer. And the two sides are already collaborating and combining their hardware and software. There will be some winners, but there will also be some blunders, and some of the new gizmos may not sell well. I, for one, am skeptical of the new Japanese washing machine that cleans people. The person climbs into a coffin-shaped machine and jets of water go to work for an eighteen-minute cycle. But who knows—this may be the modern bathtub for the next century.

Just as Asia came to dominate past waves of technology, such as car engines and memory chips and consumer electronics devices including televisions and Walkmans, so it is well positioned to be the central force in future waves, such as robotics, ceramics, cellular phone technology, fiber optics, and perhaps artificial intelligence. Japan has long been a king in gadgetry, and so one of the central questions of the coming decades will be how successfully Japan, along with the rest of high-tech-oriented Asia, can not only catch up to the West but also move with deft innovation and Draconian cost-savings to dominate the world's commercialization of new technologies.

A good place to see what is brewing in the marketplace is the house of the future built by Matsushita Electric Industrial Company. At the front door, a camera sends a video of a visitor to screens in each room, and if you are not home, the visitor's image is recorded and dropped into a home server, a storage center for the computerized, Internet-linked home. Alternatively, you can have the images of the visitor transmitted on the spot to your office PC or handheld digital device so that you can still receive the visitor in your home when you're not there. With remote-controlled security, you could even open the doors. In the living room, a fifty-inch plasma-display television screen turns the room into a miniature theater, offering hundreds of broadcast channels, video-on-demand, electronic shopping, travel booking, ticket purchasing, and family-calendar planning. An electronic program guide stores TV programs so that you can call them up by switching channels as if they were broadcast live, and you can bookmark a program and finish watching it in another part of the house. If paper tickets are necessary, they can be sent electronically to your printer.

In the bedroom, air conditioners, lights, and other appliances can be controlled by your voice command. Online education allows children to participate in classroom discussions and view themselves and other students asking questions, and two-way interactive learning programs can be tailor-made to students' level of ability and progress. The family's daily information center is a movable terminal that you can use to check messages (voice or written) from your kids, leave notes, check the kids' schedules, store health and household accounting records, and manage your use of water and electricity. In the bathroom, a health-monitoring toilet seat can measure a person's weight and body-fat ratio. It tests urine for sugar levels and automatically stores the results in the home server or sends an analysis to the local clinic by Internet. In the kitchen, the computer screen generates menus and, once you have chosen your meal, orders any necessary ingredients from a local shop and sends cooking instructions to the microwave oven. The refrigerator can register each item on the home server, so that you can glance at a computerized listing of what's inside. At the supermarket you can use a cell phone and call up the refrigerator's Internet address and check to see if you need beef or find out what you lack.

Companies around the world are scrambling to develop networked household appliances and to bring the outside world into the home through sensory online shopping. Japan can also play a major role in this virtual shopping if it builds on its skills in three-dimensional video games and in the aesthetics of retailing. Instead of clicking and shooting down the enemy, you will be strolling the virtual aisles, sniffing the aroma of teas and sweets, clicking and putting your beautifully wrapped apples or chunks of creamy chocolate into a virtual shopping cart with delivery to your door.

Exhausted and bleary-eyed, I got off a plane one evening at Haneda Airport in Tokyo. As I was trudging along with all the passengers through the dim halls, the cleaning crew was busy at work after hours. With smooth-sliding feet and stick-straight backs, the workers seemed tireless as they labored to vacuum and clean the floors. I walked over, luggage and all, to get a close-up look. The workers were the all-night crew as well as the all-day crew, the kind that never take vacations or complain or ask for raises: They were robots, roaming the corridors of Haneda Airport on their rolling boxy feet, vacuuming diligently without any adult supervision. The cleaning robots were not only vacuuming, they were also sweeping and waxing the floors. Japan leads the world in robots. Fifty-seven percent of the world's 720,000 robots are in Japan, and they are a common sight in factories and other places. Some experts believe that advances in computing and robotics will lead to huge numbers of new kinds of robots that work as personal helpers, scrubbing floors or mowing lawns or washing dishes. Likewise, smart cars may be able to ferry children to school or soccer matches without a driver, and smart diagnostic equipment may be able to check sick children at home without the need to take them to the doctor, or eventually conduct breast or prostate exams without the embarrassment of human contact. Smart personal assistants would pay bills and schedule appointments and translate conversations into foreign languages and conduct research on request. Much of this is some time away, but here and there one gets a glimpse of the potential.

Haneda Airport uses five robot cleaners, all with sensors so that they do not bump into walls or weary passengers. Though the robots don't smile and can't give directions to bewildered passengers, they are a milestone in the dream to remove the toil from human existence. "The robots are much more effective than humans," said Masaru Suzuki, an official of the airport company that uses the robots. He said that each robot can clean five hundred square meters per hour, while a human can only clean two hundred square meters in that time. And so teams of researchers have been painstakingly measuring the push and pull of muscles and tendons to mimic human movement and nudge the limits of computer manipulation to capture human-like motion. In the back of the minds of the engineers, aside from the prestige that goes with pioneering a new technology, is the hope that in the next decade or so every middle-class home may want a cleaning robot. But so far, the Haneda robots are more impressive than economically efficient, and this is at the heart of the problem of robotics—and a great deal of other technology—in Japan. The starkest sign of the dilemma is that while a half-dozen Japanese companies have developed cleaning robots, most have now dropped out of the market. The problem seems to be the cost: Packed with sensors and gyroscopes, the robots cost more than $30,000, which is more than anybody wants to pay for even the coolest vacuum cleaner. "Looking at the market," said an official of a Japanese company that has quit the field, "it seems it will not pay."

Indeed, sales of industrial robots were flat in Japan in 1999. But the robot market is robust in the United States, the second-largest market, and in Germany. And gains in computer speed and declining costs could make robots more practical. Fuji Heavy Industries, which has sold only twenty cleaning robots since it entered the business in 1994, is going full-speed ahead and is now testing a $130,000 unit that automatically takes the elevator from floor to floor, cleaning as it goes. At some point, the costs should come down because of the same force that drives both PCs and robotics: Moore's Law. That law says that engineers can effectively double the power of a chip annually while keeping the price constant. This kind of exponential growth is staggering: It is sometimes said that if automobiles had enjoyed similar gains since the beginning of the century, they would now cost a penny and travel at nearly the speed of light.

Already, robots are stepping creakily into the mainstream, and some of

Japan's robots are awesome in their achievements, if not always their practicality. Honda has created P2 and P3, human-like and human-sized robots that are probably the most advanced self-contained robots in the world today. They look like Arnold Schwarzenegger inside the armor of the Tin Man. P2 and P3 can walk and climb stairs, and they can even play soccer, though extremely badly. Robots are also beginning to move out of the factory and into the home, and again, the Japanese have been the quickest to spot the consumer opportunity and to build on their manufacturing prowess.

Take Aibo, Sony's robotic pet dog. Why would anyone want Aibo, when he could have the real lovable and cuddly thing? No matter—five thousand Aibo dogs went on sale for the first time in 1999 with a price tag of about $2,500 each. The Japanese units were sold out in twenty minutes. In the United States, the units sold out in four days. The pet dog comes preprogrammed with six emotions: happiness, sadness, anger, surprise, fear, and dislike. When Aibo is angry, he doesn't bite, but he does move away and his eyes glow red; when he is praised, his eyes sparkle green and he may sing a tune. Aibo has been programmed with various instincts, but these do not include chasing cats. That's just as well, because another Japanese electronics giant, Matsushita, has developed a prototype of a $450 robotic cat aimed at keeping elderly widows company.

"Good morning!" the cat says cheerily each morning as it wakes up, automatically. "How are you today?" And it responds with brief conversation when it is petted or spoken to. So far, it can say fifty different Japanese phrases, and there are plenty more to come. And it can pout, raise its eyebrows, and contort its face into many different expressions. Kenji Mizutani, one of the engineers who is designing the robot, proudly showed off a prototype in Matsushita's office and demonstrated that this is one plugged-in kitty. Connected to a cell phone, it downloaded and then passed on news and recorded phone messages. The eyes can also function as a clock and record when the kitty is happy or sad. And when the kitty is connected to a digital network control center, it can help monitor conversations and send a warning message if there is no talking in the house for an unusually long period of time. It's not so intrusive that it has a camera, but it's a kind of animal therapy for the elderly, who are a swelling portion of Asia's population and whose care is becoming one of the country's biggest challenges.

It's no wonder Matsushita is designing the pet kitty specifically for the elderly. Japan has the world's fastest aging society, with the proportion of

*Kenji Mizutani, an engineer at Matsu-
shita, holds a prototype of the robotic cat
that he helped design. The cat is at the vanguard of a wave of robotic devices that are
meant to function as pets and assistants.*

people over sixty-five rising from one in six people in the late 1990s to one in four by the year 2015. By the year 2025, Japan will have twice as many elderly as children. At the same time, that striking statistic will produce an even more remarkable one: The median age for all Japanese will be fifty. That burden of having to take care of the elderly has spawned a hot market in developing technologies that target the elderly. The investments may pay off as the baby boomers around the world retire in the coming decades. Equally important, a growing drive to innovate might also help spread a spirit of creation that will enable Japan to reinvent an economy that is threatening to wind down in the twenty-first century.

. . .

Haruo Saito was eyeing his doctor a bit nervously. Saito, a seventy-eight-year-old retired laborer, had been stiff and slow-moving since his stroke in the mid-1990s. He had already done his blood-pressure check and an electrocardiogram, and now he reported that he had been dizzy lately. The doctor, Shuichi Shigetomi, listened politely. But there was no warmth in his bedside manner—which was not entirely surprising, since he was thirty miles away. The consultation took place over a videophone and a small electronic monitoring box placed in Saito's home in the village of Katsurao, about 160 miles northeast of Tokyo.

In the first experiment of its kind, Japan launched a trial of tele-medicine in 1999 in Katsurao, a sleepy backwater without even a train sta-tion. Katsurao quickly became a laboratory for the kind of devices that will make life easier for its elderly, who make up 27 percent of its 1,900 inhab-itants. When I visited, each of Katsurao's five hundred households had its own videophone, and the village was planning to install electronic units in three hundred households to measure blood pressure, pulse, and other vital signs. Katsurao has no pharmacies of its own, and the only medical care is a part-time clinic open two afternoons a week. It takes a half day by bus and train to get to the nearest hospital, but the hospital is now linked electronically to the homes of Katsurao villagers, and pharmacies in the next village have agreed to send medicine by mail. All this of course was extremely expensive, though not to the villagers. Japan's Nippon Tele-phone and Telegraph (NTT) poured in fifty million yen, about $455,000, and was able to attract another $680,000 in central and local government funds. How did Katsurao, a place with no major industry, get the technol-ogy? I think it had to do with the officials. They are extremely aggressive and wanted Katsurao to become one of Japan's most wired villages. Instead of pouring money into bricks and bridges, as much of Japan does, Katsurao was pouring it into circuits and computers. The village was fast becoming a role model for the rest of the nation. Curious officials from across Japan were making the pilgrimage to Katsurao to gape and learn.

So now, Toshiko Yamada, a sixty-two-year-old retired accountant in Ka-tsurao, can rest assured that specialists are monitoring her health from the hospital. Ensconced in her home and surrounded by drawings by her grandchildren, Yamada was punching in "yes" or "no" answers to ques-tions like: "Have you eaten?" or "Have you had vertigo?" or "Do you have a problem breathing?" I watched as she then ordered an electrocardio-

*Haruo Saito has a doctor's appointment with the help of the video-phone in front of him.* (Sheryl WuDunn)

gram, whose results were automatically sent to health specialists by the machine. Every month, she gets a report summarizing her daily condition and noting any abnormalities.

"One time my pulse rate went above one hundred, and the public health official got worried and gave me a call," said Yamada, as she sat on a floor cushion beside the telehealth machine. "Then I realized that I had measured my heartbeat right after I had finished hanging up the laundry to dry upstairs."

Not everyone, though, is as receptive as Yamada to such conveniences. Her husband, Isao, who is sixty-six, staunchly resists giving in to home technologies. When he answers the videophone, he stands far enough away that the camera cannot capture him in full view. His hesitancy, how-ever, appears to be tied mostly to anxiety over the unfamiliar. "For now, I'm not using it," he says. But he adds, quickly: "But maybe I might someday."

The elderly are usually the hardest group to get hooked onto new tech-nologies, and Japan is certainly no different. For years, the same was true even for middle-aged white-collar workers. Japanese managers may have helped design the world's technologies, but when they sat at their desks, they turned to pen and paper and shunned the computer screen. That's partly why Japanese companies have strived to create easy-to-use gadgets. The problem is that by the 1990s, Japan had lost any hankering for entrepreneurship. High-tech companies around the world these days are usually small, flexible, and entrepreneurial, but in Japanese there isn't even a good word for entrepreneur. Instead, the Japanese like to borrow the term from English: *an-tore-purah-nah*.* But gradually people like Masayoshi Son, the Softbank king, emerged in Japan, Korea, China, Taiwan, and elsewhere. In the past, government ministries and large corporations recruited the nation's top talent, and most bright young people still eschew small companies. So while one-fourth of the Harvard Business School graduating class goes to work for small ventures these days, maybe one or two business graduates per class in Japan strike out at new ventures. But at least there is change. In the early years of the twenty-first century, the number of Internet users in Asia is expected to grow by more than 50 percent each year, according to estimates by the International Data Corporation. That could mean e-commerce sales of $72 billion by the year 2003, and already a growing swell of high-tech companies are recruiting and nurturing the entrepreneurs, the rebels, the risky financiers, and the creative types—people like Koichi Okawa.

Okawa is a beefy young Japanese with a short mop of black hair and a giggle bursting with joy. He started out on the conventional track, entering Tokyo's prestigious Keio University in 1989. He majored in commerce and merchandising, but he didn't much like college and hardly went to classes. Instead, he got part-time jobs, tutoring and bartending in Yokohama, a suburban city just outside Tokyo. He bartended for six or seven months, and then flunked his first year and was held back as a freshman for the second year. He was held back again after his second year, and then was expelled after flunking his third year. "I failed three times before I got kicked out," Okawa said with a hearty laugh. "I just didn't go to classes. It wasn't interesting, not that I had something to do besides school. My parents, the first time I flunked, thought it was unbelievable. The second time they said, 'I told you, don't make this mistake again.' The third time they just said, 'Go ahead and do something good for people.' I think they gave up on me.

* The Japanese have always had a word, *kigyoka*, to mean to "plan a company," but recently a similar word has appeared, also pronounced *kigyoka* but written with a different character. This new word, which is not yet in many dictionaries, literally means "one who starts a company," and it still does not capture the sense of the dynamic entrepreneurial spirit that is embedded in the English expression.

"After I got kicked out, I moved to Kyoto and worked in a liquor store for three years, carrying beer cases and other heavy things. Then I told them that I could handle a computer. The liquor store ran a franchise system and many stores weren't effectively managed. So the liquor store was trying to improve management, especially in handling distribution. I was using the computer to work out the plan for liquor storage." Okawa was still considered a young grunt in the liquor store and was always at the beck and call of the top managers. Meanwhile, he was tapping away at night on the Internet, and when he began making suggestions to management about computerization and was rebuffed, he became even more resistant to authority. Soon he came to realize that he wanted to develop an Internet business "because it is a world without any older people who grumble and supervise you and take control. It's a fresh new business. I think that in Japan, outside of the Net industry, it's difficult to try something you want to do. Older people will say, 'You better not do this or that,' or they offer advice to do something in a certain way. It's difficult to try something new. So I was attracted to the Net."

Okawa quit his job and took a year or so off "just to think" and look at web pages. There were many growing Internet businesses and he began observing different models, evaluating which ones were successful and how long they took to make money. He was chatting online with people. Then one day in cyberspace he met Eiichiro Fukami, a scrappy computer programmer with a long, flowing drape of black hair who favors worn T-shirts. The two men met in person, and six months later they started working on a new venture. Together they devised software to allow users to distribute email simultaneously to thousands of people at once. Users of ordinary email systems in Japan could send out only one hundred emails at a time. It got more complicated when the numbers soared beyond that. Okawa and Fukami also launched Magmag, Inc., a web site and compilation of Japanese magazines. Some people think of Magmag as a kind of search engine for Japanese magazines, and it offers electronic subscriptions to email magazines. Every week there are two hundred new magazines on the list, which they distribute three times a week. In the summer of 1999, their tiny shoestring operation had 1.4 million readers, four-fifths of whom were in their twenties and thirties. Advertisers showered Magmag with cash and they were profitable within a year, before they even had a chance to file the papers to set up their company. By 1999, sales were running $180,000 a month, and half of that was profit.

Why were they successful?

*Koichi Okawa answers the phone in his office. He began running
Magmag, his magazine mailing lists, out of a tiny office bursting
with wires and computers in Kyoto. A brown envelope becomes his
nameplate, with red scribbling in Japanese: "Shacho," or President.*

(Sheryl WuDunn)

"Luck," said Okawa, chuckling, and then he turned serious. He said
that Magmag has a special relationship with its readers. "With a search
engine, you can't develop a close relationship. With a mailing list, you can
create a closer relationship with readers and it's difficult to break that." He
responds to four to five emails a day, out of hundreds sent in. When he
once asked for some jokes on a certain topic, hundreds of responses
arrived the next day.

Okawa bought an apartment near the office so that his employees,
instead of sleeping at their desks in the office, can crash at night in a pad
that has a bath, a kitchen, and beds. His parents also call whenever they
see a photo of him in the newspaper or to offer comments. "If I took a year
to explain to them what I do in the Internet business, they wouldn't understand. Even as I show them articles about me, they express their concern
that the Internet business is dangerous. They say, 'It's not a good idea to be
involved in that business.' " At least for now, Magmag has an embarrassment of riches. "We haven't utilized the profits very well yet," explains
Okawa. He adds, with evident ebullience: "They're just piling up."

Okawa, like Japan, had better keep running to stay ahead. Japan is Asia's leader in technology, but other countries are also making important advances. Taiwan and South Korea are well-known competitors in various hardware components. Malaysia also wants to join the race and is developing a smartcard for all citizens, a bit like a credit card but with a chip that functions as passport, driver's license, and national identity card. Singapore has become the first country in the world to run a broad-ranging fiber-optic cable system to link ordinary homes, allowing not only super-high-speed Internet access but two-way capabilities to run burglar alarms, order pizzas, provide video conferencing, and order movies on demand. Even India is increasingly involved, training top software engineers in its educational system. America will probably continue to dominate the software business—although a growing share of the writing of the code will be done remotely, in places like India—but as homes are wired the commercial applications will increasingly come from Asia. And as technology becomes more and more important for the entire global economy, Asia stands to be a major beneficiary.

Japan demonstrated with cellular telephones that it can overcome a late start. Regulations kept Japanese cell phones expensive and little-used—indeed, one could only rent them in the beginning—until American pressure forced the business wide open in 1994. Paradoxically, that American pressure was the best thing that could have happened to Japan's cell phone companies. As prices dropped, the market took off and Japanese companies were forced by the fires of competition from Motorola and Nokia to become some of the best cell phone makers and operators in the world. They quickly overcame the late entry, and my Japanese-made cell phone always amazed American friends because it was so tiny and lasted so long without a battery charge. In 1999, Japan had fifty million twinkling and tinkling portable phones in use, and it became the early leader in the third generation of wireless technology, wideband CDMA (code division multiple access), that speeded up the flow by widening the "channels" through which data and voice were sent. A subsidiary of Nippon Telegraph and Telecommunications, NTT DoCoMo, was also the first company to develop mobile phones that let you buy and sell stocks, reserve tickets for trains and airplanes, transfer funds between bank accounts, and send and receive text messages and simple drawings. Another mobile phone has a tiny camera that sends a shaky TV-style color image to a small screen on the other party's hand-held video phone. DoCoMo was also the first company to develop a special locator system, allowing parents to call their kids on a mobile phone, which automatically faxes back a map of the exact location of the kid's whereabouts. For many Japanese, this mobile phone eased worries about where their kids or elderly parents were. For Japanese companies, it was the first stage in a dream that mobile phones will become a key accessory—as common as wrist watches—that people take when they leave home.

Ever competitive, South Korea is scrambling to outdo its Japanese rivals in telecommunications. Authorities in South Korea, a nation of forty-five million people, set a goal to become one of the world's top five leaders in information and communications technologies. Companies like LG Electronics (a subsidiary of the LG Group) and Samsung Electronics are trying to seize on these new technologies as a chance to gain a place in the global marketplace. The first company to make a portable device for playing music downloaded from the Internet was a Korean one, Saehan Information Systems, with its MPMan, and it was eclipsed by the MP3 player made by a Korean-founded company, Diamond Multimedia System, in the United States. Samsung Electronics's Yepp players have flooded the world and hope to capture 30 percent of the total market in the next few years. Japanese companies, and to a lesser extent Korean ones, are also making inroads into fulfilling their long-held dreams of putting a digital TV in every home. Though current versions are expensive, it is just a matter of time before they become cheaper and more commonplace.

South Korea also turned its late entry in cell phones into an advantage by leap-frogging technology. In fact, when Korea went cellular, it chose the state-of-the-art CDMA, which was slightly ahead of the current technical prowess of most mobile phones in Japan, America, and Europe. Long before American cars had global positioning systems, South Korean taxis already were installing GPS computer screens to give directions and alert drivers to the routes with the least traffic. In 1998, the early days of CDMA technology, two-thirds of the world's CDMA subscribers were in Asia and those left behind were scrambling to keep apace. During three months in the spring of 1999, as Indonesia was still staggering under the pressure of political turmoil and economic crisis, the growth in sales of personal computers in that country was the highest in Asia, outside Japan. And in catching up, Asian countries are sometimes leaping ahead. In China, when authorities opened their stock exchange in Shanghai, they chose the most advanced trading technology at the time, and even now the Shanghai Stock Exchange is one of the most modern in the world. Then

Tokyo, a technology exporter but a slow corporate user of technology, pulled a fast one. The Tokyo Stock Exchange was so outdated that authorities did away with it, and now traders do their transactions electronically without any physical exchange at all.

Technology is fast becoming a passkey to riches, and in some ways that are worrisome, Asians are racing into technologies with the same frenzy with which they built their tall buildings and extravagant cities. They were practically begging the world to get in on the action, drumming up schemes to get foreigners to invest in technology and upgrade it. In Malaysia, as if the Petronas Towers weren't record-breaking enough, the government opened an "intelligent city" called Cyberjaya, a special multimedia zone that it hoped would become an engine for economic recovery, and Lucent Technologies was one of the early investors to help lay the groundwork in telecommunications. Malaysia's smartcard also aimed to be one of the most comprehensive in the world. Even Vietnam was holding e-commerce seminars.

There are, of course, plenty of reasons to be skeptical about Asia's ability to transform its human resources into a technological powerhouse that rivals the West. Asian countries are still hampered by bloated bureaucracies and by a shortage of venture capital for high-tech ventures. Employees at large companies have also often been leery of using technologies for fear that this modern mechanization might ultimately rob them of their jobs. Japan and other Asian countries, for example, initially missed the PC boom. Japan was leading the way on a supercomputer project, and NEC is still building the world's fastest computer. But the center of the industry turned out to be PCs rather than supercomputers, and Asia got left behind. Moreover, the lack of venture capital made it difficult for entrepreneurs to start technology companies, and companies were late in awakening to the opportunities of electronic commerce. Japan's tardiness held back the rest of Asia as well. With English the pivotal language of the Internet, at least for now, countries such as Japan and China, which rely on Chinese characters, also have had a major handicap. Approaching a computer is nerve-wracking enough for many people, but it is particularly overwhelming when one has to cross a language chasm, as Toshiyuki Shimizu found out.

"Look at this," he complained, puzzling over a computer guide that looked like a strange mix of Japanese and English. " 'Start button.' 'Click.' 'Start menu.' 'Device.' 'Slot.' This is all in English!" he said. Well, not quite all English but pretty close. The first sentence actually read: *Sutaato*

*Asia is a dizzying kaleidoscope of technologies, home not only to robots
but also to millions of families who seem barely touched by the twentieth
century. This low-tech Ping-Pong game, played over a board on the
dirt, underscores the gaps that have arisen. For this village in China's
Henan Province, the next step is not the Internet, but rather electricity.*

(Sheryl WuDunn)

*botan* (start button) *o kurikku* (click) *suru, sutaato menyuu* (start menu)
*ga hyoji sareru.* In other words, click the start button and the start menu
will appear. It is a bit overwhelming for the Japanese person who sits down
at a *kiiboudo* (keyboard) for the first time and is told to move the *mausu*
(mouse) and *daburu-kurikku* (double-click) on the *aikon* (icon).

"I look at a computer book and I can't even figure out how to get
started," fretted Kimii Oishi, a seventy-four-year-old woman who has
joined Tokyo's Grandma *Pasukon saron* (personal computer salon) and
was clutching a *konpyutaa manyuaru.* "Look at this," she added. "*Manyuaru.* I don't even know what that is. What's a *manyuaru?* I don't even
know how to begin." A *manyuaru* is a manual. And since there is already a
word in Japanese meaning the same thing, *manyuaru* reflects the tendency to adopt foreign words even when there are already perfectly good
ones available in Japanese. So when Americans are ready to smash their

computers for generating error messages, they should recognize that it could be worse. They could be *toraburushyuutingu* (troubleshooting) using the Japanese version of Microsoft Windows and getting *herupu* (help) like the one beginning: "What to do if the *fairu* [file] does not appear in the correct *doraibu* [drive] and *foruda* [folder] of the open *fairu* [file] *daiarogubokkusu* [dialogue box]."

Educators may have done an outstanding job in teaching math and science, but they tend to be traditional and have been slow in teaching computer skills. In schools in England, there are eleven students for every computer in the eighth grade; in the United States, there are sixteen. In Japan there are twenty-five, and in Korea there are fifty-seven. American universities graduate legions of computer specialists each year; Japan hardly any. Instead, Japanese companies are supposed to hire ordinary engineers and then train them in computers. Authorities are trying to change that, and Japanese educators agreed to incorporate the application of computers more fully into the elementary-school curriculum after the year 2002.

The issues are not always cut and dry. When five Japanese publishing companies sought approval for their social science textbooks for the year 2000, four of them were turned down because the books included the addresses of private web sites and the government did not want to authorize free publicity. Another problem is that Asian technology has often not been linked to financial judgments about making money. As the Haneda Airport robots suggest, often products have been developed because they were neat and prestigious rather than because they were efficient. Throughout the region, many of Asia's high-tech projects—even in robotics—began to look like white elephants because they consumed years and years of work by intelligent researchers, along with scads of money. Such large projects are always something of a gamble and the potential is sometimes enormous. Japan is sponsoring some fascinating work on speech recognition and telephone translators, for example, so that computers can automatically translate telephone conversations between Japanese and English: One caller would speak English into a phone, and the other party would hear Japanese. It is pathbreaking technology, especially for non-English-speaking nations, and might be a magnificent dividend to globalization when it is rolled out into the market. But the research has already taken more than a decade and no one knows if the project will pay off financially.

Finally, a country can have all the basics for technological success—

creative inventors, highly trained scientists, hard workers, plenty of money—and still fail. After all, look at what happened to China. It had invented printing in the eleventh century, several hundred years before printing hit Europe. China also invented gunpowder in the tenth century. It devised the wheelbarrow, the stirrup, and the compass, then paper, silk, tea, and porcelain. The Chinese had a water-driven machine for spinning hemp in the twelfth century, six hundred years before the Industrial Revolution in England. The Chinese used coal and coke in blast furnaces for smelting iron in the eleventh century on a scale reached by Britain only seven hundred years later.

But then, what happened to technological prowess in China? Nothing. That splendid culture and its wondrous inventions developed early in the last millennium went virtually nowhere. That's because, though it had brilliant inventors, China's stratified and compartmentalized society, its state control, and its rigid educational system did not allow people to harness, build upon, or spread the use of those technologies. Instead, the state stifled and sequestered innovation in a closed and inflexible society. China withdrew into itself, and the same forces that cut short the Chinese age of exploration, which had been symbolized by Admiral Zheng He, also paralyzed Chinese science and technology and thus China's economy. Chinese leaders may certainly have recognized the value of their inventions, but they feared a loss of control and would not let them spread or cross over into other fields. That could happen again if Asia doesn't watch out. I think it is unlikely that Asian countries will impede the spread of technology and withdraw into themselves again. But success is also a matter of degree, and Asian countries are still burdened by heavy-handed bureaucracies, social rigidities, and a low tolerance for contrariness. The best and the brightest in countries like Japan and Korea still go into government ministries, burdening the economy, rather than into businesses, stimulating it. The hurdles are high for those outside the blueblood elite, and the cultural barriers are still significant. Indeed, Softbank's Son perhaps is Japan's leading entrepreneur today for a simple reason: He is not exactly Japanese. His grandparents came to Japan from Korea, where his ancestors had been for twenty-one generations after migrating from China. As a result, he is usually regarded as a member of the Korean minority, which has suffered intense discrimination over the years. If Son had been purely Japanese, he would have had more options open to him— and thus might have ended up a faceless banker or bureaucrat. It was partly because the best avenues were not open to him that he had to blaze his own trail.

Son grew up in a small town on the southern Japanese island of Kyushu. His father and other Koreans illegally built their houses on land owned by Japan National Railways, sparking a long-running conflict with the authorities. It was on that land that Son's father raised pigs and chickens and illicitly made sake. The home brew apparently was lucrative, for he became the first person in the town to buy a car. In those days, Koreans in Japan were persecuted—virtually barred from the nation's best schools, from the most prestigious corporations, and from Japanese citizenship— and Son's Korean nationality cast a shadow over his boyhood, particularly when his family moved out of their Korean neighborhood so that the young Son could attend a better Japanese school. To try to melt into society, the family took on a Japanese last name, Yasumoto.

"I was a good student, but in those days I had a darkness in my mind all the time," Son wrote in an essay. "It was because of my nationality. When I was with friends, I was very happy. When I came back home alone, I had the feeling that I was hiding something from my friends." He took on his real Korean-Chinese name, Son, only when he went to America at sixteen to go to high school and then on to the University of California at Berkeley. It was his American experience, he says, that laid the groundwork for his career. "My learning experience in the United States made me think much more open-mindedly," said Son. "If I had stayed all the time in Japan, I probably would have become much more conservative, just as other Japanese."

His wife, a Japanese, also had an unconventional fighting spirit. When they married and she took on Son's surname, the Japanese authorities wouldn't let her register the unusual name "Son" because it wasn't in their directory of names. She petitioned and after a lengthy battle the authorities relented and she registered the name. Months later, Son went to the authorities to change his name from Yasumoto to Son. The authorities looked at his application and said, Well, yes, you can register because there is now a precedent for your name: your wife's.

Son's identity as an outsider helped him in some ways once he became an entrepreneur. He developed a knack for adjusting to new situations, and he sometimes comes across as a chameleon. He can backslap and guffaw and jabber in colloquial English with American investment bankers and discuss the details of new computer chips with the techies, and then he can turn somber and bow and spew out honorifics in polite Japanese to blend into a Japanese business crowd.

One of the legacies of the Asian economic crisis is that it opened more doors for outsiders, people like Son who had no chance to climb a safe corporate ladder and were forced to take risks in high-tech start-ups. In the past, outsiders were simply locked out of the establishment—no financing, no connections, no contracts steered their way. But now, rigidities are softening and the segmentation in society is breaking down. Outsiders are building bridges into the establishment; salarymen are journeying over those bridges, leaving their corporate careers behind them; high-tech companies in Japan are strengthening their ties to research universities to develop future research; and there is much more collaboration among different parts of corporate society.

Jang Chang Ik, the Korean computer programmer at LG, wasn't left totally in the lurch. The company had given him a four-month reprieve to figure out what to do with his life, and he used that time to push ahead. After a severe bout of depression, Jang poured his entire savings of about $45,000 into starting his company. Every bank turned his company down for a loan, which wasn't surprising since they themselves were strapped for cash. Yet Jang paid calls on prospective clients—his old clients from LG—to see if they would buy his services, and he asked his old colleagues at LG if they would send software programming contracts his way. Gradually he found business, at first mostly from LG, and then he attracted more clients after he rushed through a project successfully in a couple of months. Soon he was turning a profit, and he had thirteen employees on a payroll that he planned to expand to twenty. Jang dreams that his little company will become the next-generation LG Group—or at least his new livelihood for the next couple of decades, and perhaps for his two sons, who are now thirteen and fifteen. Jang happened to have some useful skills and was taking a risk ahead of his peers. But he is like other white-collar workers in Korea and the rest of Asia: He would never have had the nerve to set off as an outsider and start his own business if life had gone as he had hoped. Moreover, his transformation from corporate conformer to entrepreneur was quick. "At LG, I was considered a conformer," admitted Jang. "I did conform, but that doesn't mean I was not individualistic."

.  .  .

All across the region, there have always been mom-and-pop stores, from noodle shops to needlecraft makers. After all, many of today's giant companies were founded by brave and calculating young men, people like Akio Morita and Masaru Ibuka, who started making tape recorders and transistor radios in an enterprise that became Sony Corporation. Konosuke Matsushita started making electric sockets with his wife and her brother and turned the company into the powerhouse that is Matsushita Electric Industrial Company. Soichiro Honda, who hooked an engine to a bicycle to make Japan's first motorcycle, built his company into Honda Motor Company. But it will take more than a few entrepreneurs to reinvent an economy and make Asia boom again. New institutions and new mechanisms need to be built to foster the trickle of entrepreneurialism. One of the difficulties for young Asian companies is that there's no money. Banks don't lend because start-ups are too risky. The memory of the speculative bubble is still recent in Japan and the pain left over from excessive lending in the rest of Asia still numbs. Up until the late 1990s, venture capital funds were investing only at later stages, if at all. So the big technology companies like NEC Corporation and Fujitsu, Ltd., have tried cultivating a new spirit by holding contests for the best spinoffs. The winners get marketing, production, and technology support from the parent company but are given free rein to make their own decisions on the belief that such independence can make them nimble enough to be competitive where the parent company might stumble. There have been some takers, but those programs have never become a major force. Instead, the pressure is coming from outsiders, like foreigners who are bringing in new attitudes toward shareholder governance and a greater reverence for profitability. And the Asian financial crisis brought about a great deal of self-reflection and national inward-thinking about how to create the right systems for regeneration. Financial systems are being shaken up and venture capitalists are emerging in Asia, particularly in Japan. Though the amounts of funds are nowhere near the $12 billion to $16 billion in venture capital sloshing around the United States, funds are forming like wildfire, foreign investors are piling in as well, and money is being handed out, perhaps faster than the entrepreneurs can soak it up. Yoji Kawakei, who started a 250-million-yen fund, worth about $2.5 million, at Future Venture Capital in the Japanese city of Kyoto, says he still has to persuade small companies to take his money because he is not a traditional source of funds, like a bank or the government. But he has invested in several companies and he has started a second fund. "It's opposite from the United States in that I visit the companies to persuade them because businessmen don't fully understand the advantages of venture capital," said Kawakei. His attempts, however, are increasingly successful: "I think the entrepreneurial spirit is on the rise." No, it is not Silicon Valley, and it may never be, but more and more high-tech start-ups are being launched everywhere—often with the labor of laid-off workers—and schools are doing more to teach English and computer skills, even if it is because companies are donating computers.

Outsiders like Son are preaching more openly about their methods of management, ones that challenge the norm and may offer an edge for the future. For instance, they are turning to venture capitalists and equity markets, rather than banks, as major sources of capital. But once again, growth is becoming a key goal, often at the expense of profits. Japan is familiar with this idea of taking losses first to expand market share, called *son shite, toku toru,* or literally, take losses, get benefits. It was a practice for which Japan was praised in the 1980s and rebuked in the 1990s, and now it is becoming a hallmark of the global Internet and information industry, with its easy access to equity. Back then, Japanese companies had a cheap call on credit, and now for the most part they don't, but they still have the experience and the know-how in building market share. Ironically, Son, the one outsider who is gaining a following, has himself been an expansionist, an imperialist in the Internet world, and the soaring value of Internet stocks has perhaps exaggerated his ability to pick individual winners. He admits that his appetite for expansion has often outstripped his financial ability. His ambitions for growth scared away his original bankers at the Industrial Bank of Japan, which had long been one of the nation's most prestigious institutions (that missed opportunity turned out to be only one of the many mistakes made by IBJ, which merged with two other venerable Japanese banks). Initially, Son was lucky, and the share prices of his start-ups exploded in their public offerings. In one of his early years, his own share price in Japan rose more than tenfold during the course of the year, from 6,610 yen, or $60, in January, to 79,400 yen, or $722, in late November. Just as his stock was soaring, however, his losses were climbing, and that autumn the company recorded a six-month loss—which he claimed was a one-off deal—of about $34 million. Indeed, months later, his stock tumbled too. The problem is that share-price bubbles may burst, saddling Son with many corporate carcasses, including his own. Son has suffered many setbacks already, and he is very vulnerable. Moreover, as Son ventures into relatively new territory—like developing a new stock exchange—he is taking risks in areas in which he has no proven expertise. For now, though, he is maneuvering through the venture landscape in the United States, Japan, and the rest of the world.

Son is banking on the prospect that a growing number of people will move, like Jang, from large corporations to their own start-ups, and he is hoping to make a good return by supplying the investment capital that has been so scarce for high-tech entrepreneurs. Likewise, his project in Japan to develop an electronic, over-the-counter Nasdaq exchange—more technologically sophisticated than Nasdaq in New York—creates an institutional flow of capital to cash-starved start-ups. In 1999, he set up a bevy of new venture capital funds to pour money into budding businesses in the United States and Japan. Then, partly to court these start-ups, Son held a grand reception for 1,400 entrepreneurs at the Royal Park Hotel, near Softbank's offices in Ningyocho. A giant hall with glittering chandeliers was filled with rows of chairs, which were snapped up by entrepreneurs as they flowed rapidly into the space. Many of them were in their thirties and forties. There were women, too.

Son began the rally explaining how easy it is to get capital or to be listed on Nasdaq in the United States, compared to the slow, sometimes twenty-year, process it traditionally took a Japanese company to prove itself with earnings and respectability before listing over-the-counter at home. Son gestured boldly with his hands as he spoke eagerly about his project to start the Nasdaq Japan exchange; his voice rose with emotion as he recounted his experience in his early days when he was struggling to establish his business. He called upon his guest entrepreneurs to join his efforts in making a new market.

"This is a historical day," Son bellowed in Japanese to the crowd. "Let me ask you some questions first. People who already have their own business, raise your hand! Ah, more than 95 percent. If you have more than fifteen employees, raise your hand. More than 85 percent. If your business is more than one year old, raise your hand. Ah, I would say 90 percent." He looked out at the audience and declared, "I am sure that there are many among you who have big dreams but who are wishing that if only you had some capital, some human resources, and some social recognition. . . . I was feeling the same. It took a very long time for me to establish my business. I wanted to take my company public earlier on. I started to think that if there is no market where entrepreneurs can raise money, then I will make such a market myself. That is the venture business.

"Is the current stock market free? Fair? I don't think so. I felt there were too many aspects that were inconvenient. And I will change that. As far as the law is concerned, the United States and Japan are not that different. But in actual practice, the two are as different as heaven and earth. . . . I would like to create a Nasdaq Japan Club with you and set up a forum like this for me to get directly in touch with you at least four times a year. If you want to join the club, please leave your business cards in the cardboard box in the lobby.

"When I started Softbank seventeen years ago," he continued, "I was standing on top of a soapbox, a crate for oranges, making a speech. I said, 'I will make my business as large as one trillion yen, two trillion yen.' I had two people [in my company] at the time. In two months, both of them quit. One time, an ex–truck driver responded to my recruitment and he said, 'I know nothing about computers.' But I quickly said, 'But your eyes are filled with aspiration. Come to my company immediately.' In fact, he was the only applicant. I know how founders of businesses feel. . . . You just want more good people, more capital. The branch office head of a bank was like a god. I begged my bankers, clinging to their sleeves, saying I would be in trouble if I didn't transmit ten million yen in one week. My heart fell whenever I received a call from the head of the personnel department because I thought, 'How many people are quitting this time?'

"But after the initial public offering, the business environment changed considerably. But then I was called 'Soft Pank' every time I made a business acquisition [*panku*, in Japanese, refers to a tire going flat]. When the price of Softbank shares came down, many people said, 'We told you.' But I was not beaten down. And I survived. This is the venture spirit. I have gone through the time of aches and pains. I have gone through a time of losing my hair. My body really shows what I went through. But things will change. You will get access to the passport.

"Now, the Japanese economy is just like the ruins after a fire. The storm of lay-offs is blowing over. Where do those laid-off workers go? They should come here! Those who want good human resources, please raise your hands. The dawn of a new Japan is near. Let's do it together."

It was a rousing speech that demonstrated a charisma that Son rarely displayed to the Japanese public. Entrepreneurs scrambled to put their *meishi*, or namecards, in his cardboard box. Some people clamored to ask questions. Some were just awestruck. Others were encouraged to see a can-do spirit that so often gets knocked down in Japan. Even for the skeptics at that meeting, it was hard not to be optimistic about Asia's prospects for cultivating new technologies and boosting its economy on their back. A millennium ago, Asia had great technologies but missed its chance to commercialize them. Now, it is finally getting another chance.

*Part Three*

# CLOUDS ON THE HORIZON

*Ryu Gu Che, a Korean-Japanese, pays his respects at the Ear Mound in Kyoto, Japan. This hill was made four hundred years ago with the ears and noses of perhaps one hundred thousand Koreans whom the Japanese army slaughtered in its attacks on Korea. As proof of their victories, army units brought back the ears and noses to Japan, and so there are several such ear mounds and nose mounds around Japan. Most Japanese have never heard of the Ear Mound, but predictably it is better known in Korea, where it is regarded as a product of typical Japanese brutality.*

### CHAPTER TEN

# Prisoners of History

## NICHOLAS D. KRISTOF

*The past is never dead. It's not even past.*

—WILLIAM FAULKNER

*History repeats itself??*

Almost every time I visited Omiya, I saw Shinzaburo Horie in his garden. A lean and rugged farmer in his early eighties, he was all muscle and gristle and thinning hair and leathery skin, tirelessly tending his crops in the hot midday sun. Even as an old man he was athletic, and I believed the tales I had heard about how as a youth he had leaped from the cliff into Omiya's swimming hole forty feet below—the only boy ever to do that. Horie lived on the main street of Omiya and always waved politely to me as I passed, adding a greeting of "*konnichiwa*" if he was within speaking range. He came across as a bit shy and formal and gentlemanly, a model of benevolence.

One day he agreed to talk to me about bygone days of Omiya and Japan. Horie sat ramrod straight in his chair, wearing nice, clean slacks and a shirt that looked as stiff as he did, and so I tried to set him at ease, joking about my poor Japanese and asking gentle questions about life in prewar Omiya. Then gradually we came to the war and his life as a soldier, and he began to fidget nervously.

"Where did you serve in the war?" I asked.

"China." He sighed, took deep breaths, looked down at his shoes, and added: "In Manchuria."

"What did you do there?"

"I was just a soldier," he replied without looking at me. "It was a terrible time. There was very little food, and it was cold and dangerous. It was awful." He fidgeted even more, shifting his weight back and forth on the chair, occasionally stroking his stubbly chin nervously.

"Did you see much fighting?" I asked.

Horie grew tense and agitated. "Some," he said briefly, and then he sidetracked the conversation with stray and irrelevant comments. Yet gradually he began to peel away his memories, and he described his military camp in China. I asked about his life and what he remembered, and his hands began to shake like dry leaves in the wind. Finally, after a long parry-and-thrust conversation, I asked: "What was the worst thing about life there?" He took a deep breath, gulped, and let down his guard.

"There was one time when I ate human flesh," he said, and he sighed deeply and paused to control himself. He leaned forward, looking me straight in the eye for the first time, and his eyes were aching with pain. "I've never told anybody, not even my wife," he whispered. "Nobody knows."

My stomach was churning, and I wondered if I had heard him right. "How did it happen?"

"My buddies and I were all hungry, because there was no food anywhere." Horie looked as if he might cry. "And then all of a sudden there was some fresh meat for sale in the local market and we quickly bought it and cooked it."

I started to say something, but he silenced me and continued: "It was the first meat we'd had in a long time, and we thought it was delicious. We were thrilled."

Horie paused and took several deep breaths as he stared down at his shoes before continuing: "And then the military police came around, asking whether anybody had bought meat in the market. We said that we had, and they explained what had happened. The meat was from a Chinese boy of about sixteen."

*Shinzaburo Horie and his wife stroll through Omiya, Japan. He
has never told his wife about his wartime experiences.*

"What had happened?" I asked softly.

"Some Japanese soldiers who were hungry had killed the boy and eaten
some of his meat and sold the rest to the Chinese merchant, and we
bought it from the merchant."

Horie stopped and stared down at the floor for a long time. Finally, I
intruded: "Was anybody punished for that?"

"I heard that the Japanese soldiers were punished for killing and eating
the boy, but I don't know," he said heavily. "It was just a rumor. And anyway, I don't know how they were punished. My buddies and I didn't get
into trouble."

"Of course not," I said, trying to reassure him. "It wasn't your fault. It
was an accident. You didn't know that it was human flesh."

"I can't forget the fact that I ate a human being," Horie said, looking at
me piercingly. "It was only one time, and not so much meat, but after sixty
years I can't put it behind me."

Nor can Asia as a whole. Just as Horie was still haunted by his past, so is
most of Asia. The continent's future remains deeply undermined by its
history, whose antagonisms could lead to new wars or to an unraveling of a

promising economic future. My optimism about Asia is tempered by these concerns, for Asia's future seems a hostage to its history, and I feel the shadow of the past acutely when I talk to ordinary people like Horie. Often they try, like Horie, to keep the past buried, but it always climbs out again.

Horie was part of an army that was as courageous as it was cruel. While every American soldier in the Pacific in World War II was backed by four tons of equipment, each Japanese soldier had just two pounds' worth. One Allied soldier surrendered for every three dead, while among the Japanese 120 died for each one who surrendered. Yet these brave, disciplined troops bayoneted babies and raped girls and beheaded prisoners on a scale that exceeded that of any other modern army.

I think of Horie as a symbol of Asia's difficulties in coming to terms with its past. Just as he can't even talk to his wife or grandchildren about what happened, so Asia is weighed down by a history that for decades has festered without healing. Although Asia has seemed remarkably peaceful since the end of the Vietnam War, the peace has been a fragile one, concealing antagonisms that could still erupt in an instant. Historical grievances still create risks of war—over Taiwan, Kashmir, and islands such as the Spratlys, Paracels, and Diaoyu/Senkakus—and lead countries to pour resources into fighter planes and submarines rather than education and fiber-optic cable. The historical burdens also stand in the way of economic cooperation. Japan's capital cannot be used to exploit Siberia's resources, for example, because of the bitterness that is one of the great legacies of World War II. And the mutual suspicions still block, for now, the kind of integration that has united Europe or knit North America together in trade. For Asia to achieve a bright future, it will still have to overcome its past.

Japan is at the nub of this problem. For more than half a century, it has refused to confront its past squarely, and this has created antagonisms in the region and encouraged nationalism in both China and Korea. Furthermore, Asia needs a leader, and a well-trusted Japan could help set Asia's agenda for trade and finance, for fighting crime and pollution, for ensuring security along sea lanes. But Japan's inability to face its past has left it unable to play that leadership role. Tokyo has been incapable of mounting a meaningful security policy even for itself, and when Japanese are asked in surveys what should be done if another country invades Japan, only 46 percent say that Japan should use force to respond. In short, one of the greatest hurdles in Asia's future is its past.

History has left many potential flashpoints, and in several of them—

such as Taiwan—a war would set back the region for decades. Some nuclear proliferation experts believe that the likeliest place on Earth for an exchange of nuclear weapons is the India-Pakistan border. There are plenty of other security crises that could erupt over Asia as well, and nearly all are rooted in unresolved historical disputes and antagonisms.

The way that Asia's past continually intrudes into the present was driven home to me during a conversation in Beijing. Sheryl and I were having a secret meeting over dinner with a leader of China's underground democracy movement, so we huddled at a distant corner table of a restaurant. The democracy leader was someone I knew well and admired greatly for his courage and commitment, and so I watched respectfully as he rapped on the table suspiciously to look for bugs. Then when the waitresses stepped away, I listened intently as he leaned forward and told us his secret plans for advancing human rights.

"We're going to kill Japanese," he said brightly.

"What?"

"We're going to kill Japanese businessmen. That'll scare them so they won't invest here. And then the government will really be screwed!"

"You're not serious?"

"Of course we're serious. We can't demonstrate these days and we can't publish. The only thing we can do for democracy is kill Japanese businessmen."

"But how can you promote democracy by killing people?"    *biased opinion*

"Not people. They're Japanese. Japanese devils."

He never did kill anybody, but the dinner left me shaken. For weeks I worried that some Japanese acquaintance in Beijing would be stabbed by my pro-democracy friend. And he was representative of a broad swath of public opinion. A poll published in 1999 by Dentsu, a Japanese public relations firm, found that 69 percent of Chinese said they disliked Japanese, while 67 percent of South Koreans said they too disliked Japanese.

Yet for all the animosities and dangers, a hugely important change is beginning to take place: Asia is gradually coming to confront its past. It is an unsteady process, and looking backward has created new disputes and resentments. Yet delicately, uncertainly, Asia is moving to face its past and scrub away at the distrust. If this process continues, it will ultimately make Asia a much more stable and vital region. This historical restructuring is almost as critical for Asia as its economic restructuring.

With Horie, I came to see that process unfolding. That day when he told me about eating human flesh, I continued to speak with him for another hour or so, neither of us touching cups of green tea that had grown cold. Finally, after a bit of small talk, I offered a final question. "Sometimes we all do things rashly, or wrongly, and later we wish we could undo them. I wonder, was there anything you did rashly during the war and now regret?"

Horie's hands began rattling again, but he scarcely paused. "One day always comes back to me," he began. "We were searching a Chinese village for guerrillas. We were sure they were around, but we couldn't find them. Then I saw a stack of dried reeds, with a bit of an arm visible, holding a gun."

"What did you do?"

"I charged with my bayonet and thrust it into the reeds at chest height, and I heard a scream. I pulled the rifle out, and there was a baby skewered on the bayonet." Horie stopped to regain control of himself, and his face twitched for a moment in grief.

"A baby?"

"The baby was maybe six months old, and the hilt had gotten caught in its belt, so it was stuck to the bayonet. It turned out that the baby's mother was a guerrilla, holding the baby as she hid in the reeds. The bayonet had gone through her as well as the baby, so she died as well."

He paused again, his face gaunt and overcome by the rush of memories.

"You're sure you saw an arm sticking out of the reeds?" I asked. "You weren't just jabbing your bayonet into the reeds to see if someone was there?"

"No, no! I saw an arm."

I don't entirely believe Horie. Chinese guerrillas were short of weapons, and it seems unlikely to me that a nursing mother with a baby would be packing a gun, particularly if she were living in the village. If I were guessing, I would say that Horie was looking for guerrillas and jabbing his bayonet at potential hiding places like the pile of reeds. It would be a natural action for a jittery Japanese soldier in a Chinese village, just as it would be natural for a young Chinese woman to try to hide when Japanese troops showed up.

Yet after talking to Horie, I felt more respect than ever for him. He was a good and brave man who had done something terrible, but it was probably unintentional and it haunted him every day. Horie wanted nothing to do with the excuses that Japan's rightists always make for wartime atrocities. "Japan did terrible things in the war," he said. "We have to show remorse. We have to apologize. What we did was wrong. We should absolutely apologize to China and Korea. Absolutely."

Horie's torment at what he had done, his own strong belief that Japan should make amends, his willingness to open up to me—these underscored the distance Japan and other countries had come over the years. The wounds of history are still festering in Asia and they are nurturing a dangerous nationalism, but they are finally being treated. With time, with luck, they will heal.

One problem is that Japan has not been able to translate into national policy the penitence that people like Horie feel. Japan has never offered official compensation to the "comfort women"—girls from Korea and other countries whom it forced to be sex slaves for army troops. In 1998, the Japanese authorities did deign to pay two Korean women pensions for their forced labor during the war at a Japanese factory. But the one-time lump-sum pension that Japan agreed to pay was twelve cents each.

A sizable segment of the Japanese population feels no remorse for the war and vehemently resists any apology. Seisuke Okuno, a former cabinet minister, led 161 members of the Diet in backing a resolution opposing any apology for World War II, and he told me that if any country is guilty of war crimes, it is the United States—for dropping the atomic bombs on Hiroshima and Nagasaki. Japan's purpose in invading its neighbors, he insisted, was entirely noble: "These countries had been colonized and oppressed by whites. Our purpose was to free and stabilize them."

The popularity of this view was underscored by the success of the film *Pride*, Japan's biggest box-office hit in the first half of 1998. *Pride* paints wartime prime minister Hideki Tojo as a national hero, a kind and honorable man thrust into war by the West and unfairly executed as a war criminal. Japanese diplomats insist that movies like *Pride* are merely a tribute to pluralism, and they argue that their country has apologized many times for its wartime conduct. But Japan's statements normally do not use a word for apology, such as *shazai*, but rather the vague term *hansei*, which can mean remorse or self-reflection. When Prime Minister Tomiichi Murayama, a bleeding-heart liberal, asked the Diet to pass a resolution of contrition, parliamentarians replaced the word "apology" with *hansei* and "aggressive acts" with "aggressive-like acts."

How can people make excuses for the inexcusable? They can do so with remarkable panache. Take Kubo, a pudgy fellow who during the war had served in Unit 731, a top-secret organization that conducted biological warfare against China. A farmer living in northern Japan, Kubo agreed to see me in a friend's office in the town center. He seemed friendly, with a frequent grin that displayed a mouthful of silver. His graying crewcut topped a round face with a week's worth of gray stubble rising from a lined, sun-darkened jaw. Muscular and powerful, with callused and weather-beaten hands, he was well scrubbed and tidied up, decked out in his best pair of gray slacks. His wife, a thin, frail, graying woman, had brought rice rolls for us to eat as we talked. The two of them seemed like perfect grandparents, the model of a sweet old Japanese couple, except that Kubo was the most evil person I've ever met.

His wife doesn't know his secret, nor does anyone else in his family. Kubo swore an oath in 1945, at the end of the war, not to tell anyone what he saw and not to have any contact with his former army buddies, and he pretty much kept the promise over the decades. Ironically, he confided in me only because he wanted to convince me that Japan's army had not been as brutal as foreigners thought. He waited until his wife had left the room, and then he began his story.

"I joined the army when I was twelve years old, in 1937," he said. "I didn't question the war at all. Everything was done for emperor and country. I thought that the emperor was a living god." Kubo was sent to China to join Unit 731, and the officers gave Kubo a bit of medical training so that he could help with the experiments. These experiments were conducted on Chinese prisoners, mostly Communists, who were called *maruta,* or "logs." One of the first experiments that Kubo saw involved an outdoor test of the effectiveness of a lethal gas. It was conducted on an open plain, in the grain fields that seem to stretch forever in northeastern China, and the victims and the experimenters drove together to the site in trucks.

"The *maruta* were chained and tied with ropes to wooden stakes," Kubo recalled. "Some were in a crucifixion position, and others had their hands tied behind their backs. I wasn't told anything about them, but they were all men, and they seemed all young or in middle age and in good health. That was best for medical testing. Then we brought out a machine that was supposed to spew out poison gas, and we measured the distance from the machine to the prisoners, so that we could figure out how far away the gas would be effective. Our goal was to make fighting more efficient.

"We ran back and watched as the machine began to produce the poison

gas. But before anything happened, the wind suddenly changed—it s.
the gas blowing in our direction. So we had to run for our lives, and ,
never did see what happened to those prisoners."

Kubo spent much of his time trying to contaminate Chinese cities with
bubonic plague, and he also tried to infect rivers and wells with bacterio-
logical agents to poison anybody in the area. At one point, he paused and
frowned as he noticed that I seemed to be paying a good deal of attention
to what he regarded as the peccadilloes of war. "When we threw germs
into rivers and wells, they contaminated our water as well," Kubo said.
"And what we did in Unit 731 was mostly academic study. I didn't see any
torture or anything."

What kind of academic study?

"Well, we would infect *maruta* with the plague to see how long it would
take them to die, to see how it would affect them. We wanted to understand better how we could use the plague germs against our enemies.
Sometimes we would dissect the *maruta* after they had been infected, to
study how the plague spread in their internal organs. Once the doctors let
me take the first cut."

Kubo recalled that the *maruta* he cut was a Communist prisoner,
thirty-four years old, who had been infected with the plague. The prisoner
was brought in and tied naked to the operating table, facing up, and Kubo
and the other Japanese approached him wearing gowns and face masks so
that they would not get the disease. The prisoner was not anesthetized,
and he looked silently at Kubo as preparations began for the first incision.

"It was the easiest part of the surgery, which is why they let me do it,"
Kubo said. "The fellow knew that it was over for him, and so he hadn't
struggled when they led him into the room and tied him down. But when I
picked up the scalpel, that's when he began screaming. I cut him open
from the chest to the stomach, and he screamed terribly, and his face was
all twisted in agony. He made this unimaginable sound, he was screaming
so horribly. But then he finally stopped. He was unconscious."

Kubo paused and shook his head genially.

"This was all in a day's work for the surgeons," he added. "But it really
left an impression on me, because it was my first time."

The atrocities that the Japanese army committed during World War II
are well known, so what struck me was not so much Kubo's brutality back
then as his lack of remorse today. Our conversation was at cross-purposes,
because he had agreed to speak in the belief that a conversation would

that Unit 731 had not been so awful after all. We became
⟨frus⟩trated with each other.

"⟨...⟩ that vivisection was wrong?" I asked. "Do you feel that
⟨...⟩ immoral?"

"⟨Peo⟩ple do experiments on live bodies all the time," Kubo replied, looking injured. "Like heart transplants and other surgery, even though sometimes those experiments fail. And those doctors are paid so much money!"

"But transplants are meant to save lives, not destroy them. And those
doctors use anesthesia."

"We couldn't use anesthesia. Vivisection should be done under normal
circumstances. If we'd used anesthesia, that might have affected the body
organs and blood vessels that we were examining. So we couldn't have
used an anesthetic."

"So you don't think you did anything wrong?"

Kubo shrugged impatiently, exasperated by my questioning. "People say
that Unit 731 was brutal, and I can't say that they are wrong. But all this
came to the surface only because we lost the war. If we had won, this
would have been kept secret. And I think Unit 731 did some good things,
because what we did in Unit 731 was mostly academic stuff. If we had won
the war, all this would have been justified."

"But what about experiments on children? I read about a thirty-year-
old Russian woman and her child. Unit 731 put them in a gas chamber
with glass windows, and the soldiers clustered around to watch as the gas
choked her, as she tried to save her child by lying on top of him. Is that
justifiable?"

"Of course there were experiments on kids. But probably their fathers
were spies."

I paused. His geniality had a harder edge now, and we were glaring
indignantly at each other.

"Do you think this could ever happen again?" I asked.

"Yes, there's a chance this could happen again. Because in a war, you
have to win."

I realized that Kubo is representative of Japan's dark side, its refusal to
show contrition, its inability to face the past. But he is unusual not only in
his wartime behavior but also in his obduracy. Polls show that Japanese
believe two-to-one that their government has not done enough to apologize for the war or help the victims. Kubo and hard-liners like him linger,
but they are slowly yielding ground and Japan is coming around.

Because in a war, you have to
win!

. . .

*Confucian tie-in*

Why is Japan so reluctant to confront its past? Apart from nations, such as a Confucian reluctance to speak ill of there is an obvious reason: Countries, far more than indi say that they are sorry. The United States, after all, has never formally apologized for enslaving Africans, invading Mexico and Canada, stealing Texas, colonizing the Philippines and Guam, or carpet-bombing Vietnam. Americans have conveniently forgotten the relish with which we slaughtered two hundred thousand Filipinos when they rebelled against our "liberation" a century ago. Take General Jacob "Hell-Roaring Jake" Smith, the military governor of the Philippine island of Samar. He ordered his troops to turn the entire island into "a howling wilderness" and specified that all males over the age of ten should be killed. "I want no prisoners," he declared. "I wish you to kill and burn; the more you kill and burn, the better you will please me." His men obliged, and the carnage was fantastic. On the main Philippine island of Luzon, a visiting American congressman said: "They never rebel in northern Luzon, because there isn't anybody there to rebel. The country was marched over and cleaned in a most resolute manner. The good Lord in heaven only knows the number of Filipinos that were put under the ground. Our soldiers took no prisoners, they kept no records; they simply swept the country, and wherever or whenever they could get hold of a Filipino they killed him."

One can argue that Americans have forgotten their atrocities in the Philippines because they occurred a century ago. But even in the case of World War II, Americans have almost no acquaintance with the brutality in which their own troops often engaged. The historian John Dower has gathered a series of horrifying accounts of Americans and Australians slaughtering wounded or surrendering Japanese and collecting grisly souvenirs such as teeth and ears—in one case, from a wounded Japanese man who thrashed about on the ground while a Marine cut his cheeks and yanked out his teeth. "The other night, Stanley emptied his pockets of 'souvenirs'—eleven ears from dead Japs," the Marines' *Leatherneck* journal reported in 1943. "It was not disgusting, as it would be from the civilian point of view." Charles Lindbergh, who accompanied American troops during the war, wrote in his diary that soldiers kicked in the teeth of Japanese prisoners, both before and after executing them. "It was freely admitted that some of our soldiers tortured Jap prisoners and were as cruel and

...rbaric at times as the Japs themselves. Our men think nothing of shooting a Japanese prisoner or a soldier attempting to surrender."

My point is not that we were all just as bad as the Japanese troops, or even that people in glass houses should not throw stones.* The Japanese troops in World War II were particularly barbaric (just as the Japanese in the Russo-Japanese War of 1905 were particularly gentlemanly). It is simply human nature to rationalize or forget our own sins and to home in on those of the other fellow. Japan's reluctance to face its past may be stupid and shortsighted and inexcusable, but it also is perfectly natural.

Moreover, most Japanese know very little of their country's dark past and thus are genuinely ignorant of what there is to repent. For decades, the Japanese government forced textbook publishers to excise any hint of the brutalities committed by the army. When one textbook writer referred to Japan's wartime "aggression," the Ministry of Education called for the sentence to be deleted, arguing that "in the interests of the education of citizens, it is not desirable to use a term with such negative implications to describe the acts of their own country. A term such as 'military advance' should be used instead of 'aggression.' "

Thanks to court intervention, the textbooks in recent years have become more honest and complete. The junior-high textbooks, for example, now mention Japanese "aggression," Unit 731, and the Rape of Nanjing (the massacre that unfolded after Japanese troops seized the Chinese city at the end of 1937). Moreover, Japanese scholars and journalists, who are disproportionately leftist, have increasingly been writing about the Rape of Nanjing, about the comfort women and other atrocities, and in fact the best research and most damning evidence of government complicity usually comes from Japanese scholars themselves. Far more, for example, is published in Japanese than in English about the Rape of Nanjing.

---

* I should also note that American troops were sometimes incredibly altruistic. In Okinawa, at different times I spoke to two elderly women who, as young girls, were both saved by American GIs who wrestled them to the ground to stop them from committing suicide. One of the girls had been in a cave where an entire village was hidden, but when the villagers were discovered they decided to commit suicide together. The American soldiers pleaded with them to give up, not to kill themselves, but the Japanese were sure they would be raped and tortured and murdered. So the mothers began killing their children. At that point, the American soldiers—at enormous risk to themselves—ran inside the cave and wrenched the knives and swords away from those who were killing themselves and their children. Many died, but the Americans saved about half of them. As I sat among the human bones in the darkness of that musty cave, which had been sealed and forgotten since that day, I felt an awe for those American veterans.

*This photograph is said to show Japanese soldiers patrolling in Nanjing after the massacre of Chinese civilians there. The damage to the city is apparent in the buildings in the background.*

—Chinese/korean aim

There is another reason why Japan has difficulty confronting its historical responsibilities, and that is the overzealousness of certain Chinese and Koreans whose aim in examining history is not uncovering truth but rather humiliating Japan. Partly because they are playing to domestic audiences, Chinese and Korean leaders tend to exaggerate Japanese sins in the same way that Japanese leaders downplay them. And ordinary Japanese understandably see all the talk about history as a cynical exercise when Chinese officials seem less interested in what actually happened than in using the past to blackmail Japan into giving more aid. The Japanese, inflamed by the exaggerations, become resentful and defensive, and the cycle of recriminations continues. To break this spiral, each country must look at history as something more than simply a debating platform to score points. History is invariably too muddled and uncertain for that. For instance, the Rape of Nanjing is the single greatest Japanese atrocity abroad, and the one that is most often raised by Chinese and Westerners alike. But it is also an example of how history tends to be written by polemicists rather than impartial scholars.

China regularly claims that there were three hundred thousand fatalities and sometimes offers a death count as high as six hundred thousand. Iris Chang, a Chinese-American, has written a book about the massacre in which she concludes that between 260,000 and 350,000 people were killed. She also writes about victims being nailed to walls, hung by their tongues from iron hooks, or buried in the ground to their waists and then torn apart by German shepherds. Japanese rightists such as Tokyo governor Shintaro Ishihara, on the other hand, claim that the Rape of Nanjing never happened.

A close look shows that both sides rely on dubious witnesses and evidence, and in that sense the Rape of Nanjing is a useful window into historiography as an international competition. The Japanese rightists are clearly wrong when they say that there was no massacre, but likewise there is little basis for the assertions that hundreds of thousands died. Just as some Japanese have tried to cover up the massacres, so some Chinese have fiddled with Nanjing to try to make it even more horrifying than it really was.

What is clear is that Japanese troops rampaged through Nanjing, butchering any young men they found. The soldiers forced their way into homes, gang-raping women and girls and beheading any brothers or fathers who protested. Girls were often killed or mutilated after being raped, and entire families were roasted alive. This slaughter and torture and rape went on for eight weeks, and the Japanese seizure of Nanjing was perhaps the most barbaric capture of any city in modern times. John Rabe, a German civilian who witnessed the slaughter and saved many lives, recorded the brutality in his diary. "You can't breathe for sheer revulsion when you keep finding the bodies of women with bamboo poles thrust up their vaginas," he wrote. "Even old women over seventy are constantly being raped."

The question of how many people were killed is deeply uncertain. Rabe, as the head of the safety zone in Nanjing, was in the center of the action and had information from his network of Chinese friends and assistants, but although his diary recounts terrible brutality and killing, there is nothing about tongues or German shepherds. Back in Germany months afterward, he wrote: "According to Chinese claims, 100,000 civilians were killed; this, however, is probably something of an overstatement. We Europeans put the number at about 50,000 to 60,000." Other early estimates by witnesses were in the same ballpark. Miner Searle Bates, a history professor in Nanjing and a member of the safety zone committee, said in Jan-

uary 1938 that forty thousand had been killed, including twelve thousand
civilians and the rest soldiers. In February 1938, a Chinese delegate to the
League of Nations put the figure at twenty thousand civilians. The Chinese Red Army newspaper reported on April 30, 1938, that the total death
toll was 42,000. These estimates have been justly criticized, however,
as based on early, incomplete evidence, possibly before the full toll in out-
lying rural areas became known.

The higher estimates, by Chinese commentators or by the War Crimes
Tribunal in Tokyo, of hundreds of thousands of deaths, are totals of various
figures. For starters, they include reports by supposed eyewitnesses such
as Lu Su, who claimed that on December 18 he hid in a cave and saw
57,418 Chinese men and women bayoneted and machine-gunned by Japanese troops. There is no explanation for how he counted the precise
number, and no accounting for how he saw the massacre if he was hiding
in a cave. When all these "eyewitness" accounts of various killings are
added together, the total number of people said to be slaughtered in these
massacres is 190,000.

Massacres did take place on a huge scale—Japanese diaries confirm
that—but the problem is that eyewitnesses like Lu Su often lie. Major
Hisao Ohta, a Japanese officer in Nanjing, is often cited for his confession
that his soldiers dumped the bodies of 150,000 Chinese victims into the
Nanjing River between December 15 and December 17, 1937. Any such
confession should be suspect because it was made when he was in a Chinese prison camp, and sure enough, it turns out that Major Ohta was not
even assigned to go to Nanjing until December 25, 1937, a week after the
killings he "witnessed." Most of the eyewitness reports of Nanjing bar-
barism are, of course, from Chinese survivors, and théy also need to be
treated with skepticism. Communist rule produced all kinds of witnesses,
and indeed during the Korean War the Chinese cited eyewitness reports
that Americans had participated jointly with the Japanese in the Rape of
Nanjing. But even if the government had not been whipping up campaigns against Japan, there is something very human about exaggerating
genuine horrors. That is why the death tolls based on eyewitness claims
usually come down dramatically when investigators get access to an area:
In Romania in 1989, the first gory reports were that sixty thousand
demonstrators had been massacred in Timişoara by the collapsing Communist regime, but that figure later fell to fewer than one thousand, and in
Kosovo in 1999, the U.S. State Department initially suggested that one
hundred thousand Albanians might have been killed, but later estimates

dropped to a few thousand. I encountered this psychology at the time of the Tiananmen killings in 1989, when there were witnesses who vividly described massacre scenes that had never occurred and insisted that the death toll was in the thousands or tens of thousands. I heard people recounting how they had seen Tiananmen Square knee-deep in blood and guts where tanks had rolled across fleeing students; since I was one of the last to flee the square, gunfire all around me, I knew these were exaggerations. Hundreds were killed, and as I remember my rage I can understand how people could exaggerate in those circumstances. But it did no honor to the dead to give credence to the wilder claims.

Particularly in Nanjing, where the government encouraged the emergence of professional victims who would recount their anti-Japanese tales to promote Chinese nationalism, and where it was in people's interest to exaggerate, we need to be wary of the resulting accounts. We need to be skeptical of victims as well as war criminals.

Then there are Nanjing's burial claims, in which two charitable groups said that they buried 155,000 people. But the figures invite doubt because 105,000 of those burials are attributed to a little-known group called Cunshandang in just a three-week period in April. Cunshandang previously had buried only 75 bodies a day, so it is difficult to see how it suddenly took on another 105,000 burials, or 5,000 a day, after the Rape of Nanjing was mostly over. In any case, some scholars believe that Cunshandang was subcontracting for the Red Swastika Society and that its burials were included in the Red Swastika Society's figure of a total of 43,000 burials, including natural deaths.

Another approach to the death toll was provided by Professor Lewis S.C. Smythe of Nanjing University, who conducted a survey in the spring of 1938 of one in every fifty households in Nanjing and one in ten in the surrounding countryside. Smythe's report concluded that about 29,400 people had been killed, mostly outside of Nanjing itself.

So in reality how many people were killed in Nanjing? The answer is simply that we don't know. But we need to distinguish between combat deaths and those of deserters and civilians. My own guesswork is that tens of thousands of Chinese soldiers died in combat and tens of thousands more after they had surrendered, fled, or been taken prisoner, in violation of international law. In addition, many, many thousands of civilians were slaughtered. I can't exclude the possibility that the highest figures are correct, but it seems to me more reasonable that the total death toll is near

Rabe's estimate of fifty thousand to sixty thousand, or Miner Searle Bates's of forty thousand, or the initial Communist Chinese estimate of forty thousand.

I have detoured into this minefield to try to show that these historical disputes are often far more complex than they seem at first, and that while Japan is responsible for its failure to apologize adequately and confront its brutality, other countries also need to act responsibly. It may seem churlish to complain about Chinese exaggerations of the Rape of Nanjing, when there is no doubt that it was one of the worst atrocities of the war and that the suffering was incalculable. But when China inflates numbers of victims to try to intensify Japanese guilt, then this stokes not guilt but anger. On all sides, history should be written with pens rather than cudgels.

Most of the responsibility for facing the past must, of course, go to Japan. But as Kim Dae Jung has acknowledged, some must also go to China and Korea and other countries. China needs to realize that while the Japanese army killed millions of Chinese, Mao killed tens of millions. Koreans need to accept that while Japan's annexation of the Korean peninsula from 1910 to 1945 was ruthless, it led to the vast expansion of roads, railroads, and modern schools, so that by 1945 Korea had half as many miles of roads as China. While nothing makes Koreans angrier— quite justifiably—than Japan's refusal to compensate the comfort women, it was Koreans themselves who, under coercion, seized teenage girls and handed them over to the occupiers. Moreover, Koreans and Chinese alike need to acknowledge that however awful Japan was in the war, exceedingly few Japanese alive today ever bayoneted babies or raped girls in Nanjing.

There is a more fundamental reason for Japan's difficulties acknowledging war guilt, and it has to do with Miyoko Inoue and all that she represents. Miyoko, a fourteen-year-old girl, was near ground zero at 8:15 a.m. on August 6, 1945, when the United States dropped the atomic bomb over Hiroshima. At that precise moment, Miyoko ceased to exist. She was not simply killed; she was vaporized. The only trace remaining behind was an impression of a foot in her left shoe. Her skin, her clothes, her bones, her blood, her other shoe—they were all atomized. The shoe is now in the Hiroshima Peace Museum, a long white building set in a beautiful green park at the epicenter of the bombing. The museum is a monument to the horrors of the atomic bombing, noted by the hundreds of thousands of schoolchildren who file through with wide-open eyes and then leave comments in the guest book like "How can human beings do this?"

The Hiroshima bombing was a tragedy not only for the likes of Miyoko but for the region, for it nurtured a sense among Japanese of themselves as victims of the war rather than its cause. In Japan, there is a nearly universal feeling that the United States was wrong, and probably racist, to drop the bombs, and this view has also spread in the West. The perception that Japan is a victim of the war has made it more difficult for Japanese to accept that they have a responsibility to apologize to or compensate their victims.

The atomic bombing is such a fundamental part of this equation—it is impossible to understand Japan today without reference to it—that it is worth a closer look even now. I arrived in Japan thinking that the bombing was a mistake, but I gradually changed my mind and concluded that it ended up saving lives of Japanese and Americans alike. What changed my feelings was my research into wartime Japanese decision-making, based on recent Japanese scholarship and newly released Japanese documents.

The minutes of cabinet meetings and other sessions show that the Japanese army was absolutely determined not to surrender but to fight on to the last man—to the last baby, for that matter. "Sacrifice twenty million Japanese lives," a senior navy official urged in one meeting, proposing a massive suicide attack on the Allies. The documents suggest that Japan would not have surrendered just because it was losing or just because Russia entered the war. Indeed, even after the atomic bombing of Hiroshima, Army Minister Korechika Anami insisted on fighting to the end. "The appearance of the atomic bomb does not spell the end of the war," he insisted at a cabinet meeting on August 9, 1945. "We are confident about the decisive battle in the homeland against American forces." At another point, he told the meeting: "I am quite sure we could inflict great casualties on the enemy, and even if we fail in the attempt, our hundred million people are ready to die for honor." Anami suggested hopefully that perhaps the Americans had built only one atomic bomb—and just then a messenger arrived in the room with the news that an atomic bomb had been dropped on Nagasaki as well.

The Japanese archives show that one of the great heroes of World War II was Marcus McDilda, an American fighter pilot shot down on August 8, 1945. He was beaten up, tortured, and quizzed repeatedly as to what he knew about the atomic bomb. McDilda knew nothing and said so. A general arrived, brandished a sword, and slashed McDilda's lip, saying he would personally cut off McDilda's head unless he spilled everything he knew about the atomic bomb. And so McDilda, his lip bleeding, his bruises throbbing, began to lie. McDilda said that the atomic bomb measured twenty-four feet by thirty-six feet and he explained how it worked: "As you know, when atoms are split, there are a lot of plusses and minuses released. Well, we've taken these and put them in a huge container and separated them from each other with a lead shield. When the box is dropped out of a plane, we melt the lead shield and the plusses and minuses come together." McDilda added that America had one hundred of these atomic bombs prepared for use. Asked about future targets, he replied, "I believe Tokyo is supposed to be bombed in the next few days."

The interrogators rushed off to call the headquarters in Tokyo, and Anami reluctantly advised the cabinet that America had one hundred more atomic bombs and that Tokyo was the next target, possibly on August 12. This dampened spirits in the cabinet room, but, incredibly, even then Anami and the generals insisted that there could be no surrender.

In reading the documents of those meetings, one gets the sense that the diehard army elements almost succeeded in forcing the war on to an endless ground battle on the main Japanese islands. Even after the two atomic bombings, even after Russia entered the war, even after the emperor intervened and demanded a surrender, hard-line elements tried a mutiny so that they could keep fighting and prevent the emperor's surrender announcement from being broadcast. The mutiny failed, but it was a close call. Without the two atomic bombings, or at least the one in Hiroshima, the "peace faction" would never have convinced the Japanese decision-makers to surrender. Koichi Kido, then the Lórd Keeper of the Privy Seal and one of the staunch advocates of making peace, said later that those in favor of surrender "were assisted by the atomic bomb in our endeavor to end the war." Kido added: "The feeling that the Emperor and I had about the atomic bombing was that the psychological moment we had long waited for had finally arrived to resolutely carry out the termination of the war. . . . We felt that if we took the occasion and utilized the psychological shock of the bomb to carry through, we might perhaps succeed in ending the war." Likewise, Navy Minister Mitsumasa Yonai, another advocate of surrender, called the atomic bombs "providential help," and the prime minister at the time, Kantaro Suzuki, later called the bombing "an extremely favorable opportunity." The advocates of peace used the atomic bombs to help the army save face, by suggesting that

Japan had not been defeated by Allied armies but by "science"—something beyond its control. This gave an excuse for the army to back down. "The atomic bomb was a golden opportunity given by heaven for Japan to end the war," explained Hisatsune Sakomizu, the chief cabinet secretary at the time.

In the battle over the small, sparsely populated islands of Okinawa, fourteen thousand Americans and two hundred thousand Japanese were killed. If the fighting had reached the main islands of Japan, millions of Japanese would have been killed. So in that context, it seems to me that nothing saved so many Japanese lives as the dropping of the atomic bombs. Far from being victimized by the bombs, Japan was rescued by them.

Why is East Asia now beginning to face up to the past? What has changed?

With the ending of the Cold War, Asians became people instead of Communists and capitalists. South Koreans, Americans, and Chinese alike increasingly began to demand that Japan confront its history. And ordinary Japanese themselves began to do the same. Gradually, Japanese politicians began to express more sincere statements of regret for World War II, culminating in Prime Minister Tomiichi Murayama's heartfelt apology on the fiftieth anniversary of the end of the war. No subsequent prime minister has spoken from the heart in the same way, but they have at least echoed the language.

More mature leaders have also emerged in other countries, most notably Kim Dae Jung in South Korea. Nowhere is Kim's statesmanship more evident than in his handling of history. One of his greatest moments was his state visit to Japan in 1998, when he spoke to the Japanese parliament and candidly emphasized the "doubts and mistrust" throughout Asia about Japan but also emphasized the need to move on. "Japan needs true courage to look at the past squarely and respect the judgment of history," he declared, but he added: "South Korea should also rightly evaluate Japan, in all its changed aspects, and search with hope for future possibilities." Kim announced that he was ending the ban on imports from Japan, and he emphasized Korea's readiness to work with Japan to build a better relationship. There was an outpouring of warmth from the Japanese, and Prime Minister Keizo Obuchi responded with an unusually forthright apology for the war. That visit was a model of how two countries can overcome the past and move forward.

*Teruichi Ukita chats about his wartime memories, saying that he terribly regrets what he did—without quite saying what it was that he did.*

The visit gives me hope because it demonstrates that this fog of recalcitrance may slowly be burning off, laying the groundwork for stronger economic cooperation and progress. I saw similar signs of maturity in many of the ordinary people I talked to, especially in Japan, Korea, and China, people like Teruichi Ukita, one of the old men of Omiya. Ukita, seventy-one, is a burly fellow with a crown of white hair shorn in a crew cut. We sat down on folding chairs in a community center, our arms on the table, and we chatted for a bit to take the measure of one another. He spoke gruffly, without the polite suffixes that a Japanese normally uses in conversation with a stranger, but this was not rudeness so much as his simple, straightforward manner. It was a wet, cold, winter day, but even as the rain tumbled down outside, the room was warm and cozy, and Ukita was friendly and hospitable.

He used a thick wooden spear to carve up an *okashi,* a delicate Japanese cake, and matter-of-factly acknowledged that he had served in China in the *Kenpeitai,* the dreaded military police. Records confirmed that. He confessed that he had killed many Chinese during the war, but he refused to provide any details. "I saw lots of torture scenes, but I don't want to talk about it or remember it," Ukita said bluntly. "It was said that even crying babies would shut up at the mention of the *Kenpeitai*. Everybody was afraid of us. The word was that prisoners would enter by the front gate but leave by the back gate—as corpses."

It seemed that Ukita himself had tortured prisoners, although he would not directly say so, and I asked what the torturers were like.

"They were just regular people doing their job. But there were two kinds of torturers. You've got to understand the difference." He paused and looked me keenly in the eye. "There were torturers who were cold, and there were torturers who were humane. That was the big difference. You understand that?"

"Not really. What's the difference between a cold torturer and a humane one?"

"A cold torturer," Ukita began, but he broke off, searching for a way to explain to me. After a long silence, he spoke up again: "If you look in a man's eyes as you torture him, then you understand him. When you ask him for information, you can tell from his eyes if he's telling the truth when he says, 'I don't know, I don't know.' The humane torturers would stop at that point, if they saw the man really didn't know. The cold ones would keep going."

His voice was quavering, and I quietly asked about the victims.

"Most of them were men, young men," he said. "But I remember some women as well. I remember. . . ." He paused, and he seemed on the verge of breaking down.

"Look, this is really unpleasant for me to remember," he said shakily. "I hate to think about it. I just can't talk about it."

It was only when Japan lost the war that he began to think about what he had done, he said. Ukita was captured by Russians and sent to a labor camp in Siberia, along with hundreds of thousands of other Japanese, and it was there, when he saw Russians casually killing his fellow Japanese, that he belatedly realized the universality of humanity. "Watching Chinese being killed, I had no emotions," Ukita said heavily. "It was like a game. But when I saw Japanese being executed in Siberia for stealing things, I got so angry and emotional."

"What about comfort women?" I asked. "Did you see any of them?"

"Oh, yeah, I often visited them. Now some Japanese say that they were volunteers, but I know from my experience that they were forced to work in the brothels. They weren't volunteers; they were kidnapped. I talked to them. I know it."

At this point, Ukita's voice choked, and he blinked back tears. "At the time of the war, I was in my twenties and single, and I didn't understand," he said, his voice breaking. "But when I had two daughters myself, I started to realize what I had done."

"But what exactly did you do?"

Ukita choked again, and ran his hand across his face. "I can't say," he said tremulously. "But Japan is wrong, absolutely wrong, to refuse to pay those girls official compensation. They are right and we are in the wrong. We should pay them for all the injuries we have done them."

He looked up. "War makes people do terrible things," he said in a broken voice, by way of apology. "Humans are so stupid. You do terrible things, and you regret them later. At first, humans seem so smart. And in reality, they're such idiots."

Most veterans are like Ukita, remorseful for what they have done, and so a historical restructuring is beginning to accompany the political and economic change. But the pace is too slow, and until the historical disputes are buried they will inflame nationalists and threaten the well-being of Asia. Yuko Tojo, the dragon lady in Tokyo, is a good example of these nationalists waiting in the wings.

*Yuko Tojo, a modern Japanese nationalist, visits a Shinto shrine in Tokyo.*

### CHAPTER ELEVEN

# My Country, Right or Wrong

## NICHOLAS D. KRISTOF

*Where but in China could you find it an act of high patriotism to fornicate?*

—THE BRITISH GOVERNOR OF HONG KONG IN 1911, AFTER PROSTITUTES SOUGHT CUSTOMERS BY
PLEDGING TO SEND HALF THEIR EARNINGS TO SUPPORT THE CHINESE REVOLUTION.

Yuko Tojo is a slight, prim woman of fifty-nine, bespectacled with dark-brown hair that is tucked back neatly behind her ears and halts just above her firm shoulders. She wears long dark skirts, sensible shoes, and blouses buttoned to her neck, making her look like a severe school mistress. Yet she greeted me warmly and plunked down on a couch in the lobby of her building to talk with me. She asked me what I wanted to drink, and then dispatched her aide to get tea. He was a burly man, three times her size and perhaps a *Yakuza* gangster, but he fawned over her and scurried off to do her bidding.

Yuko Tojo spoke with me in Japanese, seeming entirely relaxed as she recalled her girlhood. During World War II, she and her family had been sent to a remote village to avoid the American bombings, but after the war, when she was in the fifth grade, her family returned to Tokyo. Then the other children teased her by making faces as if they were being strangled. "I didn't know what they were doing," she recalled. "I didn't have a clue why they were doing it. But they would pretend there was a rope around their necks, and they would gasp and stick out their tongues." She heard the mysterious word *koshukei* whispered about her grandpa, and so one time she looked up the word in a picture dictionary. It meant "to be hanged to death," and the definition was accompanied by a picture of a man in a black hood being hanged from a gallows. Soon, everything became clear.

Her grandfather, Hideki Tojo, the wartime prime minister, had been hanged as a war criminal. Her father was ousted from his job because of the shame of it all, and other parents would not let their children play with her. The war was something to be pushed under the tatami and forgotten. So for decades, Yuko Tojo ran away from her grandfather and never mentioned her ancestry, happily taking her husband's name after marriage, but in her heart she always burned with feelings of unfairness. Then, in the 1990s, Japanese occasionally started to speak out in defense of Hideki Tojo. A growing number of Japanese scholars and journalists began to rebel against the notion that Japan had been particularly evil during World War II, speaking out affirmatively of their country's past and arguing for a more assertive future. Yuko Tojo for her part wrote a best-selling book defending her grandfather. She began using her original name again, and she launched a campaign to rehabilitate Hideki Tojo—and to honor the nationalism that led to World War II.

This kind of modern nationalism emerges directly from the region's historical wounds, and it is one of the prime risks in Asia's future. As I've said, while historical problems are gradually being addressed, they will take decades to be resolved entirely. And in the meantime, the danger of the historical antagonisms is that they spawn nationalism. While most Asians see nationalism as the source of their greatest triumph in the twentieth century—independence from colonial rule—I regard it as the reason for the greatest catastrophes that Asia has suffered in the last century. Nationalism also constitutes the greatest risk to Asia in the coming decades. It creates risk of military conflict, of diversion of scarce resources into military spending, and of economic nationalism that aims to beggar one's neighbor and ends up impoverishing oneself. The West's greatest mistake in Asia in the twentieth century was the failure to recognize the strength of nationalism as it arose, so it's worth a careful look now.

Without nationalism India might still be British and Indonesia Dutch.

But once the new flags had been raised, nationalism's influence was pernicious. It led to Japanese militarism and millions of deaths during World War II in the Pacific. It led to the Communist movements in China, Indochina, and Korea, for Mao Zedong, Ho Chi Minh, and Kim Il Sung were not so much Communists as nationalists. Nationalism, or the silly Western response to it, eventually led to such disasters as the Vietnam War, the Cambodian genocide, and the great Chinese famine that at the beginning of the 1960s killed thirty million people.

On the economic front, nationalism was equally catastrophic. It led to inward-looking economic policies that curbed foreign investment, discouraged international trade, and impoverished India, Pakistan, Burma, North Korea, and, until recently, China. Most of Asia's people live shorter lives in worse conditions than if their governments had been less nationalistic in economic matters.

Mahatma Gandhi is partly to blame. Once when I was walking Gregory to school in Tokyo he asked me who the greatest person in recent times had been. I said that perhaps it was Gandhi, and I told him the story of how this 114-pound man in a loincloth had used peaceful resistance to bring down the British Empire. I described how Gandhi had been just as tough on his own people as on the British, riding third-class in the trains and preaching equality with the Untouchables, going on a hunger strike and risking his life to force an end to rioting against Muslims. I mentioned issues that I thought would interest a first-grader, such as Gandhi's fixation with bowel movements and his tendency to ask friends for detailed reports about their feces (Gandhi gave himself a salt-water enema each morning, and one sign that he liked somebody was that he would offer to give that person an enema). But overall I stressed that Gandhi was an incomparably good man who had left a tremendous impact on the politics and ideas of the twentieth century.

I also recounted how Gandhi had had crazy ideas about how to run a country. Gandhi carried his old wooden spinning wheel with him everywhere, and he spent thirty minutes every day spinning rough cotton *khadi* cloth, and he insisted that his followers do the same. He argued for closing down the cotton mills and in their place equipping each home with a spinning wheel, and he wanted each of India's villages to be a self-sufficient unit. He trudged around India, lugging his spinning wheel and denouncing modern industry—yet he delivered his blasts against modernism with a microphone. Gandhi had been such a good man in every other respect, I told Gregory, that his foolish economic ideas had been accepted as well, and had helped keep India impoverished. Every year, 1.9 million Indian children die before the age of one, mostly from diseases of poverty such as diarrhea, and many of them could be spared if Gandhi the nationalist had been a better economist and had encouraged India to open itself to the international market economy. Gandhi was, in short, a wonderful man who in one respect left a catastrophic legacy.

For all those catastrophes, Asia has still not purged itself of the menace of nationalism. Some countries, such as South Korea, are getting over their xenophobia, while in others, such as Japan and China, nationalism is becoming more visible. "With the United States occupation after the war, there was mind control over the Japanese people about their history, and only now is the mind control being lifted," Yuko Tojo told me, explaining the popularity of her movement in Japan. "Now is the first time that many people are learning the real history of Japan." Leaning forward, she became more intense. "People always talk about Hitler and Tojo in the same breath," she said fervently. "But they were utterly different. Hitler murdered the Jews, but Tojo didn't kill his own people. Japan was encircled by hostile nations before the war, and it was strangled by sanctions and had no resources. So General Tojo, for the sake of the survival of his people, had to resort to arms. He died for his country. He died to save his people."

The message of the Japanese nationalists like Yuko Tojo is rooted in the past but is directed at the future. They are frustrated by Japan's lack of military power, and they yearn for a more muscular foreign policy. They do not claim foreign territories or salivate for overseas military adventures, but many would like to see Japan arm itself with nuclear weapons and show more gumption when pushed around by Washington.

Optimists about Asia tend to justify their rosy forecasts by extrapolating from present growth rates into the future. That is reasonable to a point, but the problem is that unforeseeable crises sometimes erupt. In 1996, a year before the Asian crisis began, I was one of a group of speakers at a conference in Tokyo on Asia's prospects. All the other speakers were much more eminent, and they went first. Every one of them used the metaphor of the flying geese, with Japan as the lead goose and the rest of Asia following behind, and in somber, reasonable tones they explained that the Asian geese should be able to fly smoothly into prosperity. The audience of Japanese businessmen nodded appreciatively. Finally, it was my turn, and I'm afraid I rather upset the restrained, dignified mood of the conference by arguing that you cannot base flight predictions of geese solely on their musculature, age, health, and past performance. "Because," I said enthusiastically, as the audience shrank back, "what if on the ground below there is a goose hunter? With a shotgun! Boom! Boom! Then there go the geese, and all those calculations are of no use." There was a long pause as everyone stared at the American maniac-idiot. But my point then and now, not a profound one, is simply that economic analysis sometimes focuses too much on economics. A nuclear war between India and Pakistan or a war over Taiwan would suddenly make laughable any assessment of Asia's economic future. So that is why nationalism is an important caveat in weighing Asia's prospects: It acts like the goose hunter.

Asian countries direct their nationalism not just at the West but at each other. In modern Europe, the key relationship was between France and Germany, and once that was sorted out the entire continent achieved a measure of harmony. In Asia the central relationship today is between China and Japan (although eventually it may become China and India). If Beijing and Tokyo can sort out their problems of history and territory, then Asia will be a safer place, but in the last few years the opposite has happened. While historical wounds are slowly healing, there are some signs of growing nationalism in both China and Japan, and these feed on each other.

Japanese nationalism manifests itself in part through the country's steady rearmament. While Tokyo nominally clings to its "peace constitution" and claims that it has no army at all, it is clear that Japan is steadily turning itself into an impressive regional power with an ability to strike its neighbors. Already Japan has the most powerful conventional force in Asia, and it is steadily becoming more comfortable with offensive weaponry and capabilities. It is building up its intelligence-gathering operations and preparing to launch reconnaissance satellites, and it is beginning to develop air-to-air refueling so that its fighters will be able to strike at its neighbors. It does not have nuclear weapons now, but its bureaucrats have kept the nuclear option alive by importing plutonium for power generation and by developing the H-2 and H-2A rockets, which could be transformed into intercontinental ballistic missiles with nuclear warheads. Within a decade or so, Japan will probably amend its constitution to make itself less pacifist, and if at some point it is provoked it will be able to become a nuclear power very quickly.

Yet although Japan is becoming more nationalistic, I do not worry so much about it. While Japan is rearming, it lacks the will and ruthlessness these days to threaten its neighbors. Indeed, Japanese nationalism has been dangerous mostly for the way in which it inflames Chinese nationalism; within Japan itself, the rightists have unexpectedly played a useful role, for they have ended the taboo on discussion of Japan's past. Now there are apologists for the war, like Yuko Tojo, and there are also scholars who continue to uncover new evidence of Japanese atrocities. For the first time, there is a debate in Japan about its past, and this is a debate that the nationalists can never win.

Japanese nationalism does create trouble in another respect. A shallower but broader nationalism leads Japan to persist in making what to me seem dubious territorial claims. These claims, which the United States has supported explicitly or implicitly, have aggravated the tensions in the western Pacific and resulted in an ongoing risk of an accidental war.

The better-known of these Japanese claims involves what Tokyo calls the Northern Territories, four clusters of islands that were lost to Russia at the end of World War II. Since these were seized by Russia in war, Japan would ordinarily have a good claim in international law to recover them. But when Prime Minister Shigeru Yoshida signed the San Francisco Peace Treaty in 1951, Japan renounced "all right, title, and claim to the Kuril Islands." These days, Tokyo says it did not mean that to include the Northern Territories, but that is fiction. Yoshida groused publicly that he regretted giving up those four island groups—which clearly meant that he knew he was giving them up. And the head of the Treaties Bureau in the Japanese Foreign Ministry formally told parliament in 1951 that the reference to "Kuril Islands" in the peace treaty included the Northern Territories. The United States, Great Britain, and Australia agreed that Japan had given up its claims to those four island groups. It was only years later that Japan revived its claims and declared that the foreign ministry official had misspoken in parliament. The Cold War was then raging, and the United States quickly backed Japan against Russia. So for decades Japan has allowed its questionable claims to these four small island groups to block trade relations between its own industry and those controlling natural resources of eastern Russia.

Japan's other dubious claim is one in which the United States played an even more central role, and one where the consequences may be even more dangerous. It concerns what the Chinese call the Diaoyu chain and the Japanese call the Senkaku Islands. They are a clump of five islets and three barren rocks two hundred miles off the Chinese coast, northeast of Taiwan. Only seabirds live there. Nobody paid much attention to them until a couple of decades ago when some preliminary research suggested that the area may be rich in oil and gas reserves. Suddenly, China, Taiwan, and Japan began clamoring that they owned the islands. The United States officially claims to be neutral, but it has effectively sided with Japan. In 1972, the United States handed over "administration" of the islands to Japan, and it has paid a Japanese owner rent for using one of the islets as a bombing range—ignoring the original Chinese title owner.

In fact, the Chinese claim is probably stronger. China's claims are based on navigational records that go back many centuries, and even a 1783 Japanese map shows them to be Chinese territory. Japan's claims are much more recent, for it purported to discover the islands in 1884 and then annexed them in 1895. That was when Japan had just defeated China in war and seized Taiwan, and so China was in no position to argue. It's unfortunate that Japan, which has so much to gain from stability in the western Pacific, is contributing to instability by insisting on dubious territorial claims both to its north and south. Japan refuses to seek adjudication of the disputes in the International Court of Justice, but Washington should push it to do so. Adjudication would not only help resolve these thorny issues but also set an example for all Asia.

Still, the bottom line is that Japanese nationalism is only a modest risk in the years ahead. Likewise, I do not worry so much about South Korea, Thailand, or most of the rest of the region. The Asian economic crisis was an incredible opportunity for political systems in the region to go through spasms of xenophobia, blaming the West for their troubles, and for the most part they did not. Malaysia's prime minister, Mahathir Mohamad, tried to blame Jews and whites who "still have the desire to rule the world," but each time he denounced some foreign scapegoat, his currency and stock market fell another 5 percent. He grew quieter. And South Korea, traditionally one of the more xenophobic countries around, where young women walking hand in hand with Western men used to be accosted by strangers and scolded or even slapped, responded to the crisis by opening its economy and making it easier for foreigners to buy Korean land.

Indonesia is more worrisome, and there is some risk of it coming apart at the seams. But my main concern about nationalism involves China and India. They are among the last major multiethnic, multilingual empires in the world, and neither is a modern nation-state. As the scholar Lucian Pye has observed, "China is a civilization pretending to be a nation-state." Both India and China are in some ways more comparable to Europe than to a particular country, and there is some possibility that in the future they will fragment or lurch into civil war. India has seventeen major languages and twenty-two thousand dialects, and although Hindi speakers are the largest group they do not make up a majority. There is very little in the way of history or culture or language that unites the country, and one of the lessons of the twentieth century is that higher levels of education and urbanization often stimulate aspirations for independence and lead countries to break into smaller bits. The last time India divided, the partition of 1947, the slaughter probably exceeded two hundred thousand, and Pakistan's division in 1971 was also exceptionally bloody.

The same risks of disintegration apply to China as well, and some experts worry that China may fall apart as it frequently has in its long history. Some see a fissure developing between north and south, or between coastal regions and the interior. For my part, I would bet against any division of the Chinese heartland inhabited by the Han Chinese majority. Northerners and southerners may complain about each other and call each other crooks, but for the most part they still identify more with China as a whole than with their province or region. And the growing migration from region to region has also undermined the sense of local identity in most of China. Provinces have been tussling with each other for many years over taxes and raw materials, even setting up roadblocks to prevent silkworm cocoons or kashmir wool from going into neighboring provinces, but I have a hard time imagining many Chinese willing to sacrifice their wealth and their lives for the sake of Guangdong Province or Fujian Province.

Where China is more likely to come apart is at the fringes—Tibet and the Muslim region of Xinjiang in the far west. Both are already boiling with pro-independence sentiment, and as their populations become more urbanized and educated, as a middle class develops, the independence movements will grow. At some point, I think, China may decide that it is not worth the expense and bloodshed and international criticism to hold on to Tibet and southern Xinjiang. That would mean the loss of a considerable amount of physical area but only a tiny part of China's population, and I do not believe that the secession of either would lead to further fragmentation. China's heartland, I think, will hold together.

In both India and China, there is also the question of whether nationalism will be directed at outsiders. Partly because of their history of abuse at the hands of Western countries, Indians and Chinese rival each other in their masterly ability to spin conspiracy theories. In China, this tradition goes back at least to the Boxer Rebellion of 1899–1900, when ultranationalists spread rumors that foreign missionaries were spreading immorality and offending the gods. The Boxers declared that the gods were punishing China with drought "because the Foreign Devils disturb China, urging the people to join their religion, to turn their backs on Heaven and forget their ancestors." The Boxers warned that "Foreign devils are not produced by mankind. If you do not believe it, look at them carefully. The eyes of all the Foreign Devils are bluish. . . . Let the various Foreign Devils all be killed." So the Boxers rampaged around China, shouting the slogan "Protect the country, destroy the foreigner." They sliced off the breasts of Western women and left their corpses on the city walls, and they killed missionaries together with their children, although the greatest slaughter was of Chinese Christians.

Various Chinese governments since then have cultivated antiforeign sentiment as a way of maintaining their own legitimacy. The Communist authorities, for example, have done this by emphasizing what they call "education in national shame." *Guochi,* national shame, is one of those words that pops up constantly in China, and any defeat or setback is portrayed as a *guochi.* China distributes a list of ten "must-knows" for elementary students focusing on this history lesson: "The Western Great Powers and Japan one after the other invaded China. By force they compelled the Qing Dynasty to sign one unequal treaty after another, and they undermined Chinese sovereignty, occupied a large part of Chinese territory, oppressed the Chinese people, and plundered China's endless wealth. They caused China to decline gradually into a semi-colonial, semi-feudal society." There is something to all this, but school textbooks point only to foreign oppression and not to China's own mistakes.

It was this environment that led Chinese university students to attack Western embassies after the May 1999 NATO bombing of the Chinese embassy in Belgrade. To anyone schooled in China the bombing was not an accident, but one more in a 150-year-old string of *guochi* at the hands of Western powers. Some of the students felt that China was now powerful enough to strike back. A banner that protesters hung across the street from the British embassy asked: "What is our atomic bomb waiting for?"

In India, there is a similar mistrust of outsiders, partly a legacy of British misrule. This nationalism has even bred an Indian version of the Boxers, who see as their enemy foreign missionaries like Graham Staines. A fifty-eight-year-old Australian, Staines was an evangelical Christian who had lived most of his life in India's poor state of Orissa, and he spoke several local languages. India was really the only country that his sons, Philip and Timothy, knew, and Staines was renowned for his work with leprosy patients. A strong, solid man with a high forehead, thinning hair, and a beatific smile, Staines ran a hospital for lepers, working with people whose fingers and toes were stubs and who had no money to pay for their care. In January 1999, he arranged a trip with a missionary friend, Gil Venz, to a remote jungle village called Manoharpur, to plan a four-day religious festival for the thirty Christian families in the area. The trips into the jungle were always nice breaks from life in the city, so Staines brought ten-year-old Philip and six-year-old Tim. The two boys, both with short blond hair askew, were thrilled by the excursion into the countryside in the family's World War II–era Jeep.

It was an eight-hour drive, exhausting the two boys, and they arrived after dark. After a brief prayer meeting and a light dinner, Venz went to sleep in a local home, while Staines and his sons retired to the Jeep. It was cool in the hills, so the boys jokingly piled straw on the roof, saying that it would keep them warm, and then they all stretched out and went to sleep in the Jeep. Shortly after midnight, a crowd of eighty anti-Christian zealots crept into the village with clubs and bows and arrows, and surrounded the Jeep. They taunted Staines and his sons, howled antiforeign slogans, and ordered local villagers to stay in their homes. Someone lit the straw on the roof of the Jeep, and then the people in the crowd brought more straw and piled it under the Jeep and lit it to create a bonfire. They smashed the windows and threw more straw inside and lit it as well. Staines was in the back seat, clutching Tim, while Philip was cowering in the front seat. They tried to climb out of the Jeep, but the mob forced them back. As Staines and his sons burned alive, the mob jeered that they were getting a proper Hindu cremation.

News of the killing seared India, and the reaction was reassuring. Some ten thousand Indians attended the funeral for the one large coffin and the two small ones, and everybody in politics denounced the murders. When I visited India shortly afterward, I was often asked by Indians what I thought of the killings, and most people seemed shaken by the incident.

An even greater risk is nationalism directed against other Asians. In the long run, India and China will scrape against each other's ambitions, as they did when they fought their border war in 1962. Already in New Delhi, officials in private speak with passion about the long-run "China threat." India did not need to develop its Agni-II ballistic missile, tested in 1999 and capable of soaring 2,500 kilometers, to hit Pakistan next door; rather, the aim was to reach Chinese cities.

The more immediate risk of war is between India and Pakistan, partly because Pakistan is obsessed with India. It sometimes seems to me quite fitting that an obstreperous, paranoid country like India would have an even more obdurate and jittery country—Pakistan—next door. The two sides are still fighting a ridiculously savage war over some of the world's most desolate real estate: the Siachen Glacier, a spectacularly beautiful and strategically irrelevant hunk of ice in the Himalayas. The Indians have army camps on the glacier as high as twenty-one thousand feet, higher than any point in North America, so high that the slightest exertion leaves a soldier with a pounding heart. The troops live in igloos and are shot at by the other side when they step outside to relieve themselves. They survive because snipers are handicapped when bullets fly unpredictably in the thin air. Both sides sacrifice soldiers to avalanches, altitude sickness, and more mundane misfortunes like freezing to death. Each day, India spends about $4 million on its defense of the glacier; that sum could save, by my reckoning, more than one thousand lives a day among Indian children if it were spent on public health projects.

Pakistani adventurism led to bitter fighting in Kashmir in 1999, and some analysts believe that Pakistan and India came quite close to a general war. American intelligence specialists were horrified when their satellite images revealed that India's "strike force" in Rajasthan was loading tanks and artillery onto railcars in apparent preparation for a broad offensive against Pakistan. If it could not evict Pakistani infiltrators from Kashmir, India seemed to be prepared for a full-scale war. Fortunately, the infiltrators were pushed back, and the immediate crisis was averted.

Yet American spooks are disheartened because whenever they do wargame scenarios on the Indian subcontinent, Pakistan and India invariably end up nuking each other. With such tiny arsenals, it turns out that there is a huge incentive for each side to strike first and take out the other's nuclear capability. Moreover, the knowledge that the other may attempt to do this keeps each side on a hair trigger that increases the risk of a mistaken launch. The fact that India and Pakistan came close to war in 1999 underscores that the risks will remain for decades.

In the case of China, the main risk is also territorial—Taiwan. And Taiwan is also the most fundamental stumbling block in Chinese-American relations. As Admiral Dennis Blair, commander-in-chief of America's Pacific forces, remarked, "Taiwan is the turd in the punchbowl of U.S.–China relations." America finds itself truly caught between competing emotions over Taiwan. On the one hand, a nation that two hundred years ago split off from its mother country in search of freedom cannot help but sympathize with another such aspirant today. On the other hand, while the United States may sympathize with Taiwan's yearning for independence and freedom, it is not eager to risk American lives for it.

While most Chinese do not insist on gaining control over Taiwan immediately, they do want to see some progress. Instead, Taiwan has been developing its own identity, separate from China. When I lived in Taiwan in 1987–88, the people there called themselves *Zhongguo ren,* or Chinese people, and it seemed very natural. But now many insist that they are not *Zhongguo ren* but *Taiwan ren,* or Taiwan people. Democracy in Taiwan has helped forge the island's own identity, differentiating it from China in a process that culminated in the election in 2000 of President Chen Shuibian. Born to uneducated parents, Chen grew up dirt-poor, studied diligently and won honors as perhaps the most brilliant student in the country, then became the top scorer on the bar exam and the nation's youngest lawyer, and ultimately emerged as a Taiwan nationalist, political prisoner, opposition leader—and, now, president. But if Taiwan pushes too far in the years to come, then there is a real risk that China will respond and that war will break out.

Most Westerners are too quick to assume that China would necessarily win the war. China could, of course, use nuclear warheads to destroy Taiwan, but presumably it would not. And in a conventional conflict, it would find it impossible to launch an invasion—it simply does not have the sealift capacity. A Chinese invasion would be a Million Man Swim. Taiwan has air superiority over the Taiwan Strait, so the only thing China could do would be to use submarines and missiles to impose a quarantine around Taiwan and hope that choking off supplies and wrecking the stock market would force Taiwan to capitulate. Maybe it would. But China increasingly has to worry about its own stock market as well. When Beijing began threatening war against Taiwan in the summer of 1999, the stock market index in Taiwan fell 20 percent. But an index of shares in Shanghai fell 40 percent.

While most of the attention has focused on Taiwan, I believe there is another danger spot: those uninhabited Diaoyu Islands that Japan continues to claim. The risk is that China will seize the Diaoyu Islands by force, in the same way that it has effectively seized Mischief Reef off the Philippines. Japanese officials tend to say, a bit nervously, that China would never do such a thing, but in fact there are three reasons why China might. First, Beijing is looking for ways to put pressure on Taiwan, and seizing uninhabited islands near Taiwan would do that. Second, China is extremely sensitive to the fact that it is now a net oil importer, and the Chinese navy is telling the Politburo that the petroleum reserves around the Diaoyu Islands are huge. Third, Chinese overwhelmingly believe that the Diaoyu are rightly theirs, and any Chinese move to seize them would set off nationwide celebrations and strongly boost the legitimacy of President Jiang Zemin and other leaders.

The United States is, amazingly, committed to defending the islands for Japan. The Japanese-American Security Treaty stipulates that the United States will protect not just Japanese territory (which arguably does not include the islands) but also "the territories under the administration of Japan." That is clearly what the Diaoyu Islands are. The upshot is that we have a treaty obligation to side with Japan after any Chinese seizure of the islands, even though we acknowledge that they may be Chinese. It is a crazy situation, and America probably would not risk war with China over a few uninhabited islets that nobody has heard of and that are probably China's in the first place. But if America does not intervene, then the security relationship between Tokyo and Washington will be stretched to the breaking point.

The bottom line is that China and India are both rising powers, and throughout history the most difficult challenge in international relations has been to accommodate emerging powers. America's rise led to the Mexican-American War, the Spanish-American War, and countless smaller interventions and skirmishes. To speak of the China threat can be misleading, because the problem is not China but the structural difficulty of what to do with a nation that is emerging into the big leagues. Yet if it is wrong to demonize China, it is also wrong to paint it as a particularly peace-loving country. Supporters of China often emphasize that it has no history of invading its neighbors, and it is true that in modern times China has been much too weak to tackle surrounding countries. But, if Chinese are intrinsically nonaggressive, then how did a few tribes along the Yellow River end up controlling a continental empire? And what about the fifteenth-century invasion of Vietnam, when China claimed to have killed seven million Vietnamese? And why is China now moving toward precisely the technologies, such as air-to-air refueling and aircraft carriers, that will allow it to project power beyond its borders? Some elderly Asians are edgy precisely because they remember how Japanese industrialization was accompanied by militarization. As an aging Japanese member of parliament confided to me: "China worries me so much precisely because I look at it and feel a terrible sense of déjà vu. It's a nation that had been humiliated and now is industrializing and gaining military power, and it's under the sway of nationalism and the army. I know all about that—it's what happened here in Japan. And in those circumstances, look at what we did!"

China has only a tiny nuclear arsenal, but this includes at least a dozen DF-5 and DF-5A missiles whose intended targets are in the United States. Each can carry a single nuclear warhead that would destroy an American city. Moreover, the evidence is strong (though not conclusive) that China is refining its warheads with information stolen from America about the W-88 warhead. Then again, China's nuclear weapons husbandry is in some respects more prudent than America's. The United States keeps nuclear weapons on a hair trigger, so that it can launch them very rapidly. Thus while Washington announced with much fanfare that it was no longer "targeting" China with missiles, it would take only about a minute to punch the coordinates back in and retarget Chinese cities. China, in contrast, operates on a nuclear doctrine of delayed second strike, meaning that it has no plans to launch its own missiles when it detects incoming warheads, or even immediately after it has been hit. Rather, its doctrine is to strike back days or even weeks after it has been hit, reducing the possibility of an accidental launch. Moreover, China's missiles are liquid-fueled, and just as you cannot leave gasoline in a car for years on end the missiles cannot be stored with fuel inside them. When China prepares to launch, it will have to send out the fuel trucks and fill up the missiles—a process that takes time and is observable by satellites. Likewise, China does not actually keep nuclear warheads on its missiles. In the event of a launch order, the warheads would have to be trucked out and fastened onto the missiles. All this makes it very unlikely that some rogue commander could spend several days fueling up missiles and attaching warheads without being stopped.

Still, China is the only nation in the world that now prepares to target nuclear missiles at the United States. On at least three occasions I have heard of, Chinese officials warned visitors that in a conflict they would strike America (Los Angeles has been mentioned twice). No doubt this is a bluff, but it is a worrying bluff. In addition, some intelligence specialists believe that China is developing biological weapons in a couple of mysterious factories in western China, and they point to strange outbreaks of hemorrhagic fever near those factories. China may be contemplating other weaponry as well. Two People's Liberation Army colonels, Qiao Liang and Wang Xiangsui, argued in a recent book that China might have to use unconventional measures—such as terrorism, drug trafficking, and destruction of the environment—to deal with a powerful adversary, by which they clearly mean the United States.

Ever since the aftermath of the American Revolution, or at the latest the War of 1812, the United States has had only one potential adversary that could destroy it—the Soviet Union. But now that is changing. For the first time in five hundred years, Asian countries are emerging as potential military rivals of the West, and missile technology is giving even tiny North Korea the capacity to kill enormous numbers of Americans. North Korea is believed to have a few nuclear weapons and it is developing Taepodong missiles that may be able to reach the American West Coast, although it is unclear whether it has the ability yet to attach the nuclear weapons to the missiles. In any case, North Korea almost certainly has biological and chemical weapons that it could attach to the warheads; among these are sarin nerve gas and probably the virus that causes smallpox.

In many ways, Asia today resembles Europe a century ago, when rising incomes and education and urbanization spurred nationalism and antagonisms that provoked two world wars. Now these same forces are changing Asia in similar ways. The risk is that Europe's past will be Asia's future. That is one reason why nationalism is one of the greatest threats to Asia in the twenty-first century. I do not believe that war is inevitable, just possible, but this bleak reality must be placed alongside the region's tremendous economic potential. Asia is not only the place on the globe with the greatest economic opportunities, but it is perhaps also the most dangerous place in the world today.

*Girls in areas like this village in West Timor, Indonesia, are always last to get food, education, and medical care, and this discrimination has hurt not just women, but all of Asia.*

### CHAPTER TWELVE

# From the Back of the House

## SHERYL WUDUNN

*Being a woman is a terribly difficult task since it consists principally in dealing with men.*

—JOSEPH CONRAD

When I was living in China, I tracked down Zhang Hanzhi to invite her to dinner one evening. I had heard that she was close to Jiang Qing, Chairman Mao Zedong's widow, and this turned out to be false, as I discovered over appetizers. But during the rest of our dinner, Nick and I found ourselves fascinated and dazzled by Zhang. A tall woman with a faint hint of gray peeking through her neatly permed hair, she is still pretty in her sixties, and it is easy to see how Chairman Mao and others adored her. She is a natural storyteller in both English and Chinese, and with a twinkling eye she carries you into her past world of political intrigue. Her house, for instance, is tied up in history. In the heart of Beijing, it is one of the grand old courtyard homes that are now cultural relics. High red walls ring the entire compound, part of which used to belong to Hua Guofeng, who took over briefly as China's top leader after Chairman Mao died in 1976. When

I visited most recently, Zhang was sitting in her home office, computers whirring. Scrolls of her late husband's calligraphy hung on the walls in nearby rooms, and Chinese antiques were nestled in the many corners of her meandering, maze-like home. It was chilly in the open-air courtyard as we moved back and forth between the rooms. Chaos reigned. A tailor visited. A top government economist dropped by. She got a couple of calls from Zhongnanhai, the sprawling compound of China's top leaders, and the telephone seemed to jangle continuously. Zhang offered me a box of European chocolates and some French tea, and I sat spellbound as I heard her tell a very personal tale. I thought I knew all about her, after a decade of friendship, and then she told me of the women in her family.

It is a yarn that underscores the ways in which the role of women is changing in Asia. On the one hand, discrimination against women holds Asia back because the talent and cleverness of half the population are grossly misused. On the other hand, the gradual inroads women are making in society and the workplace are creating new opportunities—not just for women, but for Asia as a whole. This hugely neglected resource is now beginning to be utilized properly, as women increasingly work not only as mothers and farmers and prostitutes but also as lawyers and writers and commodity traders. As women slowly move into the economic mainstream in Asia, they are bolstering the economic life of the region and becoming a new source of economic vitality. The paradox is that the gains are potentially so large precisely because women historically have been regarded in much of Asia as so insignificant.

In ancient times, there were some strong and dynamic women, such as Empress Wu Zetian in seventh-century China. She worked her way up from a lowly concubine to run what at the time was the most important nation in the world. But around the year 1000, the social noose around women tightened. Scholars developed a strict Confucian code of daily conduct for women in hopes of imposing stability and virtue on society. Women were praised and rewarded with money and gifts if they behaved as "proper" women should, particularly if they declined to remarry when they became widowed. Although sexual infidelity was the norm for men, it was brutally punished among middle- or upper-class women until the nineteenth century. Streams of books, pages upon pages, describe punishments for women who broke the code of honor. One kind of ancient torture, if a woman had a *yehe*, literally a "wild gathering," was to tie her to a Wooden Donkey, an apparatus that mechanically raped her with a wooden phallus. Adulterous women were sometimes punished by having their skin peeled off until they died. Flaying was still on the legal code at the end of the nineteenth century, and widows were sometimes encouraged to commit suicide and thus avoid temptations. Stacks of chronicles list the names of virtuous women who committed suicide. If family members objected, widows who wanted to die would kill themselves discreetly by swallowing a handful of needles.

India was equally repressive, and the ancient practice of suttee—a woman's burning herself to death on her husband's funeral pyre—was not uncommon until the nineteenth century, when the British outlawed the practice. By the twentieth century, it had basically disappeared, and then in 1987 a village woman named Roop Kanwar revived it. When the funeral pyre was made for her husband, an unemployed college graduate who had died of appendicitis, Roop sat on the pyre, a lit match was thrown in, and she burned to death. Her act threw the nation into hysterics, as traditionalists prayed to her honorable soul and feminists were horrified. But as time went on, it seemed that she may not have been so grandly self-sacrificial, after all. Rather, she was compelled by people around her to commit this "honorable" act and apparently was forced back onto the burning pyre several times. In the end, the parliament passed a tougher law to ban suttee. But it was clear that no one had tried to stop her and that millions of people wanted to believe that Roop had voluntarily thrown herself to an honorable death after her husband had died.

Even the languages in Asia expressed and reflected the discriminatory attitudes. A few hundred years ago, when a Korean girl was born, her parents frequently named her Gutsuni, or "last girl," in hopes that she would be the last girl born to the family. China also embraced those values, and even now rural parents occasionally name their daughters Laidi or Yingdi, which mean "bring forth a brother." In the recent past, Chinese men used to call their wives *nei-ren,* or "inside person." That is better than what a Chinese peasant might have called his wife: the *kang shangde,* the "one on the bed." Even now in Japan, the word for another person's wife is *oku-san,* or "person in the back of the house."

The women in Zhang Hanzhi's family emerged from that milieu. The earliest of the clan who anybody remembers is the great-grandmother, a spunky peasant who lived in a village near the famous town of Suzhou. Her name is not known, and it's not clear that she even had one: Chinese women in the nineteenth century were sometimes just called Daughter Number One, Daughter Number Two, and so on. But whatever she was called, that matriarch had a shrewd mind and apparently good looks and she uprooted her family from the countryside to move to the shadowy night district of Shanghai, creating a Chinese revolution in her own family. The result was breathtaking opportunities for her progeny, as well as terrible risks. The great-grandmother eventually started up a nightclub on Hui Le Li, the most famous street for bordellos in Shanghai. These clubs were the intersection for political debate, as revolutionaries sought the secrecy of them to map out their political campaigns.

The great-grandmother's daughter, Xi Cuizhen, who was born in about 1900, grew up partly in the nightclub and thus met some of the most wealthy and well-known men in Shanghai. One of those was a famous literary scholar and lawyer, Zhang Shizhao, a married man who was a former minister of education. This man became Zhang Hanzhi's father. Zhang Shizhao began to spend more time at the bordello, enjoying the charms of vivacious entertainers who poured wine, made sweet talk, and performed a dance or two. Xi was gracious with her guests and obviously caught Zhang's eye, but for her, dancing was virtually impossible because of her very small feet. Her mother and father had begun binding them, wrapping her tiny feet around and around in white cloth, when she was about four years old. Her mother would unravel the cloth every evening, wash Xi's feet, and then rewrap the cloth before her daughter went to sleep. It was extremely painful as Xi's feet began to grow, and it was often difficult to sleep with the constant throbbing pain, but soon the bones of her small toes began to curl under, as they were supposed to. Footbinding breaks the arches and the toes, which curl under to form a foot shaped like a crescent, with a sharp point at the big toe. Chinese women began binding their feet around 1000 A.D.; it was clearly seen as a means to curb women. The attitude was captured by a poet who penned this explanation: "Why must the foot be bound? / To prevent barbarous running around!" Indeed, the twelfth-century philosopher Zhu Xi decreed that in his region in Fujian Province women were by nature so unchaste that the feet of all of them should be bound to prevent them from sin. The Mongols, who came to power in the year 1270, opposed footbinding and condemned the practice, but it still spread because men craved the beauty of the slender and pointed foot. Footbinding lasted for many centuries and began to disappear only in the early twentieth century. Critics dubbed it abusive, newspapers printed the names of families who bound their daughters' feet, and a women's movement began to take shape.

Zhang took Xi Cuizhen on as his second wife, setting her up in her own home, and spending some nights with her and other evenings with his other wives and families. Zhang ended up with three wives, each of whom lived in her own home and complemented his career at different moments in his long life. "Most of the time before 1949, all three wives were living in Shanghai, but not together," said Zhang Hanzhi. "It was part of society. It became the status quo of society and that's how women had to live." Zhang Shizhao and Xi adopted Zhang Hanzhi from a friend, and the girl went to school in Shanghai. This was just after the Chinese Communist revolution, and it was a thrilling time, especially for women. Mao Zedong preached that women held up half the sky, and he established the marriage law in 1950 that gave women the freedom to choose whom they marry. Child weddings were banned, concubines were outlawed, and brothels were closed. Women went to night school, they studied sewing, or they joined the neighborhood factory. Women drove trucks and became pilots.

"I felt the old system was so rotten," recalled Zhang Hanzhi. "I could see that the new society brought new hope, new feeling, new friendship." Her father, still a prominent scholar, was recruited to the leadership of the National People's Congress, the rubber stamp legislature, and moved to Beijing with Zhang Hanzhi. When she was fourteen, her father took her to a party hosted by Mao Zedong. "I could feel the atmosphere after the revolution in 1949," she recalled. "It was so revolutionary, you could really feel that everyone was equal."

Zhang excelled in her studies, particularly in her command of English, and she went to college at the Foreign Languages Institute, an achievement that women in her mother's generation would never have dreamed of. She became a freethinking academic there and married Hong Junyan, a Beijing University professor. Together they had a daughter, Hung Huang. Then in 1962, after meeting Mao again at his seventieth birthday party, the Communist leader asked Zhang to give him his first English lesson. He was impressed by her, and she began to give him regular English tutorials. Then in 1970 he sent her to the Foreign Ministry. "We need women diplomats," he said. "China needs a woman spokesman."

At first, it was an awkward fit: Zhang with her free-spirited academic ways and the Chinese Foreign Ministry with its bureaucratic formalism. On her first day as a diplomat, Zhang went to work carrying a green army bag with the phrase "Serve the People" spelled out in red characters. From it, she took out her teacup—a jam jar held by a plastic net so that she wouldn't burn her fingers. Her conservative colleagues used porcelain teacups. "They all examined my jar when I left," she says. "I was like someone from outer space dropping into the Foreign Office." Then she was given a ruler, scissors, glue, and a small desk and told to read cables of foreign news articles from Chinese embassies abroad and to scan for news about Pakistan. Her male boss explained, "Use the ruler to draw a line around the article, cut it with a scissors, stick it onto a piece of paper, and give it to me."

Zhang, demoralized, was ready to quit. But she persisted, and her support from Mao and her command of English led her to become one of China's top translators, interpreting for Henry Kissinger on his secret mission to Beijing and then for President Nixon on his visit to China in 1972. She worked closely with Mao and was privy to some of the confidential talks that helped establish the foundations of Chinese-American relations.

In November 1971 Mao had nominated her to be an interpreter for the first Chinese delegation to the United Nations. It was on that trip to New York that she got the attention of Qiao Guanhua, the deputy foreign minister and a widower. Zhang had to get Qiao's signature for a document, and when she finally got a chance to see him, he said he was too tired and wanted to take a nap. Disgusted, she tossed the document on the desk and said, "Well, it's up to you!" and stalked out. The deputy foreign minister was shocked that a woman dared to behave so boldly. Still, he must not have been too appalled, for two years later, in 1973, after Zhang had divorced her first husband, she and Qiao married.

As the twenty-first century unfolds, one of the most promising engines of growth in Asia is its women. David S. Landes, an economic historian at Harvard University, has written that the best gauge of whether a society has the flexibility and open-mindedness to sustain an economic boom is the way it treats its women. "The economic implications of gender discrimination are most serious," he writes. "To deny women is to deprive a country of labor and talent, but—even worse—*to undermine the drive to achievement of boys and men.*" In general, he says, "the best clue to a nation's growth and development potential is the status and role of women." One of the fundamental reasons, for instance, that Europe thrived during the high Middle Ages and in the Renaissance was the growing education of women in Europe. Women had some independence in the convents and although they were also victimized, women had successful careers and began to participate more in economic society. From Thomas More to Baldassare Castiglione in the early sixteenth century, scholars were calling for the education of women.

*Juliana Aoetpa (left), an eight-year-old Indonesian girl whose parents pulled her out of school because they could not afford to buy a uniform for her. Parents in Asia are far more likely to take their daughters out of school than their sons.*

For all the injustices and discrimination directed at women in the West, they have done well by international standards, while Asian women have done pretty poorly. In China, for instance, outright cruelty to women still lingers. They are sometimes kidnapped and sold for cash. India, too, still tolerates bride burnings when a new groom is unhappy with his dowry. Child marriages and prostitution, domestic abuse and cruelty to widows still persist in much of developing Asia. And these dark spots will temper growth in the future unless the problems are addressed. In particular, 44 percent of females in India aged fifteen to twenty-four still cannot read or write a short and simple statement about daily life. In Pakistan the figure is 63 percent, so that for the whole of South Asia, the rate of illiteracy among women is 48 percent, the weakest showing of all regions captured by World Bank statistics. Though this ratio is an improvement over the past, it is nearly twice the illiteracy rate among men in the region.

Moreover, parents are much more likely to pull their daughters out of school than their sons. In some places in rural China, even elementary school classes are overwhelmingly boys. And throughout the region, girls are much more likely than boys to suffer the fate of Juliana Aoetpa, an eight-year-old girl with olive skin, big black eyes, and long black hair, who lives in the village of Toeneka in eastern Indonesia. Her region of West Timor had been hit by the Asian economic crisis, by a drought, and by political turmoil that had ravaged the economy, and Juliana was one of the family's main victims. Her parents told her to drop out of the local elementary school and spend the days fetching water and gathering food. "School is free," said her mother, Josisna Banue. "But the children have to buy a uniform, and we just couldn't afford it." The uniform costs a bit less than $2.

After the economic crisis struck Indonesia, most of the school dropouts were girls. "People say it's better for girls to stay at home so that they can save money for the boys," said Meriana Kulla, a seventeen-year-old girl on the Indonesian island of Sumba. "Parents are afraid that their money will run out, so they are pulling the girls out of school." This wasn't surprising, for even before the crisis, girls in Indonesia were six times more likely than boys to drop out of school before the fourth grade. Females are discriminated against not just in access to education but in every aspect of life, even at the dinner table. Efriendi Bea, a twenty-seven-year-old mother of two, was eight months pregnant when she talked about her troubles. She sat on a creaky wooden bed in her dirt-floor hut, decorated with a 1990 calendar and glossy advertisements ripped out of an Indonesian magazine. She said that despite her pregnancy she was eating nothing but bark and roots foraged in the woods. Her two girls, aged ten and four, were eating the same crude diet and looked malnourished. The problem was that when the family comes across more nutritious food, it goes elsewhere. "When we get some meat, my husband eats it," Bea explained. "My husband has to work hard, farming and fishing, so he takes the meat so he'll have energy."

Bea and her family have two chickens, six pigs, and two goats, but they do not eat the livestock. Instead, they sell the animals to get cash—a chicken sells for about $1.25—and Bea's husband uses the cash himself. He spends a total of about twenty cents a week buying tobacco and betel nuts. He rolls the tobacco up in scraps of paper to make his own cigarettes, and he chews the betel nuts, which produce a mild natural high and are widely consumed in rural areas of Asia. "The pattern is for families to save resources for the fathers," said Dr. Anugerah Pekerti, the chairman of World Vision Indonesia, an aid organization. "When the fathers are asked

*Efriendi Bea, a pregnant Indonesian peasant who was eating nothing but bark and roots. The best food, she said, was going to her husband.*

why they smoke cigarettes instead of buying food for their hungry children, they say, 'We can always make more children.' "

The result of attitudes like those in Bea's area is that in times of difficulty the scarce bounty goes to the males. It is not that parents deliberately starve their daughters, but rather that they take the choicest bits of meat out of the pot and set them on the plate of the father or the eldest son. Or parents rush their sick son to the doctor, but when their daughter is ill they feel her forehead doubtfully and say, "Well, let's see how you are tomorrow."

As a result, in much of Asia girls die at a higher rate compared with boys than in most other parts of the world—whether rich areas like the United States or poor areas like sub-Saharan Africa. In fact, Asia has arguably discriminated against women more than any other continent. One measure of this is that women, while a majority of the population in most regions around the world, constitute significantly less than half of all Asians. Nature has made us so that at birth there are always about 5 percent more boys born than girls. But then boys die much more often than girls. Thus by about the age of twenty, girls and boys exist in roughly equal numbers, and after that there are more women than men. In the overall sex ratio for the population, most countries have more females than males. Japan has 51 women for every 50 men, the United States has 50.7 women for every 50 men, and even Nigeria has 50.7 women for every 50 men. Asia stands out as having the world's lowest ratios of female populations, for East Asia (dominated by China) has just 48.9 women for every 50 men, and South Asia (dominated by India) has just 48.5. How did there get to be so many men? Or, more aptly, what happened to all the women? These differences seem tiny in overall percentages, and I don't want to exaggerate the figures, but in practice they mean that 80 million to 100 million girls and women are missing from the statistics. In effect, girls died because they were not given the same food and health care as their brothers, or because they were killed as infants, or selectively aborted because they were female.

In other parts of Asia where the discrimination doesn't mean life or death, it is still an uphill battle for women, and even the men sometimes admit it. "I was married at twenty-eight, and I'm fifty-two now," said Lee Un Kee, a man who lives in Punsooilri in South Korea. "How could I have been married all these years and not beaten my wife?" He paused, looked down the dirt road that cuts through the little hamlet of tile-roofed homes thirty miles northwest of Seoul, and added that it is sometimes unhealthy to suppress the urge. "I would hit her, and she would grab on to me, and then I would go out and drink and calm down," said Lee, who farms a rice paddy beside the village. "For me, it's better to release that anger and get it over with. Otherwise, I just get sick inside. Of course, you have to apologize afterward. Otherwise, you can have a bad feeling in your relationship with your wife." Lee's attitudes are surprisingly common in rural Korea, for studies have shown that wife-beating remains relatively frequent. In one survey, 42 percent of South Korean women said they had been beaten by their husbands at least once. Wife-beating is still considered part of normal life and the woman doesn't always blame just the man. "Of course my husband beats me," said Chong Chin Suk, a fifty-six-year-old woman who runs the village store. "But it was my fault because I scolded him."

"Maybe there are some cases where it's just the man's fault," added Chong, a small, plump grandmother who used a broom of twigs to sweep the dirt in front of her shop. "But ultimately the woman is to blame because if she won't argue with her husband, he probably won't beat her." In fact, Chong counseled her daughter not to resist. "I told my daughter

*Lee Un Kee (right) and Chong Chin Sook talk about wife-beating in the village of Punsooilri, South Korea. Lee says that he has beaten his wife, and Chong says that she has been beaten by her husband.*

not to fight back. I told her, 'If he hits you, just sit back and take it.' " But in fact, Chong added, her daughter never took that advice and when she is hit by her husband, she slugs right back—"like this," Chong explained, shadowboxing as if she were in the ring. Fistfights, in that sense, are a sign of progress. But both men and women acknowledge that beating is wrong and women admit to covering up bruises. Police consider wife-beating a domestic matter and don't get involved, but women also say that it is on the decline.

The status of women in South Korea is certainly improving, and there is virtually no illiteracy among women, who also are nearly as well educated as men. But South Korea is a deeply disturbing puzzle in its attitudes toward women because it is a modern industrialized country and yet no other industrialized country treats females so disgracefully. A 1996 ranking of 125 countries by their proportion of female government employees found that South Korea ranked 107th and North Korea 114th; almost all those that ranked lower were Arab countries or tiny island nations. In that respect, Korea reflects the tenacity of discriminatory traditions that survive and tussle with modern values of gender equality. Korea is adjusting its views toward women, but it will be a long and twisted path ahead. Parents are still making daily decisions that discriminate against daughters. When money became scarce and prospects for the future were uncertain during the Asian economic crisis, families began pulling their daughters out of cram schools so that they could devote the money to their sons. "My older sister has four kids, three girls and then the youngest is a son," said Lee In Sook, a bubbly, self-confident, twenty-five-year-old woman working in Seoul for an advertising company. "Each child used to go to two or three after-school classes a week, but after the economic crisis hit, their dad ordered the girls to drop out of everything but art classes. And since the boy will carry on the family name, he was forced to continue taking three classes, even though he didn't want to." Is that fair? Lee paused and looked a bit perplexed. "It would be best if everyone could get opportunities," she said thoughtfully, "but I think it's right that a son gets the most attention."

At least Lee's older sister kept her three daughters, for one of the most complex and troubling trends in recent years has been that not every mother in Korea does that. When Lee Young Sun (no relation) was pregnant for the second time, she secretly paid a doctor to learn the gender of the fetus. He told her she would have a girl, and she took off with her family on a vacation in misery. She and her husband already had a daughter, and after considering the issue very carefully, they reached their decision. Lee went to the doctor and had an abortion. "I suggested it to my husband, and now I feel differently, but at that time, I felt driven to think that an abortion was necessary," said Lee, who was thirty-five when I met her. "My husband says that he doesn't need a son. But when I ask him, 'Will it be good to have a son?' he keeps silent. In that case, I assume his answer is yes." Echoing the contradictions of her generation, Lee was torn between the demands of tradition and a growing appreciation for females in Korean society. She happily had another daughter later, but even as greater numbers of women like her stand by their baby girls, they also feel an age-old obligation to bear sons. So they secretly abort fetuses of females, and try again.

South Korea has thirty thousand fewer girls born each year than would be the case if there were no such abortions. Three hundred thirty thousand are born annually, suggesting that about one female fetus in twelve is aborted because of its gender. China, India, and other countries have also discovered that expectant mothers are aborting female fetuses, thanks to ultrasound and other modern technology, and the result is shortages of women and girls in society. With forty-five million people in South Korea, there are nearly 116 boys born for every 100 girls, one of the highest such ratios of any country in the world. The only comparable figure is in China, where 118.5 boys are born for every 100 girls, according to a nationwide survey by the Chinese government in 1992. The survey so shocked officials in Beijing that they never formally released the results. In other countries of all races and income levels where data are reliable, the ratio is 105 or 106 boys born for every 100 girls. In some regions of South Korea, the figure soared to as high as 125. I was saddened by the distortion and deaths in China, but I was even more disturbed by the trend in South Korea because it is one of the wealthiest and most educated societies in Asia, and it is sometimes college-educated urban Korean women, not peasants in China, who are making decisions to abort their female fetuses.

"It makes women very nervous, especially if they are married to the first son in a line of first sons, and if she doesn't have a boy, she may fear she will be divorced," said Kwak Bae Hee, who helps run the Korea Legal Aid Center for Family Relations. "Say a family has no son and only a daughter, who gets married. Then from the family's point of view, when the father dies, the family dies with him." Lee Sea Baick, a demographer at Seoul National University, told me bluntly: "This country is a male-dominated country. . . . We look down on women. This concept comes from Confucianism. And we can't develop women's status without destroying some traditional Confucianism." In the 1970s, according to Lee, survey data showed that 27 percent of Korean women allowed their husbands to have concubines if they could not bear sons themselves. That is no longer true, and concubines have disappeared. But already, there are fewer girls in the elementary schools. For example, Lee Yon Ha, a seven-year-old first-grader, and her thirteen girlfriends in the coed classroom at the Segom-jong Elementary School are surrounded by twenty-three boys. "I don't like all these boys around," said Yon Ha, speaking shyly as a few boy pupils were leaping on their desks. The boys were sensing the shortage of girls as well. During folk dances at traditional festivals, several boys had to dance together because of the shortage of girls.

Soon after Lee Young Sun had her second daughter, her father-in-law came to her to ask her when she could get pregnant again. Then one day, he handed her a newspaper advertisement on how to give birth to sons. Lee obediently took the advertisement, stuffed it in her wallet, and never followed up. "My mother-in-law never said a word before, but lately she's been suggesting: 'Why don't you have another child, before it gets too late?'" Lee said. "My father-in-law doesn't put pressure on his own son, but at the family ancestral worship ritual, he prays that the ancestors will bless my husband with a son." Lee says she loves her daughters and does not want a son, but there are moments of indecision. When she rides the bus or the subway with her two daughters, elderly women often come up to her with faces full of pity. "They ask me, 'Have you no son?' And I say, no," Lee said. "Then they say, 'Oh, you must bear a son.' That kind of makes me wonder for a few seconds: Am I doing the right thing by not having a son?

In Japan, discrimination still lingers as the remnants of a tradition in which women for centuries trailed behind their husbands, scrubbing away their muddy footprints, preparing their baths, and, once upon a time, paying for infidelity with their delicate heads. It took three decades for the contraceptive pill to win approval, in 1999, long after it had arrived in other industrialized countries. That victory came only after Viagra, the potency pill for men, sailed through the bureaucratic barriers and into drug stores in six months. Though the portion of women in the labor force inched up from 38 percent in 1980 to 41 percent in 1997, most women workers are only part-timers or hold low-level jobs, partly because the tax code encourages part-time income. Over lunch, Nick once asked Hiroshi Okuda, then the president of Toyota Motor Company, who the highest-ranking woman in the company was. Okuda laughed and said: "I have no idea. She's so low that I don't know." Then he and his aides conversed for a long while, tossing out names and positions and scratching their heads. It turned out that the most senior woman was hundreds of positions down. Perhaps it's not entirely fair to expect a woman on the board of a major Japanese car company, and of course the scarcity of women at the top is not as true at cosmetic companies or department-store retailers, where women are the target consumers. But still, women tend to be given non-career-track jobs that get eliminated more readily in economic downturns, which is exactly what happened when Japanese companies strived to cut costs in the late 1990s.

By the early 1970s, Zhang Hanzhi was at the top of her game. Her husband had become foreign minister and she herself was now a close associate of Chairman Mao, with whom she continued to spend a great deal of time. After Nixon's visit to China, Mao decided that he wanted to send some Chinese youngsters to America to grow up there and learn American ways from the ground up, and so Zhang's daughter, Hung Huang—then twelve years old—was one of twenty-eight children chosen for the experiment. Hung Huang attended the Little Red School House in Manhattan and lived with a family of New Yorkers, who introduced her to *The Cat in the Hat, Sesame Street,* and Ray's Pizza. In 1977, however, Hung had to cut her schooling short and return to China. With Mao's death, the political tides had turned against her mother, who had been put under house arrest. Zhang's guards wanted to get rid of her but didn't want to be blamed for it, so they dropped hints. "They left a pair of scissors one day," said Zhang. "Another day they left a rope. But not for a moment did I ever think of killing myself. I knew how to survive." Hung remained in Beijing until her mother was released in 1980. She then returned to the United States to attend Vassar College. On graduating, she returned to China to become a metals trader in Beijing.

She was enormously successful, and as we became friends in Beijing and I visited her office, I came to admire her intuitive business savvy. She was a natural boss, a strong woman whom strong men did not resent but looked to for leadership. She would bark commands in Chinese while speaking on two phones in English and monitoring her computer screens. She could come across as incredibly American—once when she described someone as "a bitch on wheels" in her customary rapid-fire English I realized that anyone who met the two of us and was told that only one of us was born an American would guess that it was she—but she had that perseverance, that *gaman* that so characterizes Asia. The discipline, the work ethic, and the incredible drive all helped explain her tremendous success.

Of course, as a woman Hung was always a bit out of place in the Chinese business world, and occasionally it showed. Once when she was desperate to win a $60-million contract, she stayed for hours in the offices of the two bureaucrats responsible for awarding the deal. She answered their phones, pleaded with them, but won the contract only after she broke down in tears. She went drinking with male customers, although she did not buy them hookers as a male executive might have; the first time out she drank too much and ended up vomiting in the laps of her customers.

Slowly the status of women in Asia is improving, reflecting and triggering a greater open-mindedness, and this is good not only for the women, but also for the future growth of the nations as a whole. Women entrepreneurs are in abundance in China, Hong Kong, Singapore, and Taiwan, and there are more and more women starting new ventures in the rest of the region.

Based on the way education is spreading and values are changing, the trend seems likely to continue. The progress, ironically, has been greatest in places like India and China where women traditionally were treated most dreadfully, partly because there is so much potential for improvement. Asia has made tremendous strides in education, and more girls are going to school today than ever before. Illiteracy rates among girls have dropped drastically compared to two decades ago; in China, where 14 percent of young women were illiterate in 1980, now only 4 percent are. Even in India, illiteracy rates among women have fallen to 44 percent today from 61 percent in 1980. Of course, Afghanistan under the Taliban marks a retreat of several hundred years for women—the Taliban generally do not allow girls to go to school or women to be examined by male doctors. But in the cities, which represent the future of Asia, it is increasingly common to see educated young women holding important jobs alongside men. More and more women in Asia are being given—and are taking—an opportunity to play a role in economic life. So now, one of the largest potential pools of labor is opening up, and the impact is already showing.

Women were the engine of China's boom, for example, for the factories in coastal China that produced the shoes and toys and clothes that poured into markets all over the world were staffed by young peasant women from the villages who in past generations never entered the paid labor force. Soon the factory managers began to prefer women, because their hands were thought to be more nimble and quicker than those of young men.

Companies that put the talents of women to better use also tend to have stronger economic performance. Kathy Matsui, an analyst at Goldman Sachs in Tokyo, has compared the performance of the fifty companies in Japan that have the highest proportion of female employees with the fifty companies that have the lowest proportion. Companies with more females performed nearly 50 percent better on the Tokyo Stock Exchange than those with the lowest ratio of females. One major reason for the difference in performance is that those companies that recognize the potential for women are also more open-minded and flexible in their approach to business.

As in China, the past discrimination creates opportunities for quick improvement. One measure of that is female participation in the labor force. In the United States, 46 percent of all workers are women, a very high figure that helps explain some of the bounce in the American economy. The United States has boomed in part because more and more women have joined the labor force, often in very productive jobs. In con-

*Indian women are a hugely neglected re-
source, for in rural areas few participate in
the economy. This grandmother and mother
in Rajasthan spend most of their time in this
cave-home where they live with the children.*

trast, only 41 percent of workers in Europe are women, and worldwide the figure is 40 percent.

In East Asia, there is some room for gains as more women enter the workforce, but not much. In Vietnam, 49 percent of the workforce is made up of women, in Thailand it is 46 percent, and even in China it is 45 percent. There are not many unemployed women to add to the economy in those countries, although there are many who could be employed more fruitfully. Elsewhere there is some room for gains in the years ahead: In

Japan and South Korea, the figure is 41 percent; in Indonesia, 40 percent; in Malaysia and the Philippines, 37 percent. But the greatest potential gains are in India and the other countries of South Asia. Only 32 percent of Indian women are in the labor force, and just 27 percent in Pakistan. As those women get jobs, they will help fuel Asia's industrialization.

In the past few years, a few selected women have become political leaders, such as Benazir Bhutto in Pakistan, Indira Gandhi in India, Megawati Sukarnoputri in Indonesia, Sirimavo Bandaranaike and Chandrika Kumaratunga in Sri Lanka, Khaleda Zia and Sheikh Hasina in Bangladesh, and Corazon Aquino in the Philippines. Yet one should not make too much of this, since every one of them inherited the mantle of power from a father or husband, and their rises speak less of equal opportunities than they do of a political aristocracy. When Megawati (the daughter of Indonesia's first president, Sukarno) emerged as the leading vote-getter in Indonesia's elections in 1999, one of the factors working against her was her gender, for many Indonesians argued that their country simply was not ready for a woman president. She ended up as vice president. Now, at least, Megawati and the other female leaders serve as role models, and others will follow.

Hung sees her tearful outbursts and messy drinking sessions in China as growing pains, the awkward acts that come with any transition. Now Hung is a partner at a high-powered consulting firm in Beijing. While her mother is an enlightened traditionalist in her views about women, Hung is modern, individualistic, and multicultural. She is on her third marriage—this one to a French diplomat. But unlike her forebears, Hung is much less dependent on men. Like a growing number of women in China today, her achievements are varied and distinctly her own. Women may still be treated like dirt in many rural areas, but in the cities, the relationship between the sexes is not all that different from the way it is in the United States.

The Zhang family's own troubled journey underscores some of the changes in gender relations. For the great-grandmother and the grandmother of the clan, the only opportunity to rise was to appeal to men's passions. By the time Zhang Hanzhi came along, it was possible for a woman to demonstrate her talents, but even Zhang was aided by her marriage and her association with Mao. Now the next generation, Hung Huang, is finally able to do whatever she can on her own, as a person rather than as a woman.

When Zhang's memoirs became a best-selling book in China, readers got a glimpse of how Hung's mother, like other women of her generation, views her own success. All they had to do was read the title—*Ten Years in the Storm: Remembering My Father, My Husband and Chairman Mao.* While her success was very much her own, she still saw her life path as intertwined and enhanced by the three most powerful men in her life. That is demonstrably different from the way Hung and the younger generation of educated women in Asia today see themselves.

"I would never have given that title to my book," says Hung. "Link my achievements to the men in my life? Never."

Young women in Asia may not be challenging the status quo as aggressively as American women did in the 1960s, and there is no bra-burning or marching to "take back the night." But from India to Malaysia to Japan, there is a broad resentment at discrimination and an equally broad yearning for greater career opportunities and burden-sharing in the home.

"My father almost never steps inside the kitchen," said Chie Suzuki, a twenty-seven-year-old systems engineer whose father didn't want her to go to college and study computer science. "If Mom is around, he wouldn't even serve tea—he'd just yell, 'Tea!' But of course if my mother isn't around, he has to do it by himself." Suzuki paused reflectively and added: "Would I marry someone like my dad? No way!"

Takashi Ikoma, a forester in Omiya, summed up the traditional male view by recounting his own domestic skills: "I can't light a stove. I don't know how to use the washing machine. I've never washed a dish." As Ikoma saw it, he did the outside work and earned the income, and his wife cooked and ran his bath and scrubbed his back. Yet even Ikoma is a great improvement over earlier generations. An elderly woman in Omiya, Toshie Yoshida, said that her late husband would put his underwear on after stepping out of the bath, and then she would have to pick clothes for him and dress him each day, helping him to put his shirt and trousers on as if he were a small child. "He didn't even know where his socks were kept," she said.

One of the hidden strengths of women, in Japan and elsewhere in Asia, is that traditionally they tended to be the ones who dealt with money. In peasant families, they were the ones who took goods to market and sold them, and even now in Thailand or Indonesia the market-sellers are mostly women, as are the people who run the tiny streetside restaurants and shops. All this gives women a sense of money and bargaining, a savoir

*Women traders in a market on the island of Sumba, Indonesia. In much of Asia, men do the farming while women take charge of selling the produce in the markets. This means that in rural areas women have more experience than men in commerce, negotiation, and money, and some women are able to move up from spreading their wares on a cloth on the ground to opening stalls or shops or tiny restaurants. But very few have made the next leap, to operating larger businesses.*

faire that helps them move up one notch on the commercial ladder to run larger businesses or work in corporations. Even in Japan, where women have been denied much of a role in the business world, women play a far more important economic role than is generally recognized—as consumers. Women control the purse strings in the home, make most decisions about purchases, and give their husbands only modest allowances for spending money.

In Omiya, a postal worker named Norikazu Okuyama explained with a sparkle in his eye that his wife gives him $300 a month from his paycheck, and he can spend it as he wants. His wife is in charge of the rest of the money. "My wife keeps the accounts very strictly," Okuyama grumbled good-naturedly. "I can't cheat her out of even one yen." As his workmates egged him on, Okuyama said he spent his allowance in large part on a common Japanese pastime—drinking in bars with colleagues. "I'm very stingy," Okuyama said, grinning. "So I spend money only on what I can consume."

One survey a few years ago found that half of Japanese men were dissatisfied with the size of their allowances, and some have to plead with their wives for an advance if they run out early. Okuyama sees this at his job at the post office, which in Japan also functions as a savings bank. Husbands sometimes slink in toward the end of the month, asking to withdraw money secretly from family accounts. "But then we could get complaints from the wives," said Okuyama. So someone at the post office first calls the wife to get her approval.

One might think that cash machines would undermine the financial authority of the wives. But many wives refuse to give their husbands a cash card for the family account. "Generally speaking, I think the leadership of households in Omiya is taken by wives," Okuyama said. "Things go best when the husband is swimming in the palm of his wife's hand." The upshot is that women have almost no corporate economic power, but enormous influence on the buying end.

Still, what matters for economic growth is production, and women in Asia have not been encouraged to produce much except children. The Asian economic crisis helped change those attitudes, though, by engendering massive layoffs of men and forcing their wives into the marketplace to make some money in their stead. When Jang Chang Ik, my friend the Korean entrepreneur, had to raise cash to start his new software company, the person who took on the task was his wife, Kim Gwi Seon. Kim looks like a petite and docile wife, a pretty woman with soft cheekbones and active eyes that dart around under her sharp black bob of a haircut. A wife who stands firmly behind her man, she spent fifteen years raising her two boys and cleaning house. When visitors come, her first thought is, "I have to clean my house!" because she hasn't scrubbed the floors of her already tidy apartment. She makes sure her two boys do their homework and behave nicely to neighbors. She is gracious to her in-laws and makes a good Korean meal with kimchee for them every night. When the crisis began, Kim was forty-three and the only thing she wanted in her staunchly middle-class existence was to be able to say that she was the wife of a successful man in a big company.

Jang had first floated the idea of starting his own company a few years earlier, but Kim had rejected it flat out. "He was too young, and it was too risky to start a new business at that time," she recalled telling him. "We

*Kim Gwi Seon is an invisible force on behalf of her husband's company. He asks her to stay away from the office to avoid embarrassing him, but she still does much of the key work for the firm.*
(Sheryl WuDunn)

had no money, so I said no." He brought it up again the next year, when they were living in the southern city of Kumi, South Korea. She hemmed and hawed before relenting, but then he got cold feet and stayed at LG Group. Only after he was fired did they agree that they would become entrepreneurs. So Kim embarked on her part of their plan. While her husband was setting up an office in Seoul, she was out knocking on the doors of bankers to see if she could get loans to help start their new company, which they called JCI Information Technology.

She was turned down everywhere. So she went to a state corporation that lends to start-ups. She had heard that they offered a very favorable rate, 0.6 percent. But when she talked with them, they told her that the deadline for new loans had passed. She found another lending corporation for small- and medium-sized companies and she filled out a stack of application forms. She handed it over and was told that a decision would be made later. And the banker gave her the familiar refrain: "What is necessary to get a loan is a successful business record." Kim and Jang ended up pouring in money from friends and family to start JCI, and Kim now takes care of much of the accounting, banking, and other administrative errands for JCI. But changes in attitudes come slowly, and although Jang is happy to have his wife do the work, he does not want her showing up in the office. It would appear too "family-like" in front of his employees. "He wants the company to be strictly a company," Kim explained. So she works out of their home, while she also takes care of the kids and their homework, the housecleaning, the laundry, the gas bills, and the cooking. She feels uncomfortable taking any credit, saying proudly that she is just a wife. Yet at JCI, Kim is a hidden treasure, a behind-the-scenes chief financial officer, a catch-all administrator, and an occasional accountant. She is also a housewife who, like many women in Asia, continues to define herself in terms of her husband and his career.

Throughout Asia, there are unsung heroes and saviors like Kim, women who are gaining the confidence and skills to help form a business or manage a company. Not all women are as hidden from view as Kim, and more of them are stepping out onto stages traditionally dominated by men. In the long run, the emergence of women like Kim or Hung Huang into the business world is one of the hallmarks of the change that is coming to Asia and invigorating it.

*Wei Haiyun (left) and Liu Yingchun with Kong Degui, getting polluted drinking water from the Yellow River. The children are stunted and mentally retarded because of the effects of the pollution.*

### CHAPTER THIRTEEN

# The Filthy Earth

## NICHOLAS D. KRISTOF

*The environment is everything that isn't me.*

—ALBERT EINSTEIN

Whether or not rising nationalism results in missiles flying around Asia, a war is already under way in the region. It kills three million people each year, mostly children and the elderly, and yet it is scarcely noticed. It is the war between humans and the environment, and it is one that both sides are losing. The environment is one of the bleakest prisms through which to view Asia, for it is becoming a brake on development and a challenge to the rest of the world as well. This environmental catastrophe is one reason to temper one's optimism about Asia.

The costs of Asia's industrial revolution are etched in little hamlets like Badui, a Chinese village in rural Gansu Province. It was a dazzling autumn day with just a hint of crispness in the air as I strode into Badui, and at first it looked like a big mud pie. Badui is a warren of high mud-brick walls, within which are mud-brick huts and mud-brick outhouses and mud-brick storage sheds containing stacks of mud bricks. The village is perched beside the upper reaches of the Yellow River, a great expanse of inpenetrable gray about 150 meters wide. The river simply gives this part of China a glance and then moves on, without leaving any water behind, so the landscape is dry and barren. On the far bank of the Yellow River from Badui, the land rises from the water as a series of jutting cliffs, and even the close side has only a few trees and a bit of grass before giving way to the same moonscape of barren silver crags.

Badui is five miles from the nearest road. The average family has a patch of dirt, a few chickens, a rickety table and a couple of chairs, and sometimes a basin for washing clothes. Families with a grandfather or grandmother at home keep a spare coffin tucked away in a corner of the courtyard. The village is resoundingly quiet—most of the time, there are no radios or televisions to interrupt the overwhelming quiet, just an occasional barking dog or shrieking child. Framed as it is by rugged silver mountains on one side and the meandering river on the other, the majesty of the natural setting is overpowering.

I roamed through the dirt paths and looked into the doorways. The first home had a small courtyard with a woman washing clothes in a great metal pan as two teenage boys stood behind her idly. The woman said her husband had just died in his thirties—"of a stomach ache," she explained—but what struck me was the way the teenage sons stared at me, their heads lolling to the side and their mouths creasing into monstrous grins. Their hair was shaggy and unkempt and their expressions preposterous.

"Yeah, they're not right in the head," the mother said, as she saw me looking at them uneasily. "Nobody is in this village. That's why people in these parts call this the 'village of idiots.' I wasn't born here; I married into it. But the same thing is happening to me. I can feel it every day. My brain's getting fried up until eventually there'll be nothing left. My mind goes blank sometimes, as if everything in there has been poured out somewhere. That's what happens here."

My skin began to crawl.

In the next courtyard, a young man with a thicket of untrimmed hair and a stupid smile just stood staring at me, unable to say a word or summon the rest of his family. I roamed about, more and more uncomfortable, but every courtyard seemed haunted by the same twisted faces and hideously silly smiles. The words "village of idiots" rang in my ears.

Then, smack in the middle of the path, was a lanky grandfather with laughlines all over his face, wearing a blue cap and dark work clothes. He looked fine, but he was holding the hand of a little girl—not just a little girl, but a miniature girl, who came up only a bit higher than his knees. She was very cute, in red flowered suspenders, red shoes, and a pink jacket, her head shaved and her cheeks and stomach plump. She was the size of a toddler, and her split pants and lack of underwear showed that she was not yet potty-trained. But she stood and walked effortlessly on her own, and she gazed at me with solemn black sparkling eyes that were those of a child, not a baby. I looked at her, confused, and she looked back at me, equally confused.

"What's her name?" I asked her grandfather, who was beaming with pride at the attention I was focusing on her.

"She's Liu Yingchun, my granddaughter," he said, and he tried to tickle her to get her to smile. She simply stared at me in curiosity.

"How old is she?"

"She's seven years old," he said, although I later worked out that by American conventions she was six.

"Then why is she so short?"

"Oh, kids here are like that," protested the grandfather, still beaming lovingly at her. "Plenty of the kids just never grow up, never learn to speak. But this girl, she's a smart one. She may yet learn how to speak. And she's growing. She's a growing girl."

I looked at the proud grandfather, but my spine was tingling. Despite the bright sunlight, Badui no longer felt charming but rather sinister and grotesque. I felt I was in the Twilight Zone.

"Kids like her are all over," the grandfather said. "Right in here, this home here," he said, pointing to the mud-brick wall beside us. "There's a boy like that."

I stepped into the doorway of the compound he had pointed to. A big yellow dog barked furiously and strained at its chain as he lunged at me, and so I stopped there and looked inside. The courtyard was all dirt, and on the far side was a one-story rectangular block of a house made of white-washed mud bricks with a concrete addition. A young woman in a green sweater was stringing beads, perhaps making necklaces to sell, and her baby sat beside her, also dressed in green. A few other children and grown-ups were standing around as well.

"Hi there," I called out. "Can I come in?"

The dog barked more furiously, and the peasants looked at me in astonishment. But the young mother waved me in, and I entered, giving the dog a wide berth. I walked over to the woman in green and nodded toward her baby, who looked about one year old.

"What a cute baby!" I said ingratiatingly. It was perhaps the wrong moment, for he had just urinated where he was sitting. Everybody looked at him, and he began to play with his fingers in the urine. His mother picked him up, scolded him, and moved him away. "You dumbo!" she said to him lovingly, tapping on his chest. "You melon-head!"

"What's the baby's name?" I asked her.

"Wei Haiyun." She explained that his name was made up of the characters "hai" for ocean and "yun" for cloud. Haiyun grasped his mother tightly as I approached, and he looked away, as everybody laughed. She cradled him like a nursing infant.

"How old is the baby?"

She mumbled something under her breath.

"What was that? How old?"

"Eight years old," she murmured softly.

"Eight? He can't be eight! When was he born?" I grilled her for a time about his birthdate and his sign in the Chinese zodiac and then asked the neighbors as well. But Wei Haiyun was indeed eight years old. I was so stunned by his height that I took a piece of string and held it against him, cutting it off to record his height. (On returning home I measured it— twenty-nine inches. That is the height an average American baby reaches at twelve months.)

I looked closely at Haiyun. His head was shaved, his ears stuck out from the side of his head, and his cheeks were red and chapped from the wind. He had piercing black eyes that stared at me anxiously, so that looking at his face alone I would have judged him a handsome boy of eight or ten. But he was miniaturized, roughly in proper proportions, and he behaved like a baby: He ran to his mother to be cradled when he was upset, and he had never learned to use the toilet. His green pants were stained dark where he had repeatedly soiled himself, and they were left unzipped. In the back they were split so that they opened whenever he squatted. He wore a matching green jacket, old and patched, with an emblem of a soccer-playing squirrel on the chest.

It turned out that one-third to one-half of the 180 people in Badui have some serious physical disorder, and nearly all the peasants die early— often in their forties. Many lose their minds, or become deaf or blind before they die. Women report frequent miscarriages and stillborn children, as well as periodic birth defects. Shortly before I arrived, a baby had been born with fingers fused on both hands. But what struck me most was how many tiny children there were like Haiyun, many not just short but also mentally retarded or deaf.

Similar problems, on a more modest scale, also confound thousands more peasants in other nearby villages, and everyone knows what the problem is: the effluent water dumped into the river by the Liujiaxia Fertilizer Factory just upstream. That river water is the only source of drinking water for Badui. The peasants know that the water is contaminated and that it will destroy their minds and bodies, but they are thirsty and there is no alternative.

People are dying of pollution not just in Badui but all over Asia. The entire continent is an environmental nightmare, for rapid industrialization has produced some of the filthiest air and water ever seen in human history. One United Nations study found that of the fifteen cities with the worst air pollution in the world, thirteen were in Asia. "The worst pollution in the world is unequivocally in Asia," says Daniel C. Esty, a specialist on international environmental issues at Yale University. "The statistics about China are stunning, and right behind those Chinese cities stand almost every other major city of Asia: Bangkok, Manila, and Jakarta are all right up there among the top polluted cities of the world."

Every year, more than 1.5 million Asians die from the effects of air pollution alone, and another five hundred thousand die from the dirty water and bad sanitation, according to estimates published by the World Health Organization and the World Bank. Another study by the World Bank, using different assumptions, calculates that air and water pollution together kill two million people annually in China alone—suggesting that the toll throughout Asia is three million or more. In short, more people die annually from pollution in Asia than died in the entire course of the Vietnam War (1.4 million, from the 1950s through the 1970s). To put it another way, roughly ten times as many people die in China every day from pollution as were killed in the Tiananmen massacre of 1989.

The upshot is that environmental degradation is one of the structural flaws in Asia's economic architecture. For decades, Asia's factories churned out more and more goods, and these were factored into stellar GDP growth rates while the environmental ruin was ignored. Yet the pollution is now a major constraint on Asian growth and on Asian life expectancies, and it also poses increasing problems for the rest of the world as well. While there has been progress on most fronts of human development in Asia, with regard to the environment things have gone steadily downhill. Environmental issues are often separated and dealt with apart from broader issues of the economy or society, but that is short-sighted. There are some signs that Babylon and the Fertile Crescent, after having pioneered human civilization, collapsed because they destroyed their local environment. Asia is poisoning its land, water, and air so severely that it is impossible to judge the economic prospects without taking a whiff of what is going on: All these poisons are subverting the economic foundation that Asia is building, and they are a legitimate reason for caution about the future.

Take Badui and the villages around it, for if ever a compelling case could be made for closing a nearby polluting factory, this should be it. The area is China's frontier, and it was settled in 1501 by a branch of the Kong clan, descendants of Confucius (in Chinese, Confucius is Kong Fuzi, or Mr. Kong). Some of the land where the river regularly overflowed and dumped its silt was particularly fertile, and the local peasants grew relatively prosperous. Prospects looked even better when the Communists took over and promptly planned a series of grand dam and hydroelectric projects along the Yellow River. One of those power projects began generating electricity in 1961, and it attracted companies like Liujiaxia Fertilizer Factory that needed cheap electricity and plentiful water. The fertilizer factory was built beginning in 1966, on the site of the original Kong graveyard.

The villagers began dying soon after the factory went into operation. The middle-aged simply got thin, weak, and then died. Nursing women had no milk, and their babies died. Children developed a rash that lasted until their late teens. And those babies who did live sometimes stopped growing.

The peasants told me all this, but it was the sight of Wei Haiyun that shook me the most. He sat in his mother's arms, frail and tiny, more an infant than an eight-year-old, peeking out at me and then hiding his face in her shirt when he saw I was watching. She was ambivalent, eager to talk about her misfortunes yet embarrassed about her son's condition and fearful that I would think her a bad parent.

"Is he toilet trained?" I asked.

"Not really," she sighed, looking into his face as he tried to hide it. "No. We hope he will be."

"Does he go to school?"

"Not yet. I hope he'll go to school later, when he's a bit older."

"Does he speak much?"

"Yeah, a little."

"What does he say?"

" 'Ma.' Things like that. He can say 'Ma-Ma.' "

"Anything else?"

She bit her lip and shook her head.

"Can he say 'Ba-ba'?"

She shook her head again and looked as if she would weep.

"Has he ever seen a doctor?"

"No, no, no!" A bitter laugh. "No doctor has ever come to this village."

"What are you going to do?"

She shrugged helplessly, and put out her finger to tickle her son's cheek. I turned to the village chief, Kong Fanli, a gaunt peasant who said he was thirty-three years old but did not seem to be altogether right in the head himself. He wore a Chicago Bulls T-shirt, probably discarded a decade earlier in America, and his skin showed through a half-dozen holes in the shirt. He smoked a home-rolled cigarette wrapped in newspaper, and his speech was slurred.

"What are you going to do?" I asked him.

"We're peasants," he said, puffing nervously on his cigarette. "We don't know what to do."

"So?"

"So, if the kids grow, they'll grow. And if they don't, they won't."

I said nothing, and after a few more puffs he continued.

"I don't know what to do. There's nothing to do. Everybody just dies. The water, you know. Even the goats—you watch them. When they get old, their brains go and they become blind and they stagger around and run into things. It happens to anything that drinks this water."

"Where do you get the drinking water?"

"I'll show you." Kong took another puff and led me—and everyone else, including little Wei Haiyun, who could walk well despite his tiny size—down a trail to the Yellow River one hundred yards away. The grassy bank was pleasant and deserted, and the scene was majestic with the great muddy river slowly flowing past. Kong gestured to the water, and said: "Here's where we reach over and get the water. With buckets."

I looked at the water, all brown and mucky and smelly. It did not look potable, and I said so. "Actually, it's pretty good right now," laughed Kong Xiangrong, a middle-aged man who had sneaked away from his wife for a nap by the river. "This time of year the water level is fairly high, and that helps. And this time of day, in the late afternoon, the river is higher, too, so that's why we get the water about now. In the morning, it's lower and so it's really dirty. In the seasons when the water really gets low, then it gets so dirty that the fish die. Their bodies come to the surface and float on their backs down the river."

He cackled and added, "They call it the Yellow River. But when the river level falls, it becomes the Black River."

"There must be somewhere else you can get water," I told them. The peasants all shook their heads vigorously.

"Where?" said Kong Fanli, scratching his Bulls T-shirt and looking around.

"You saw how far away we are from the road," said Kong Xiangrong, who had given up on his nap. "We talked about laying a pipe, but it would be much too far. And there's not much rain here, and there aren't any streams. We've tried wells, but there's no water no matter how deep we dig. You think I want to drink this river water? You think I want to give it to my kids? To my goats? I feel sick every time I pull a bucket out. But there's no other water."

Factory officials, when I contacted them, were unsympathetic. They acknowledged the pollution problems but noted that there was no firm scientific proof that they were the cause of the birth defects. The officials argued that the biggest problem is not pollution but indolent peasants. "The villagers are lazy and unreasonable," argued Zeng Qingang, a factory director. Zeng argued that the peasants were simply seeking payoffs from the factory instead of trying to make a living themselves, and he added: "They say, 'We should get rich by living off the factory.' "

I was never able to establish the precise health problem in Badui. The evidence that the cause of the problem was factory effluent was strong but circumstantial: The problems started when the factory began operations, they affected animals as well as people, and they went away in a group of villages that began piping in their water from another source in 1989 and 1990. Water samples that I took with me and had analyzed in Japan showed the presence of arsenic and other poisons, but not in levels that would be deadly—and in any case, the chemists I consulted were hard-pressed to explain just what could cause all the symptoms found in Badui. Arsenic and heavy metals may be part of the explanation, but heavy metals should cause more birth defects while arsenic should cause darkened skin. Some experts suggested that something in the water might be combining with a mineral deficiency in the peasants, or that a dangerous chemical might accumulate in fish or in the potatoes that are the peasants' staple food. That uncertainty is fairly typical. We tend to think of environmental issues as scientific and thereby precise, but in fact causal connections are very difficult to establish.

Asian pollution mostly kills Asians. But increasingly, filth is becoming as cosmopolitan as a business executive, traveling around the world—and this makes environmental problems particularly difficult to tackle. If the theories of greenhouse gases causing global warming are correct, then a carbon molecule emitted in China will threaten the Long Island shoreline as much as a carbon molecule that wafts up from a New York City smokestack. Asia is still a minor source of greenhouse gas emissions, but the trendline is ominous: The two fastest-growing major sources of greenhouse gases are China and India. Within the next decade or so, China will surpass the United States and become the leading source of greenhouse gas emissions. So if the seas rise and the world's climate changes, it will be Asia that will push the world over the edge. In the twenty-first century, the battle over carbon emissions may be one of the most poisonous confrontations between Asia and the West.

I sympathize with the Chinese and Indians who say that they are within their rights. The United States has been spewing out carbon for 150 years, while China and India are just getting started. Of the human-source carbon out there in the atmosphere, only an infinitesimal portion is from Asia. Thus it seems unfair for the United States to say: "You've got to industrialize more slowly because we've already pumped out as much carbon dioxide as the atmosphere can absorb." The American position seems particularly unfair because the United States is continuing to spew out vast amounts of carbon to support the American lifestyle. China puts out only one-ninth as much carbon per person as the United States. As Shu Kongzhong, a Chinese environmental expert, put it: "In the developed world, there are often only two people in a car. Yet you want us to give up riding in a bus." But, realistically, the problem of global warming will be resolved only if China, India, and Indonesia change their position and agree to mandatory cutbacks in their emissions. Since the United States has made clear that it is not going to do much to curb its own emissions unless Asian countries do so as well, the fate of global warming ultimately depends on whether Asia does its part and then some.

If global warming does take place and the seas rise, then that could be a significant blow to the prospects of some Asian countries. While northern countries like China and Russia might enjoy some benefits—a longer growing season and a more temperate climate—there are vigorous debates among scholars about how the benefits would weigh against the losses, such as lost coastland. Certainly tropical island countries like the Philippines and Indonesia would be hard hit. Bangladesh would be especially vulnerable, for huge areas of its delta are barely above sea level. Even worse off would be the island countries of the Pacific, like Kiribati and Tuvalu, which would vanish beneath the seas.

A related global concern is the resources that Asia will require as it industrializes. Pessimists see Asia as a huge vacuum cleaner growing exponentially, eventually sucking up so much of the world's grain and oil that scarcities will be inevitable. Already, Asia's annual grain imports have increased from six million tons in 1950 to more than ninety million tons today. Lester R. Brown, one of the Cassandras of food security, argues that by the year 2030 China alone may annually need to import two hundred million tons of grain, a quantity equal to current total world exports. He adds: "Food security is likely to emerge as the defining issue of the era now beginning, much as ideological conflict was the defining issue of the historical era that recently ended."

Similar arguments are made about oil supplies. Suppose, for the sake of argument, that China eventually achieved the American level of automobile use and oil consumption. It would then consume eighty million barrels of oil a day—compared to present global production of sixty-four million barrels a day. Even with more realistic assumptions about Asian oil consumption, there are real questions about where the petroleum will come from.

I'm a bit skeptical of these calculations, partly because, historically, pessimists have been wrong on issues of scarcity. They have always anticipated shortages, while in fact new technologies or higher prices have generated far more additional production than anyone dreamed. In 1914, for example, the United States Bureau of Mines suggested that American oil reserves would last ten years. In 1939 and again in 1951, the Department of the Interior concluded that the American supply of oil would run out in thirteen years. Thus it is reasonable to be skeptical of alarmist claims today. But Asia's industrialization will test the world's supplies of resources as never before.

. . .

Take a deep breath in Seattle, and you can inhale Asia. Chinese air pollution drifts over the Pacific and has been detected on the U.S. West Coast. Asia's worst pollution problems have to do with the air, especially in the gritty industrial cities of China and India. The danger level is generally considered to be reached when the particles in a cubic meter of air weigh more than one hundred micrograms. That is well above the level on the streets of New York City. But Lanzhou, China—perhaps the most polluted city in the world, at least in terms of suspended particles—has 732 micrograms per cubic meter. And worst of all is the "indoor air pollution" caused when people cook food on coal stoves or heat their homes in winter with coal briquettes. Indoor particulates while meals are cooking have been measured at eleven thousand micrograms. This indoor air pollution probably kills far more people than normal air pollution, and it is relatively easy to tackle: Improved stoves with good chimneys dramatically reduce the smoke.

**NUMBER OF DEATHS ANNUALLY FROM AIR PARTICULATES, INDOOR AND OUTDOOR**

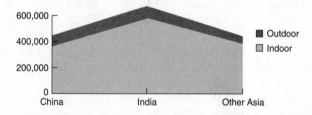

Source: World Health Organization, *Health and Environment in Sustainable Development*

**AIR POLLUTION IN SELECTED CITIES**
SUSPENDED PARTICULATES IN CITIES AROUND THE WORLD,
IN MICROGRAMS PER CUBIC METER (DANGER LEVEL IS 100)

| | | | |
|---|---|---|---|
| Stockholm | 9 | Manila | 200 |
| Paris | 14 | Shanghai | 246 |
| Tokyo | 49 | Jakarta | 271 |
| New York | 61 | Calcutta | 375 |
| Seoul | 84 | Beijing | 377 |
| Kuala Lumpur | 85 | Delhi | 415 |
| Los Angeles | 100 | Lucknow | 463 |
| Hong Kong | 132 | Lanzhou | 732 |

Source: *World Development Indicators 1999* and *1997;* United Nations Environmental Programme; World Bank data.

One of the saddest aspects of air pollution is lead. It is difficult to imagine a greater scientific mistake of the twentieth century than the decision to add lead to gasoline to improve performance. The lead in the air from car exhaust maims children intellectually. The tragedy is that this lead can be removed easily; it simply takes the willpower to switch to unleaded gasoline. China is now in the process of changing, but in Shanghai, where citizens pride themselves on all the cars that now clog the streets, various studies have shown that at least 65 percent of the children—100 percent in one study—have lead levels in their blood higher than the point considered dangerous to mental development. The retardation is permanent, and half a century from now the victims will still be around as the flotsam of Asia's industrial revolution.

Foul water kills fewer people than the air—half a million a year in Asia. The biggest problem may be a bit difficult for people accustomed to drinking Evian or Perrier to comprehend, but here goes: People drink from rivers or ponds that are also used as toilets. Perhaps the worst slum in the world is the ethnic Vietnamese enclave on the muddy slopes of the Bassac River in Phnom Penh, Cambodia. Rickety one-room huts are built on stilts above the putrid, garbage-strewn slopes, and children play and defecate in the mud below. Grown-ups use public toilets set up on plywood platforms every fifty feet along the river, so the waste drops down into the river below. Mothers reach over and pull buckets of drinking water from the river just a few feet away from where other people are defecating. I looked in the buckets and was disgusted by the black, slimy liquid sloshing inside.

Preung Sriy, like most mothers in the slum, has lost a child because of the filth. A round-faced twenty-seven-year-old woman with lackluster eyes, Preung Sriy was sitting on a board beside her shack, preparing lunch for her three surviving children. They stood around her, a small girl and a small boy, both stark naked, both staring at me with dull eyes, and a sick infant wrapped in swaddling clothes. The stench from the mud and the river was overpowering, and so was the sense of chaos, with old boards and bones and rags scattered around. Preung Sriy said hesitantly that an eight-year-old son had died a few years ago after a severe bout of diarrhea, and that her other children also regularly get diarrhea.

"His name was Sok Chea," she said dreamily of her dead son. "He was my first-born child. He was sick for three weeks, and I even took him to the doctor, I was so scared. But he still died."

The two small children paid no heed to the story of their brother. They

*Two people use a particularly public toilet in Phnom Penh, Cambodia. Waste drops into the Bassac River below, and local residents use buckets to pull out their drinking water twenty feet away.*

simply stared at me nervously, occasionally brushing aside a fly if it lingered too long on their faces or on the sores on their arms.

"Did you ever go to school?" I asked Preung Sriy.

"A bit. Maybe six months in all. Never could read."

"What about your children?"

"No, never."

"Do you use the river water?"

"Of course. We have to. It's the only water, and so I use it for washing vegetables, for bathing the kids, for drinking, for washing up."

"Do all of you wash your hands?"

"I sometimes wash my hands before making food, and my kids sometimes wash their hands before eating and sometimes they don't. My husband and I use the toilet over the river, and the kids just go down below the house. My kids are lazy—they don't wash their hands afterward."

Preung Sriy seemed lackadaisical and fatigued. Part of that may be simply that she was exhausted, but she almost certainly suffered from intestinal worms—along with just about every other person in the slum. Worms are a problem in the Third World on a massive scale, and some public health experts say that the majority of human beings alive in the world today have them in their guts. Of course, very few Americans or Europeans have worms, but in the slums and poor villages in Asia, the infestation rate is virtually 100 percent. In small children, the worms can cause anemia and mental retardation, even death, but most of the time they simply make people tired and weak. So in school, as these children struggle to learn to read and count, their insides are being eaten up.

The ailments of pollution are, in a sense, the consequences of poverty. In Badui, for example, the Liujiaxia Fertilizer Factory is allowed to continue to discharge its effluent into the river because it is a backbone of the local economy. It is barely breaking even, and if it spent large sums on purifying its emissions it would probably go bankrupt. The factory is a pillar of the region's economy, employing three thousand workers at better than the prevailing wage. Just as important, it produces two hundred thousand metric tons of urea each year, and that fertilizer vastly increases the output of marginal farmlands in provinces like Gansu. In some sense, the factory saves lives, in that it raises incomes for its employees and for the farmers who use the fertilizer, and as a result they are able to visit doctors and get medication that they would not otherwise be able to afford. So Liujiaxia Fertilizer Factory, if it is a villain, is a complex one, and it is entirely possible that it saves the lives of more people than it kills.

The result is that environmental decisions, for factories and for individuals, reflect an excruciating balancing act. For families near a polluted river, there is an easy way to make water drinkable: boiling it. But this requires fuel, which is relatively expensive in the cities, and so families choose to spend their money in other ways. In a slum in Thane, India, I talked to a twenty-eight-year-old woman named Usha Bhagwani, as she watched her five- and seven-year-old sons scamper about the muddy paths outside her hut. Bhagwani, a rail-thin woman with a long, bony face and sharp eyes, is always fretting about how to spend her rupees. Should she buy good food so that her boys get stronger? Or should she buy them shoes so that they will not get hookworms? Or should she send them to school? Or should she buy kerosene to boil the water?

"There isn't enough money to do everything, and kerosene is expensive," Bhagwani complained. "I try to boil the water. But the boys some-

*Usha Bhagwani offers dirty water to her sons to drink, in her home in an Indian slum. She has already lost two children to sickness, perhaps because of polluted water.*

times insist on drinking right away because they're thirsty. And there isn't always enough money to buy the kerosene anyway."

Bhagwani told me about Santosh, her fifteen-month-old son who had died two years earlier, and Sheetal, a frail seven-month-old girl who had just died a few months before my visit. Both had died after suffering from diarrhea, and although there were never autopsies, it is a good bet that they died because of contaminated water. Bhagwani knew that it was wrong to give her children unboiled water, but she said that it would cost her about $4 a month in kerosene to boil all her family's drinking water. That would amount to one-third of her income as a housemaid. "I could probably afford that," she said, "but then there would be less food for the boys."

She showed me the pipe where she gets her water. The pipe theoretically brings in water from a relatively clean river, but the pipe is cracked and runs in the ditch that is filled with sewage, carrying waste from the neighborhood's outhouse. Too much tea had caught up with me at this point, so I asked directions to the nearest toilet. Bhagwani's eldest son took me into the local outhouse, and a rat watched me balefully as I went about my business. The urine trickled down a little gully, past the rat, and into the ditch with the pipe where the Bhagwanis get their water. It was the first time that I had ever urinated in my host's drinking water, and I shuddered.

For people like the Bhagwanis, nothing would make more difference in their life than a proper toilet and clean water. We talked about this inside her tiny hut, the size of a closet, and then the boys raced in and asked for a drink. "There isn't any water that's boiled," Bhagwani said. But then she shrugged and reached for the water bottle and poured it into the family's white plastic cup. First one boy and then the other drank a cup to the last drop, and her eyes softened as she watched them gulp the water.

If poverty is one reason for the terrible pollution, another is overcrowding and urbanization. The traditional image of Asia was the timeless scene of a peasant in a rice paddy, but increasingly the more representative picture would be of a child in a gutter. For example, the population of Dhaka, the Bangladeshi capital, has risen from 420,000 in 1950 to eight million today. Of the fifteen biggest metropolitan areas in the world today, nine are in Asia.

### WORLD'S LARGEST METROPOLITAN AREAS

| IN 1950 | | IN 1995 | |
|---|---|---|---|
| 1. New York City | 12.3 million | 1. Tokyo | 26.8 million |
| 2. Shanghai | 10.3 million | 2. Sao Paulo | 16.4 million |
| 3. London | 10.2 million | 3. New York City | 16.3 million |
| 4. Tokyo | 6.7 million | 4. Mexico City | 15.6 million |
| 5. Beijing | 6.6 million | 5. Bombay | 15.1 million |
| 6. Paris | 5.4 million | 6. Shanghai | 15.1 million |
| 7. Tianjin, China | 5.4 million | 7. Los Angeles | 12.4 million |
| 8. Buenos Aires | 5.1 million | 8. Beijing | 12.4 million |
| 9. Chicago | 4.9 million | 9. Calcutta | 11.7 million |
| 10. Moscow | 4.8 million | 10. Seoul | 11.6 million |
| 11. Calcutta | 4.5 million | 11. Jakarta | 11.5 million |
| 12. Los Angeles | 4.1 million | 12. Buenos Aires | 11.0 million |
| 13. Osaka | 3.8 million | 13. Tianjin, China | 10.7 million |
| 14. Milan | 3.6 million | 14. Osaka | 10.6 million |
| 15. Rio de Janeiro | 3.5 million | 15. Lagos | 10.3 million |

Source: United Nations Environmental Programme; United Nations Population Division, *World Urbanization Prospects.*

The boom in the cities underscores a central paradox: In most of Asia, people are not fleeing the filth but embracing it. Peasants are voting with their feet, moving from rural areas with relatively clean air and water to the urban slums where they and their children may die of dirty air and water. To an American, the fetid lanes of Dharavi—the shantytown in Bombay that is the largest slum in the world—seem hellish intersections of gritty air and stinking water. But to many rural Indians, the slums sing of opportunity, of jobs, of schools, of hopes to break out of subsistence poverty. Indeed, it is possible for parents to decide quite rationally that they will move from a village to a slum, because even if one child dies, the others will have far greater opportunities than they would at home. The kids may go to a decent elementary school and, if they are smart enough, conceivably to high school as well.

Aside from poverty and overcrowding, a third reason for the enormous toll from pollution in Asia is ignorance. Two million people may die each year of pollution in Asia, but just try and find *one* victim. The numbers calculated by scientists are inferred from mortality statistics, and most people in Asia are so used to pollution that they do not realize that it is killing them. Cars are dangerous, they allow, and so are airplanes, even medicines. But air and water are not. So when their loved ones die, they blame bad hearts or weak lungs, not airborne particles.

Almost every summer, a vast cloud of smoke from forest fires rises over Southeast Asia. The fires are set deliberately each year to clear land, and usually they burn out by the early fall. But in 1997 the El Niño currents created unusually dry weather, and so the fires burned for several more months. The smoke was everywhere, an unimaginable cloud that stung the eyes and blotted out the sun across hundreds of thousands of square miles in six countries, affecting two hundred million people. Some experts argued that it exceeded Chernobyl as the worst man-made environmental catastrophe in history.

The smoke caused many boats and cars to collide, as well as a fatal plane crash, but the main toll came in respiratory tract infections across the region. The experts I spoke with said that such smoke would clearly cause many deaths. But when I journeyed to Jambi, a city in Indonesia that was in the center of the haze, everybody insisted that it was no more than an inconvenience. Even the doctors in the local hospitals described the smoke as simply a nuisance. I visited a school in Jambi and watched the kids play tag on the grounds as they waited for the bell. Tag was an ideal game, because the smoke made it easy to hide. The principal, a matronly woman named Ratnajuwita, invited me into her office and cheerfully advised me that the smoke was not a health hazard. "We have

*Schoolgirls in Jambi, Indonesia, walking home through the thick haze
left by forest fires.*

no health problems and no drop-off in attendance," she said, sending an
aide to get attendance records. "Everyone is fine. The only problem is that
we can't use the blackboards in the classrooms."

"Why not?" I asked, puzzled.

"The smoke is so thick in the classrooms that the students can't see
what is written."

When I visited surrounding villages, I found that huge numbers of people were sick and dying—even if they had no idea what made them ill. In
the little hamlet of Penyengat Rendah, a cluster of shacks in the jungle, I
sat on the crude plank floor of a hut and talked with Dariah, a twenty-
seven-year-old housewife. The hut was raised on stilts, to keep out floods
and wild animals, and it leaned precariously as if a gust of wind might
send us all hurtling to the ground. The plank floor was rough, with cracks
through which I could see the earth below, and a large cockroach roamed
the wall as we spoke. The walls were similar: broad, rough planks that
didn't always meet, nailed crudely together. The cracks let in some light,
along with a window that had no glass, just a cloth covering it. Dariah's
skin was as weathered and rough as her home, and her stringy black hair
was brushed and tied back. She had buck teeth that had never seen a den-

*Dariah, a villager in Indonesia, with two
of her children in front of their home.*

tist, and a prominent chin that jutted forward as she fussed over her three
little girls. All of them coughed regularly from the smoke, and a mound in
Dariah's stomach showed that another child was on the way.

"When are you due?" I asked.

"I don't know," she laughed, before breaking into a coughing fit. "We'll
see."

"Have you been to a doctor?

"No. That would be too expensive."

Dariah's family had lost its financial stability when her husband, Ramli,
had died two months earlier. A thirty-seven-year-old sawmill worker, he
had caught something like a cold that left him coughing, but he never got
better.

"He had big racking coughs that would shake him and shake our
house," Dariah recalled. "He would cough and cough and cough. And

then he lost his energy and just lay on the floor, gasping for breath. He gasped like a fish out of water. He just couldn't get air. His chest hurt. But we thought it was just a cold, and so we never got a doctor. And then one morning—it was dawn—he coughed and gasped more than ever. And then suddenly he didn't move anymore."

"What was it that killed him? Do you know?"

"Well, he hurt his shoulder last spring, carrying some lumber. Maybe it was that."

"But had his shoulder been hurting him before he died?"

"No, not really. But what else could it have been?"

I looked out the open door of the shack at the smoke swirling outside. Dariah had just described the classic symptoms of a fatal respiratory infection, and yet she thought her husband had died of an old shoulder injury.

"What about the smoke?" I asked. "Could it be the smoke that killed him?"

"Oh, yeah, that might have been it," Dariah agreed simply, and she gazed out the door as well. The garden was visible through the haze, but everything else was simply gray—like what you see out the window when an airplane flies through a cloud.

I left Indonesia profoundly distressed, not just about the thousands of people who were dying from the smoke but also about the inattention to the risks. If some guerrilla force had staged an uprising in Southeast Asia and killed fifty thousand people, then there would have been an international effort to restore peace and ensure that such slaughter never happened again. But so long as people were unaware that pollution was killing them, they were unlikely to do anything about it. And, indeed, on that trip I repeatedly encountered ordinary farmers who were making the problems worse by burning land to clear it.

Purwadi, a gentle peasant strolling barefoot over the smoking ashes of the forest he had just burned down, was typical. He was unflappable, even when I ordered my taxi to come to a screeching halt beside him and ran out to snap two rolls of film of him surrounded by plumes of smoke. Purwadi was forty-two years old, a farmer who had just moved to the area in hopes of improving his family's life. He saw himself as a pioneer, building a shack and living without electricity or water, and he said that he simply had to burn down the forest if he was to have a field to sustain his family. I asked him about the health effects of the smoke, and he shuffled his feet and said he didn't know about any of that. "There's no other way of clearing the land," he added. "And I've got to plant my chilies."

*Purwadi, an Indonesian peasant, plants
chilies on his new farm. Purwadi cleared
the land the way everybody else does: by
burning down the forests.*

The general pattern has been for countries to mess themselves up in the initial stages of industrialization, and then to clean themselves up. In the late 1960s Tokyo arguably had the dirtiest air in the world. But over the next two decades, Japan managed to make itself one of the cleanest of the industrialized countries. Taiwan and South Korea are behind, so that they have probably just about reached their filthiest point and soon will get better. But every other country in Asia is still getting dirtier and will continue to do so for many years to come. Thus the annual death toll from pollution in Asia may well double to five million or more in another decade or so.

Governments are tackling the problem, but they are also often doing what they can to cover it up. Malaysia tried to gag scientists from discussing the health risks of smoke from Indonesian forest fires. And when I applied for an Indian visa so that I could learn more about pollution there, the prime minister's office ordered the Foreign Ministry to reject my visa application. The American ambassador, Frank Wisner, interceded with the prime minister's office and the Foreign Ministry, but the Indian government refused to budge. The visa refusal was a fluke, having to do with a hard-line official, and it was not very effective: In Cambodia, I sweet-talked the Indian Embassy into giving me a quick visa. So the next night I attended a dinner at Ambassador Wisner's home along with the Indian health minister, who was startled to see me.

When I visited China to investigate its pollution, the State Security Ministry caught up with me because of their taps on the telephone of Dai Qing, China's leading environmentalist. After that, I was tailed by teams of police goons everywhere I went. Concerned that the authorities might try to seize my film and water samples, on my last day I left for the airport at 7:30 a.m., figuring that no Chinese government organization manages to do anything before 8:00 a.m. But then I looked back and saw a Mercedes-Benz and two motorcycles emerge from beside the Jianguo Hotel to follow me. I pointed out the tails to my taxi driver and we experimented by making a couple of turns to see if they would follow. He was amused, and a bit frightened, to see that they followed everywhere we went.

"What are you?" my taxi driver asked. "A murderer?"

The authorities did not take my film or samples. But as my United Airlines plane banked toward Tokyo, I mused that if the same resources were directed toward cleaning up China's environment as to harassing environmentalists and journalists, the air and water would be considerably cleaner.

Yet responsibility must go not just to governments and factories but also to ordinary people. If the sight of pint-sized boys like Wei Haiyun in Badui was wrenching, it was just as depressing to talk to some of his neighbors. They were not just victims of the pollution but also its agents. Take Cui Tengxiong, a middle-aged man who is the richest peasant in the area. An entrepreneur who bounced into a home I was visiting, he was pure energy. "Hi!" he declared, pumping my hand. "I heard a foreigner was here. Where are you from? Can I do anything for you? You here to do business?"

Cui said that he was the first local farmer to dig fish ponds and that they all use Yellow River water to fill the ponds. He complained vigorously that the Liujiaxia Fertilizer Factory effluent often kills his fish, up to half of them. Too busy to sit down, Cui strode back and forth in the shack, ranting at the factory and the way it was damaging his business.

"Where do you sell the fish that survive?" I asked.

"To the market in Lanzhou," he replied. "People around here won't buy the fish because they know what water the fish are raised in."

"Do you think it's safe to eat the fish?" I asked.

"I think so," he said vaguely. "People around here sometimes eat fish from the river."

"Maybe that's the problem here," I suggested. "Have the fish ever been tested?"

"No. The fish taste different from the fish raised in cleaner water. I'm a bit afraid that they'll test the fish and then tell us not to sell them."

*What a difference a couple of generations can make! This emaciated old man in China's Fujian Province is a vision of Asia past, with its famines and chronic hopelessness. His granddaughter, an emblem of Asia future, may end up dieting.*

### CHAPTER FOURTEEN

# Tryst with Destiny

## NICHOLAS D. KRISTOF
## AND SHERYL WUDUNN

*Long years ago we made a tryst with destiny, and now the time comes when we shall
redeem our pledge, not wholly or in full measure, but very substantially. . . .
A moment comes, which comes but rarely in history, when we step out from the
old to the new, when an age ends and when the soul of a nation long
suppressed finds utterance.*

—JAWAHARLAL NEHRU, SPEECH ON INDIA'S INDEPENDENCE, 1947

Three seconds are left in the men's basketball final in the Kuala Lumpur
2040 Olympics. The United States is ahead by two points, but then Ji
steals the ball and passes it to Qian. The fans in the gigantic stadium are
all on their feet, screaming in a dozen languages as Qian heaves the ball
over his shoulder like a baseball at the basket more than a half-court
away. As the buzzer sounds, it swishes through the net.

The plastic bubble over the stadium erupts in huge letters in English

*and Chinese: CHINA WINS GOLD MEDAL!!! The Chinese fans are deliri-
ous, but controversy erupts immediately. In an interview with Walter
Wang, the legendary anchor of NHKCCTVCNNBBC, the world's largest
media organization, the American coach angrily accuses Korean and
Indonesian referees of favoring China. He demands that the Chinese players submit to additional tests for nanobots, the tiny robotic and computer
devices that allegedly have been installed in their bodies to improve their
stamina and shooting accuracy. And he grumpily suggests that China
bought its medal. "They aren't better than us, damn it!" he roars. "It's just
that they're bigger! Why, we had only one starter over eight feet. And we
just play for fun—we don't scour 1.6 billion kids for the ones with the best
bone structure for basketball and then fill 'em with nanobots and genetic
material and computers until they're more silicon than flesh!"*

*The coach's comments trigger widespread indignation in China, where
Zhongguo.com, the world's largest Internet portal, tartly notes that the
Chinese players have submitted to routine nanobot screening of their
urine and stool samples. "The Yanks are simply frustrated because they're
in eclipse, like the Brits a hundred years ago," Zhongguo.com editorializes
condescendingly. "And their basketball technology is very backward." In
the new virtual United States capital, I'mthePrez.gov, President Juan
Sepulveda wears a cardigan for his fireside chat in the home of every
American, urging people to wear WIN! buttons as a sign of their determination to put America right again. "Yeah, it's been a tough year, what with
the Indian landing on Mars, the Kim's Riceburger acquisition of McDon-
ald's, and now this basketball loss," President Sepulveda says earnestly,
through his three-dimensional image appearing in living rooms around
the country, thanks to Hyundai technology. "But we still have the world's
second-largest economy by most measures, and the world's most accurate
nuclear warheads. We have a lot to be happy about!"*

*No one pays much attention. The Park-Neilson Rating Service reports
that 62 percent of Americans evicted President Sepulveda from their living
rooms, ranking him fourth in the evening's entertainment. First was an
astonishing and titillating Terebi Asahi documentary on the messy sexual
practices of the twentieth century, before Matsushita's sensorial brain
stimulation made a physical partner redundant. Second was a virtual
pay-per-participate vacation on Softbankmicrosoft's Time Channel to
travel back to ancient Rome and watch professional wrestling by gladia-
tors in the Coliseum. Third was an alarmist documentary on PBS about*

*China's construction of a new canal in Central America, in addition to its*
*de facto control over those in Nicaragua and Panama. . . .*

No one has a clue what the world will really look like in 2040. China may
never win the gold medal in basketball, and riceburgers may never be a
hit. But we do believe that in myriad ways Asia will be a more important
place, and that it will gradually displace the United States as the "center
of the world." America and Europe will still be important, for they have
enormous strengths and will be less troubled by the internal conflicts and
jockeying that will confound Asia, but at some point economic primacy is
likely to return to Asia after a five-hundred-year absence.

Yet the Asia that gains primacy will also be very different from the one
today. Indeed, those changes within Asia will be almost as important to the
world as the relative changes in power between East and West. And while
we cannot see into the future, at least not until Softbankmicrosoft
launches its Time Channel, already one can see the beginnings of the
reordering within Asia. Some countries are rising and others faltering, just
as European and American states have risen and fallen in past centuries.
Hints of these changes are visible in the most unlikely places.

In the northwest of Tokyo is Kabukicho, one of Asia's largest "entertainment zones." It is a cluttered neighborhood of narrow alleys, neon signs,
beckoning touts, and raucous laughter, an area that wakes up at noon and
parties until dawn, where gamblers and gangsters run rings around the
police, where prostitutes and strippers undress for success. Kabukicho is
packed with massage parlors, strip shows, porn stores, gambling dens,
bars, hostess clubs, and S&M services. There are even distinctively Japanese parlors called "image clubs," where customers act out fantasies by
spanking prostitutes who pretend to be schoolgirls in uniform or by grop-
ing young women who pretend to be subway commuters—all in private
fantasy rooms built to look like school classrooms or subway cars.

Beyond the razzle-dazzle, Kabukicho offers a glimpse of the directions
in which Asia is evolving. In the aftermath of World War II, when vast
stretches of Tokyo were rubble as far as the eye could see, all this bustle
was directed at Americans. Indeed, the Japanese government ran brothels
for the Americans so as to dissipate the sexual energies of the GIs harm-
lessly on prostitutes, and the authorities ran recruitment campaigns asking war widows to sacrifice their own virtue by working in these brothels so
as to "save" young Japanese women from the American brutes. Then, as

*Revelers stroll through Kabukicho, Japan's*
*"entertainment district," at night.*

Japan prospered, the clientele became increasingly Japanese, and eventually in the 1980s Western women began to show up in the brothels to cater to Japanese men. Prosperity had reversed the tables.

Yet ultimately, it is the Chinese who have come to dominate Kabukicho. Most of the prostitutes are now Chinese, and many of the gangsters and touts and petty thieves are from Shanghai or Guangdong or Fujian. "None of us like Japanese men," said a twenty-five-year-old Chinese woman working as a prostitute in a Kabukicho bar. "They're so different from Chinese people. They're cold, and we're warm. They like distance, and we like to be close. I wouldn't choose them for pleasure." She shrugged, and added, "But this is business." The woman has prospered because of the same fierce drive that is lifting much of the rest of Asia: She takes classes in Japanese and English during the day, then goes to work in her bar and the nearby "love hotels" from 9:00 p.m. to 5:00 a.m. "It's tough, but I'm making a lot more money than I was in China," she said. "With the money, I hope I can go to the United States. I have some relatives in Florida, in a city called Miami. That's where I'd like to go next."

The Chinese inroads into Kabukicho reflect a weakening of Japan's competitive position within Asia. Japan was the dominant player in Asia in the twentieth century, colonizing China and other countries, waging a war that reshaped the continent, and emerging as an economic power. But now Japan is slowly fading. Its economic, cultural, and even political influence over Asia is gradually receding, and the East is moving from a unipolar continent to a tripolar region. Japan is still by far the most important economy in Asia, but China is gaining ground and behind it is India. Over the course of the twenty-first century, our guess is that all of Asia will become much more important economically and politically but that the landscape within it will change so that China will become the most important player, followed eventually by a rising India and a declining Japan. Of course, these are prognostications based on current trends, and in the past such forecasts have often been wrong. In the early 1950s, analysts of Asian affairs often said that the countries with the greatest prospects were Burma and the Philippines—two of the countries that did the worst over the next four decades.

The Chinese success in taking over Kabukicho has a good deal to do with the reasons that Asia has prospered more generally: flexibility, drive, and social stability. It may seem unorthodox to discuss a red-light district in terms of social stability. And yet anyone who visits Kabukicho will know what we mean. It is raunchy, but not in a threatening or oppressive way; Kabukicho is a Norman Rockwell kind of red-light district, with well-lit and spotless streets, clean-cut barkers who ask men to step inside with a polite "please," and pimps who wear neckties. Crime is rare, the streets are safe, and when one Chinese prostitute stole some bills from a customer's wallet at a love hotel, she was banished from the industry forever.

The sex industry is, of course, unpalatable and offensive to most Asian women, but in Kabukicho it is not staffed by abused girls, runaways, and drug addicts as in the West, but rather by a surprising number of female Horatio Alger characters. "Here, if you work hard, then you can make money and get ahead," explained a twenty-seven-year-old doctor from Harbin in northeastern China, a tall woman whom Nick interviewed while she was working as a prostitute in Kabukicho. "The Japanese complain about unemployment, but there's good money to be made here. You just have to be willing to work hard and take the tough jobs. This is my ticket to get ahead in life."

Then she turned to Nick and asked him his shoe size and date of birth. "Oh," she squealed, "you're the one! My astrologer told me that I would marry someone with just your combination. We would make a great couple!"

The Japanese authorities try to keep the Chinese prostitutes and gangsters out, but the restrictions have little impact. The gangs make phony Japanese passports and visas, and they sell real ones that have been stolen. Some of the women slip into Japan as phony university students or enter fake marriages with Japanese men in exchange for $10,000. Or else they simply sneak into Japan by boat. Much of this evasion of the law is masterminded by Chinese gangs, who have overseen this gold rush to Japan and who have in the process outmaneuvered the Japanese gangsters, or *yakuza*.

"Our biggest problem is the rise of the Chinese mafia," one *yakuza* lamented. "The Chinese gangs are taking business from us in every area—in prostitution, in gambling, in fencing stolen goods." He added, "The difference between us is that Japanese *yakuza* think of long-term business relationships, but the Chinese mafia thinks just of the short-term. Their only goal is money, money, money." His comment was strangely reminiscent of what Japanese industrialists often say of Chinese rivals.

The Chinese gangs prospered partly because they have been quicker than Japanese crooks to enter new fields and adopt high technology, like equipment to forge passports or magnetic strip cards that fool *pachinko* arcades. Chinese mobsters also won business by competing effectively on price: They offer contract killings, for example, for as little as $2,700. "The Chinese mafia is very, very good at business," the *yakuza* acknowledged. "Whether in fake magnetic cards or fencing stolen goods, they go about things with a real system. They are very serious about making money." The *yakuza* then sputtered that the Chinese gangsters are so brazen that they are robbing the *yakuza* themselves. "They know that we have money, and that if they rob us we cannot go to the police," he said. "So it's terrible: A *yakuza* will be walking down the street, and these Chinese dogs will hold him up at knifepoint or gunpoint and demand his money. There is nothing more humiliating for a *yakuza* than to be robbed by another gangster, but if he fights back he will be killed. For Japanese *yakuza*, the most important thing is staying alive, and making money is second. But for the Chinese gangsters, the first thing is mon[ey, the sec]ond thing is money. And the third thing is money."

The Chinese brothels and massage parlors in Kabukich[o beat] their Japanese rivals because they fought harder, charged less, and were more entrepreneurial. One Taiwan bar owner circulates a four-page list of rules to her women employees, underscoring the science of indulging drunken Japanese customers. For anyone who thinks of prostitution in terms of American streetwalkers in hot pants, the rules are an eye-opener. "If a guest complains, immediately refund him his money," says rule 29. "If any girl gets three complaints, she must immediately resign." The rules stipulate that women must smile and wear makeup at all times, and that chewing gum is punishable by an $80 fine. Asking a customer for a tip is a firing offense, and the women must flatter customers about absolutely everything they do. "When a customer sings karaoke, please, everyone clap," says rule 37. "This is compulsory."

China's rise in Kabukicho underscores the way relationships within Asia will be scrambled around. Of course, the future of individual countries is even less certain than that of the continent as a whole, but some likely directions are apparent. What follows are not forecasts exactly, but rather the scenarios that we believe are most likely for the countries that the Chinese might call the Three Bigs and the Three Mediums of Asia in the twenty-first century.

# *Japan*

A bit more than a century ago, Japan emerged on the globe as a dazzling new star, stunning the world with its military defeat first of China in 1895 and then of Russia in 1905. Its postwar economic boom of the last half-century has been equally spectacular. But now after an awesome century Japan seems poised to recede again in importance to the rest of the world, and our guess is that we will look back on the twentieth century as the period of Japan's greatest strength. Japan's share of global GDP probably peaked in 1989 (or in early 1995 if economies are valued at official exchange rates), and from now on it will be downhill. Japan in the mid-twenty-first century will look a bit like England in the mid-twentieth century: It will still be a great power, with some of the world's greatest companies, and it will continue to be the dominant economy in Asia for years to come. It may even gain military importance as it becomes more assertive and perhaps even turns to nuclear weapons. Japanese firms will still thrive and even benefit from Asia's continuing rise, and companies like Sony and Toyota will continue to be top-notch international brands. Moreover, Asia's demographic prospects are in some respects a good thing: Many Japanese will live more enjoyable lives in a less crowded country. But for all those caveats, the fact remains that Japan's share of global economic output will be fading and that for all its strengths it will have the air of a has-been.

That conclusion emerges when one crunches the numbers. Japan's working-age population peaked in 1995 and is now dwindling quickly. The overall Japanese population will still rise a tiny bit until 2007 because of the long life expectancy of today's retirees. But after that, the Japanese government's official projections show the country's population tumbling rapidly, from 126 million today to one hundred million in 2050 to sixty-seven million in 2100. Of course, those predictions are highly uncertain, and Japan can squeeze some extra work out of women and the elderly. But it would take a huge increase in working women or late retirements to make a major difference in Japanese trends.

Likewise, with fewer workers, Japan would need dramatic boosts in productivity—output per worker—to maintain a growing economy, but in fact Japan's productivity increases have been getting smaller each year. Using calculations based on productivity trends and the government's own fairly optimistic fertility assumptions, it seems that Japan's economy in the year 2025 may be a hair smaller than it is today, and that by 2050 it will be much smaller, largely because the country's workforce will contract sharply in the coming decades.

There are a few solutions that Japan could turn to in order to boost its long-term economic prospects. One solution would be a vast increase in immigration, but Japan remains deeply conscious of its relative homogeneity, and it is difficult to imagine the government allowing large numbers of workers into Japan. Another solution would be an economic restructuring to allocate capital and labor more efficiently, for that would boost productivity. And that is happening, but not at a fast enough pace to make a major difference. Japan remains deeply committed at a fundamental level to certain pleasant inefficiencies, such as companies that are loyal to employees and do not throw them away like old socks; government protection for small farmers, construction companies, and shopkeepers;

*Yoshie Kokou visits the graves of his parents
in the cemetery of Akashima, where he is one
of the last remaining residents.*

and subsidies to people living in remote areas. When Daiki, the boy who
has his own one-student school, is forced to go to a larger school, then the
new wave of cruel efficiency in Japan would be a bullish sign for the economy, but for now there is little sign that Japan is willing to sell its soul for
greater productivity.

In thinking of the future of Japan, one parable is the little island of
Akashima in the Goto archipelago near Nagasaki. Yoshie Kokou, a friendly
seventy-year-old fisherman, stood on a bluff on Akashima, smiling shyly
and speaking lovingly of the throngs of friends and family members who
surrounded him. The only catch is that Kokou was standing in the cemetery, and the throngs were all buried there. Akashima's hospital, school,
stores, and most of its homes are abandoned, and aside from Kokou only
four people still live on the 128-acre island. Akashima, its seaside cliffs jut-

ting out of a blue-black ocean that is hospitable mostly to the passing whales, has lost people (it had three hundred inhabitants at its peak a few decades ago) partly because women had fewer babies but mostly because people moved to the cities. More important, Akashima offers a glimpse of Japan's difficulties in generating the kind of boom in productivity that might help make up for a shrinking workforce. Akashima, a minnow in the Sea of Japan, is taking up a whale's share of the national resources. As Kokou spoke of the island, several barges were chugging into Akashima's port to begin a $2.5-million project to expand it and build a new pier.

It may seem odd to be spending so much money on a project that serves only five full-time residents, but that is just the beginning. The government also provides a $490,000 annual subsidy to the twice-daily ferry to Akashima and a neighboring island, Oshima, which has seventy residents. At a huge cost, the government has also laid down not just one but two undersea cables to Akashima to carry electricity to the five residents, demonstrating its absolute disregard for expense and efficiency. "That is to ensure a stable supply of electricity," explained Choji Tanikawa, an official in the regional office on the main island of Fukue. Then there are the other subsidies: the underwater telephone cable, the postal delivery, the weekly clinic by a government doctor. The school on the island of Oshima next door has what must be one of the best student-teacher ratios in the world: There are three students and nine teachers.

Because it lays down undersea cables to places like Akashima, Japan charges unified telephone rates across the country so high that they have stifled Japan's growth of the Internet. Likewise, servicing such remote places results in high electrical charges, postal rates, and taxes that have made it increasingly difficult for Japanese businesses to compete. It is, for example, more expensive to mail a letter within Tokyo than to mail it from America to Tokyo. Japanese companies began to do their mass mailings from America to save on postage, so the Japanese government banned the mailing of domestic advertising from abroad. Japan, in short, has fostered a gentle brand of capitalism, so that mercy does indeed seem to "droppeth as the gentle rain from heaven," as Shakespeare wrote. But Shakespeare never pondered the plight of a country with such a flood of mercy that it cannot restructure its economy. The effort to run a country as if it were a Disney movie is deeply admirable but hopelessly naïve, and so Japan today abounds with charm but not much efficiency. In a system too squeamish to let industries or islands die, taxes increasingly go to rescue the feeblest competitors, and to keep islands like Akashima alive. There has not even been any discussion of cutting back the ferry service to once daily, and islanders seem stunned when they are asked whether the government should continue to provide expensive services to a tiny, aging population. "They've never talked about cutting off services," said Mankichi Kokou, seventy-three, another Akashima resident. "Even if this becomes a ghost town, the services will continue. They have to." So Akashima endures, and Japan withers.

*In 2040, Tokyo looks like a very pleasant place. The move of the imperial family to Kyoto has opened up the Imperial Palace as a grand new park for the elderly in central Tokyo. Sprightly men and women in their eighties and nineties, many sporting bionic legs and the new artificial skin that does away with wrinkles, walk their robotic pets through the park, allowing them to lift their legs on trees and emit a stream of fragrant perfume.*

*Decentralization and the diminishing importance of government bureaucracies have led businesses and professionals to move elsewhere in Japan, and the 30 percent reduction in Tokyo's population has been catastrophic for property prices but a huge benefit for renters and for the livability of Tokyo. The old crack about Japanese living in rabbit hutches has disappeared now that the average Japanese has more housing space than the average American. Japan's population decline has been even greater than anticipated because many elderly people are moving to Japanese retirement communities in the Philippines and Indonesia, where they can be pampered inexpensively by nurses and assistants. In Japan, in contrast, labor shortages have made elderly care a bit of a nightmare.*

*The new Murdoch-owned* Nippon Today, *which with its daily diet of sex, crime, and tips on gum care has eclipsed the* Asahi *and* Yomiuri *to become Japan's leading newspaper, is delivered electronically to homes around the country and is condemning the way American banks now dominate Japan's economy. "Tear It Down," had been* Nippon Today's *banner headline the day the new Citicorp Tower had opened as the tallest building in Japan. But most people seem resigned to the changes—and a bit reassured that Sony-Toyota, Inc., is the largest and most profitable company in the world, dominating the market for driverless automobiles and pilotless airplanes as well as for personal-assistant robots. "Japan may be a lesser country today," explains Prime Minister Makiko Son, "but we Japanese are living better than ever."*

# China

No country is more an amalgam of enormous frailties and tremendous strengths than China, and judgments about its future depend on how one weighs them against each other. In our judgment, China will face periodic economic and political crises in the coming years, may experience more massacres like Tiananmen, may endure a banking crisis, will be savaged by continuing corruption on a scale that Americans find unfathomable, will face growing urban and rural unrest, will suffer growing separatist violence in Tibet and Xinjiang, and may experience an army coup d'état. And yet we believe that China is likely to continue to develop and prosper and move fitfully toward a more democratic system.

The economic vulnerabilities are Brobdingnagian, having to do largely with the inefficiencies and interrelationship of state banks and state-owned companies. In the old days, the Chinese government subsidized money-losing state enterprises, but in the 1990s it tried to back out of that. So officials curbed subsidies and instead ordered state-owned banks to increase their loans to state enterprises to keep them going. In effect, the burden of keeping inefficient companies alive was moved from the national budget to the banking system. This meant that the savings of bank depositors were forwarded into a black hole and became unrecoverable, and China's banking system is now insolvent. If depositors ever demand their money back, they will get a rude surprise—and bank runs are a real possibility, along with the political unrest that they would engender.

The larger problem is the chronically money-losing state enterprises that led the banks into insolvency. These enterprises mostly have no hope of ever making money, but the government does not put them out of their misery for fear that laid-off workers would riot in the streets. And, in fairness, it is not always right to blame the enterprises, as many of them lose money because their product prices are fixed too low or because they are responsible for social welfare payments and pensions for retired workers. The entire state enterprise system needs major surgery, but the government has been fearful of the political consequences of that surgery.

The other economic vulnerability is a bit like that of Japan or the old Korean *chaebol:* Some Chinese companies borrowed too much and invested too much, creating overcapacity and a property bubble. In Shanghai's Pudong district, the occupancy rate is less than 30 percent and yet more buildings are going up—including the 1,509-foot-high World Financial Center, which is supposed to soar above Malaysia's Petronas Towers to become the tallest building in the world. The World Financial Center is being built and financed by Minoru Mori, a Japanese construction tycoon regarded as something of a visionary in Japanese business circles. Mori, who reveres the French architect Le Corbusier and aspires not just to put up roofs but also to reshape society, is still optimistic that any property glut in China will work itself out. Yet on the wall of his thirty-seventh-floor boardroom in Tokyo, there is a painting from Mori's large collection of Le Corbusiers, bearing what may be an appropriate inscription by the artist: "*Je revais,*" or "I was dreaming."

China's economic frailties are closely linked to a political one: The Communist Party knows that it has to get across the chasm to a more democratic system of government, but it is not sure how it can cross or whether it can get there in one piece. Because the government is weak and does not have much legitimacy, it is reluctant to close the money-losing companies and recapitalize the banks and fully privatize the housing market. China is not a Communist country these days, and almost no one in China believes in communism. But the leadership insists on Communist Party rule, even if the party is taking the country to capitalism, and its bottom line is: Anything is possible, but we've got to stay in command. It is not Marxist-Leninist, but market-Leninist: The party has traded Marxist economics for market economics, but it still wants to preserve a centralized, authoritarian political system of the kind that Lenin dictated. In this sense, China today resembles not Russia of old or the other Communist countries, but rather Taiwan in the 1960s, South Korea in the 1970s, or Spain in the 1960s. It is much closer to fascism than to communism, and that's a good thing because Spain, Chile, and Taiwan showed that the path from fascism to democracy can be reasonably smooth.

For all its vulnerabilities, China also has enormous strengths. Its banking system may be insolvent, but it can afford to recapitalize it with bonds or by issuing bank stock. State-owned enterprises are a mess, but that mess is a smaller and smaller part of the overall economic pie. Economic management is steadily improving. Most important, China is successfully engendering the crucial psychological revolution that it missed five centuries ago: Chinese now respect profit and seek it, and China is flexible enough and curious enough to absorb foreign technologies and develop its own. Even the Communist Party leadership, for all its nervousness, has made the leap by embracing the Internet, telecommunications, and photocopiers, despite the political risks.

Skeptics point out that China will not be able to follow the trail of South Korea or Taiwan and export its way to industrialization, for it is too huge to expand its exports at this pace indefinitely. So the engine for growth will be China's gargantuan market at home. In particular, its service sector—education, health care, tourism, retailing—is primitive, meaning that it has enormous room to expand. The service sector accounts for less than 30 percent of China's economy today, compared to about half in the economies of other countries at a similar income level, or two-thirds of richer economies. New private schools, dental offices, investment houses, video clubs, cosmetic surgeons, and beauticians are setting up shop, and there is tremendous potential for growth. In recent years, the only element of the service sector that has become sated is prostitution.

Plenty can go wrong, of course, including domestic political upheavals, a sharp slowdown in reforms, or foreign military adventures. But in general, poor countries, if they maintain sound economic fundamentals and open their economies and absorb foreign technologies, can enjoy catch-up gains for many, many years. China is still so poor that this process can continue for decades, and there is broad consensus within China that it must build a modern market economy—even if there are disputes about the pace of change. Under a variety of economic leaders ranging from the liberal premier Zhao Ziyang to the conservative Li Peng and back to the reformist Zhu Rongji, China has overseen a consistently sensible economic policy and a deepening of reforms, and there is every reason to think that China will continue the steady improvement in its fundamental economic policies. But there are several factors suggesting that Chinese growth rates will probably slow. One is demographic: Fewer children and an aging population mean that China's labor force will grow more slowly and then pretty much stop growing altogether by 2020. Another is that the easiest reforms have already been adopted and the most inefficient industries already restructured, so that productivity growth will probably slow. There was a huge one-shot gain by moving underemployed peasants from the rice paddies, where they contributed negligibly to GDP, to factories where they contributed significantly, but most of that shift has already taken place. All this means that China's growth rates may be 5 or 6 percent a year or so over the next couple of decades, down from 8 to 10 percent in the last twenty years.

The World Bank calculated that even if total factor productivity growth drops significantly to 2 percent per year and the savings rate falls to 30 percent, then China's average annual growth rate in the years to 2020 will still be a roaring 7.2 percent. Even if total factor productivity growth slumps to 1 percent a year, then growth would still be 5.4 percent per year until 2020. Those are way down from the rates in the 1980s and 1990s, when China was the fastest-growing economy in the world—indeed, if China's thirty provinces were counted as individual countries, then the twenty fastest-growing countries in the world between 1978 and 1995 all would have been Chinese.

Still, those slower growth rates are enough to allow China to surpass the United States as the world's biggest economy, measured in purchasing power, before the year 2020, and then to continue on from there. The United States, after well over a century as the largest economy in the world, would have to yield to China, which has held the role for most of human history. China will still be a poor country in 2020, with only about one-fifth the per capita income of the United States. Its standard of living would be about what Portugal's is today. The Communist Party's traditional monopoly on information will have disintegrated, and ordinary Chinese will have a realistic sense of what is going on in their country. The Communist Party will try desperately to hold on to power, possibly with a Mexico-style democratization, in which the ruling party allows a measure of freedom and competition but tries to rig the system in its own favor. Indeed, this might well work, for it is entirely possible that China could hold a quasi-free election that the Communist Party leaders would win resoundingly, depending on the pliant peasant vote, and thus dramatically increase their own mandate and legitimacy. But it is clear that the pressures for democratization and openness will grow.

At some point, the Chinese will probably decide that Tibet is not worth the headache of holding on to, and that it is not worth risking their prosperity to fight a war over Taiwan. The risk, of course, is that the war will already be over by then. China in the coming couple of decades will be deeply anguished, torn between frustrations and resentments and growing nationalism on the one hand and new opportunities and responsibilities on the other. Our bet is that China will behave responsibly and temper its nationalism, but we wouldn't give odds.

*In 2040, China is the leading industrial country in the world. Sony-Toyota and General Electric-Motors auto plants are scattered along the*

*Communism has lost its role as an ideology that any Chinese believe in, and religion is gaining strength in China. This church is in Wenzhou, on the Chinese coast, and ironically Christianity is making far more headway in China today than it was a century ago when missionaries were free to travel around the country and proselytize.*

coast, where the newly minted electronic cars are shipped out to markets around the world on Cosco, the Chinese-owned shipping line that is the world's largest. The new craze for space vacations has propelled the stock of Sichuan Space, and founder Jia Mingzi is now the world's richest man. China's extensive explorations of the moon and its new space colony there have worried the United States and India, but the G-3 countries have been unable to reach agreement on the issue.

The upcoming Chinese elections are attracting enormous attention *around the world, particularly among the 25 million Chinese-Americans and the countless other Chinese scattered throughout Australia and Canada (where Mandarin has surpassed French as the second language). The People's Party, formerly known as the Communist Party, is still likely to win because of its strong organization in rural areas, but the vigorous Democratic Party has a chance of wresting power for the first time ever. The Democratic Party's main issues are corruption and the horrific environment, and it is also benefiting from anger among elderly voters who are irritated that the People's Party has allowed Tibet and Taiwan to become independent. Both parties say that they would do more for education, but already China's average educational attainment is higher than in Europe or America, and Qinghua University is now regarded by many as the finest scientific university in the world. Chinese students are also studying in huge numbers in every university in America and Australia, making up 10 or 20 percent of the student body at Harvard University and many West Coast campuses. Chinese scholars, many of them bearing foreign passports, are an enormous presence in Western universities, and it is common to hear Mandarin spoken in the corridors of international scientific conferences. Chinese songs regularly appear on the Top 40, and China's domination of the Olympics and of several key sports has made it a center for international athletics. Most American schools now teach Chinese, using the revolutionary new brain-cramming technology pioneered at Qinghua, and Chinese movies often show at the multiplex in Texas, while qi gong exercises are popular in Kansas and Nebraska.*

# India

One of the tragedies of the twentieth century was the rot of the Indian subcontinent. Home to one of the great civilizations and possessing boundless potential, India remained mired unnecessarily in misery and wretchedness. What stands out when one walks through the Howrah slums of Calcutta or the shantytowns of Karachi in Pakistan is simply the waste of human lives and the withering of hopes, the squandering of an entire century. Every year, 118,000 Indian women die in childbirth and 2.37 million children die before the age of five; include Pakistan and

Bangladesh, and the totals for the subcontinent are 162,000 mothers dying in childbirth each year and 3.1 million children dying before the age of five. Counting the small children alone, that amounts to a Holocaust every two years, an even more rapid pace than Hitler's.

In modern times, no great country has been more savagely misruled for so long—by such well-meaning leaders—as India. Jawaharlal Nehru was an uncommonly brave and decent man whose follies are only now being untangled. Under his leadership, India neglected agriculture and effectively forced peasants to subsidize hugely inefficient factories, and the "license raj" bureaucracy became a Kafkaesque nightmare. In the 1950s, India and South Korea were at roughly equal levels of development, and India might have seemed more likely to prosper. But today South Korea's forty-two million people produce more than India's one billion, Korea's manufactures are twice India's, its exports four times India's—and its infant mortality rate one-eighth of India's. Corruption is endemic, so that government officials operate by what Salman Rushdie has called the "Indian theory of relativity": "everything is for relatives." India's lost century will haunt it for decades to come, for even now primary schooling is abysmal and health care inadequate. India is trying to enter the information age with three hundred million adult illiterates.

Yet India is putting that tragedy behind it. In the summer of 1991, India's economy came perilously close to collapsing, and the crisis forced Prime Minister P.V. Narasimha Rao and Finance Minister Manmohan Singh to launch the beginning of an economic revolution. The reforms are grossly inadequate, but they seem to have a momentum of their own and they have triggered a new psychology in favor of market economics. At first, the experts assumed that the reforms would be maintained only if the Congress Party stayed in office, but then the nationalist Bharatiya Janata Party staggered to power and deepened the restructuring. The pace is far too slow, and millions will die as a result, but economic reform is now an Indian consensus. The racist idiocy of the "Hindu rate of growth"—which suggested that India was capable of only 3 to 4 percent growth a year—has been abandoned, and India has been chugging along at 6 or 7 percent in recent years.

If all goes right, then Rao and Singh will be remembered for transforming India as profoundly as Deng Xiaoping changed China. There are many pitfalls ahead, but the naysayers are wrong to doubt India simply because it is a mess. India in 2000 was comparable in messiness to where China was in 1987, also nine years after its reforms began. Our guess is that

*Can India turn into an Asian tiger? In rural areas like this remote part of Rajasthan, it is difficult to imagine. But slowly, gradually, India is beginning to improve its economic fundamentals, and it seems poised to gain back in the twenty-first century the ground it lost in the nineteenth and twentieth.*

India's growth rates will not match what China's were in the boom years, because India's reforms are more tentative, its administration weaker, its savings rate lower, its leaders less commanding. And India does not have Taiwan and Hong Kong next door to invest in it and mastermind its industrial revolution. But India's demographics look like East Asia's did twenty-five years ago, with the bulge of the population now moving into the workforce, and it has a huge pool of underutilized females whom it can mobilize for enormous national gain. India's savings rate, though not as lofty as China's, is still high and rising. And the end of the license raj has forced a decentralization, with Indian states competing against one another for investors and for economic growth. When N.R. Narayana Murthy founded Infosys Technologies, Ltd. in 1981, it took him nine months to get the company a telephone line and three years to get permission to import a computer. Company executives had to get permission from government bureaucrats to travel abroad. Yet Murthy persevered, winning a growing business writing software for foreign clients, and in 1999 Infosys became the first Indian company to be listed on an American stock exchange, where it quickly reached a market capitalization of $17 billion.

The result of the economic liberalization is that India is likely to gain steady influence in the world. Its share of global trade and GDP will increase, and because its birthrates are higher than China's it will overtake China by the year 2050 to become the most populous country in the world. Its cultural importance is now felt mostly in England, but steadily Indian authors and films will continue to find greater markets in America and other regions as well. In 1835, Lord Macaulay of England jeered that "a single shelf of European books [is] worth the whole literature of India and Arabia," but that attitude is disappearing. Already, the $1 million advance paid to Arundhati Roy for her manuscript of *The God of Small Things* is among the largest ever paid for a first novel.

Still, India remains a gamble. It has not yet proven that it can put its government on a sound fiscal foundation—huge deficits are constrained only by cutting necessary infrastructure spending—and there is still a neurosis about foreign investment and a tendency to blame the rest of the world when India has problems. India's economic trajectory will depend on how this psychology changes, how quickly it can create equity and social mobility among all castes, how well it can maintain political and economic stability, how quickly it can build a fuller market economy, how well it can curb corruption and how skillfully it can harness the energy and knowledge and savings of Indians abroad. It is striking that while those who knew China best—the businesspeople of Hong Kong—raced in after China's opening, the Indian entrepreneurs and doctors in places like Silicon Valley have been much more cautious about investing in their native country. India also faces a political and military minefield ahead, and it confronts the challenge of having Pakistan as a neighbor. Sometimes it takes two to keep a peace, and that may be a problem in India-Pakistan relations. Pakistan is even more backward than India, for it is not just an economic disaster but a social one as well: Feudal landowners control the countryside (sometimes literally enslaving people) and dominate the political process, blocking prospects for political change. Bangladesh, on the other hand, is also desperately poor but is beginning to make the economic and psychological transition to a modern market system.

Nehru was one of the greatest orators of the twentieth century, and one's blood still stirs today to read his declaration on the new assertive "spirit of Asia": "Asia is no longer passive; it has been passive enough in the past. It is no more a submissive Asia; it has tolerated submissiveness for so long. Asia of today is dynamic; Asia is full of life." Or there was his proud peroration, quoted at the beginning of this chapter, on the birth of modern India after the end of English colonial rule, about the moment "when we step out from the old to the new." Reading those speeches today, it is striking that they seem much more true of the epoch that India is now entering than of the one in which Nehru spoke. Only now that India has shed the mantle of Nehru's policies is it becoming dynamic and giving utterance to his prophecy.

*In 2040, India has become the world's leading software producer. Most of the code for Sony-Toyota cars and airplanes, for Sichuan Space shuttles, for General Electric-Motors electronic kitchens and even for Windows '40 is written by Indian engineers. India has also become, with China, the leading labor exporter in the world, supplying cooks, nannies, gardeners, and nurses to countries where labor is tighter. English has supplanted Hindi as the leading language in India, although for most Indians it remains a second language. India's boom of the last twenty-five years has prompted a surge in foreign investment in India, and the number of Indians living in England, Canada, and the United States has soared. The success of Prime Minister Chaudhury in England has led to a major improvement in Indian-English ties and a renewed burst of Indian emigration to England.*

*India still has huge troubles, though. Air and water pollution have reached a crisis point, and rising sea levels are threatening the coastline— although not so seriously as in neighboring Bangladesh. Pakistan-India tensions have subsided a bit, partly because Islamabad now realizes it cannot challenge Delhi, but India-China relations have become increasingly strained. Each country has dozens of nuclear warheads targeted at the other, and they have massed huge numbers of troops on their disputed border. The Indian-engineered coup in Burma, toppling a pro-Chinese government, has aggravated tensions further, and intelligence experts say that each side is preparing for an "information war" to incapacitate the electronic systems of the other. Government sites are secure, of course, but defense ministry hackers on each side have figured out how to disable the other country's private Internet sites and email communications en masse. In a test run, Indian hackers wiped out all the Bank of Zhejiang's records, so that it had no firm idea who its depositors and borrowers were.*

*Chinese Defense Ministry hackers were itching to respond with computer assaults that would destroy India's economy, and United Nations officials were desperately trying to avoid a new-style war that would risk battering the global economy. Only in France, where the new best-seller* Le Défi Indien *is sailing off the Internet order lines, is there some relish at the prospect of an inter-Asian electronic war.*

# Korea

Although the triumvirate of Japan, China, and India will dominate Asia over the twenty-first century, there will be many other important players. In other words, Asia will look less like the Americas—dominated in the north by the United States and in the south by Brazil—than like Europe, where Germany is the major power, but England, France, Italy, and even Sweden are also major economies with world-class companies. One of those leading second-rank economies, significantly more important than it is today, will be Korea. At that point it will be unified, following the collapse of North Korea, and it will have one of the most highly educated, hardworking populations in the world. A nation of seventy million people (the combined populations today in the north and south) cannot be a force on the order of China or India, but it will still be a very important player, and its per capita income will steadily come closer to Japan's. Because Korea has proven far more willing to engage in painful restructuring than Japan, the Koreans will eventually realize their dream of achieving some kind of parity of living standards with Japan.

One of the challenges will be the absorption of the north by the south. Indeed, it is entirely possible that North Korea, in the process of collapsing, will unleash a murderous attack of artillery and poison gas on Seoul, conceivably even a nuclear attack. But that is unlikely, and Korea is not going to be bankrupted by unification in the way that Germany almost was. The reason is simple: South Koreans are not going to be nearly as generous to North Koreans as West Germans were to East Germans. Korea will, of course, gradually move to improve the north's infrastructure and it will encourage investments there. But social welfare payments will be minimal, as they are in South Korea, and it is entirely possible that the south will not even allow people from the north to move south. The barbed wire and minefields that cut across the peninsula may stay in place for years after reunification.

Korea's biggest problems are not unification or even the psychology of restructuring; they are nationalism and xenophobia. This xenophobia is the legacy of Japanese colonialism, just as India's was the consequence of British colonialism, and they are both terribly debilitating. Kim Dae Jung made important strides in leading Koreans to accept the need for foreign investment and a more open economy, but this national reeducation will take time. One crucial test will come after North Korea's collapse, for South Korea still claims for the Korean motherland a strip of Chinese territory adjacent to North Korea (for its part, North Korea concedes that the territory is Chinese). If Seoul continues to press China for that land after it has military forces on the border with China, then there will be a serious border dispute. So Korea's leaders and ordinary people alike have to learn to be patriotic without being fiercely nationalistic. The saddest sight in Seoul is of the countless young Korean-Americans, sent by their parents back to their ancestral homeland to learn Korean. They hang out by the language schools, miserable, homesick, and frustrated, exchanging tales about being roundly insulted by taxi drivers and pushcart vendors for not knowing Korean language and culture. Suddenly they feel far more American than they ever did in Los Angeles. If Korea is to achieve its potential, the parochialism that feeds that bullying must stop and Korea must embrace the world.

# Indonesia

Indonesia is the giant of Southeast Asia, and its two hundred million people make it the fourth most populous country in the world. It is also one of the most troubled, and the loss of East Timor in 1999 has led to the prospect of further fragmentation. But Indonesia could lose quite a few fragments and remain a mighty country. The regions where there are secessionist movements—Aceh in Sumatra, Irian Jaya, and a few others—are more important psychologically than economically, and there is no thought of splitting up the Javanese heartland. Indonesia is also noteworthy for its brand of exceptionally tolerant Islam, making it a model for the

*Children playing at the garbage dump that is their home in
Indonesia. With luck and hard work, this will be the last generation in Indonesia that will live this way.*

Muslim world, and there seems a reasonable prospect that Indonesia can
reestablish a measure of order and resume the business of enriching its
people. One of the critical tasks will be to accept ethnic Chinese instead of
discriminating against them, and fortunately President Abdurrahman
Wahid is an eloquent spokesman for equality and tolerance.

## Vietnam

Vietnam and its neighbors were a great disappointment in the 1990s.
When we first backpacked through Vietnam and Laos in 1989, we were
optimistic that Vietnam would emulate China's entrepreneurial knack
and its rush to prosperity. And it has, but only to a point. Vietnam has not
made the political transition to a more democratic system, and economically it is still wary of full-fledged capitalism as well. Partly for these reasons, it has also been unable to exploit one of its great assets: the many
overseas Vietnamese living in America and Australia. It should be begging

them to come home and teach and start factories and invest, but instead it has been distrustful of them. Still, Vietnam's seventy-seven million people abound with the same drive and vibrancy that have enlivened China, and they are blessed with a long coastline and an impressive 94 percent literacy rate. When the leaders get their policies right, Vietnam will take off.

Most Asian countries, even the catastrophic performers like Burma and Pakistan, would do all right if only they had effective governments. And one advantage of being in a thriving region is the effect of neighbors who adopt successful market policies—a reflection of what the Chinese call the red-eye disease, or jealousy. India, for example, was content with its old "Hindu rate of growth" until it saw how Deng Xiaoping's market reforms allowed China to enjoy rates of up to 10 percent per year. India reformed itself as a direct result of its envy of China, while Malaysian envy of Singapore had a similar effect, as did Thailand's envy of Malaysia. Now Vietnamese and Lao envy of Thailand is working in the same way, and the proximity and sense of competition in Southeast Asia seems to be working for everybody's benefit. These countries have problems—Thailand's infrastructure and poor education system are real impediments to long-term growth—but they seem eager to overcome them, if only to catch up with the neighbors.

On the other hand, we are quite pessimistic about the island states of the South Pacific and Micronesia. The Pacific islands have a bleak present and an even bleaker future, which is odd because they have the image of paradise. And on a brief visit the image seems largely earned. Many of the countries are coral atolls, slivers of land the shape of crescent moons rising from the turquoise sea, with gorgeous sand beaches and palm trees and exceptionally friendly people. Our sense of the mellow lifestyle on the islands was shaped by an early visit to Tonga, where King Taufa'ahau Toupou IV had embarked on a weight-watching program. Nick strolled over to a main street and watched as a policeman put up a ROAD CLOSED sign as the king then pedaled his bicycle furiously up and down the street, accompanied by a few beefy bodyguards jogging beside him. The scene seemed straight out of Pippi Longstocking. Then there are the outer islands of Yap, where the women go topless but are exceptionally modest where their legs are concerned. American women missionaries on the islands have been taken aback by delegations of topless women coming to them and complaining that the missionaries' skirts are indecently short.

The islands have almost no resources to export, other than a dwindling fish catch, and everything has to be imported at tremendous cost. Countries like Tuvalu briefly tried to rent out their phone systems to international pornographic services, and Tonga pioneered the practice of making money by selling fancy postage stamps to overseas collectors, but none of these strategies have worked well. Meanwhile, rising seas are threatening the atolls, which barely peep out of the water, and it is possible that countries like Kiribati and the Marshall Islands will have to be entirely abandoned to the ocean. Already some of the small islands are being abandoned for economic reasons. Nick had always wanted to visit Yap's Sorol atoll, one of the most isolated and traditional places in the world, an island in the middle of the ocean with just one family living on it as it had lived for many centuries, but by the time Nick got around to planning his trip, the family had moved away.*

The course of the East will to some extent depend on policies in the West. But as one listens to the great debates in Washington or London about Asia policy, it is hard not to feel that we Westerners exaggerate our own importance. Half a century ago, we fretted and argued about "who lost China," when of course it was never ours to lose. Even now, some critics of China make impassioned arguments about the need to threaten economic sanctions, maintaining that sanctions can help promote human rights or preserve Pacific security. Meanwhile the rival camp insists that by engaging China and building ties, we will strengthen democracy and make Asia safer. In fact, we can have an impact on countries like China only at the margin, and often in unpredictable ways. In the early 1990s, pressure from Western capitals really did make a difference in getting dissidents out of prison. Some of our friends were spared torture because of that pressure. On the other hand, that same pressure tended to bolster the position within the politburo of hard-liners like Li Peng, so that broader democratic reforms suffered a setback. Likewise, in Britain there was a vigorous debate in the 1980s and 1990s about whether to adopt a tough or conciliatory policy over Hong Kong, and in the end there was a nice experiment: David Wilson was governor of Hong Kong and took a conciliatory stance, and then Chris Patten arrived and was much tougher on Beijing. The soft approach allowed China to walk all over Britain, while the hard

---

* Memo to tourists: Visit the Pacific islands before they sink. Kiribati is one of the most charming, Bikini is dazzling for its beaches and diving, and the island of Tanna on Vanuatu has a traditional lifestyle that makes it one of the most fascinating places in the Pacific.

approach made China lash out. In the end, neither approach elicited the kind of mellowing that advocates had hoped for (although Patten's strategy did at least allow Britain to hold its head high when it left Hong Kong).

The American policy of "strategic partnership" with China is absurd and creates impossible expectations, for whatever it is we have with China, it is not a strategic partnership. Washington has no more of a strategy toward China than Beijing has toward America. And while there are important areas of cooperation, China and America are also economic, diplomatic, and even military rivals. It is hard to describe two countries as partners when they are each prepared, at least in theory, to destroy the other with nuclear weapons.

Our own take on policy is that economic sanctions are counterproductive, and that engagement—in the form of more economic, political, business, cultural, and nongovernmental ties—is the best way to bring about change. The West's policy toward Burma, isolating it and applying economic sanctions, has been a disaster that has harmed ordinary Burmese and probably strengthened the position of the obstinate generals who run the country. But we have to acknowledge that engagement is not always very effective either, and it can take decades to work. The United States engaged nationalist China for many decades, and as recently as the early 1980s Taiwan was still imprisoning dissidents and occasionally even killing them. Only in the 1990s did Taiwan truly become a democracy. So we could be engaging China or Burma for decades without seeing a democracy emerge.

Still, even small bits of progress are important. China these days imprisons dissidents but usually does not torture them—and although that improvement sounds rather feeble in Western salons, it is pretty important if you happen to be in a Chinese prison cell. Likewise, while it is difficult to improve the lives of dissidents very much, we can help improve the lives of other Chinese or Burmese. Western efforts to help distribute iodine to mineral-deficient rural areas can reduce by tens of thousands the number of mentally retarded children in China, and assistance on the environment can help ensure that there are no more tiny boys and girls like those who live just downstream from the Liujiaxia Fertilizer Factory in Gansu Province.

It's also worth noting that just because sanctions are ineffective in getting China or other countries to improve their human rights records does not mean that we have no tools. The bully pulpit is modestly effective in embarrassing countries to improve their human rights records, and probably more effective than sanctions. A war over Taiwan is one of the greatest threats to security in the Pacific, and there we have some leverage in ambiguity: We must encourage Taiwan to think that it is on its own if there is a war, while we must make China think that we will back Taiwan in a conflict. We can suggest that if Taiwan takes the initiative, by declaring formal independence or taking similar steps that lead to war, it will have to fight its own way out of its mess, while if China takes the initiative and moves on Taiwan we will send help to Taipei. The result would be that Taiwan would be more careful about provoking China, and China would be more careful about military intervention. But the United States has found it hard to maintain this kind of ambiguity, and it may not be very effective in the long run. Another tool we have is diplomacy, and we can make it clear to Beijing that the moment it starts any assault on Taiwan, we will favorably consider a request from Taiwan to recognize its government as that of an independent country. If that were known, it might be one more reason for the doves in the Chinese politburo to preach caution regarding Taiwan. Chinese leaders would realize that an assault on Taiwan might result in its permanent separation from China and their own disgrace in the annals of Chinese history.

Yet ultimately China is right: Americans are unwilling to risk the nuclear destruction of Los Angeles so that Taiwan can choose its own future. If China eventually becomes the world's dominant economy and acquires military sea-lift power to match, without losing its determination that Taiwan is Chinese territory, then we in the West may be forced to sit on the sidelines as the giant engulfs the dwarf.

If Western influence on Asia is easily exaggerated, neither should we overstate the consequences for America from Asia's rise. We do not believe the United States will be overtaken as dramatically in the twenty-first century as England was in the twentieth, for the United States has a combination of technological expertise, cultural and business hegemony, linguistic dominance, and military superiority that are unrivaled. Even after the United States has lost its status as the world's largest economy in a couple of decades, people all over the world will probably still use IBM computers, shop at Amazon.com, watch Tom Cruise movies—and perhaps tremble at the sight of a B-1 bomber overhead. But America will itself become more Asian, with a growing legal and illegal Asian population in the United States, especially in universities and the high-tech sector, and every aspect of the economy will become more integrated with Asia. Hawaii led the way in the 1980s and 1990s, becoming virtually an Asian outpost heavily dependent on tourism, trade, and investment from Japan, Korea, and other countries. Even Nick's rural hometown of Yamhill, Oregon, has become sensitive to Asia's heartbeat, with local logs selling to Japan and wheat to China and Japanese electronic companies building factories in the Willamette Valley. The local county jail now regularly has a half-dozen or more forlorn Chinese peasants who have broken no law but are awaiting hearings on their immigration status.* The country high school now offers not just welding but also Japanese.

All this will not so much change history as revert to it. When China and India turned inward, when the scholars destroyed Zheng He's fleet and banned ocean-going shipping, when Japan subjected visiting missionaries to the unimaginable *ana tsurushi* (the torture of the pit), they handed themselves a setback that would last centuries. But now Asia is finally regaining its ground, and it has the greed, curiosity, and outward drive that it so fatally lacked five centuries ago. When Chinese Prime Minister Zhu Rongji made a state visit to Australia, he excused himself to go to the restroom. When he had not reemerged after a few minutes, security guards became worried and barged in. They found that Zhu, an engineer by training, had become fascinated by the high-tech toilet, made by an Australian company called Caroma. The toilet, operated by a two-button flush system, uses only one-third as much water as regular toilets. So Zhu had disassembled the toilet and laid it out on the floor to study how it worked. "We must introduce this toilet in China," Zhu declared.

If Asian leaders in the 1400s had been like Zhu, they would never have dismantled Zheng He's fleet, and the world would be entirely different. But in the end, the arrogance of ancient Asians did not destroy their countries' hopes, they only delayed them for half a millennium. Now, finally, Asia is getting a second chance.

In short, Western dominance of the globe in the nineteenth and twentieth centuries will, we think, be remembered as a reflection of the real "Asian economic crisis," the one that lasted two centuries. In the longer run, Asia will—even if it remains far poorer per capita than the West—recover some of its traditional economic strength. Consider these two graphs:

---

* We volunteered as interpreters for five of these Chinese peasant women in the local jail, moved not only by their courage in crossing the seas to try to improve their lives but also by the thought that our situations could have been reversed. If the Ming Dynasty rulers had been brighter, it might be us Westerners sitting in jails in China as illegal immigrants pleading for a chance to settle there.

**ASIA'S SHARE OF GLOBAL GDP**

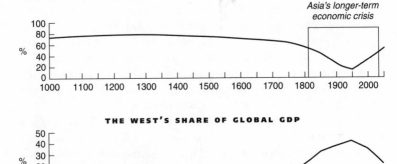

("THE WEST" INCLUDES WESTERN EUROPE, THE UNITED STATES, AND CANADA)

Source: Derived from Maddison and also incorporating projections from the World Bank and private economists.

People occasionally ask us what this means for investments. In the short run, nobody knows. But when people ask, we tell them to look for good Asian companies that will prosper with an emerging middle class and an education boom or that will cater to the elderly in an aging population. We think Americans have not yet adequately appreciated the Philippines' strengths or India's long-term potential, and that attitudes toward China foolishly alternate between hot and cold. So buy when cold and sell when hot. Asia's industrialization will also create demand for certain commodities, such as timber and oil, and it will lead to a boom in demand for Asian antiques. This rush for antiques could clearly be seen in East Asia. First, as Japanese tycoons themselves became rich, the price of ancient Japanese pottery and paintings began soaring in value, and scrolls that had gone for a few dollars at the end of World War II began fetching hundreds of thousands of dollars by the late 1980s. Then the same happened to Koreans: A newly prosperous elite began to buy ancient Korean porcelain, and so high-grade Yi Dynasty porcelain that we could have bought inexpensively when we first traveled to Seoul in 1983 was priced out of sight by the late 1990s. Likewise, newly rich Chinese entrepreneurs began snapping up Chinese antiques, sending prices soaring through the stratosphere. Nick had always loved a seventeenth-century map of Asia that he had picked up at a good price in Singapore, so years later he tried to pick up another—and was staggered that the maps had become unaffordable. As East Asians became richer, they sought bits of their past. Our bet is that the same will happen to Indian tapestries, Khmer relics, Thai Buddhas, and Indonesian furniture.

Analysts sometimes rave about Asia's prospects based on how it has done in the last few decades. But that is actually poor ground for optimism. Several careful scholarly studies, one partly conducted by Larry Summers when he was at the World Bank, have shown that past economic growth is not an indication of future growth. Another sophisticated study showed that when a region runs into a banking crisis, its postcrisis growth rates are not correlated to its precrisis growth rates. The danger of extrapolation based on current trends is that underlying conditions can change drastically, and new paradigms can emerge. A century ago, anyone extrapolating about Asia based on the then-prevailing situation would have predicted that the East would steadily decline into a quivering, quarrelsome little bundle of poverty and irrelevancy. Even if economic fundamentals remain sound in Asia, wars could erupt that would destroy Asia's bright hopes, or civil unrest could spread havoc within several key countries. The mobs in Turen, Indonesia, hacking off the heads of "sorcerers" in a country that had been praised for its stability, speak to a fragility that lingers in much of Asia. This fragility reflects the unfinished political and social evolutions in the East, and as the industrial revolution shakes up these countries and broadens the middle class and promotes urbanization and education and emancipates women, it is difficult to be sure what the result will be. Countries like Indonesia or India could become liberal democracies, or they could become nationalist Muslim or Hindu dictatorships that oppress minorities and threaten the neighbors. It isn't likely, but that underlying fragility is very real.

For all of our optimism about Asia's long-run prospects, it is impossible to be sure of what will happen or when. Asia has been in a slumber for so many centuries, with so many false awakenings, that it is difficult to be sure that this one is real. Likewise, the changes now taking place—building more of a market economy and governments based on democracy and law—are important, but they are not enough. The direction is sound, but we cannot be sure that either the direction or pace will be sustained. Asia has been too slow in embracing the information age, and one can argue that the sense of social hierarchy that is at the core of much of the East is inimical to the casual democracy that the Internet is all about.

Moreover, Asia faces important challenges in the coming decades. In the recent past, East Asia thrived because it adopted capitalist policies while much of the rest of the world dabbled in socialism and protectionism. Now that just about everybody believes in markets, Asia will face more competition. Already Latin American countries like Chile and African ones like Uganda are starting to look more like East Asia; the competition to lead the growth sweepstakes will get tougher.

That competition will also impinge on the West. To Americans, proud and content as they dominate the globe, United States leadership in everything from nuclear weapons to Internet sites may seem so overwhelming that it is difficult to imagine Asia chipping away at this preeminence—although of course that is precisely what has already happened for more than half a century. America has been in relative decline, measured by its share of global GDP or even by its share of global nuclear weapons, since 1945. Yet of course this relative decline has been accompanied by tremendous gains in prosperity, and that offers a lesson: We need not fear Asia's economic strength. As the East enriches itself, it will also enrich us, economically as well as culturally. But chip away it will, we think.

At this shining moment of American glory, with New York City pretty clearly the "center of the world," it is worth contemplating what has happened to past centers. In the year 1000 B.C., the center of the world was probably the Zhou Dynasty capital of China, on the Wei River near the present city of Xi'an. In 1 A.D., it was probably Rome, although there is also a strong case to be made for Chang-An, China. In the year 1000, it was Kaifeng, China, then the capital of by far the greatest country in the world. To visit Kaifeng today—a dirty, dilapidated, and dreary midsized city in China's heartland—is to recall how much politics matter. A few catastrophic calls by some Chinese emperors in Zheng He's time in the fifteenth century helped send all of Asia into a tailspin from which it is only now recovering. The same thing could happen again, either to Asia or to the West. Or a nuclear war or another environmental catastrophe could reshape the entire global habitat. It's natural these days to wonder where the center of the world will be in the year 3000, but the main lesson of history is simply uncertainty. Our hunch is that the twenty-first century will mark the return to preeminence of Asia, but history demonstrates that we can only make educated guesses.

Yet if the past is an imperfect guide, the present is a better one. And as we have tried to describe, the outlines of those new strategies are becoming visible. Asia's economic engine increasingly will be its internal market and the transition to services. Countries strong in English, such as the Philippines, India, and Sri Lanka, may do comparatively better in the future by providing outsourcing such as phone banks and transcription for American customers. In the long run, growth rates will slow, but there is still room for even mid-level countries to generate increased growth. The average Korean worker labors with only 40 percent of the capital of the average American worker, and the average Thai worker uses only one-eighth as much capital as the average American. So as the capital investments increase over time, there is considerable room for output to rise as well. Likewise, for all its strengths in education, even in East Asia the average mid-career worker has had only seven years of education, compared to about a dozen in the West. As the educational levels increase, so too will the output. Most important, as countries in the region rely more on market discipline—and that trend is clear—productivity will increase.

Thus the reason for optimism about Asia is not that it has done well in recent decades, but rather that it has a dazzling combination of factors that we've described: flexibility, discipline, social stability, drive, and greed. These, coupled with increased reliance on markets and improved financial systems as a result of the Asian economic crisis, are good reasons for believing in Asia's future. But fundamentally our optimism comes not so much from the economic analyses as from our interactions with the people, from encountering that extraordinary *gaman,* that ferocious will to succeed. That drive carried Sheryl's grandparents from tiny villages in China's Guangdong Province to America, where they forced their children and, alas, grandchildren to study harder.

The United States has thrived and grown partly because of that drive from immigrants, not just those from Asia but primarily the waves of Irish, Scandinavians, Greeks, Italians, Poles, Jews, and others who saw America as a land of opportunity and made it so. In many cases, the immigrants came from farms or small towns in the old country, where their way of life and their futures were rigidly stratified and circumscribed, where they could expect to do the same things that their parents and grandparents had done, where their station in life was largely predetermined. Serfs came from central Europe and settled land in the Midwest, realizing that if they worked hard enough they could achieve the impossible and own their own farms. Miners realized that with time and labor they could save enough so that their children would not necessarily be miners. In the

United States, these immigrants encountered a flexible land where outputs seemed to respond to inputs. The immigrants, especially the first generation, reacted by working harder than they ever had before. A few became Andrew Carnegies, but most became the workers toiling in Carnegie's steel mills, performing difficult, dirty, and dangerous work that helped industrialize America.

Now Asia, it seems to us, is creating its own version of the American spirit. People whose lot was largely fixed in the villages and small towns are finding that they or their children can do new things and can dramatically raise their station in life. If they work harder, they will get more. So many dream of becoming a Li Ka-shing, a refugee from China who started selling plastic flowers and became one of the world's richest men, but most end up toiling in Li Ka-shing's factories. Young men and women in the huts and villages of Vietnam, China, and Indonesia take off and look for factory jobs or go to night school or struggle with friends to disassemble and reassemble computers so as to master the world's new technologies. The same sense of possibilities that fired immigrants in America has arisen in Asia. Of course, Asian economies are not driven by immigrants themselves. Chinese sneak into Japan, Indonesians into Malaysia, and Burmese into Thailand, but they are secondary in the economic equation. So the dynamo is not immigrants but rather domestic workers who are inspired by a sense of new opportunity. They will include the poor, barely educated Chinese peasants who travel to Guangdong Province to work in shoe factories, the laborers in Malaysian factories who study accounting at night so as to move up in the world, and the well-educated Indian bureaucrats who become frustrated with low pay and limited authority and launch their own high-tech start-ups. It may sound difficult to re-create an immigrant mentality without immigrants, but the common denominator in nineteenth-century America and twenty-first-century Asia is migrants. In America, they were migrants from overseas; in Asia, they are migrants from other areas of the same country (although the gulf from Manchuria in China's northeast to Guangdong, with a dialect that is incomprehensible to most Chinese, is perhaps greater than the one bridged by the Irish who settled in Boston). The migrant mentality is already evident in Asia, and Japan industrialized with armies of rural farmworkers who took buses from the villages and started work in factories the same afternoon. The mindset of those laborers from places like the farm town of Omiya in the Kii peninsula settling in the industrial districts of Osaka was not so dissimilar from those of the Irish or Poles settling in Boston or Chicago, and there has been something similar going on in China, Indonesia, and Bangladesh. The psychology of America is arising in the East.

One way of looking at the change is to recognize that in the twentieth century Asian drive was directed partly at economic prosperity but much of it was also expended on nationalist causes: In India, it forced the British to pack up and leave; in China, it resulted in a Communist revolution and decades of social upheaval; in Vietnam, it forced the greatest military power in the world to flee in humiliation. One of the most amazing sights in Asia is the tunnels that the Vietcong used in South Vietnam to hide and to infiltrate soldiers. In Cu Chi, a former tunnel fighter told us that the entrance to one was within a few feet of us, but although we searched the ground we could not find it. Then he brushed away the leaves and dirt and removed a small plug, and there was a tunnel barely bigger than a woodchuck hole. The tunnels are just big enough for a small person to crawl along in, and they are also occupied by rats and snakes and bats. We crawled along one such tunnel for just one hundred feet, and we still shudder at the memory of a strange animal that zipped by us in the darkness. Yet some Vietcong lived in those tunnels for years at a time. We emerged into the light, frantically brushing out our hair for any odd insects or bats that might have found a new home, better understanding why Vietnam won the war and feeling a new respect for local determination. The trick will be to harness that determination to the economy, but that is now beginning to happen all over Asia.

Those who have read our earlier book, *China Wakes,* may remember that we began the book with the story of a young Chinese woman named Tang Rimei. To us, her plight underscored China's dark side, for her experience seemed emblematic of all that goes wrong in China, of all that is grimmer and more complicated than tourists ever imagine. Tang Rimei, a tall, slender woman with glasses, attractive and scholarly, had been working as a secretary in the southern city of Shenzhen, next to Hong Kong. Her boss was corrupt, and she quickly figured out that he was earning huge sums by embezzling funds and cheating other companies. He asked her to forge documents for one of his ventures, and she refused, so he fired her.

When Tang Rimei went to the police, they turned out to be in league with her boss—who paid them bribes and took them on trips to local brothels—and they told her boss what she had done. She was warned a few times to be quiet, but instead she tried to denounce her boss and the police to higher authorities, and that is when a company manager and nine gangsters showed up at her door. Tang's beloved older brother, Tang Richeng, a tall, strong man studying at a sports institute, had come down to protect his sister, and the two of them were the only ones home. The gangsters began breaking down the iron door to the apartment, shouting that they were going to kill her, and when Tang telephoned the police, they refused to respond.

When the gangsters broke in, Tang Richeng tried to protect his sister, and the gangsters beat him to death with iron pipes as she watched helplessly. "I was screaming, 'Help! Help!' " she recalled later. "They hit me a little bit, but because my big brother was protecting me they mostly hit him. Then some people came by, and they got scared and ran away. My big brother was bloody and lying on the floor. He was still breathing, but he had no reactions. I was pleading with people for help. Finally, after fifty minutes, the police came and took my big brother to the hospital. By that time, he had stopped breathing. He was dead." Tang Rimei, more outraged than ever, continued to denounce her boss in posters and letters and gave interviews to Hong Kong reporters. That's when the Chinese police arrested her and warned her to keep quiet. When she was released, she fled to Hong Kong, where she seemed a broken, teary woman. We worried about her and feared that the thugs would catch up with her, and she had seemed so shattered that it was difficult to imagine her overcoming the experience.

We heard nothing more for years about her, and we assumed that she was working in some third-rate job in Hong Kong, hiding out from her enemies. Then, as we were finishing this book, we got an email from her, along with her cellular phone number, and we gave her a call. Now she speaks fluent English and goes by the name Linda Tang.

It turned out that after a few years in Hong Kong, pestering the courts and diplomats and journalists in the struggle to avenge her brother's death, she won a student visa to Canada to study law (the United States consulate turned down her visa application). She earned her degree, won Canadian nationality, learned English, and took on the name Linda—all without telling her classmates what she had been through. But then she went back to China in 1999, as a Canadian this time, and filed a series of lawsuits against the men who had killed her brother. She is still doggedly pursuing the case even as she launches her own legal career. We should never have bothered feeling sorry for a person like her; with that gumption, as long as her heart beats she will never be kept down.

So what was meant to be a warning about Asia's darker side ultimately is something more hopeful: an instance of a tenacious woman overcoming insurmountable obstacles and emerging triumphant. Tang Rimei is different now—and not in name alone—but her story in the end turns out not to be a cautionary tale so much as an inspirational one, and a reminder that if you bet against Asians, you do so at your own risk.

# NOTES

We did not want to clutter up our text with footnotes, but we did want to provide some citations and references for readers who wish to delve more deeply into these subjects. In addition, there are several books that have also wrestled with the larger issue of changing economic centers in the world and that helped stimulate our own thinking. One of them is *The Wealth and Poverty of Nations* (New York: W.W. Norton, 1998), a magisterial 635-page tome by David S. Landes, professor emeritus of history and economics at Harvard University. Landes is not an Asia specialist and his book does not focus on the East, but he provides a marvelously intelligent and erudite history for those seeking a global context. A generation earlier, the late Mancur Olson explored similar issues in *The Rise and Decline of Nations* (New Haven, Conn.: Yale University Press, 1982), and his analysis remains as wise as ever.

Our analysis of the Asian economic crisis in several of the early chapters is rooted in a four-part series that we and several other reporters worked on collectively and that appeared in the *New York Times* in February 1999. Some of the quotations about the crisis in chapters three and five come from reporting done for the series by our Washington colleagues, particularly David E. Sanger, the brilliant and indefatigable *Times* correspondent who covered the Treasury Department and international economics for most of the Clinton administration. Other excellent and perceptive reporters whose material we relied on for the book were Jeff Gerth, Richard Stevenson, and Edward Wyatt.

By far the best place to find scholarly articles and intelligent analysis of Asia and its economic crisis is the homepage of Professor Nouriel Roubini of the Stern School of Business at New York University. His homepage has become *the* clearing house for academic analysis of the crisis, and we found it invaluable. It is at http://www.stern.nyu.edu/~nroubini/asia/Asia-Homepage.html. We particularly benefited from articles there by Paul Krugman, Jeffrey Sachs, and Nouriel Roubini.

Several books offer an excellent overview of Asian development issues. Among them are Jim Rohwer, *Asia Rising* (New York: Touchstone, 1996), and David Bloom and Jeffrey Sachs, *Emerging Asia: Changes and Challenges* (Manila: Asian Development Bank, 1997). *The East Asian Miracle* (Washington, D.C.: World Bank, 1993) is also useful, though a bit dated. It was financed by the Japanese government so as to legitimize government intervention in the economy, and in retrospect the book's sympathetic analysis of industrial policy seems foolish. Scholarly works by the World Bank, the Asian Development Bank, the International Monetary Fund, and the Organisation for Economic Co-operation and Development have also explored these issues with intelligence and insight. For data, we've normally used World Bank figures, principally from *World Development Indicators 1999* (Washington, D.C.: World Bank, 1999).

3    **Extremes are followed:** The Cheng Yi quotation is from *Yi Zhuan,* the works of
     Cheng Yi in four volumes. Cheng Yi lived from 1032 to 1085 and advocated the use of
     reason rather than superstition.

15   **What happened:** The best discussion of the demographic issues is in David E. Bloom
     and Jeffrey G. Williamson, "Demographic Transitions and Economic Miracles in
     Emerging Asia," National Bureau of Economic Research Working Paper 6268; and
     Nicholas Eberstadt, "Population Prospects for Eastern Asia to 2015: Trends and
     Implications," unpublished essay. Some of the best work on demographic constraints
     in Japan has been by Robert Alan Feldman, an analyst at Morgan Stanley Dean Witter
     in Tokyo.

25   **Awake:** The Tagore poem is from *Later Poems of Tagore,* Aurobindo Bose, trans. (New
     Delhi: Orient Paperbacks, 1974).

26   **It all seems sad:** The best comprehensive source on Zheng He is the Chinese-
     language, two-volume set *San Bao Tai Jian Xi Yang Ji Tong Su Yan Yi* (Shanghai: Guji
     Chubanshe, 1985). By far the best work in English is Louise Levathes, *When China
     Ruled the Seas* (New York: Simon & Schuster, 1994). One of Zheng He's aides, Ma
     Huan, wrote an interesting account of the voyages in 1451, and it was translated by
     J.V.G. Mills and published by the Hakluyt Society in 1970 through Cambridge Univer-
     sity Press. Also useful is Edward L. Dreyer, *Early Ming China* (Stanford, Calif.: Stan-
     ford University Press, 1982). No better known today than Zheng He's voyages are the
     Franciscan missions from Rome to China, lasting from about 1250 to 1350. This
     period of East-West communication was a fruitful one, and there is some evidence
     that the Chinese goddess Guanyin, who still inspires devotion in southern China and
     overseas Chinese communities, was based on Western representations of Mary
     brought by the Franciscans. See the beautiful and fascinating book by Lauren Arnold,
     *Princely Gifts and Papal Treasures* (San Francisco: Desiderata Press, 1999).

28   **Asia's Lead:** Information for the graphic comparing inventions of the East and West
     came from various sources, but a starting point was the *Far Eastern Economic Review,*
     "Asian Millennium" section, April 15, 1999. By far the most comprehensive examina-
     tion of technology in ancient China is Joseph Needham, *Science and Civilisation in
     China* (Cambridge, England: Cambridge University Press, 1983), a massive multivol-
     ume study replete with illustrations and fascinating asides. Incidentally, the invention
     of gunpowder demonstrates the usefulness of serendipity and curious minds even in
     ancient research. Chinese scholars initially developed something like gunpowder
     while trying to make elixirs for immortality. Then the scientists discovered that while
     gunpowder was not a useful nutritional supplement, it would explode.

29   **Share of World GDP:** Angus Maddison's data are from his books *Monitoring the
     World Economy 1820–1992* (1995) and *Chinese Economic Performance in the Long
     Run* (1998), both published in Paris by the OECD as Development Centre Studies.
     The China book, in particular, is a first-rate summation of China's growth and
     decline. The calculations for "Entire Asia" in the chart of "Share of World GDP" are
     not his, except for 1820, but we calculated them based in large part on his figures for
     China, India, and Japan.

30   **Asia was a grand trading network:** A useful resource for historical information
     such as that about the rhinoceros in China and the estimate of two million taxpayers
     in ancient Chang-an are from Joanna Waley-Cohen, *The Sextants of Beijing* (New
     York: W.W. Norton & Co., 1999).

39   **The average Chinese:** The comparisons between eighteenth-century China and
     Europe, in terms of nutrition and living standards, draw from some thoughtful and

provocative research by the economic historian Kenneth Pomeranz. It will be published in a forthcoming book, but for now it is in two unpublished papers, "Rethinking the Late Imperial Chinese Economy" and "East Asia, Europe, and the Industrial Revolution."

43    **"One senses . . .":** The Nehru quotations come from Jawaharlal Nehru, *The Discovery of India* (Calcutta: Signet Press, 1946), p. 54. This terrific book was written in six months while Nehru was in prison; one of Britain's lasting legacies of Indian rule was imprisoning Nehru and giving him the time to write.

44    **One lesson:** Paul Kennedy discusses his theory of imperial overstretch in his book *The Rise and Fall of the Great Powers* (New York: Random House, 1987).

### CHAPTER THREE

49    **Let us all be happy:** The Artemus Ward quote comes from *Natural History*. Ward was a pseudonym for Charles Farrar Browne, and he often used spellings like "borrer" to reflect New England dialect.

50    **His father, Mongkol Kanjanapas:** Bruce Gilley, "Crawling Back," *Far Eastern Economic Review,* October 21, 1999, pp. 56–60. Gilley has some nice touches in his discussion about Anant Kanjanapas and the family.

63    **Tiger Management:** Callum Henderson, *Asia Falling: Making Sense of the Asian Currency Crisis and Its Aftermath* (New York: McGraw-Hill, 1998). Henderson has a good description of the events on the trading floor during the crisis.

### CHAPTER FOUR

69    **On a small back street:** Kiccho is the standard Japanese romanization for the two characters that make up the name of the restaurant. But in English, it often refers to itself as Kitcho, and it is also sometimes written as Ki-cho.

74    **One careful study:** The study showing that MITI's work backfired and that the best Japanese industries arose through fierce competition is by Michael E. Porter and Hirotaka Takeuchi, "Fixing What Really Ails Japan," *Foreign Affairs,* May/June 1999, pp. 66–81.

### CHAPTER FIVE

91    **If thou be poure:** The Chaucer quote comes from the prologue to "The Man of Law's Tale."

### CHAPTER SIX

121    **Jackie Chan:** The Jackie Chan material comes from a first-rate profile of him in the *Los Angeles Times,* December 27, 1998, p. 5.

126    **The eeriest vignette:** The incident is best described in Don Oberdorfer, *The Two Koreas* (Reading, Mass.: Addison-Wesley, 1997), pp. 47–55.

136    **Asia's boom:** The argument that Asia grew by increasing inputs rather than by boosting productivity was popularized by Paul Krugman in his 1994 *Foreign Affairs* article, "The Myth of the Asian Miracle," Vol. 73, No. 6, but it was first made by another scholar, Alwyn Young. Krugman's article generated an enormous academic debate, but one of the most striking effects was in Singapore. Officials in Singapore initially blasted Krugman's analysis, but then they began to worry that he might be right—and so they launched a national campaign to boost productivity.

137    **Already India:** The discussion of countries like India and the Philippines performing services like telephone calling for Western companies benefited from an excellent cover story in the *Far Eastern Economic Review,* September 2, 1999, pp. 8–13. The information about G.E. Capital and AOL comes from this article.

139   **Korea's most famous:** The adulation for people like Sim Chong who sacrifice them-
      selves for family may seem odd in the West. We think of human sacrifices as some-
      thing bizarre that people like the Aztecs did. But in fact that is, of course, what war is
      all about—human sacrifice, not for the sake of appeasing gods or saving one's family,
      but for the sake of the nation. In some cases, such as Germany in World War I (though
      not just Germany), the sacrifices have been justified not only by goals of national
      integrity but also by economic interests of the state. The nationalistic Western version
      of the Korean praise for Sim Chong is expressed in what Wilfred Owen described as
      "the old Lie, *Dulce et decorum est, Pro patria Mori*"—it is sweet and fitting to die for
      one's country.

**CHAPTER SEVEN**

143   **There is nothing:** The quotation from Niccolò Machiavelli comes from *The Prince*
      (New York: Mentor edition by Oxford University Press, 1952), Luigi Ricci, trans.,
      chapter six, p. 55.

145   **Thailand is divided:** For a very informative discussion of Thailand's economic crisis,
      see Pasuk Phonbgpaichit and Chris Baker's *Thailand's Boom and Bust* (Bangkok:
      Silkworm Books, 1998). Income gaps are hard to measure, but in general, the gaps in
      Asian countries are not as acute as the gap in the United States. But in some cases,
      the Gini Index, which measures the distribution of income in an economy, shows a
      high inequality in Asia. The index for the United States, for instance, is 40.1, while it
      is 46.2 for Thailand, 41.5 for China, and 48.4 for Malaysia, but only 29.7 for India and
      36.5 for Indonesia. An index of zero means perfect equality; an index of 100 means
      perfect inequality. There were no statistics available for Japan and South Korea. Our
      source for these figures was the *World Development Indicators 1999* (Washington,
      D.C.: World Bank, 1999).

159   **Defeated by the market:** The convenient expressway exit from the Bangkok Airport
      to Muang Thong Thani was closed in early 1999 because of a dispute between
      Bangkok Land and the operator. At the time of this writing, it was not clear when it
      would be reopened.

**CHAPTER EIGHT**

163   **Interviewer:** The Gandhi quotation at the beginning of the chapter is widely attrib-
      uted to him, but we could not find a citation for it in his papers and we do not know
      who the interviewer was. There are several instances, however, where he made simi-
      lar comments in his own writings about Western civilization.

165   **The writer Francis Fukuyama:** One of the most thoughtful books on the changing
      social patterns of crime and family around the world is Francis Fukuyama, *The Great
      Disruption* (New York: Free Press, 1999).

175   **It is the same:** A discussion of the family structure around the world (although it has
      less about Asia) is in J. Bruce, C.B. Lloyd, and A. Leonard, *Families in Focus* (New
      York: Population Council, 1995).

177   **The foolishness:** The story of Omasu is from Lafcadio Hearn, *Writings from Japan*
      (New York: Penguin, 1984).

178   **Education is:** Most of the education statistics come from *Education at a Glance,
      OECD Indicators 1998* (Paris: OECD, 1998).

180   **Particularly in Japan:** The best book we found on Japanese elementary education is
      Catherine C. Lewis, *Educating Hearts and Minds: Reflections on Japanese Preschool
      and Elementary Education* (New York: Cambridge University Press, 1995).

186   **A runner ran:** The math problems come from Toshio Sawada, "Mathematics and
      Science Education in Japan," an unpublished paper presented for the symposium on
      science education at National Taiwan Normal University, June 1992.

187    **Many Asian intellectuals:** The Aristotle comment on education comes not from
       Aristotle's own writings but from Diogenes Laertius, *Lives of the Philosophers*, in his
       section on Aristotle.

193    **"Well, I hope . . .":** Ray Kurzweil has some remarkable insights into the future of
       smart machines in his book, *The Age of Spiritual Machines* (New York: Viking Pen-
       guin, 1999). Quotes on p. 50.

202    **Fifty-seven percent:** For recent statistics on robots, see the *Economist,* October
       16–22, 1999, pp. 108 and 109.

212    **The first company to make a portable:** For a discussion about Korea's advances into
       Internet technology, see: "It's a Digital World," *Far Eastern Economic Review,* Decem-
       ber 16, 1999, pp. 8–12.
       **two-thirds of the world's subscribers to CDMA:** *Telephony,* Intertec Publishing
       Corp., August 3, 1998.

215    **In schools in England:** *Education at a Glance: OECD Indicators, 1998,* Centre for
       Educational Research and Innovation (Paris: Organisation for Economic Co-
       operation and Development, 1998), p. 308. The data on number of students per com-
       puter in different countries is from 1995.

216    **But then, what happened:** For a discussion of the problems with China's inventions,
       see Landes, *The Wealth and Poverty of Nations,* chapter four, "The Invention of
       Invention."

217    **"I was a good student . . .":** Son's essay appeared in the *Harvard Business Review,*
       1992.

220    **Just as his stock:** Softbank had mid-year losses on September 30, 1999, of about
       $33.6 million, most of which the company said were due to poor performance of
       investments in the United States. Growing concerns about Son's empire and volatility
       in Internet stocks in the United States then punished his stocks for months.

227    **The past is:** The Faulkner quote at the beginning of the chapter comes from *Requiem
       for a Nun* (New York: Random House, 1950), p. 92.

229    **While every American:** Rates of surrender and figures for supplies in the Pacific the-
       ater for Americans and Japanese are from Meirion and Susie Harries, *Soldiers of the
       Sun* (New York: Random House, 1991), pp. vii, 348.

231    **A poll published in 1999:** The poll data on liking or disliking the Japanese comes
       from "Comparative Analysis of Global Values," by the Dentsu Institute for Human
       Studies, 1999.

236    **Americans have conveniently:** The Philippines material is from Richard O'Connor,
       *Pacific Destiny* (New York: Little, Brown & Co., 1969), pp. 276 *et seq.;* and from Stan-
       ley Karnow, *In Our Image* (New York: Random House, 1989).

237    **"The other night . . .":** The *Leatherneck* quotation and the material after the refer-
       ence to Dower is from John W. Dower, *War Without Mercy* (New York: Pantheon,
       1986), pp. 64 *et seq.*

239    **China regularly claims:** The Nanjing massacre is widely discussed in Iris Chang's
       book, *The Rape of Nanking* (New York: Basic Books, 1997), and in John Rabe's diary,
       and in many Chinese and Japanese books and essays. We benefited from the scholar-
       ship of Ikuhiko Hata, a Nihon University historian who has also spent time at Har-
       vard, Columbia, Princeton, and the University of Michigan. He is the author of
       Japanese-language works such as *Nankin Jiken (The Nanjing Incident)* and a shorter
       English-language monograph, *Nanking: Setting the Record Straight.* The work we
       recommend the most is simply Rabe's diary, for although it does not get into the

debates about historiography it is a gripping, first-person account of what he saw in the center of the action. Erwin Wickert, ed., *The Good Man of Nanking: The Diaries of John Rabe,* John E. Woods, trans. (New York: Alfred A. Knopf, 1998). Wickert, incidentally, suggests that Rabe's estimate of fifty thousand to sixty thousand casualties may be too low.

241 **I encountered this psychology:** Regarding Tiananmen, hundreds of people were killed in the crackdown, but the slaughter was scattered around Beijing rather than concentrated in Tiananmen Square. In recent years, some have asserted that no one was actually killed within Tiananmen Square, but that is probably incorrect and depends on a very narrow definition of the square. The Chinese authorities normally refer to Tiananmen Square as the area that includes not just the plaza but also the Avenue of Eternal Peace and the area north of it, up to Tiananmen itself. Nick saw perhaps a dozen people killed in that area, mostly on the Avenue of Eternal Peace. And even if one uses a narrow definition of the square and excludes the avenue, he saw a couple of people shot that night on the plaza just beside the avenue. He was running away and has no idea whether they survived their wounds.

243 **The minutes of cabinet meetings:** The accounts of Japanese decision-making during World War II owe a great deal to ideas and quotations in unpublished papers by Professor Sadao Asada of Japan's Doshisha University. Professor Asada's work is brilliant, and we particularly recommend an unpublished essay called "The Shock of the Atomic Bomb and Japan's Decision to Surrender," 1995. McDilda is also discussed in William Craig, *The Fall of Japan* (New York: Penguin, 1967), and some of the quotes are from Craig's book. We were unable to locate McDilda, who appears to have died. The view contrary to ours—that the atomic bombing was not justified—is best argued by Gar Alperovitz. See his brilliant book, *The Decision to Use the Atomic Bomb* (New York: Alfred A. Knopf, 1995), or his article "Hiroshima: Historians Reassess," in *Foreign Policy,* Summer 1995.

### CHAPTER ELEVEN

258 **The Boxers declared:** The quotations about the Boxers come from Louis L. Snyder, *The Dynamics of Nationalism* (Princeton, N.J.: Nostrand, 1964), p. 322.

261 **As Admiral Dennis Blair:** The punchbowl quotation comes from Edward Timperlake and William C. Triplett II, *Red Dragon Rising* (Washington, D.C.: Regnery, 1999), p. 151, which attributes it to the *Washington Times,* July 30, 1999.

264 **Two People's Liberation Army colonels:** The book by the two Chinese colonels is discussed in an article by the *Washington Post*'s ace China correspondent, John Pomfret, "China Ponders New Rules of 'Unrestricted War,' " August 8, 1999, p. A01.

### CHAPTER TWELVE

269 **India was equally repressive:** For an excellent analysis of women's status in India, see: Elisabeth Bumiller, *May You Be the Mother of a Hundred Sons* (New York: Random House, 1990). See especially pp. 44–74 for a discussion of suttee.

272 **David S. Landes:** David S. Landes, *The Wealth and Poverty of Nations* (New York: W.W. Norton & Co., 1998), p. 413. Landes has a stimulating discussion of the status of women and economic success.

**From Thomas More:** Baldassare Castiglione, *The Book of the Courtier,* George Bull, trans. (New York: Penguin, 1967). In a dialogue recorded by Castiglione, Lorenzo di Medici defends women; pp. 220–21.

274 **And throughout the region:** A group called the Kasumisou Foundation is now assisting Juliana and other people in her village. The foundation is a small tax-exempt charity incorporated in California and doing wonderful work in Southeast Asia and China. A Tokyo-based American couple, Mark and Barbara Rosasco, founded Kasu-

misou as a way to use their own savings to help poor Asians, and although they now accept contributions they still cover all administrative expenses so that donations are fully used on behalf of the needy. For information, write 1300 Hillview Drive, Menlo Park, CA 94025, or contact the Rosascos at rosasco@tkb.att.ne.jp.

275  **As a result, in much of Asia:** World Bank statistics also show that African women have a stronger presence in the workplace than Asian women, and this does seem surprising. It is possible that the gap is partly due to some distortions in the gathering of the figures.

276  **These differences seem tiny:** For a discussion on missing babies in China, please see Kristof and WuDunn, *China Wakes* (New York: Times Books, 1994), chapter eight.

280  **Though the portion of women:** In Japan, one reason women do not pursue more full-time jobs is the tax code. The code encourages women to remain working part-time because taxes and pension contributions jump dramatically above earnings of about one million yen, or about $9,000.

282  **Kathy Matsui:** Matsui has a good analysis of the female economy in *Women-omics: Buy the Female Economy,* Goldman Sachs Investment Research, Japan, August 13, 1999. Matsui cites a report in the Japanese-language *Nihon Keizai Shimbun.* That report says that if the female labor participation rate, which is the proportion of eligible women workers who work, rises from 50 percent to 56 percent, which is the level in the United States, then gross domestic product could rise 0.3 percent a year in the first decade of the twenty-first century. Her report also cites a survey conducted by the Japan Economic Planning Agency on the working environment for working women in the OECD countries.

283  **In Japan and South Korea:** Korean women started out slightly ahead in their numbers in the workplace in 1980. In that year, Korean women made up 39 percent of the labor force, compared to 38 percent in Japan, according to the *World Development Indicators* (Washington, D.C.: World Bank, 1999). However, Korean women progressed slightly less in the workplace in recent years than women in Japan.

## CHAPTER THIRTEEN

300  **Similar arguments:** Some estimates of oil use by Asia appear in "Fueling Asia's Recovery," *Foreign Affairs,* March/April 1998, pp. 34 *et seq.* Also see *Newsweek,* Asia edition, March 3, 1998, p. 52.

301  **Number of deaths:** The estimates of global annual deaths from air pollution, indoor and outdoor, come from *Health and Environment in Sustainable Development* (Geneva: World Health Organization, 1997), p. 89. This is an excellent resource on the public health consequences of pollution in Asia and elsewhere.

## CHAPTER FOURTEEN

315  **Three seconds:** The discussion of future scenarios benefited in particular from *China 2020* (Washington, D.C.: World Bank, 1997) and *Global Economic Prospects and the Developing Countries* (Washington, D.C.: World Bank, 1997).

333  **When N.R. Narayana Murthy:** The information on Murthy comes from an excellent article by our colleague Celia W. Dugger, "India's High-Tech, and Sheepish, Capitalism," *New York Times,* December 16, 1999, p. 1.

342  **We can suggest:** Our proposed Taiwan policy sounds catchier in Chinese than in English. The present Beijing policy to Taiwan is equivalent to *Ni du, wo da,* or "You go independent, and we'll attack." Our suggestion is that Taiwan counter with *Ni da, wo du,* meaning "You attack, and we'll go independent." This would give the United States some flexibility, because despite misperceptions to the contrary, Washington has not exactly had a one-China policy. Rather, the original American position in 1972

was that since both Taiwan and the mainland agree that Taiwan is part of China, the United States does not dispute that. Obviously, if Taiwan were to announce that it is not part of China after all, then that would leave an opening for the United States to declare its policy inoperative and to recognize Taiwan. It would be foolish to change American policy if it were Taiwan that took the first step. But Washington should point out to Beijing that an unprovoked mainland attack on Taiwan could lead to Taiwan immediately declaring independence and being recognized by the United States.

# ACKNOWLEDGMENTS

The first time Nick visited Asia, in 1982, he was a student and backpacking around on the cheap. He stayed for free on the floor of the Golden Temple in Amritsar, India, surrounded by equally penniless beggars and Hindu pilgrims. A local man—evidently feeling sorry for such an impoverished youth—suggested that Nick go to a temple-run feeding station. "The temple gives out free food there," he suggested. "You can get lunch and you won't have to pay for it." So Nick trundled off to the feeding station and joined the line for free food. A temple worker came by and gave each person a battered tin bowl, then a spoonful of dhal, and finally a chapati bread to eat it with. So there were one hundred of Amritsar's sorriest, filthiest beggars grubbing away at the free food, and in the middle was an American law student.

We have been imposing on Asian hospitality ever since, and we have been staggered many times by the wonderful people who enveloped us with their warmth and helped us in the years since then. Our jobs often meant that we landed exhausted in remote areas where we knew nobody, and time and time again some local businessman or peasant or scholar appeared as a guardian angel and rescued us. We saw some terrible things in Asia as well, but our abiding emotions are warmth and gratitude for all those who helped us in our Asian adventure.

Still, it's hard to know quite where to begin thanking people in these acknowledgments. Should we start with the kids at Yamhill Grade School who went to an organizational meeting for a student newspaper and, not wanting to edit the paper themselves, chose Nick in absentia to be editor in chief, thus propelling him into journalism? Or the professors at Harvard Business School, who made the business world seem so compelling that Sheryl fled to journalism instead?

Then there are those who trained us in journalism, from Sheryl's editors at the *Miami Herald* to Nick's at the *News-Register* in McMinnville, Oregon. Above all, there are those who made the leap of faith and hired us at the *New York Times* and sent us to Asia. John M. Lee and Abe Rosenthal hired Nick to write about business, mercifully without determining that he didn't know a thing about the subject. Joe Lelyveld and Max Frankel hired Sheryl, ignoring catcalls that it was wrong to hire somebody as a foreign correspondent who had never worked in the head office.

It probably looks obsequious when *Times* authors lard their acknowledgments with thanks to the Sulzbergers, the royal family of the *Times*, but the gratitude is heartfelt. Punch and Arthur Sulzberger have been helpful beyond all expectations and are both strong arguments for the divine right of monarchy. Punch's grace first shone through when Nick, a new employee at the *Times*, mistook Punch for an even newer one and was about to offer him some hints for getting along at the *Times;* to spare Nick embarrassment, Punch delicately hinted at his identity.

Foreign correspondents have relatively little adult supervision, but what we did get came from the *Times* foreign desk, whose professionalism was staggering. On Nick's first reporting trip to Taiwan in 1986, he wrote an article about Madam Chiang Kai-shek and calculated her age from the date of birth in her official biography. Then a note came back from the foreign desk, politely asking if that was really the best age to use for her and noting that she had made many contradictory statements about her birthdate over the years. The note amounted to a scholarly disquisition on the uncertainties of Madam Chiang's birthdate, and it ended: "But you know all that."

Yeah, sure he did. Among those who worked on the foreign desk at one time or another over the years and to whom we owe particular thanks are Susan Chira, Marie Courtney, Tom Feyer, Bernie Gwertzman, Bill Keller, Joe Lelyveld, Ed Marks, Jeanne Moore, Jeanne Pinder, Kathy Rose, and a succession of very hardworking young clerks—some of the hardest-working people in American journalism, and certainly the most patient. Some of the material about the Asia crisis first appeared in a series in the *Times* in February 1999 and originated with other reporters who worked on the series with us. David E. Sanger, an old college friend who is one of our generation's most brilliant and tenacious reporters, knows the Washington and Asian terrain intimately and was the main source of information about what was going on in the Treasury Department and White House during that period. Jeff Gerth and Edward Wyatt, two other terrific *Times* journalists, also worked on that same series and gathered information that ultimately ended up here as well. Our hats off to all.

While in Asia, many presidents and prime ministers and other towering figures gave generously of their time. Zhu Rongji, Ryutaro Hashimoto, Keizo Obuchi, Lee Teng-hui, Kim Dae Jung, Kim Young Sam, Tomiichi Murayama, and others all took the time to explain issues to us, and President Imata Kabua of the Marshall Islands went further and discussed his views about America when he was dead drunk, ensuring an unusual level of candor. It was a treat to chat with Emperor Akihito and Empress Michiko, and to have a play date with Prince Akishino and Princess Kiko so that Gregory and Geoffrey could climb trees with the delightful princesses Mako and Kako. It would be difficult to imagine an imperial family that is brighter or more level-headed than Japan's, or one whose princesses are better tree-climbers.

Yet while we benefited from the insights from presidents and princesses, they make few appearances in this book. The most memorable times were spent not with the leaders but rather with peasants in rural China or Bangladesh, with the bus driver who smuggled Nick into closed zones in Pakistan by putting him with the baggage on top of the bus, with ordinary families whose homes we barged into in North Korea to be sure of interviewing typical citizens, with Mitsuo Fujishima, a convicted murderer awaiting execution in Tokyo, who helped Nick sneak into death row as a suddenly deputized social worker. It would be impossible to enumerate all of these ordinary people, but they enriched our lives in Asia and taught us about the East and about ourselves.

Diplomats, particularly Americans, often gave us their insights and roared in like the cavalry when we got into trouble. When Nick was arrested in Fiji, when Sheryl was barred from reporting in China, when Nick was denied a journalist visa to India, U.S. ambassadors and other officials helped save the day. Lots of others also helped in those crises, like the Japan Airlines pilot who took a bulletproof vest to Nick during riots in Jakarta.

Other journalists were our soulmates and teachers every step of the way. Some were prominent writers for major publications, and others were anonymous and underpaid stringers; those stringers are often the heroes of journalism, amassing language skills and local knowledge, living within the culture of their country rather than in five-star hotels, taking enormous risks when the bullets start flying. But whomever they worked for, other journalists were generous with help and friendship and jokes. When your light plane has lost its controls and is coming down for a crash landing without even being able to jettison its full load of fuel, as happened once to Nick, there are no more witty people to have aboard than other foreign correspondents. In particular, thanks to a few fellow *Times* foreign correspondents who helped with work that ended up in this book: John Burns (and Jane, of course); Seth Mydans; and our former Tokyo colleague, Andy Pollack.

Stuart Isett, an intrepid and creative photographer based in Tokyo, was generous in furnishing the photograph of Masayoshi Son.

We also owe a special word to those who hated our work—and there were plenty—especially when we wrote from China or Japan. We recognize that your complaints were sincere and thoughtful, and we found the vituperations as useful as the compliments. We weighed those complaints and in some cases made adjustments in our coverage, although perhaps not as much as you would have liked.

In our previous book, *China Wakes,* we offered thanks to people who helped us while we lived in Hong Kong, China, and Taiwan. For this book, we owe additional thanks for help in China to Zhu Mei, Howard Xu, and Peng Zheng. We owe a special debt to Zhang Hanzhi and Hung Huang, both wonderful and generous teachers about China. In Japan, we benefited from the most wonderful staff a newspaper bureau could possess. Kanji Takamasu and Yasuko Kamiizumi are our heroes, even if we left each of them with a few additional gray hairs. Warmest thanks also to Kaoru Fujimoto, Chieko Mori, Emiko Koishi, Miki Tanikawa, Sayaka Yakushiji, Junko Nonoyama, Chieko Tsuneoka, Tatsuhiko Kawashima, Tomoko Miyokawa, Kazuyuki and Yumiko Hamada, and Akira and Yuko Chiba.

In Korea, similar thanks to Sam Len, Kim Heung-sook and Stella Kim; in Indonesia, to Retno Soeti; in India, to Hari Kumar; in Thailand, to Jeerawat Na Thalang.

Hiroo Towers was a wonderful home for us in Tokyo, and we and our kids will always miss Tadokoro-san, the very epitome of Japanese warmth. The Japanese schools in our area were magnificent: Mochizuki Sensei at Aiiku Hou Iku En, Mori-san at Nanbuzaka Youchien, Ikeda Sensei at Kougai Shogakko—they all left our children with warm memories and much better Japanese than their parents. Ditto for Nishimachi International School. For our own Japanese, we are deeply grateful to Yasuko Asuke, the finest Japanese teacher in history, and Reiko Sassa and the others at the Japan Society in New York. The Japan Society does a first-class job in the sometimes challenging role of introducing America and Japan to each other. *Honto ni, iroiro osewa ni narimashite, arigatou gozaimashita.*

The little town of Omiya in Mie Prefecture became our favorite place in Japan, a second home, and we are in debt to those who opened their hearts and their houses to us there. Michiko Yoshida and her family in Omiya helped teach us how wonderful Japanese society can be, and we will always have a special warmth in our hearts for Japan because of the hospitality and generosity of the Yoshidas and the other good people of Omiya.

We wrote this book largely at Linfield College in McMinnville, Oregon, and we are deeply grateful to president Vivian Bull, Dean Marv Henberg (whose outstanding judgment has been evident ever since he served on Rhodes Scholarship selection committees in the 1980s), and the rest of the Linfield community for welcoming us so warmly. Linfield's beautiful campus, with the reddest maple leaves we have ever seen, made a wonderful home and impressed us with its hospitality and strong sense of community, all in Oregon's own God's Country.

Our agents, Anne Sibbald and Mort Janklow of Janklow & Nesbit Associates, are the best in the business, as well as the nicest. We worship at their altar.

Alfred A. Knopf is not only the best publishing house around, but one where the old-time publishing values of quality still survive (meaning that editors actually edit). Jonathan Segal, our editor, may have a second career in alchemy, judging by the way he can take raw ideas and copy and with a bit of pencil lead transform them into something much better.

Several people read all or parts of the manuscript and saved us from folly with their tactful and helpful suggestions. They include Graham Duncan, Ladis Kristof, David Sanger, Akira Chiba, Kanji Takamasu, William D. Campbell, and Brian Walker.

Our most important thanks go to family members and our parents: Ladis and Jane Kristof in Yamhill, Oregon; David and Alice WuDunn in New York; Darrell WuDunn; and Sondra WuDunn. There is a wonderful Chinese poem from the Tang Dynasty, more than one thousand years ago, called "Traveler's Song" and written by Meng Jia. It goes like this:

> *My loving mother, thread in hand,*
> *Mended the coat I have on now,*
> *Stitch by stitch, just before I left home,*
> *Thinking that I might be gone a long time.*
> *How can a blade of young grass*
> *Ever repay the warmth of the spring sun?*

We are also grateful to our kids, Gregory, Geoffrey, and Caroline, who put up with our constant scribbling, even as we fielded their questions about stars and bugs and everything in between. Finally, there is one more person we need to thank, someone who worked tirelessly to improve the manuscript and boost our spirits and who shared our grand adventure and made it all worthwhile: my spouse.

# INDEX

## ALSO BY NICHOLAS KRISTOF
## AND SHERYL WUDUNN

CHINA WAKES
*The Struggle for the Soul of a Rising Power*

"When China wakes, it will shake the world," Napoleon predicted. In this heroically researched book, Nicholas Kristof and Sheryl WuDunn illuminate both the Chinese boom-state and the tottering dictatorship. With the same vigor and empathy that won them the Pulitzer Prize for journalism, they travel from the highlands of Tibet to the bloody environs of Tiananmen Square and produce a canvas that takes in peasants and real estate speculators, dissidents and corrupt officials. Insightful, affecting, and bursting with color on every page, *China Wakes* is an exemplary work of reportage.

"Gives us the rough and rich texture of a peasant empire now transforming itself. Kristof and WuDunn are passionate interpreters." —*The Washington Post Book World*

Asian Studies/0-679-76393-7

VINTAGE BOOKS
Available at your local bookstore, or call toll-free to order:
1-800-793-2665 (credit cards only).